Coast-to-Coast Empire

Coast-to-Coast Empire

Manifest Destiny and the New Mexico Borderlands

William S. Kiser

UNIVERSITY OF OKLAHOMA PRESS : NORMAN

This book is published with the generous assistance of the Kerr Foundation, Inc.

Library of Congress Cataloging-in-Publication Data

Name: Kiser, William S., 1986– author.
Title: Coast-to-coast empire : Manifest Destiny and the New Mexico borderlands /
    William S. Kiser.
Description: Norman : University of Oklahoma Press, 2018. | Includes bibliographical
    references and index.
Identifiers: LCCN 2017046329 | ISBN 978-0-8061-6026-9 (hardcover : alk. paper)
Subjects: LCSH: New Mexico—History—19th century. | Manifest Destiny.
Classification: LCC F801 .K57 2018 | DDC 978.9/04—dc23
LC record available at https://lccn.loc.gov/2017046329

The paper in this book meets the guidelines for permanence and durability of the Committee
on Production Guidelines for Book Longevity of the Council on Library Resources, Inc. ∞

1 2 3 4 5 6 7 8 9 10

In loving memory of
Tom Burch and Emily Hughes

Contents

ILLUSTRATIONS

Figures

Maps

Cartography by Bill Nelson

Acknowledgments

As with all book projects, this work benefited from the assistance of many scholars, archivists, colleagues, and friends. I thank Amy Porter, Ed Westermann, and John P. Wilson, each of whom read a draft of the manuscript and provided valuable suggestions for improvement. I also appreciate Philis Barragan-Goetz, who helped me access government reports, and Andrés Reséndez, who provided his personal notes on documents in Mexican archives. I have benefited from many conversations on the topics discussed in this book, including discussions with Durwood Ball, Donald Critchlow, Brian DeLay, Donald Fixico, Francis Galan, Charles Harris, Rick Hendricks, Janne Lahti, Kyle Longley, Katherine Osburn, Charles Rankin, Louis Sadler, Calvin Schermerhorn, Brooks Simpson, Ed Sweeney, and Robert Wooster.

I thank my department chair, Bill Bush, for his support, and my home institution, Texas A&M University–San Antonio, which not only funded production costs for the maps contained in this volume but also provided a generous summer stipend to complete final manuscript revisions. Archivists at the New Mexico State Records Center and Archives in Santa Fe and the Center for Southwest Research at the University of New Mexico were instrumental in providing access to documents. Thanks are also in order for the librarians at my university, including Pru Morris, Sarah Timm, and Emily Bliss-Zaks, who are always quick to acquire research materials and other sources that I request.

Finally, as always, I appreciate the love and support of my wife, Nicole; my parents, Dan and Jerine; and all of my friends and family members.

COAST-TO-COAST EMPIRE

INTRODUCTION

In the summer of 1852 a former St. Louis mayor left his home state of Missouri and traveled to New Mexico, where he had been appointed to serve as territorial governor. Although he could claim little familiarity with the region, William Carr Lane arrived in Santa Fe with an optimistic outlook. By the time he delivered his first annual message to the legislative assembly in December, however, Lane had almost nothing positive to say. His speech began with a diatribe outlining the discouraging shortcomings that he saw. The landlocked territory was a long way from the eastern states and difficult to reach. Indian tribes surrounded the settlements in all directions and frequently raided them for livestock, provisions, and captives. The Hispanic and Pueblo Indian population, dispersed over more than 200,000 square miles, barely approached 60,000 souls. Because of its geographic enormity, Lane believed that the region required more than twenty companies of troops for permanent military service, since most civilians lacked the means to resist Indian raids. Stock raising and agricultural production fell far short of potential output, and nearly all mining operations had been abandoned. Roads were in poor condition, and very few schools existed. Finally, he complained, most inhabitants spoke only Spanish and refused to embrace American customs.[1] Why, then, had the United States gone to such great lengths and expended so much blood and treasure to acquire and retain a place that many Anglo-Americans looked down upon as worthless, primitive, and degraded?

Governor Lane was not the first newcomer to express pessimism regarding New Mexico and its Hispanic inhabitants, nor would he be the last. Disparaging remarks appeared over and over again in reports from civil officials, military officers, merchants, and others who traveled to the Southwest. Following a bloody battle at Taos in 1847, for example, a distraught Lieutenant A. B. Dyer described New Mexico as a "fatal" enterprise for Americans and believed that "this country is not worth what it will cost to keep it." After watching his commander, Captain John Burgwin, die alongside many others trying to sustain the recent conquest, Dyer realized that keeping New Mexico under American control would not be cheap or easy.[2] Ten years later Lieutenant William W. Averell caught his first glimpse of Santa Fe and was "grievously disappointed" by what he saw. "So much of expeditionary force had been expended by the government to acquire this great Territory," he sighed, "and here was its capital of jacal and adobe boxes."[3] After the Civil War General William T. Sherman summarized the feelings of many when he muttered that "we have held this Territory since 1846 . . . at a cost to the national treasury of full a hundred millions of dollars, and I doubt if it will ever reimburse to the country a tithe of that sum."[4]

Despite such negative perspectives, most people who disliked the Southwest understood its importance to the United States in terms of expansionistic nation building. Governor Lane himself recognized the territory as critical to his country's future. After blatantly condemning New Mexico in his aforementioned legislative address, he placed it directly in the context of Manifest Destiny, explaining that "this Continent must soon be crossed, from east to west, by railroads and telegraphic lines," and predicting that at least one, if not more, of those railways and telegraphs would pass through the new territory. New Mexico, he realized, provided a crucial geographic link between the Atlantic and the Pacific, and thus it constituted an indispensable national resource. The governor lauded the "Anglo-Saxon wave which is now rolling from East to West" and believed, as did other adherents to the idea of American exceptionalism, that providential design favored United States rule over the territory.[5]

Adolph Wislizenus, a doctor who passed through the region in 1846, described New Mexico as an arid desert "entirely worthless for agriculture." He abruptly changed his tune, however, when explaining the area's significance for "a great commercial nation like the United States," pointing out that the Southwest would provide a pertinent connection between the preexisting nation and its new Pacific shoreline. Once geopolitically absorbed into the American union, New Mexico would become the "new thoroughfare" between the Atlantic and Pacific Oceans, conveying emigrants westward, enticing commerce eastward, and facilitating economic development in all directions. When the doctor's report reached Congress in 1848, senators found its expansionist rhetoric so inspiring that they printed five thousand copies for public distribution.[6]

When Lieutenant William H. Emory ventured through New Mexico as a topographical engineer with the Army of the West, he affirmed what Wislizenus had observed and expounded on the true meaning behind the impending annexation. Despite its barren soil and seemingly limited resources, Emory wrote, the territory would prove essential as an "all-important military possession for the United States." Upon construction of a transcontinental railroad, which could follow the well-worn wagon ruts of the Santa Fe Trail, "immense quantities of merchandise" would pass through New Mexico and enrich the entire nation. With this in mind, Major General Thomas Jesup of the Quartermaster Department identified six possible railway avenues from the existing states to California, noting that the two most logical routes both passed directly through New Mexico. As an army officer, Emory perceived not only the commercial possibilities but also the strategic military importance of the region. Its extensive international border allowed Apaches and Comanches to pass back and forth from Mexican to American soil when trading and raiding—creating a complicated diplomatic issue that would attract a strong army presence for much of the nineteenth century—and indeed his remark on transnational human trafficking across a militarized border remains relevant today for different but equally pressing reasons.[7]

When he connected railroads with military imperatives, Emory struck on a second important purpose for a transcontinental connection. In the mid-1850s Secretary of War Jefferson Davis adopted this same line of reasoning, regarding the so-called Pacific railway in terms of national defense and pointing out to the president and Congress that a reliable linkage between the Mississippi valley and the Pacific Ocean would be imperative in the event of war with any major maritime power. A railroad would vastly improve communications between the two coasts in an age before telegraph wires reached across the continent. Locomotives could also haul vast quantities of supplies and transport troops to coastal California and Oregon if an invasion of the United States were ever to threaten the Pacific Northwest. Because of the vast distance separating the East from the West, this could mean the difference between victory and defeat for America. According to Davis, the 32nd parallel of latitude through Texas and New Mexico Territory (which at that time included Arizona) offered the most plausible route for a railway, and the Southwest therefore served a critical purpose for the common defense of the American people.[8]

President James K. Polk shared these views and fully appreciated New Mexico's strategic importance in the growing American empire. When delivering the State of the Union address in December 1848, he specifically mentioned the newly acquired Southwest as a place that might one day become profitable for agriculture and mining. Its immediate national significance, however, trumped all future possibilities. "From its position," Polk declared, "it is the intermediate and connecting territory between our settlements and our possessions in Texas, and those on the Pacific coast." To ensure American hegemony over California's goldfields and ocean ports, Polk asked Congress to establish a territorial government for New Mexico, urging lawmakers to set aside sectional differences for the country's greater good. In making these remarks, the nation's most powerful expansionist endorsed New Mexico as a critical possession and added impetus for its political incorporation and infrastructural development.[9]

In fact, the president mentioned New Mexico quite frequently over the course of his four-year term, cementing the region's position at the forefront of national growth. Referring to the Mexican Cession generally, and to sparsely settled New Mexico specifically, Polk said that the monetary worth of the land was inconsequential compared to its geographic importance, and he stressed that, in line with the Monroe Doctrine, no European power should ever again claim jurisdiction over it. These two factors alone constituted an "immense value" to the United States as a burgeoning hemispheric superpower and justified any troubles and expenses that the government might incur in retaining sovereignty over the area. "Although none of the cities on our coast of California may ever rival the city of New York in wealth, population, and business," the president prophesied, large municipalities would nonetheless rise around Pacific harbors and stimulate the American economy, provided that reliable routes of commerce could be established and maintained. Secretary of State James Buchanan echoed the president's sentiments when he wrote that California formed "an integral part of this great and glorious republic," so much so that the government would remain fully dedicated to its development.[10] James D. B. DeBow, editor of a proslavery magazine in the South, wrote in 1856 that "the growth of California constitutes one of the most remarkable chapters in the history of America." The dollar value of customs receipts at the port of San Francisco had skyrocketed by a factor of eight since the Gold Rush began in 1849. Only New York, Philadelphia, and New Orleans exported more goods annually than San Francisco, which had grown from a small seaside town to a bustling center of global commerce in just seven years. Farther south, Los Angeles and San Diego offered additional enticements for economic expansion. At one point DeBow estimated that western commerce would yield an astronomical $350 million in wealth each year. Fearful that European interests might gain a foothold on the

Pacific coast, financiers and politicians in the South and North alike clamored for exclusive access to and control of this lucrative new market.[11]

Between the eastern United States and California, however, lay New Mexico, which thus bore strategic significance for the country's ambitious imperial agenda. Polk and other expansionists wanted California, but to retain possession of it and realize its full economic and geopolitical potential, they needed New Mexico as a connecting thoroughfare in their nation-building project. After 1845 this perceived need held especially true for southerners—among whom Polk, a native of Tennessee, could be counted—because New Mexico linked slaveholding Texas to coastal California. For the following two decades, the political implications of the territory's existence and the daily lives of the people living there would be firmly grounded in notions of Manifest Destiny, American imperialism, and the sectionalism surrounding slavery debates.[12] None of this is meant to diminish the significance of places such as California, Oregon, or Utah in the broader context of westward expansion; rather, I argue that New Mexico, primarily because of its geographic location, was much more important to nineteenth-century U.S. expansion and the evolving sectional crisis than historians have previously appreciated.

Politicians and newspaper columnists ranked among the nation's most avid proponents of expansion. Indeed, it was a journalist, John O'Sullivan, who coined the phrase "Manifest Destiny" in 1845 to describe the idea that Americans acted with God's approbation when annexing territory, assimilating people, populating the continent, developing resources, and spreading democracy. Senator Thomas Hart Benton of Missouri, a leading spokesperson for American supremacy, delivered a speech entitled "The Destiny of Race" in May 1846, just as hostilities commenced between the United States and Mexico. His paean to Anglo-Saxon exceptionalism typified the rhetoric of an era during which many leading citizens viewed themselves and their nation as the world's leading light of moral democracy. "Since the dispersion of man upon earth, I know of no human event, past or present, which promises a greater, a more beneficent change upon earth than the arrival of the van of the Caucasian race upon the border of the sea which washes the shore of eastern Asia," Benton gushed in characteristic purple prose. "The van of the Caucasian race now top the Rocky Mountains, and spread down to the shores of the Pacific. In a few years a great population will grow up there, luminous with the accumulated lights of European and American civilization." Because of its geographic position, New Mexico fit nicely into these progressive schemes. Alluding specifically to the Southwest, editors of a Santa Fe newspaper duplicated Benton's feat of diction when writing in 1848 that "the wave of Freedom, that rose so proud and powerful on the

Atlantic shore—that rolled onward with its irresistible might across the Mississippi waters, is now dashing its sparkling spray along the base of the lofty mountains that tower around us—soon to mingle its torrent with the Pacific wave." Similar verbiage graced the pages of periodicals throughout the nation, disseminating the Manifest Destiny ideology to all who would read or listen.[13]

Within this context and outlook, the United States went to war with Mexico in 1846, with a primary purpose being the acquisition of land. For many, the notion of providential design—coupled with a prevailing view of Mexico as socially degraded, religiously and racially inferior, politically corrupt, and financially insolvent—justified such a hawkish course of action. Polk recommended as early as December 1845 that Congress buttress existing naval forces and enlarge the standing army, under the pretense of protecting American emigrants as they trekked westward. As disagreements with Great Britain over the Oregon Territory continued to complicate matters, the president reiterated the need to provide for the "public defense" and suggested that two-thirds of all U.S. troops be stationed on the Texas frontier to protect the new state from Indian raids on white settlements as well as from British meddling. As this diplomatic posturing played out during the early months of 1846, the perceptive Dr. Wislizenus proclaimed—quite accurately, as it turned out—that "the fate of Mexico is sealed." He prophesized that the United States would assume the paternalistic role of "enlightening the masses" in foreign regions that it acquired through legal purchase, political annexation, or military conquest. Another commentator, James Madison Cutts, phrased it even more bluntly. Mexico had failed to put California to optimum economic use, he said, and it therefore became America's moral duty to assume ownership of a territory that was otherwise wasting away. He praised his fellow countrymen as emigrants and entrepreneurs "whose intelligence, enterprise, and capacity might well be confided in to develop the character of the country."[14]

By the mid-1800s the national population had grown larger and more diverse, prompting American citizens to trickle and then stream westward. The economy expanded in stride, and a market revolution predicated on capitalism and democracy permeated many aspects of society. With its extensive coastline and numerous harbors, California fell into the fixed gaze of U.S. imperialists. The commercial possibilities attendant upon the acquisition of California seemed endless, and the overriding weakness of the Mexican government that claimed sovereignty over it enticed many of the era's most powerful politicians and businessmen. Possession of the Pacific coast would effectively globalize the American economy, creating a continental empire that could trade with the Orient as well as Europe. Both the raw materials harvested on the backs of southern slaves and the finished textiles flowing out of northern factories and mills would then reach Asian markets with relative ease. The vertical breadth of the California coast made it even more desirable and attracted the interest of both northerners and southerners, thrusting the region into the increasingly virulent sectional agitation that traced its origins to the dawn of the republic. The port at San Francisco could tangibly send and receive goods over a northern railway terminus at Chicago, while harbors at Los Angeles and San Diego could do the same for the benefit of southern cities like New Orleans and Galveston.[15] These eventualities, however, depended not only on the acquisition of California but also on the conquest of New Mexico.

As a Spanish colony, New Mexico was not an economic boon to the United States, nor did it have much appeal to early migrants, largely because of the many nomadic Indian groups who claimed the region as their own and fought violently to protect their homelands from invasion and settlement. This lethal reality, compounded by the arid climate, rough topography, lack of navigable waterways, and unfamiliar Hispanic Catholic society, caused many U.S. citizens to resist the thought of incorporating New Mexico into their political nation. But in 1821 the opening of the Santa Fe–Missouri trade began to alter such opinions, and by midcentury the region's importance to federal nation-building projects had become apparent. If the United States was to have California, it must also possess New Mexico; without the latter, the economic potential of the former could not be fully realized.

Prior to completion of the first transcontinental railroad in 1869, an expensive and time-consuming alternative for shipping goods from one U.S. coast to the other was to circumnavigate the faraway tip of South America. The absence of a canal or railroad linking the Atlantic and Pacific Oceans near the hemisphere's center did not, however, preclude ambitious Americans from trying to create overland connections through the narrower parts of Central America. In the 1850s, for instance, Cornelius Vanderbilt and a group of speculative financial backers maneuvered to gain foreign approval for railroads through Panama and Nicaragua, hoping to shorten the distance that ships would have to sail or steam when delivering cargo. At the same time, filibusters attempted to take control of Central American nations using the clandestine force of mercenary armies, the most famous effort being that of William Walker in 1855, whose initial success in Nicaragua gave way to his eventual execution by firing squad. Although many federal leaders hoped that these missions of intrigue would work—President Franklin Pierce went so far as to recognize Walker as the legitimate ruler of Nicaragua in 1856—the political and diplomatic implications of foreign meddling prevented open state sponsorship of such endeavors, and interested Americans had to hope for the best from afar. New Mexico, however, was a different story. After 1848 the United States held undisputed possession of the Desert Southwest and could develop the region accordingly, provided Americans could nationalize and assimilate Hispanic inhabitants, pacify Indian tribes, and agree on a pathway toward development. Despite the prospects for privately funded commercial arteries across Central America, New Mexico remained a more practical geographic solution to the nation's transportation needs prior to the Civil War.[16]

As these events played out during the antebellum era, territorial Utah still seemed like an implausible avenue for a railway linking the two coasts. Throughout the 1850s the American democratic state and Brigham Young's Mormon theocracy faced off in quarrels of wit and rhetoric that very nearly erupted into open warfare in 1857. Secretary of War John B. Floyd complained that the Mormon settlements in Utah "lie in the great pathway which leads from our Atlantic States to the new and flourishing communities growing up upon our Pacific seaboard." Young's religious followers, the secretary regretfully concluded, "stand a lion in our path."[17] With ongoing tension between the United States and Zion, government officials and private capitalists saw New Mexico as the most viable route through which to construct a railroad to the Pacific Coast. In the fifteen years following the Mexican-American War, nobody could have foreseen that the first transcontinental rails would come together at Promontory Point, not far from Salt Lake City.[18]

As with most aspects of American life prior to the Civil War, sectionalism came prominently into play whenever the Southwest was mentioned in political debate or private conversation. Once the United States secured possession of California, Utah, and New Mexico, what would be the ultimate political disposition of those places? Their geographic seclusion and mostly arid climates effectively precluded intensive plantation-style agriculture, and the actual implementation of chattel slavery in those areas hardly seemed practical. Furthermore, the preexistence of Indian captivity and debt peonage as alternative forms of involuntary servitude already satisfied regional demand for labor.[19] But the benefits entailed in the development of those regions bore significant ramifications for the national economy, and once the Mexican Cession lands did become a part of the United States after ratification of the Treaty of Guadalupe Hidalgo in 1848, people from all parts of the country vied for supremacy over the vast new territorial appendages. The conquest and retention of New Mexico occurred within the context of the political crisis leading up to the Civil War, during which citizens from both the North and the South first argued—and then fought—for control over the Southwest.[20] Southerners sought to make New Mexico a slave territory or state not because they actually intended to transport large numbers of black slaves there, but rather to exercise ideological control over the area in advancement of their own sectional economy and political relevance. On the other hand, northerners who hoped to contain slavery where it already existed (or abolish it altogether) and to check the proliferation of southern political power endeavored to make New Mexico a free-soil territory or state. Debates over the Pacific Railroad Surveys in the 1850s came to epitomize the sectional strife that accompanied admittance of the Mexican Cession lands into the United States.[21]

In 1821, when Mexican independence prompted the nullification of restrictive Spanish commerce laws and the Santa Fe trade opened as a result, foreign merchants filtering into New Mexico had little, if any, imperial purpose attached to their endeavors. Their primary motivation in traveling to the Southwest was profit—not settlement, conquest, or annexation. But even as a handful of American merchants and French Canadian fur trappers began operating in and around Santa Fe, two larger and more powerful economic forces were simultaneously unfolding in the United States. Starting in the early 1800s, the proliferation of a capitalist market revolution and the emergence of a Southern Cotton Kingdom would have a profound impact on the purposes that Americans attached to business and settlement in the Southwest. The market revolution and Cotton Kingdom were largely interdependent, indelibly linking southern slavery to northern industrialization and facilitating the growth of America's increasingly global economy.[22] One aspect of these broader economic phenomena involved the Santa Fe trade and merchant capitalism, which pulled the Hispanic Southwest into the commercial orbit of the United States and laid the groundwork for future military conquest.[23]

The rise of the Cotton Kingdom during this age of commercial intensification and technological innovation also helped to sectionalize New Mexico's political existence. Southerners held considerable sway in the Southwest, because trade with the region mostly involved merchants from Missouri—a slave state—who influenced regional opinion on issues like slavery and popular sovereignty.[24] Territorial expansion for the purposes of geographic conquest and political hegemony—rather than just commercial profit—originated in part with southern efforts to spread slavery beyond its existing boundaries, and New Mexico became a pawn in federal debates revolving around sectionalist politics and westward migration.[25] The far-reaching implications of the South's growing economic power and political self-identity can be gleaned in part from events in contemporaneous New Mexico. During the 1850s a new territorial constitution prohibited chattel slavery but left peonage and captivity fully intact as alternative forms of coercive labor; legislators enacted strict slave codes modeled on those of eastern states; proslavery interests aimed to build a railroad from Texas to California; and the Confederacy hatched an ambitious plot at the onset of the Civil War to invade New Mexico and establish a coast-to-coast empire of its own.[26]

In the nineteenth-century popular imagination, Manifest Destiny was romanticized as a rapid, unilateral process of peaceful American expansion and settlement, one that pulled millions of square miles of western land into the national domain while civilizing groups of people seen as culturally, racially, or religiously inferior. But in New Mexico, Manifest Destiny operated in mysterious, multifarious, and manipulative ways for a period of almost three decades before the climactic Mexican-American War brought the region into America's geopolitical fold. Imperial expansion was not always overt, purposeful, and immediate; it sometimes involved indirect and measured tactics. From the 1820s through the 1840s, gradual processes of multilateral acculturation between trappers, merchants, and Hispanos in New Mexico enabled communities to hybridize for their own prosperity and livelihood. After more than two decades of merchant capitalism, intermarriage, and increasing land ownership through Mexican grants, Americans had created an atmosphere ripe for military conquest, prompting a swift and systematic (though somewhat superficial) nationalization of New Mexico's land and people. Although the region's inhabitants remained predominantly Catholic and retained Indian and Hispanic majorities in ethnicity and culture, its economic orientation leaned more and more toward the United States, and its political attachment soon followed.[27]

By the time U.S. troops marched on Santa Fe in 1846, pro-American elements of society exercised significant political power in the province, largely because of the growing influence of American businessmen and their ideas about trade and democracy. Thus, while most outsiders who traveled between Missouri and New Mexico after 1821 had economic incentives foremost in mind, they also set in motion the imperial and ideological processes that enabled military occupation twenty-five years later. Part of that gradual evolution involved the emergence of shared and even competing nationalisms, which took shape in New Mexico's Hispanic factions of liberal pro-American and conservative anti-American leaders. Once U.S. forces occupied Santa Fe, federal officers sought to control the region by appointing members of the congenial pro-American clique to positions of authority, but in so doing they alienated a significant portion of the population and drove them to open rebellion. More than two decades of exposure to merchant capitalism created a complex society that had become, in many ways, economically dependent on the United States but politically allegiant to Mexico. When nomadic and Pueblo

Indians—whose loyalties often lay with their tribes of origin—were mixed into this cultural crucible, America's conquest and retention of the Southwest became exceedingly complicated and remained so for many years.[28]

Many historians of nineteenth-century New Mexico have treated the Santa Fe trade, Stephen W. Kearny's occupation, the antebellum Indian Wars, debates over slavery, the Pacific railway, and the Confederate invasion as separate events. In contrast, the present work approaches these topics as comprising a single, interconnected process of imposed political and ideological transformation. Armed forces played a critical role in these events. Concentrating on the activities of a large standing army in a civilian setting informs our understanding of how powerful nation-states obtain territory through warfare and retain it during peacetime. Soldiers and their commanders left an indelible imprint on the social, cultural, political, judicial, and economic systems that developed in the Southwest. They marched into the territory at the onset of the Mexican-American War and ensured possession of it through continuous occupation. Even after territorial organization in 1850, army officers continued to hold enormous influence in local matters. Tens of thousands of Hispanic and Anglo citizens relied on soldiers for protection from Indian depredations and for the stability of their local economy, and the War Department pumped millions of dollars into New Mexico each year for supplies, forage, shelter, and troop salaries. Regiments of infantry and cavalry participated in nation-building projects by escorting explorers, settlers, boundary adjudicators, and railway surveyors across the territory. When the Civil War began, the Southwest again became the backdrop for armed conflict, and federal troops backed by regiments of Hispanic volunteers united to repel a Confederate invasion. For the remainder of that war, citizens lived under martial law and suffered its attendant hardships, while thousands of Navajos endured the devastating Long Walk and subsequent incarceration at Bosque Redondo, all under military supervision.[29] The federal government's unwavering commitment to these military projects stemmed from the broader importance of New Mexico in the context of nineteenth-century expansionism.

Having been born and raised in a frontier community where danger lurked in all directions—a place where endemic hostilities with numerous Indian tribes impacted most peoples' lives—Hispanic residents of New Mexico understood the interconnectivity of martial and civil affairs all too well. When not otherwise occupied with pastoral or agricultural pursuits, many of them enlisted in local militias and embarked on aggressive expeditions into Apache, Comanche, Navajo, or Ute country. This did not, however, mean that all New Mexicans welcomed

American soldiers into their territory with open arms, nor did they enthusiastically assimilate or acculturate to Anglo customs and politics. A New Mexican *rico* named Mariano Chávez told his son in 1841 that "the heretics are going to overrun all [of] this country." Using "heretics" as a catchall term that by that time included Texan filibusters, Missourian merchants, French Canadian fur trappers, German-Jewish businessmen, and a seemingly boundless cadre of other Euro-American interlopers, he instructed his son, José Francisco, to "go and learn their language and be prepared to defend your people." The assault on New Mexico to which he referred had begun more than three decades earlier, even before Mexican independence, and perceptive men like Chávez realized that the climax was drawing near. The next two decades, from the U.S. conquest in 1846 until the end of the Civil War in 1865, would determine the long-term role of New Mexico in America's growing political nation.[30]

⇛ 1 ⇚

MERCHANT CAPITALISM
AND THE SANTA FE TRADE

In 1807 Lieutenant Zebulon M. Pike—for whom Colorado's best-known mountain peak is now named—found out the hard way about Spain's restrictive foreign-commerce laws. Ostensibly reconnoitering a portion of the recently acquired Louisiana Purchase, the twenty-eight-year-old military officer and his fifteen companions wandered a bit too far west. By March of that year Pike found himself incarcerated in Santa Fe, where he desperately tried to explain the situation to a New Mexico governor who gave him a "haughty and unfriendly reception." Conversing in broken French, the officer-turned-voyager swore that he had "no hostile intentions toward the Spanish government," insisting that his sole purpose was to explore American territory. Unconvinced, the governor confiscated Pike's personal belongings, disarmed and arrested his cohorts, and sent them all south—under a military guard commanded by Facundo Melgares—to plead their case before the commandant general in Nueva Vizcaya. Wary of generating an unwanted diplomatic debacle between Spain and the United States, the governor treated Pike to a lavish dinner before sending him away, and indeed the entire group enjoyed relatively humane treatment throughout the ordeal. The wayward Americans eventually returned unharmed to the United States, and in 1810 Pike published an account of his tribulations on New Spain's far northern frontier.[1] His descriptions of the region elicited considerable attention in the United States and sparked his country's earliest economic interest in the Southwest.[2] In Santa Fe inhabitants began speculating about "whether the Anglo-Americans will come and the possibility that they may make themselves masters of this Province."

A concerned Governor Joaquín del Real Alencaster noticed that some citizens even seemed excited about the prospects of an American takeover.[3]

After being arrested and marched through a thousand miles of foreign territory, Pike became more acquainted with northern Mexico than he intended or wished. Explaining the strictly regulated commercial structure of New Spain, he noted "the extreme dearness of imported goods" to inhabitants who seldom owned items of overseas manufacture because of Spanish laws prohibiting most forms of international exchange. He also saw that many locally produced wares could be acquired cheaply, providing an attractive two-way market in which Americans could sell their own goods at high prices, obtain local products like mules and bullion inexpensively, and transport them back to the United States for profitable resale.[4] According to Pike, legalization of trade with New Mexico might offer American businessmen a lucrative enterprise, if only Spain would lift its embargo. However ill-fated the 1806–7 expedition might have been, it aroused American interest in New Mexico, and thus Pike initiated the process of settlement and conquest that played out there over the ensuing five decades.[5]

Despite the prospects for profitable trade, no demonstrable evidence yet existed that such commerce could be sustained, nor did Spain's protective laws allow traders or trappers to toil in Spanish territory without risk of imprisonment and confiscation of property. Pike was just the first of many Americans to encounter difficulties in the precarious borderlands separating the far western United States from northern New Mexico. Others followed in his footsteps over the ensuing years, and many of them similarly landed in jail as accused spies. A group of ten men, including fur trappers Robert McKnight and James Baird, went to prison in New Mexico in 1812 and did not return to the United States for nearly a decade. After learning of the arrest, Missourians were "astonished at the barbarity" of Santa Fe's officials and hoped that the U.S. government would take immediate steps to have the men liberated.[6] The State Department did indeed take up the cause, but not until five years later, when John Quincy Adams began prodding Spain's minister plenipotentiary, Luis de Onís, to affect their release. Onís sent a dispatch to Don Ruiz de Apodaca, the viceroy in New Spain, but his communication was either lost or disregarded and nothing came of it. A year later, under increasing pressure from Secretary of State Adams, Onís renewed his efforts to free the hapless prisoners but was again ignored, demonstrating both the ambivalence of royal officials as well as the stiff enforcement of Spanish commerce laws.[7]

Foreigners caught near New Spain's northern borders faced serious risks, but American and French Canadian opportunists could not resist the temptation of

Zebulon M. Pike, c. 1814.
Courtesy National Archives and Records Administration, Washington, D.C.

profit and continued to venture into the region. In 1817 Auguste Chouteau and Julius Demun were trading with Indians near the headwaters of the Arkansas River in today's southeastern Colorado (the international boundary at that time) when Spanish military authorities apprehended them, confiscated their merchandise, shackled them in irons, and deposited them "in the dungeons of Santa Fe" for six weeks. When the men finally appeared before Governor Pedro María de Allande, the schizophrenic head of state started pounding tables with his fists and became so enraged that he temporarily lost the ability to speak, lapsing into a bizarre state of psychological impairment. After returning to his senses, the governor realized that the party had remained on the American side of the river, traded only with Arapahoes and other Southern Plains tribes, and possessed a passport from the governor of Missouri. Based on these facts, the men were set free with instructions to return immediately to their homes. The aggrieved traders submitted a claim to Congress for remuneration in the amount of $30,000, stating that the seizure of their possessions "brought us to the brink of ruin," but they experienced considerable hardship in seeing their petition executed. Chouteau and Demun were still appealing for redress in 1836—twenty years after the fact—and eventually received the disheartening news that stipulations in the 1819 Adams-Onís Treaty mandating that Spain pay certain indemnities did not apply to their case.[8]

In 1820 David Meriwether—who later succeeded Henry Clay as a Kentucky senator—encountered similar circumstances. Spanish troops confronted his encampment
on the Canadian River, arrested Meriwether and his black servant, Alfred, and killed
a number of the Pawnee Indians accompanying them. The two men, accused of
spying for the United States, were ushered into Santa Fe to appear before Governor
Facundo Melgares, the same man who, thirteen years earlier, had escorted Zebulon
Pike to Nueva Vizcaya under identical pretenses of espionage. "This was the most
miserable day of my life," Meriwether recalled of his capture, "for I felt as though I
would as soon die as live." Once in Santa Fe, the nineteen-year-old was tossed into a
tiny prison cell at the Palace of the Governors. During the interrogation, Melgares
told Meriwether that "Americans are bad people," mentioning Andrew Jackson's
forceful occupation of Spanish Florida the year before as evidence of this universal
indictment. When asked about the purpose of his expedition, Meriwether assured
the governor that he intended only to "find out if it was practicable to make a road
to New Mexico by which we could transport our articles of merchandise in wagons
and exchange them for gold and silver." Upon hearing this, Melgares shook his head
in disbelief and ordered that the Kentuckian be returned to his cell. Eventually,
authorities freed the young man and his slave after they promised never to return
to New Mexico.[9] Meriwether broke his promise thirty-two years later when he
came back to Santa Fe, ironically carrying an appointment as territorial governor.

Although such injurious and humiliating occurrences irked some Americans
and offended their nationalistic pride, there was little that could be done to reverse
Spanish policy at that time. With the War of 1812 having recently ended in stalemate,
the fledgling United States had come to realize that its military might still lagged
behind that of leading European powers. Humbled by the failure to achieve decisive
victory over Great Britain, uncharacteristically apprehensive war hawks balked at the
thought of a costly conflict with Spain over seemingly petty commercial laws and
an unproven trade with Santa Fe. But fortuitously for those wishing to initiate such
commerce, Spain's New World possessions fell into an irreversible process of mass
rebellion, with one Latin American colony after another declaring independence
in the decades after America's own democratic revolution set an example in 1776.
Mexico would be among the last colonies to break free from Spanish dominion;
as one of its earliest independent acts, in 1821 the new country abolished restrictive
commercial codes and established free trade with the United States and other
nations. In 1825 Augustus Storrs explained that the Spanish government had "viewed,
with extreme jealousy, an intercourse of other nations with her American depen-
dencies," and he lauded the fact that Enlightenment-era revolutions and Mexican

independence "entirely altered its policy in this respect."[10] For Anglo-Americans itching to capitalize on the potential wealth of New Mexico, the foremost obstacle to commercialization—Spanish hegemony—had been removed.

Santa Fe and Taos lay at the extreme northern terminus of the Camino Real, and prior to 1821 New Mexico remained a widely neglected and highly dependent economic entity at the periphery of the Spanish empire.[11] After Mexican independence and the abrogation of commercial restrictions, the advent of trade with Missouri transformed these two towns into international crossroads and vibrant ports of entry. This placed them in a position for capitalist development and, incidentally, for the concomitant processes of Americanization that culminated in military conquest twenty-five years later. Just as this burgeoning inland commerce between the United States and Mexico permanently altered the configuration of the latter's economy, so too did it prove important for Missouri, an infant state born just one year before Mexico's independence in the sectional compromise bearing its name. As Mexico's northernmost province and America's most westerly state, New Mexico and Missouri became mutually interdependent frontier zones, sparsely populated regions whose inhabitants benefited from multilateral trade networks that helped to ensure political legitimacy and economic viability.

For Missouri, international trade with New Mexico augmented its preexisting north-south commercial orientation astride the Mississippi River, rendering the new slave state important for the national—and particularly the southern—economy. During the early 1800s millions of dollars in American goods crossed the southern plains to Santa Fe, from whence caravans and teamsters transported much of that merchandise to markets in California, Sonora, Chihuahua, and even Mexico City. At the other end of the trail, St. Louis served in a similar capacity as a conduit through which Mexican products and specie filtered into U.S. markets for resale and redistribution, and many Missouri residents benefited from their position at the interstices of these business networks.[12] It comes as little wonder that Missourians so feverishly clamored for the establishment of this trade, so fervently defended their commercial interests in New Mexico, and so adamantly demanded federal support to sustain these economic endeavors.

The Missouri–Santa Fe trade that developed in the 1820s provided a prototype for transcontinental commerce and economic policy in the United States. Unlike the Oregon Trail and other routes westward, the primary purposes of which were to convey one-way settlers to new frontier homes, the Santa Fe Trail retained a predominantly commercial and military imperative from the time of its founding in 1821 until its abandonment after the railroad entered New Mexico in 1879. Ports of

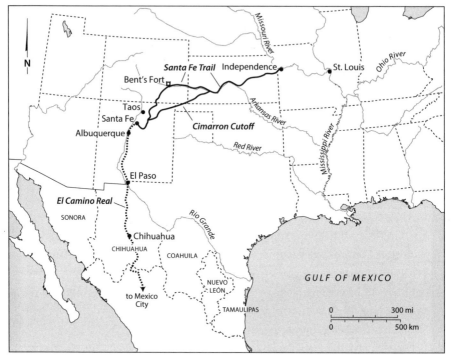

Map 1. Santa Fe Trail Network, 1820s–1860s.

entry were established at opposite ends of the lengthy overland highway, connecting two separate nations with a wagon road in a region where navigable waterways did not exist. This transnational connection allowed for the dissemination of a wide array of goods across an entire continent through mutually negotiated laws and treaties, such as that signed in 1831 promoting "amity and commerce" between the United States and Mexico and ensuring free trade by sea and by land.[13] The Missouri–Santa Fe–Chihuahua trading network also necessitated government action in the form of drawback and debenture measures that relieved American capitalists from excessive foreign fees and double taxation, further invigorating the commercial system.

As Lieutenant Pike and others had already proven, a wagon trail across the south plains would be the only practicable trade route connecting the western United States with northern Mexico. Neither the Arkansas River nor the Rio Grande could be navigated far enough inland for freighting purposes, eliminating any possibility for the use of steamboats.[14] For New Mexico the nearest major seaport was Vera Cruz, located more than 1,600 miles from Santa Fe and almost twice as far away as Missouri.[15] Thus, when William Becknell placed an advertisement in a St. Louis newspaper on June 25, 1821—two months before the Treaty of Córdoba officially recognized Mexican independence—seeking men to accompany him on a maiden voyage to New Mexico, he was pursuing what seemed to be a logical course of action.[16] Although the inaugural journey to Santa Fe carried only $15,000 worth of goods and did not produce the astronomical profits that later caravans enjoyed—U.S. Consul Manuel Alvarez downplayed Becknell's venture as "merely an experiment" by a handful of "enterprising individuals"—the expedition succeeded in "awakening the attention of speculators" and ensured continued American interest.[17] According to Augustus Storrs, Becknell and subsequent U.S. merchants (*extranjeros*) encountered a New Mexican population that seemed largely amenable to foreign trade. "The door of hospitality is opened with a cheerful welcome," he observed after traveling to Santa Fe in 1825, "and in all their principal towns the arrival of the Americans is a source of pleasure, and the evening is dedicated to dancing and festivity."[18] As late as June 1846, just two months before General Stephen W. Kearny's arrival in New Mexico, Donaciano Vigil gave a speech to the legislative assembly praising the American trade for spreading "the spirit of mercantile enterprises" throughout the country.[19]

As Becknell and his teamsters worked to establish commerce with New Mexico, others began eyeing the region for beaver trapping and fur trading, an extractive undertaking that, unlike the merchant trade over the Santa Fe Trail, entailed little to no benefit for the Mexican economy.[20] Prior to their arrest in 1817, Chouteau and Demun had petitioned Spanish authorities for permission to trap beaver along the northern tributaries of the Rio Grande, but that request was denied and they instead wound up in prison.[21] In 1822 William H. Ashley led the first organized expedition of American trappers into the southern ranges of the Rocky Mountains. Similar excursions, sometimes including up to one hundred men, occurred annually until the mid-1830s, when the combination of overhunting and insufficient natural increase began to take a heavy toll on beaver populations.[22] Southwestern trapping and the Santa Fe trade began and grew contemporaneously throughout the 1820s, and both activities had a complementary commercial impact within New Mexico.

Men like Charles Beaubien, Jim Beckwourth, William and Charles Bent, Jim Bridger, Kit Carson, Antoine Leroux, Robert McKnight, Antoine Robidoux, Jedediah Smith, Ceran St. Vrain, William Sublette, and Bill Williams became household names in northern New Mexico during their own lifetimes.[23] Many trappers of either American or French Canadian origin dabbled in peltries as well as mercantilism over the course of their lives, which in many cases spanned the Mexican national and American territorial periods. Most of them married Hispanic or Indian wives, learned Spanish and even some Indian languages, and became naturalized Mexican citizens as strategies for commercial success and social stature.[24] Matt Field, a journalist for the *New Orleans Picayune* in the 1840s, observed in Santa Fe that any American who became fluent in Spanish and resided in New Mexico for an extended period "becomes a man of great importance." He specifically mentioned Robidoux as one foreigner whose local influence rivaled that of the Hispanic priests and governors.[25] With men like these as intermediaries, the early American West became inextricably linked to the Mexican north, not only commercially but also culturally and ideologically, through processes of acculturation and mutual accommodation.[26] Senator Thomas Hart Benton once referred to these assimilative strategies during a congressional speech about race and American expansion: "Commerce is a great civilizer—social intercourse as great—and marriage greater."[27]

These processes, as they played out after Mexican independence, would prove pivotal to the American takeover at midcentury. Missourians understood the benefits that emigrants derived from marrying Hispanic women, informing Congress in an 1838 petition that such liaisons created "mutual advantages" that in turn allowed Americans "to pass their goods favorably through the custom-house."[28] Between 1821 and 1846 there were at least 122 marriages between white men and Hispanic women, most of which took place in the Taos region. An unknown number of informal liaisons, in the form of concubinage and cohabitation, also transpired without church sanction and beyond the official record. Intermarriage became an important social strategy in New Mexico, allowing male outsiders access to goods and services, relieving them from excessive taxation as foreigners, and preventing misunderstandings within the community that could undermine their economic interests and even endanger their lives. Because paid Spanish interpreters were in high demand among American merchants, those who married Hispanic women could eliminate that cost by employing their wives to translate documents and mediate verbal transactions. Even Americans who naturalized as Mexican citizens and spoke Spanish fluently had difficulty writing the formal language and enlisted the services of native speakers for official documents like bills of sale and commercial passports.[29]

Mexican law in fact encouraged miscegenation between foreign men and Hispanic women as a method for naturalizing entrepreneurial American outsiders, providing them with a pathway to citizenship, and, theoretically at least, stripping them of their allegiance to the United States through national incorporation. Traders and trappers often adopted Hispanicized versions of their names (James Giddings, for example, became Santiago Girens) and needed only to marry into a local family, reside in New Mexico for two years, and join the Catholic Church to become Mexican citizens.[30] In a culturally negotiable borderland environment, nationality remained moderately fluid, and many foreigners changed citizenship multiple times as opportunity and caprice dictated. Ceran St. Vrain and Antoine Robidoux both evolved in nationality from French Canadian to Mexican to American during their lifetimes. Notions of cultural hybridity and hyphenated nationalities have remained firmly implanted in the multicultural Southwest and trace their precedent back to this early period of interaction.[31]

For Charles Beaubien, intermarriage and naturalization brought far more than access to prime beaver streams and lower taxes. After marrying a member of the influential Lobato family in 1827, Beaubien became one of New Mexico's most powerful land owners when Governor Manuel Armijo issued large tracts to him, including the Beaubien-Miranda (or Maxwell) Land Grant. Voluntary assimilation made him a candidate for landownership and increased his economic and social clout. It also augmented growing foreign control over the region, undercut Mexican political power, and perpetuated the process of Americanization that began with the liberalization of commerce laws and concomitant influx of merchants and trappers.[32] For these reasons such men eventually became the targets of armed uprisings in the months following the 1846 U.S. conquest, when Beaubien and others of foreign ancestry were suddenly viewed as occupiers and conquerors among their adoptive kinfolk.[33]

Ironically, the governor who awarded several of the largest tracts to foreign settlers, Manuel Armijo, would be the same man faced with the American invasion in 1846, a takeover that his own generous land policies helped to encourage. Armijo bore responsibility for doling out the Sangre de Cristo Grant (1,038,195 acres), the Beaubien-Miranda Grant (1,714,764 acres), and additional conveyances totaling more than 15 million acres. He initially hoped to attract entrepreneurial immigrants who, with the backing of personal funds and financier investments, might develop commercial infrastructure and bring material wealth into New Mexico.[34] Instead, his incredibly liberal land-giving scheme empowered foreigners in much the same way that Mexican settlement policies elevated American *empresarios* like Stephen F. Austin to positions of control in Texas during the 1820s.[35] As a result, by the mid-1840s both New Mexico and Texas fell into the orbit of American geopolitical control.

Armijo was hardly alone in his attempts to attract American investment in a region that suffered from the political and economic neglect of its fledgling and fragile national government.[36] Most Hispanic politicians and citizens had good reason to support international traffic and trade. Between 1800 and 1860, Mexico's federal revenue declined by approximately 10 percent, while that of the United States increased by 1,270 percent, an economic disparity attributable in part to the market revolution and ongoing industrialization in the latter country. Trapped in the doldrums of an insolvent economy and an indifferent government, some New Mexicans began to see the logic of international commerce and aligned themselves with the more-prosperous United States. Recognizing the financial benefits of import duties and external markets for local products, Governor Bartolomé Baca dispatched commissioners to Missouri and Washington, D.C., to discuss the prospects for free trade. Voicing support for the establishment of an international highway connecting the two frontiers, Baca also took unprecedented action when he issued beaver trapping licenses to foreign applicants, with the sole condition that they be accompanied by a native New Mexican when in the field. This small concession initiated a domino effect, wherein trappers first secured a license and then established residency and applied for Mexican citizenship, thus eliminating any supervisory provisions and enabling them to operate free of regulations and fees. Baca ranked among the more open-minded of New Mexico's governors when it came to free trade with the United States, just as Armijo would one day prove amenable to foreigners seeking land. Both heads of state contributed to an ongoing process of commercial liberalization, although only Armijo would be around to witness the effects of it during the Mexican-American War.[37]

While simple profit motives might have been the original objective of American merchants and investors, a more powerful but less apparent force also attended their efforts. Hoping to secure federal funding for the survey and demarcation of the Santa Fe route, Missourians explained to Congress in 1825 that trading with Mexico's internal provinces would "promote the spread of republican principles and diffusion of knowledge."[38] Utilizing the stereotype of a politically, culturally, racially, and socially backwards Mexican republic, Missouri governor Alexander McNair appealed to Secretary of State John Quincy Adams's sense of patriotic duty when assuring him that federal support for trade with New Mexico would "awaken the inhabitants . . . to the blessings of a republican system of government."[39] Senator Benton, too, gave speeches in Congress voicing support for the Santa Fe trade. He believed that commerce would not only benefit the United States but also uplift New Mexicans through capitalism and democracy, thus providing for "the improvement of their moral and social condition."[40] Benton thought that the new trail to New Mexico would be "a stage only in the progress" of American

Senator Thomas Hart Benton, c. 1840s.
Courtesy National Archives and Records Administration, Washington, D.C.

expansion, with Santa Fe serving as "a new point of departure for our invincible citizens."[41] The first-term senator made no attempt to deceive his colleagues about the multifarious nation-building purposes that the Santa Fe trade entailed. He proudly boasted that the new overland highway would "open an easy channel of communication . . . not for merchandise only, but for thoughts and ideas," and would therefore enable "the preservation of the republican system" through its geographic and ideological spread into New Mexico.[42]

Within three years of Mexican independence, merchant caravans consisting of over one hundred men and every imaginable type of dry goods were setting out for Santa Fe on an annual basis.[43] In 1824 one expedition left Missouri with $18,000 in merchandise and returned from New Mexico with an estimated $180,000 in Spanish coins and bullion, an astronomical profit margin of 1,000 percent.[44] Less than a decade later Secretary of War Lewis Cass reported with satisfaction that the volume of commerce between the United States and Santa Fe steadily increased with each passing year, Missouri was awash in Mexican silver and gold, and "many of our citizens are profitably engaged in the trade."[45] When the Panic of 1837 struck America's financial institutions, Missouri weathered the economic crisis more easily than other states because so much specie, in the form of Mexican silver, circulated there, and merchants relied less heavily on risky paper money and unbacked credit.[46] In 1837 alone, more than $4.5 million in Mexican pesos (which remained legal tender in the U.S. until 1857) filtered into the American economy, and the total amount from 1821 to 1842 exceeded $74 million in face value.[47]

This economic growth occurred despite Mexican governors who charged exorbitant and allegedly illegal import fees on each American wagon entering their country. Governor Baca, for example, levied a 25 percent customs duty on all goods bound for Santa Fe.[48] Referring specifically to Manuel Armijo, who taxed each wagonload at the rate of $500, one disgruntled trader wrote that customs fees served "the sole use and benefit of his obesity, the Governor."[49] Augustus Storrs complained that officials imposed duties arbitrarily, noting that none of the citizens professed any knowledge of such a tax being mandated by the Mexican government. The customs-house officer in Santa Fe could produce no credentials when asked, and one Chihuahuan legislator, Manuel Almeja, confirmed that he knew of no nationally imposed import fee. "There is very little system or consistency in the political arrangements of this Provincial Government," Storrs grumbled, "[and] they look to temporary expedients, rather than permanent and general results."[50] In a letter to Secretary of War Cass, another informant hinted at clandestine schemes when explaining that "the unsettled state of the Mexican Government gives encouragement, and ensures success to the machinations of crafty men."[51] According to Josiah Gregg—whose 1844 travelogue influenced American popular opinion in much the same way as Pike's published account had three decades earlier—governors collected duties that averaged fifty to eighty thousand dollars per year, "of which nearly half has been embezzled by the officers of the customs."[52]

Americans quickly developed their own methods to dodge excessive fees and circumvent regulations. As individual traders or entire caravans approached the New Mexico settlements, customs officers would stop them to search the wagons, check their *guías* (commercial passports), and assess import duties. Because some governors, including Armijo, charged a flat fee per wagon, crafty merchants simply combined the cargo from multiple carriages, cramming a single cart to overloaded capacity before reaching the location where they expected to encounter Mexican officials. They either abandoned the empty wagons or stashed them in the mountains and recovered them on their return trip to Missouri. Traders also removed contraband items like gunpowder and tobacco prior to inspection and smuggled them into Santa Fe on pack mules.[53]

Trappers devised similar strategies to avoid paying Mexico's fees and eventually developed an underground trade in furs and peltries. As a transient profession in which many men worked alone in remote areas, trapping was exceedingly difficult for authorities to regulate. James Baird, a naturalized Mexican citizen who had spent time in a Santa Fe prison during the Spanish period, estimated in 1826 that foreigners without trapping licenses smuggled $100,000 worth of pelts out of the Southwest each year.[54] One person nonchalantly termed such tactics "sub-treasury operations."[55] Occasionally, however, trappers did get caught and were punished for working illegally. In 1826 Mexican authorities detained Silvester Pratt for unlawful beaver hunting near Taos; in 1828 three Americans—Richard Campbell, Philip Thompson, and Vincent Guion—were arrested for unlicensed possession of pelts; and later that same year Antoine Leroux and Simon Carat underwent extensive questioning in Santa Fe for similar charges. Legal proceedings could be drawn out over a long period, as Ira Emmons learned when authorities charged him with illicit fur trading, confiscated his belongings, and then took two years to settle his case.[56]

These circumstances led Senator Benton to begin pressuring Congress to approve funding for a national highway between Missouri and Santa Fe. On January 3, 1825, he introduced the Storrs report to the Senate, explaining that "the journey to New Mexico, but lately deemed a chimerical project, has become an affair of ordinary occurrence." Recalling the sectional turmoil surrounding Missouri statehood just five years earlier, he pointed out that cotton would be among the main articles of trade with New Mexico and wisely emphasized that commerce with Santa Fe would benefit both the South and the North, because the former grew the raw materials and the latter produced the finished textiles in New England factories.[57] In so doing, however, he drastically overstated the actual impact of trade with Mexico in the context of the overall American economy. In 1826, the year after Benton made his proposals, imports from Mexico totaled over $3.9 million in value, but that sum constituted just 5 percent of United States imports from around the globe. That same year, the $6.3 million worth of American goods sent to Mexico represented 8.6 percent of all national exports.[58]

Benton also introduced a bill to finance the survey and improvement of a new international wagon road and to fund military assignments to escort merchant caravans and supervise Indian treaty negotiations. The senator even took personal responsibility for the Santa Fe Trail when referring to it as "my road to Mexico."[59] Benton sought to convince congressmen of the necessity for such a trade route by outlining multiple justifications for federal funding, despite the fact that a considerable portion of the proposed road (320 out of 746 miles) traversed Mexican territory.[60] In the four years since Becknell blazed the trail, commerce between Missouri and New Mexico had, according to Benton, already proven "sufficiently valuable to merit the favor of the national protection." His fellow statesmen and constituents repeatedly urged him to promote the project and requested that the government appoint consuls in Santa Fe and Chihuahua to protect Americans on foreign soil. Appealing to national interests, Benton again couched his persuasive exposé in the language of shared sectional prosperity. "It is not the West alone which has benefited by this trade," he declared. "The North and the South participate in her profits. The South grows the cotton, the North works it up, and the West exports it, thus displaying one of the most beautiful operations of agriculture, manufactures, and commerce, mutually dependent upon and mutually aiding one another." Perhaps unwittingly, the Missouri senator had acknowledged the interconnectedness of southern slavery and northern industrialization, a reality that few in the North would have readily admitted.[61]

Given the controversial nature of federally funded internal improvement projects—an obstacle that grew even larger once Andrew Jackson became president in 1829—Benton knew that his proposal to build a road into a foreign country would meet with opposition, especially from northerners who understood that the trail would mostly benefit a southern slave state. Senator James Lloyd of Massachusetts offered the most legitimate objection, pointing out that almost half of the route to Santa Fe, beginning at the Arkansas River, traversed Mexican territory and should not be funded by the U.S. treasury. He first wondered if it was even legal for Congress to underwrite such a project, and secondly, he questioned whether it constituted an appropriate expenditure of taxpayer dollars. Federal legislators had a difficult enough time agreeing to fund internal improvements in the eastern states—as Henry Clay had come to realize after proposing the American System—much less a transnational project across a faraway frontier. "There was a very great difference between making a road in our own territory and in that of another Power," Lloyd concluded, explaining that he felt a "strong impropriety in making roads for other people."[62]

Another potential problem involved the ability and willingness of the Mexican government to pay for portions of the Santa Fe Trail in their own national domain. Senator William Kelly of Alabama had little faith in newly independent and cash-strapped Mexico to fund the development of their section of the road. Concerned about wasting money, Kelly had a hunch that the United States would have to subsidize the entire project; otherwise, the road would go only part way to Santa Fe and end abruptly at the international boundary. Even if Congress paid for and developed the entire route, however, permission from Mexican leaders would be needed in order to build the road over foreign soil.[63] Despite these misgivings, the

Senate approved the measure and the president signed it on March 3, 1825.[64] Passage
of Benton's Santa Fe Trail bill was, in the words of one observer, "strong evidence of
the fostering care of the government" and represented the country's earliest national
investment in what would become the American Southwest.[65]

A few months later Secretary of State Henry Clay wrote to Joel Poinsett, the U.S.
minister to Mexico, regarding the Santa Fe road. Poinsett would be responsible for
negotiating a free-trade agreement to allow for construction of the new international
highway. This would be no easy task, as Clay himself acknowledged when informing
the minister that both he and President Adams expected Mexican leaders to balk
when asked to sign off on such a project. The slew of legal requirements that applied
to foreign businessmen—passports, import tariffs, per diem taxes, subjection to
search and seizure, and risk of imprisonment—betrayed the Mexican government's
paranoia about American meddling, although authorities in Mexico City had difficulty enforcing most of these laws.[66] Poinsett assured his diplomatic counterparts
that "the road was intended for purely commercial purposes" and would benefit
citizens of both nations, stressing that the United States harbored no intention of
geographic expansion or territorial acquisition. According to Clay, no harm would
come to either country by marking the road and providing a safe passageway, and
bureaucrats therefore had a duty to their constituents to approve the project.[67]

Assuming they could strong-arm foreign leaders, antsy U.S. officials (Benton
foremost among them) had no intention of waiting for Mexican dignitaries to grant
permission, and a surveying party was outfitted and dispatched before Poinsett
even began his negotiations. With George C. Sibley, Benjamin H. Reeves, and
Thomas Mather serving as co-commissioners, the group left Missouri in mid-1825
and proceeded as far as the Arkansas River, hoping to receive word en route that
Mexico would allow the project. After arriving at the international boundary,
however, "they were obliged to suspend their operations for want of the expected
authority to proceed through Mexican Territory." Sibley marched on to Taos with a
small surveying corps, while the remaining commissioners and employees returned
to Missouri without completing the mission.[68] Arriving at Santa Fe in November
1825, Sibley spent the winter there while awaiting news about ongoing negotiations in
Mexico.[69] He met multiple times with Governor Antonio Narbona, who assured the
American commissioner that "he hoped the two Governments would agree perfectly
in relation to the Trade between the two countries." In contrast to the cool receptions
that Pike, Chouteau, and Meriwether had once received, the New Mexico head of
state not only welcomed Sibley but feted him at every opportunity, inviting him
to fandangos and weddings on an almost nightly basis.[70] Narbona clearly felt little

apprehension about American interference, although the same could not be said for administrators in Mexico City. In December Sibley received news that President Guadalupe Victoria refused to allow the demarcation of any roads until a formal treaty stipulated precise national boundaries.[71] The exasperated commissioner could do nothing but attend parties in Santa Fe and await further instructions.

Poinsett finally obtained permission to survey the remainder of the Santa Fe Trail on May 13, 1826—exactly twenty years to the day before the United States declared war on Mexico—but the agreement allowed only for a visual examination of the route.[72] The commissioners subsequently informed the president and Congress that it would be "a very useless expense of money & labor" to actually mark the path through Mexican territory, because it followed easily identifiable landmarks and traversed mostly flat and unobstructed plains. Referencing the restrictive Spanish laws that landed earlier traders in prison, the commissioners proclaimed that "that barrier is now removed; the way is open, plain, and direct; and a stream of Commerce is already flowing upon it."[73] Unable to envision the technological innovations that the transportation revolution would soon bring, an elated Senator Benton gushed that the new wagon road from Missouri to New Mexico would be an important thoroughfare "for Ages and Centuries to come."[74]

In granting permission for the United States to supervise activity on the international highway, Mexico unwittingly consented to the future conquest of its far north, as it was the Santa Fe trade that sparked early American interest in the region, provided an avenue for the flow of American people and ideas, and quite literally conveyed General Kearny's army of conquest into the capital in 1846. During the Mexican-American War, the well-worn wagon ruts also provided the primary route for the resupply and reinforcement of troops in New Mexico, making it a pivotal wartime lifeline. With Fort Leavenworth in Kansas serving as the supply depot for most western forts, the trail retained an important military purpose until railroads reached New Mexico several decades later.[75]

Because of the military value of a road to Santa Fe, Senator Benton prevailed upon Congress in 1825 to pay for the highway that American troops would one day use to conquer New Mexico and to sustain that takeover for three decades thereafter. Although this may not have been the intention of lawmakers in 1825, it proved to be a convenient outcome in the broader context of Manifest Destiny. Aside from mapping the route, cementing a diplomatic agreement to ensure its permanence, and subsidizing the road's maintenance, American legislators also understood the necessity of negotiating treaties with Southern Plains tribes whose homelands lay astride the trail. Foreshadowing a flurry of pacts that the United States would arrange in 1825 and 1826, Benton suggested that rights-of-way be purchased from the Indians, allowing traders and settlers to pass through their territory peacefully. Summarizing several Indian attacks that had occurred since trade with Mexico commenced in 1821, the senator insisted that Congress had a duty to protect American citizens and create an "unmolested passage" to New Mexico. Derisively referring to Indians as "miserable barbarians" and "Arabs of the desert," Benton believed that a new highway through the southern portion of the Louisiana Purchase would serve the grander moral purpose of civilizing and assimilating them. He also cited numerous roads through Cherokee and Creek country in the Old Southeast as precedent for congressional appropriations to underwrite the Santa Fe Trail.[76] When Commissioner Sibley completed his surveys in 1826, he offered specific advice for dealing with the Indians, suggesting that Mexico and the United States "act in concert" to alleviate what he believed to be the only real hindrance to international trade. Echoing Benton's unflattering perception of Indians—whom Sibley called "Pirates of the Plains"—he explained that "*none* of them have *any* Respect for the Mexican authorities" and believed that only Americans could negotiate effective and lasting agreements with Indian groups.[77]

Following the advice of Benton and Sibley, U.S. commissioners set out for the southern plains in 1825 to arrange treaties with the Cheyenne, Crow, Kansas, Maha, Missouri, Osage, Otoe, Pawnee, and Sioux tribes. Nearly identical in their stipulations, the treaties mandated that each group refrain from hostilities with any Americans on the trail, allow surveyors to construct stone markers along the route, render aid to travelers in distress, permit emigrants to hunt along the way, and keep the road open year-round. In exchange for these concessions, the commissioners distributed $800 worth of gifts to each tribe that signed an agreement.[78] The compacts essentially purchased terrain for the international road while stripping Indians of their sovereignty and laying the groundwork for more aggressive land-grabs like the 1862 Homestead Act and 1887 Dawes Act.

As with most treaties between the U.S. government and the Indians, neither side abided by the terms for long. The Pawnees, whom Josiah Gregg called "the Ishmaelites of the Prairies," violated their end of the bargain less than two years later by raiding a caravan near Pawnee Fork on the Arkansas River and carrying away most of the merchandise and animals.[79] Fur trappers also suffered from Indian attacks, as the tendency to work alone or in small groups at remote locations imperiled their operations. Between 1826 and 1830 the trapping partnership of Smith, Jackson, and Sublette lost $43,500 worth of goods during raids, and in 1831 a group of Comanches killed Jedediah Smith, one of the most famous trappers, along the Santa Fe Trail.[80] In the first decade after legal trade began, contemporary accounts claimed that Indians murdered or robbed 234 people on the road, and pecuniary losses totaled an estimated $150,000 in merchandise and animals.[81] Gregg later concluded, rather simplistically, that "these wanton cruelties had a most disastrous effect upon the prospects of the trade."[82] For their part, American emigrants disregarded the stipulation that they remain on the road, straying at will onto Indian lands and further aggravating tense relations that grew increasingly violent as years passed. As one careful observer wrote in 1831, "I have no doubt that, in most of the misunderstandings . . . the fault is with the white people."[83]

Over the next two decades the U.S. government continued to increase its stake in the Santa Fe trade. Payments to Indian tribes for rights-of-way constituted just one of the many costs of doing business in New Mexico. Where gifts and bribes failed to secure peace, military intervention would be used as a more forceful and expensive alternative. To this end, Congress in the 1830s created the First and Second Regiments of Dragoons to provide the War Department with cavalrymen trained to fight Indians, a move that reflected increasingly firm commitments to national commerce and expansion in the Southwest borderlands despite the financial strains entailed in such operations.[84] In 1829, 1834, 1843, 1845, and 1846 military escorts accompanied merchant caravans across the plains, costing taxpayers considerable sums for troop salaries and army supplies.[85] Such campaigns, according to Missouri congressman John C. Edwards in 1842, were necessary because they "impressed upon the wild Indians an idea of our determination to protect that trade."[86] By 1848, as Americans assumed sovereignty over New Mexico and commercial traffic on the trail further intensified, military officers realized that periodic troop movements would be insufficient for discouraging Indian raids. In addition to mobile columns in the field, permanent forts needed to be built to control and subdue powerful tribes like the Arapahoes, Cheyennes, Comanches, and Kiowas.[87] Referring to the Plains Indians generally, Secretary of War Charles Conrad complained in 1850 that "all the roads leading into [New Mexico] are infested by them, and cannot safely be traveled without a military escort."[88] Superintendent of Indian Affairs James Collins proposed a three-pronged military campaign, citing recent depredations and suggesting that the Comanches and Kiowas "will certainly have to be chastised before we can have any security in passing the Plains."[89] With the military already stretched thin across the western frontier, these bureaucrats could do little to ensure safe passage to all emigrants.

In 1850 authorities received a stark reminder of the dangers that attended American travelers on the Santa Fe Trail. In May of that year, allied Utes and Jicarilla Apaches attacked a caravan near Wagon Mound, killing eleven civilians and littering the prairie with unopened letters that the mail contractors had been carrying. When Lieutenant Ambrose E. Burnside investigated the scene, he discovered the bodies stripped naked and two of the men scalped; all he could do was collect what remained of the mail and deliver it to nearby Las Vegas.[90] President Millard Fillmore used his 1850 State of the Union address to bring national attention to Indian raiding along western trails, complaining that "the great roads leading into [the Mexican Cession] are infested with them, whereby traveling is rendered extremely dangerous, and immigration is almost entirely arrested."[91] Throughout the 1850s New Mexico legislators memorialized Congress, seeking additional military aid to control Indian raiding by pointing out that "hardly a [wagon] train passes that is not compelled to give tribute to these red freebooters."[92] Dealing with these issues cost immense sums of money, and by the 1850s New Mexico had become the costliest military department in the nation to equip and maintain.[93]

The Indian wars, which erupted in part because of irresponsible or irreverent civilian travelers, cost the government significant blood and treasure. And, as with all highways, basic maintenance required continuous funding. Categorizing trail upkeep as an internal improvement, Congress repeatedly passed subsidies for the Santa Fe road beginning in 1825, when Benton's first bill secured $35,000 for that purpose. Almost annually thereafter, lawmakers approved additional appropriations totaling at least $20,000 per year, so that by the time the Mexican-American War began in 1846, the United States government had invested hundreds of thousands of dollars in road maintenance alone.[94] When paired with War Department expenditures for patrolling the route and fighting Indians, the salaries for agents and commissioners who dealt with the tribes, and other contingent expenses, the commercial network between Missouri and New Mexico became a considerable national expense that, in the eyes of many imperialistic Americans, justified the conquest and geopolitical incorporation of the region at midcentury.

As conflict with Indians continued, Americans participating in the Santa Fe trade also began to develop grievances revolving around double taxation. Trader Alphonso Wetmore suggested in 1831 that relief measures be enacted; almost every year thereafter, memorialists from both Missouri and New Mexico petitioned Congress for drawback and debenture statutes that would provide financial assistance for overburdened traders and financiers.[95] Essentially, both concepts represented nineteenth-century versions of today's corporate tax breaks that limit operating costs and cushion profit margins. Drawback involved a refund of duties imposed on an imported product that was directly exported again for resale, thus alleviating the merchant from paying two tariffs on the same item. Debenture allowed rebates of American customs fees, since businessmen paid an import duty when they entered New Mexico, and much of that merchandise had already been taxed prior to leaving the United States.[96] Without these benefits, overland traders operated at an estimated 25 percent disadvantage compared to European seagoing merchants who brought similar goods into Mexico through the port at Vera Cruz. Passage of drawback and debenture bills would "infuse into the trade new vigor and life" by leveling the commercial playing field.[97]

The most vigorous attempt at this came in 1842, when a group of Missouri merchants in Santa Fe enlisted U.S. Consul Manuel Alvarez to lobby Congress on their behalf. Thinking strategically, Alvarez played on American exceptionalism and aspirations for hemispheric hegemony. He pointed out that drawback privileges for U.S. merchants would undermine transatlantic commerce between Mexico and powerful European nations like France and England, diverting some of that business to Americans operating out of Missouri and thus solidifying the national economy. Tax benefits would elevate the United States as a regional powerhouse by strengthening trade with neighboring countries at the expense of Europe. Alvarez estimated the value of foreign commerce at Chihuahua City (where much of the merchandise transported to Santa Fe eventually wound up) at $2 million annually, and emphasized the positive economic impact of this trade on the U.S. economy. With demand for foreign goods "steadily increasing" throughout Mexico, Alvarez noted that the ultimate benefactors of drawback and debenture would be American manufacturers in the North and farmers in the South, who collectively supplied most of the raw materials and finished goods that filtered into New Mexico.[98]

Even though the fundamental economic logic of this reasoning was sound, it took Congress seven years to finally approve the first drawback bill. Passage of the measure in 1845 brought almost instantaneous financial stimulus. Trade between Missouri and Santa Fe skyrocketed from $342,000 in goods to more than $1 million within one year.[99] By the time federal lawmakers approved the tax breaks, however, it made little difference. The American conquest of New Mexico in 1846 eliminated all import and export duties, domesticated the overland trade, and created benefits that far exceeded reduced taxation on international commerce. Even more ironic was a claim that Alvarez made in 1842 when he wrote that vibrant trade between the United States and Mexico "would tend greatly to promote and strengthen those feelings of mutual amity and confidence" between the two nations.[100] In reality, the profitability of the Santa Fe trade, which rose dramatically after passage of the drawback bill, gave added impetus to the expansionist policies that soon wrested the Southwest from Mexico.

Indian attacks and thefts along the trail provided a constant concern for American merchants and bureaucrats, and Missourians lobbied obsessively for tax perks like drawback and debenture, but it would be the fledgling Republic of Texas that had the most immediate impact on American commerce with Mexico. In his inaugural address incoming president Mirabeau Buonapart Lamar revealed his expansionistic agenda, envisioning a Texas empire that would soon span "from the Sabine to the Pacific."[101] When Lamar dispatched a contingent of several hundred troops and a merchant caravan into New Mexico in 1841—ostensibly to initiate trade but covertly, many believed, to conquer and annex the territory—the aggressive maneuver startled Santa Fe officials. Governor Armijo and his colleagues scrambled to thwart the invaders, capturing General Hugh McLeod's beleaguered Texan force on the eastern plains of New Mexico and forcing the prisoners of war to march in brutal winter conditions all the way to Mexico City. Many of them died along the way, and those who survived—including a deeply embittered New Orleans journalist named George Wilkins Kendall, who in 1844 published a narrative of the event that conjured widespread American hatred toward Mexico—held a grudge for the remainder of their lives. The ill treatment of several U.S. citizens accompanying the expedition, all of whom purportedly held valid passports, infuriated federal politicians who felt that Mexican authorities had blatantly disregarded international law. A group of Kentuckians sent a memorial to Congress imploring lawmakers "to use the most prompt, vigorous, and efficient means to restore to liberty and their country those men, and to vindicate, to Mexico and the world, the proud declaration that American citizenship is a shield against wrong and oppression throughout the globe."[102]

Some hawkish American expansionists, including former president Andrew Jackson, saw this not only as an opportunity to gain support for annexation among Anglos living in Texas but also as justification for a war with Mexico that would take additional territory from that country.[103] Although the expansionists initially failed in this objective, the groundwork for conflict had been established, and war would become a reality in just a few years. Most immediately, however, Americans became concerned about the impact that the Texas invasion might have on international trade, as many Mexican officials drew little distinction between Texans and U.S. citizens and feared what was fast becoming an insatiable thirst for expansion among both groups. As a kneejerk reaction to the Texan–Santa Fe Expedition, Governor Armijo suspended activity along the trail, and shortly afterwards, on August 7, 1843, Mexican President Antonio López de Santa Anna issued a formal decree closing the customs houses at Taos, Santa Fe, and Paso del Norte.[104] Concerned that recent events had jeopardized his constituents' profitable commercial network, Senator Benton remained committed to Texas annexation but now implored his congressional colleagues to consider peaceful means toward that end, in order to avoid disrupting trade with New Mexico.[105]

Although American politicians began discussing Texas annexation in the 1830s, they revisited the topic in earnest near the end of John Tyler's presidency, at which point the geopolitical absorption of Santa Fe and its hinterlands suddenly became a real possibility. When Texas achieved independence in 1836, its leaders had staked a disputable claim to the Rio Grande as its western boundary, placing Taos, Santa Fe, and most other New Mexican towns within its limits. Were the United States to annex Texas and recognize its controversial border claim, most of New Mexico's residents would be absorbed into the American nation. Benton thus found himself in a quandary. A fervent expansionist, he remained committed to the commercial infrastructure between Missouri and New Mexico that he himself had helped to establish two decades earlier, and his constituents depended on him to protect their interests in Congress. On the other hand, Benton ranked among the leading voices of American exceptionalism, delivering bigoted and even slanderous speeches throughout his career denouncing Hispanics and Indians as unworthy of political participation in the enlightened American democracy. If Texas were annexed with the Rio Grande as a western boundary, tens of thousands of Mexicans and Pueblo Indians would be "suddenly converted, by a stroke of the President's pen, into American citizens, or American rebels." Vacillating between the pros and cons, Benton believed that the absorption of Texas and New Mexico represented "an act of unparalleled outrage on Mexico" and would be a veritable declaration of war. In the next breath, however, he returned to the imperialist rhetoric for which he was known, proclaiming with characteristic bravado, "We want Texas . . . for great national reasons, obvious as day, and permanent as nature. We want it because it is geographically appurtenant to our division of North America, essential to our political, commercial, and social system."[106]

Debates over the Texas boundary claim often took on sectional overtones, with northern representatives like Luther Severance of Maine, Charles Hudson of Massachusetts, and Jacob Brinkerhoff of Ohio speaking adamantly against any annexation that included portions of New Mexico. Brinkerhoff pointed to the 1831 treaty of commerce between the United States and Mexico, noting in his objection that "we ourselves are daily in the habit of recognizing the right of Mexico to this province by the protection we afford to the Santa Fe trade, and by the payment of duties we export to that city." Alluding to the disastrous Texan–Santa Fe Expedition three years earlier, he quipped that the only Texans ever to step foot on New Mexico soil had done so as prisoners of war. "If, therefore, New Mexico shall ever become a part of our territory," the Ohioan prophetically concluded, "we must first acquire it by purchase, or take it by conquest."[107] Phrasing his support of annexation in the parlance of Manifest Destiny, another politician saw New Mexico as the most pivotal component of the entire expansionist scheme. "We must not suffer a rival power to supersede our greatness," he began. "The trade of New Mexico may be lost to us; the trade of the Californias may be transferred to other hands, and even that great commerce which is opening with China may, through the revolution of steam and railroads and Panama canals, be diverted from the Atlantic and, crossing the Pacific and the Isthmus, center in Texas. . . . Empires rise and fall, but their mutations are consequent upon the actions of men." With the simultaneous political incorporation of New Mexico and Texas, he declared, the United States would comprise "a great family of nations that may defy the world."[108] These arguments conveniently sidestepped the central issue of slavery and free soil that so deeply divided the nation over Texas annexation, indicating the complexity of the topic and the desire of some lawmakers to downplay the most incendiary issue of all in pursuit of broader Manifest Destiny goals.

Ultimately, Congress refuted Texas's claim to the Rio Grande as its western boundary, but this would be a moot point once General Kearny's Army of the West invaded New Mexico and seized the entire province in 1846. In a matter of less than two years, Texas, California, and New Mexico fell permanently into American hands, altering the nature of trade in the West and forever redefining America's commitment to the region. With seaports on the gulf coast of Texas and the Pacific coast of California, New Mexico became a critical geographic connection between the two oceans, and the vast desert region suddenly took on tremendous importance for a nation seeking to develop and sustain a continental empire. The early Santa Fe trade, as it turned out, was only the beginning of an even larger process.

The Santa Fe Trail physically and materially linked New Mexico's capital city to a hemispheric economy. Goods from factories and mills in New England traveled down a network of turnpikes and waterways to the Mississippi River, while the South's raw materials—and even some European imports—were loaded onto steamships at New Orleans and sent upriver to the same points of embarkation in Missouri. From there, annual caravans shipped the merchandise overland to New Mexico. Prior to these formalized commercial mechanisms, the closest Santa Fe came to a continental trading network was an eighteenth-century frontier exchange economy in which a number of Indian tribes served as intermediaries between Spanish New

Mexico and French Louisiana.[109] Some merchandise did filter up the Camino Real from central Mexico, but during the colonial era that flow of goods was nominal in the broader context of the Spanish economy, and it never equaled the quantity or value of commodities coming from Missouri after 1821. To be sure, New Mexico's economy was not entirely stagnant prior to American investment but was instead largely dependent on Chihuahua and Mexico City.[110] The international highway between Santa Fe and Missouri invigorated and reoriented an internal commercial relationship between New Mexico and Chihuahua that had previously relied on pastoral and agricultural produce as the primary articles of exchange.[111] The Santa Fe trade therefore shifted New Mexico's economic dependency from Chihuahua to Missouri, effectively externalizing the local economy to the eventual detriment of Mexico.[112] By the Civil War era, these economic processes had wrought significant social change, propagating the emergence of a powerful Hispanic class of mercantile elites who skillfully transitioned from pastoral land barons to market capitalists.[113]

Commercial intensification and the concomitant tariff revenue that it pumped into New Mexico's coffers also provided money to pay local militiamen, who in turn protected residents from the debilitating Indian raids that had plagued the region's settlers since colonial times. As Missourians were quick to point out whenever confronted with accusations that they exploited Nuevomexicanos for the benefit of American capitalists, "The local authorities of the province of New Mexico, by their custom-house receipts, would be enabled to maintain a sufficient military force to reduce into subjection her Indian neighbors."[114] This made the inhabitants indirectly dependent on the Santa Fe trade for protection from Indian groups. In the years following Mexican independence, for example, both regular army and militia struck the Navajos in their homelands during several expeditions, the size, scope, and frequency of which would not have been possible prior to the increasing infusion of capital and supplies after 1821.[115]

From the 1820s through the 1840s, merchant capitalists and fur trappers integrated New Mexico into a growing continental trading network—one that the United States worked with increasing determination to control—by fostering multiple levels of dependency among Hispano inhabitants. In 1843 alone some 350 traders stuffed 230 wagons with half a million dollars in American merchandise (over $16 million today) and transported it overland to New Mexico, constituting a major component of the local economy. By 1861 the average value of yearly imports had reached $3 million (about $81 million today). Prior to the American conquest, tax revenue from such goods provided more than 70 percent of the entire territorial budget, paying the salaries of three militia companies and all provincial administrators, including the governor.[116] By the 1840s political officeholders, military leaders, and landholders—three elements of Mexican society that fostered dependency among the masses through coercive labor systems like captivity and peonage—had ironically become dependent on American commerce for their own prosperity. Furthermore, forceful rhetoric and unilateral declarations like the Monroe Doctrine of 1823, which forbade European countries from meddling in the western hemisphere, reaffirmed the United States as a burgeoning regional power broker. While their primary objective may have been profit, trappers and traders also served as a conduit for the westward flow of American democracy and capitalism, and in so doing they primed the region for military and political conquest during the Mexican-American War.[117]

American interest in New Mexico began in 1810 with the publication of Zebulon Pike's narrative and was legalized in 1821 when William Becknell opened formal commercial relations between Santa Fe and Missouri. That tenuous economic link, however, could not persist between two nations so disparate in political power and imperialistic aspiration. Within twenty-five years of Becknell's inaugural trip, the United States came to see New Mexico as far more than a foreign trading partner. With the Jacksonian era's transportation and communication revolutions creating technological possibilities for efficient long-distance commerce, American capitalists saw a new future for the Southwest, one in which Mexico played no political part. The annexation of Texas, along with the election of the expansionist James K. Polk as president, affirmed that Americans were casting their gaze westward with increasing vigor, all but cementing New Mexico's role as a critical piece in the mosaic of Manifest Destiny. In the summer of 1846, it would be up to a group of 1,600 U.S. soldiers to officially initiate this process of conversion from Mexican to American dominion.

= 2 =

THE OCCUPATION AND CONQUEST
OF NEW MEXICO

Of all the men who might have overseen America's midcentury military conquest of the Southwest, Brigadier General Stephen Watts Kearny ranked among the most qualified but least likely candidates. Born in 1794 to Irish parents in Newark, New Jersey, he attended Columbia University in New York City and went on to become a decorated military leader, serving in the U.S. Army from 1810 until his death in 1848. When Congress created the First Regiment of Dragoons in 1833, Kearny received an appointment as the second in command, and a direct order from President Andrew Jackson promoted the strict disciplinarian to full colonel just three years later. An admiring observer referred to Kearny as "the idol of the west," and Susan Shelby Magoffin, one of the first American women to enter Santa Fe after the occupation, found him to be a polite gentleman.[1] Although he campaigned throughout North America during his thirty-eight-year career, the lifelong soldier never permanently settled in the Southwest, nor did he express much personal or professional interest in the region beyond his duties as an army officer. Given his impressive résumé and military pedigree, Kearny might have been well suited to lead troops in the occupation of central Mexico, and in so doing earn the battlefield honor and political laurels that colleagues like Generals Zachary Taylor and Winfield Scott enjoyed, but his orders to command a contingent of soldiers out of Missouri would instead cement his place in history as the so-called conqueror of New Mexico.

Despite his lack of familiarity with Mexico's far north, the War Department placed the veteran Kearny in command of some 1,600 troops—collectively christened

Brigadier General Stephen Watts Kearny, c. 1840s.
Courtesy National Archives and Records Administration, Washington, D.C.

the "Army of the West"—whom he marched down the Santa Fe Trail from Fort Leavenworth at the onset of the Mexican-American War.[2] In a testament to the importance that the United States placed on the economic relationship between Missouri and Santa Fe, one of the first instructions that Kearny received required him to avoid disrupting trade and commerce between the two regions and to protect American merchants from any injury to their property rights that might occur during the military operation.[3] Additional orders directed Kearny not only to occupy Santa Fe but also to provide for its safe and permanent retention, and he was therefore authorized to requisition the governor of Missouri for volunteer reinforcements if needed. Kearny also was instructed to establish a civil government under wartime military rule before proceeding to Southern California for the same purpose. In the course of creating laws for these new bureaucracies, federal officials informed him that it "would be wise and prudent" to retain former Hispano officeholders in their positions of authority, provided that they first recite an oath of allegiance to the United States and express a favorable disposition toward American democracy. To this end, Secretary of War William Marcy told Kearny to maintain a conciliatory temperament toward all peaceful inhabitants and to reassure them that "it is the wish and design of the United States to provide for them a free government."[4]

Like the Mexican-American War itself, the activities of Kearny's Army of the
West came under harsh criticism from those who saw the conflict with Mexico as
nothing more than an antagonistic project of expansion.[5] Congressional debates
on the causes and prosecution of the war seemed at times interminable, and some
politicians specifically criticized Kearny's conquest of New Mexico as an egregious
example of American imperialism under the guise of wartime strategy. Northerners
in particular opposed both the war and Polk's purported agenda for extending slavery
westward, an accusation that the president himself fervently denied throughout his
incumbency.[6] Vermont representative Solomon Foot pointed to Kearny's expedition
to New Mexico and California—two sparsely populated provinces located far
from Mexico City—as evidence that Polk and his cabinet were waging the war for
more than just a quick and conclusive military victory.[7] Representative Alexander
Harper of Ohio ventured a step further when he asked, somewhat rhetorically,
why the War Department had not simply dispatched all troops "into the heart of
Mexico" to strike a decisive blow. He read aloud Kearny's orders from the secretary
of war, citing those instructions as evidence that Polk and others intended to gain
territory in the Southwest.[8] "Two days after the declaration of war," Massachusetts
congressman Charles Hudson grumbled, "the president had resolved to make it a
war of conquest."[9]

Whatever the misgivings of antiwar politicians and protesters, the invasion of
New Mexico went forward as planned. Accompanied by a melting pot of soldiers
that included army regulars, Missouri volunteers, and even a battalion of Mormons,
Kearny's virtually uncontested military triumph—not a single shot was fired while
occupying Santa Fe—signaled the conversion of the province from Mexican to
American jurisdiction.[10] Major General Winfield Scott, commanding the Army of
Occupation in central Mexico, assured Kearny in November 1846 that his remarkable success would win him "the emphatic approbation" of the president.[11] Just one
month later, Polk did indeed praise Kearny in his annual message to Congress,
declaring that New Mexico "has been captured without bloodshed," and commending the officers who affected that outcome.[12]

Despite the lack of fanfare as U.S. forces took possession of Santa Fe, their
march from Fort Leavenworth to the distant southwestern capital was not entirely
without incident. As Kearny's column approached New Mexico on August 1, 1846,
he scribbled the first of several communiques to Governor Manuel Armijo and
entrusted it to Lieutenant Philip St. George Cooke and a small advance party that
would meet with the head of state in the days ahead. "I come as a friend," Kearny
began, "and with the disposition and intention to consider all Mexicans and others

as friends who will remain quietly and peaceably at their homes." He gave his word that this objective would be fulfilled to the utmost of his ability.[13] Cooke delivered Kearny's dispatch to the governor on August 12, the same day that he and Santa Fe merchant James W. Magoffin—whom President Polk tapped as a confidante to "render important services" during the occupation of New Mexico—met privately with Armijo to dissuade him from fighting the Army of the West.[14] Senator Thomas Hart Benton later took credit for hatching the plan and convincing Polk and his cabinet of Magoffin's capabilities.[15] Affixing a white handkerchief to the point of his sword as a flag of truce, Cooke and his small party approached the New Mexico capital and were escorted to the governor's palace. Entering the building, he found Armijo seated amongst half a dozen military officers and wearing a formal blue army coat, complete with shining epaulettes and a red sash. The governor—whom an acquaintance once insulted as "a mountain of fat"—received the commission politely, offering to quarter them overnight and graze their horses while they parleyed.[16]

As attendants passed around chocolate and whiskey, discussions between the opposing sides began.[17] Once presented with Kearny's letter, the seemingly defiant governor set pen to paper in response, mockingly addressing it to "Your Lordship" in a thinly disguised accusation of tyrannical imperialism. New Mexicans, he told Kearny, "have risen *en masse* as an immovable force" and would turn back the invasion at all costs. In a confusing reverberation between direct threats and implicit submissiveness, Armijo admitted that his forces were unlikely to defeat the Americans and suggested that they meet north of Las Vegas to discuss the conditions of occupation. Emphasizing his people's right to "self-preservation," he concluded his letter by harkening back to the menacing claim that "I have more than enough forces to repel your aggression."[18]

The most difficult man to placate was not the governor, but Diego Archuleta, a colonel in the Mexican army who would go on to mastermind an insurrection four months later. As a career military officer, the ambitious Archuleta saw armed conflict as a stepping stone to prestige and political office, and he at first seemed unwilling to allow the American occupation to proceed unopposed. Magoffin assured the colonel that Kearny's sole purpose was to "give peace and quietude to the good people of the country" and that no harm would befall any of the inhabitants. Cooke later commended the merchant-turned-diplomat for "neutralizing the contrary influence of young Colonel Archuleta," but he did not specify the methods used to do so. Magoffin informed Secretary of War William H. Crawford that Archuleta "would have fought [but] I quieted him," thus preventing a violent clash like those that Generals Taylor, Wool, and Scott experienced in other theatres of the war.

"Bloodless possession of New Mexico was what President Polk wished," Magoffin concluded, proudly emphasizing that "it was obtained through my means." In 1849 he submitted a claim for $37,780 to the U.S. government and asked to be remunerated for expenses incurred and business lost as a result of his activities during the war. "As for the services themselves they cannot be valued in money," Magoffin reminded federal officials. "The bloodless conquest of a province and the conciliation of the feelings of an invaded people, are services above money value."[19]

Kearny's dictate and Magoffin's entreaties, coupled with the efforts of U.S. Consul Manuel Alvarez just weeks earlier to dissuade Armijo and his political cohorts from mounting any resistance, may well have had a psychological effect on the already nervous and insecure New Mexico governor.[20] The meeting with Cooke and Magoffin also convinced Armijo of the Americans' military superiority and the futility of resistance; he suddenly recanted earlier assurances that he would fight to the death and instead began telling officers that he could not in good conscience sacrifice troops for a hopeless cause.[21] Ironically, while Kearny's manifesto and the persuasive testimonials of Cooke's advance party convinced Armijo that he would die in shame if he needlessly allowed New Mexicans to be butchered at the hands of U.S. soldiers, the opposite came to pass. It was Armijo's decision to flee and give up the capital that propagated his political and personal downfall.

Directed toward the New Mexico people generally and Governor Armijo specifically, Kearny's next edict explained his orders to occupy the province and assured enemies that he would be "amply sustained in the accomplishment of this object," an allusion to his superior manpower and the military might of the United States. Hoping to avoid civilian resistance and unnecessary bloodshed, Kearny told New Mexicans that if they stayed at home and remained peaceful, the occupying American forces would not harass or otherwise inconvenience them, nor would their religious or civil rights be jeopardized. With this affirmation, however, came a stern warning to those who might consider resisting the invaders. All who took up arms against the United States, Kearny swore, "will be regarded as enemies, and will be treated accordingly."[22]

An increasingly frenzied Armijo issued a proclamation of his own in which he bluntly acknowledged the "strength and power" of the United States and his vain hope that God might side with Mexico. It sounded like the desperate appeal of a downtrodden leader who knew that his government would fail to reinforce him but who nonetheless saw the political prudence in broadcasting a nationalistic public statement. "Behold, fellow patriots," Armijo declared with feigned bravado, "the invasion is the sign of alarm that must prepare us for the combat . . . to defend the most just and holiest causes." Criticizing the Americans as arrogant and greedy, the governor invoked memories of Father Hidalgo's 1810 revolution in hopes of inspiring a similar patriotic fervor among his own people. He begged New Mexicans to contribute their money and their lives for the cause of freedom and disingenuously assured them that he himself was "ready to sacrifice his life and interests in defense of his beloved country."[23]

If Armijo enjoyed one advantage, it was that he had plenty of time to prepare. As early as January 10, 1846—four months before the first shots of the war were fired in the contested Texas space between the Nueces River and the Rio Grande—the governor had issued a circular to the prefects of various New Mexico towns warning them of a possible conflict.[24] In March, Armijo received a notice from President Mariano Paredes y Arrillaga relative to deteriorating relations between the United States and Mexico.[25] Once the war between the two nations began, Armijo circulated a proclamation imploring New Mexicans to defend their homeland from the onslaughts of a neighboring enemy.[26] And on June 30 Armijo received news of the coming invasion from Adolph Wislizenus, a German doctor who arrived in Santa Fe two months ahead of U.S. troops.[27]

Two days after speaking with Wislizenus, a disturbed Armijo attended a meeting of the legislative assembly and informed his fellow administrators that a large contingent of soldiers accompanied the annual caravan of Missouri traders as they moved westward toward the capital. During a special session of the assembly that convened just days before American emissaries entered Santa Fe and met with the governor, Armijo swore that approaching U.S. forces numbered more than five thousand men, a gross exaggeration that reflected both his anxiety as well as conflicting reports from spies in the field.[28] The legislators present on August 10—the last time that the assembly met under the Mexican flag—criticized Armijo for failing to inform them of the circumstances earlier, so that they might have "secured for him the funds necessary" to mount a concerted defense of the capital.[29]

On August 14, as Kearny's army approached the village of Las Vegas just seventy miles east of Santa Fe, four Mexican soldiers "dressed in their best bib and tucker" rode up waving a white flag. They delivered a message from Armijo "expressing his determination to resist," claiming that 600 armed men had congregated ahead and suggesting that the two leaders meet north of the town. Undeterred by this bold posturing, Kearny probed forward without opposition.[30] With a crowd of Mexican citizens looking on, the general and his interpreter, longtime fur trader Antoine Robidoux, climbed atop an adobe roof in Las Vegas and addressed the townspeople "to the purport that they no longer owed allegiance to the government of Mexico" and would henceforth be considered American citizens. Seemingly unmindful of his audience's lifetime fidelity to a foreign nation, and naively believing that the entire population would instantaneously embrace American democracy, Kearny declared that "we come amongst you as friends—not as enemies; as protectors—not as conquerors. We come among you for your benefit—not for your injury."[31]

As Kearny approached Santa Fe over the coming days, he gathered the villagers at each town he came to and "harangued them much in the same manner" as he had at Las Vegas, assuring all who listened that "resistance is useless" and asserting that they must therefore succumb to the inevitable. He also required each village *alcalde* (mayor) to look him directly in the eyes and take an oath of allegiance to the United States—an act that Lieutenant Emory called "a bitter pill" that invariably elicited "downcast eyes"—although a few hinted of coming unrest by refusing to make the pledge.[32] The general strategically forced the town leaders to promise loyalty to the American government in a public spectacle as a method of encouraging villagers to do the same, essentially coercing the alcaldes into a disingenuous profession of American nationalism in hopes that others would follow their example without questioning the meaning or intent behind such action.

The immediate extension of citizenship to this foreign population irked some of the soldiers, particularly those of nativist proclivities who perceived Hispanic Catholics as unworthy of political participation in the American system. Lieutenant Cooke, for one, lamented that with Kearny's proclamations "the great boon of American citizenship thus [was] thrust, through an interpreter . . . upon eighty thousand mongrels who cannot read,—who are almost heathens." While his comments might have been rooted in racism, the young lieutenant, who led the Mormon Battalion during Kearny's conquest, also discerned a serious tactical blunder in naturalizing the population of an enemy nation during wartime. "The people of this territory are declared citizens of the United States," Cooke grumbled, "and the invaders are thus debarred the rights of war to seize needful supplies."[33] The insinuation of citizenship would also have serious legal and political ramifications a few months later during revolts at Taos and Mora.

As the Army of the West approached the steep defiles of Apache Pass east of Santa Fe, Kearny received another boisterous notice from Armijo, who threatened battle if the Americans advanced any further. As it happened, however, the Mexican soldiers came "under the effects of fear and discord" and retreated before U.S. troops arrived.[34] Susan Shelby Magoffin, the teenage wife of merchant Samuel Magoffin, mocked Armijo in her diary, writing that "a trembling for his own personal safety seized his mind and he dispersed his army."[35] The trader Josiah Gregg, who knew

Armijo personally, called him "an ambitious and turbulent demagogue."[36] His exorbitant import duties on goods arriving over the Santa Fe Trail added to his unpopularity, and his issuance of immense land grants to foreigners like Charles Beaubien further demoted him in popular opinion. Widely known for his shameless self-aggrandizement, Governor Armijo was disliked and even despised throughout parts of New Mexico.[37] While some Americans—especially those associated with the ill-fated Texan–Santa Fe Expedition of 1841—expressed stronger distaste for Armijo than others, his resonating unpopularity can be gleaned from the fact that even fellow Hispanic officeholders like U.S. Consul Manuel Alvarez repeatedly chastised the governor.[38]

Armijo took what personal belongings he could carry and left his wife behind at the family home in Albuquerque as he fled south toward Chihuahua.[39] As a final gesture, he dispatched a messenger to Kearny, who had already occupied Santa Fe, informing him that he planned to return the following day with a large body of Mexican troops. The warning turned out to be nothing more than "a ruse to obtain time to make a more effectual escape," leaving one U.S. officer to echo the opinion of American troops and the New Mexican people alike when he wrote him off as nothing more than "a coward and a rascal."[40] Realizing that his failure to engage American troops at Apache Pass would tarnish his reputation and might even result in disciplinary action, Armijo commenced a letter-writing spree to clear his name of wrongdoing. He first wrote to Colonel Mauricio Ugarte, commandant-general of Mexican troops in Chihuahua, explaining his decisions. Expressing sorrow at the circumstances and aware that everything he said would be entered into the official record for government authorities to review, the embattled governor told Ugarte that he had spiked his cannons and retreated with a few dozen loyal men, whom he dubbed "The Valiant Seventy."[41] He believed that the majority of New Mexicans had turned against him and harbored pro-American sentiments, despite the fact that more than 3,000 of them had picked up arms and rallied behind him just days earlier. Claiming that Kearny's force numbered at least 2,500—a number that Armijo exaggerated by almost 40 percent—he explained that he had no alternative but to abandon Santa Fe, "where the United States flag is at present raised."[42]

Armijo eventually arrived in Chihuahua, where he was placed under arrest and escorted to Mexico City for a meeting with government officials.[43] He found time before departing to compose his official report of the incident, which he dispatched to the minister of foreign relations. Armijo no doubt hoped his written account would smooth things over before he arrived in the Mexican capital. The United States—"that perfidious and faithless power"—had sent nearly 4,000 soldiers to conquer New Mexico, a number that Armijo now exaggerated by 60 percent instead of 40. He also understated the number of New Mexicans who answered his muster call in August, claiming that only 1,800 people came to his service when in fact the figure was at least 3,000. By flip-flopping the statistics, he made it appear that the numerical advantage belonged to Kearny, when Armijo in fact led the larger body of fighting men. Furthermore, he claimed to have taken every possible preparatory measure by sending out scouts, enlisting citizens as militia, and communicating with authorities in Durango and Chihuahua to request reinforcements that never arrived. The failure of the commanders in those two districts, the governor believed, was to blame for his inability to organize an armed resistance to the American invasion.[44]

A group of 105 New Mexico citizens, including many members of the most prominent and influential Hispano families in the province, had a very different story to tell. In a formal proclamation to the Mexican president, these eyewitnesses lambasted Armijo for his actions. In the vitriolic language of these men can be discerned the seeds of discord that would sprout in violent climax at Taos and Mora four months later. Indeed, one of the first signatures on the document was that of Tomás Ortíz, an acknowledged mastermind behind the initial plans for a civilian revolt in December 1846. Hoping to preserve their "good reputation and fame" after Armijo's embarrassing capitulation, the supplicants pointed out that the governor knew of Kearny's expedition months ahead of time. They explained the muddled process of vacillation whereby Armijo ordered all men between the ages of sixteen and fifty-nine to arms, sent them back to their homes a week later, recalled them yet again as U.S. troops neared Santa Fe, and finally dispersed the volunteers a second time as the Americans approached.[45]

"We wish that the conduct of our governor and commandant-general, Don Manuel Armijo, had been other than it was," the exasperated individuals concluded, noting that the governor's actions alone were to blame for Santa Fe having been occupied "without the slightest resistance." Had they been permitted to mount military opposition, the New Mexicans felt certain that they could have at least maintained some semblance of pride. "It would be a great deal for us to venture that victory would have crowned our efforts," they admitted, "but at least we would have had the honor of having tried." Instead, they lamented, "nothing, absolutely nothing, was done. And Sr. Armijo can say full well, *I have lost everything, including honor.*"[46] Many New Mexico citizens felt humiliated by the uncontested occupation of their homeland and nation. But some of the more politically attuned signatories also realized that, in the event Mexico won the war, they might be punished for their failure to resist the American invasion. In defense of their reputations and

Governor Manuel Armijo, c. 1840s.
Courtesy Palace of the Governors Photo Archives,
New Mexico History Museum/DCA, Santa Fe (negative no. 050809).

future livelihood, many Nuevomexicanos sought to distance themselves from Armijo while reaffirming their own patriotism as Mexican citizens.

Armijo eventually appeared before a tribunal in Mexico City. Donaciano Vigil, a New Mexico official who became temporary governor after the American occupation, claimed that Armijo accepted a bribe of 24,000 pesos from James Magoffin just days before Kearny's arrival; others claimed that the payoff consisted of 500 ounces of gold. Fortunately for the ex-governor, proof of these accusations never surfaced, and hearsay alone did not convict him. During the course of the hearings—which included official statements from New Mexico legislators and military leaders—the events surrounding Armijo's flight were recounted in what to him must have seemed like excruciating detail.[47] Citing his meritorious gubernatorial service dating back to 1837, the embattled Armijo hoped to rationalize his political and military decisions and clear his name of wrongdoing, dismissing the accusations against him as slanderous inaccuracies and assuring the tribunal that he had committed his life, family, and fortune to the protection of Mexican nationhood.[48]

With Armijo thus preoccupied, Kearny entered Santa Fe on August 18, 1846, and took quarters in the Palace of the Governors, a symbolic gesture that cemented the occupation he had accomplished.[49] The remainder of the troops encamped on a bluff overlooking the town and aimed their cannons at the houses below, a further demonstration of militaristic power and political authority.[50] As Lieutenant James W. Abert put it, the troops positioned themselves in such a manner that "ten guns may be brought to bear upon the city" should the need arise.[51] After settling on the high ground, the army of over a thousand men marched directly through the city streets to the central plaza, where they raised an American flag over the adobe governor's mansion to the tune of a thirteen-gun artillery salute.[52] Awestruck locals looked on in "gaping wonder" at the scene unfolding before them.[53] A sympathetic Lieutenant Richard Smith Elliott could not help but notice the "surly countenances and downcast looks" among many Hispanos as he rode through Santa Fe. "Strange, indeed, must have been the feelings of the citizens," he wrote, "all the future of their destiny vague and uncertain." The young officer realized the fear and anguish that many New Mexicans must have felt as they were subjected to unknown rulers whose customs, culture, language, and religion differed so starkly from their own.[54]

As straggling detachments of U.S. troops ventured into Santa Fe over the coming days, their first sight was a flagpole "from which the banner of freedom now waves" over the town plaza.[55] "In this way," trader Lewis Garrard wrote with a hint of condescension, "the province was Americanized."[56] At Kearny's insistence, what remained of Santa Fe's presidial garrison of Mexican troops presented themselves to the victorious general and surrendered their guns.[57] There would be no violent defense of the capital like the one that Major General Scott's army faced at Chapultepec. Their conquest seemingly complete, Kearny and his ranking officers enjoyed several bottles of wine and slumbered peacefully in the Governor's Palace that night.[58] "Here we are in Santa Fe," Lieutenant Elliott exclaimed, "and New Mexico is ours!"[59]

Kearny, who seemed to relish oratorical grandstanding, once again climbed a roof and spoke through an interpreter to the New Mexican people, hundreds of whom congregated in the open spaces below him. All individuals who quietly subjected themselves to American rule would be respected in their person and property, could continue worshipping as Catholics, and would enjoy protection from the Indian raids that had plagued Rio Grande settlements since the colonial era. Those who left their homes and took up arms against his troops, however, would "be considered as enemies and traitors." Pending the organization of a new civil government, Kearny informed his listeners that preexisting Mexican statutes would remain in force "until changed or modified by competent authority." Finally, he absolved all residents of their Mexican nationality and pronounced them American citizens. This unauthorized unilateral action later met with the disapproval of President Polk, who refuted immediate citizenship for New Mexicans in a special congressional address.[60]

Having secured possession of New Mexico, Kearny's officers began drafting a set of civil regulations for the new government.[61] Intended to be temporary until Congress could enact more permanent measures, these "rigid but just and equitable" laws came to be called the Kearny Code, although the commanding general himself played no role in actually writing them and merely lent his name and endorsement to the treatise.[62] Instead, Colonel Alexander Doniphan, who had formerly worked as an attorney in Missouri, would be tasked with writing most of the new legal apparatus. With the assistance of a well-educated team that included Private Willard Hall (graduate of Yale), Captain David Waldo (graduate of Transylvania College), and Francis P. Blair Jr. (graduate of Princeton), Doniphan based the Kearny Code on several preexisting codices, including the Missouri organic law and Texas state statutes. In a testament to the conciliatory nature of the new government, even some of Mexico's laws were integrated into the document.[63] Kearny sought to assuage the Hispanic inhabitants by appointing a number of former Mexican officials to head the new bureaucracy, including Donaciano Vigil as secretary, along with Antonio José Otero and Charles Beaubien as superior court judges.[64] To fill the office of governor, he selected Charles Bent, a longtime resident of northern New Mexico whose well-established trading networks and marriage into the prominent family of María Ignacia Jaramillo strengthened his connections to local society and culture.[65]

Officially entitled the "Organic Law of the Territory of New Mexico," the Kearny Code was over fifty pages long and outlined all aspects of civil government authority. Secretary Manuel Alvarez was paid $500 to translate the lengthy document into Spanish, and Oliver P. Hovey printed five hundred copies for local distribution.[66] The law established three branches of government, extended voting rights to "all free male citizens"—a phrase that implicitly recognized the existence of slavery in the form of unfree Indian captives and Hispanic peons—and even concluded with a bill of rights. The statutes codified the promises that Kearny made during his numerous proclamations to the New Mexican people, protecting their rights to religious freedom, private property, free speech, and due process of law. Finally, the organic law attempted to maintain brevity and simplicity by retaining all preexisting laws "which are not repugnant to, or inconsistent with, the constitution of the United States and the laws thereof."[67]

The Kearny Code came under harsh criticism later that year when President Polk condemned portions of it as overbearing and unconstitutional.[68] In a special message to politicians on December 22, 1846, Polk worried that portions of New Mexico's organic act established a permanent rather than temporary territorial government and that in so doing Kearny had overstepped his wartime authority as a military officer. Such stipulations, the president bluntly declared, "have not been approved and recognized by me." While seeking to correct this mistake, however, Polk carefully refrained from criticizing the victorious leader of the Army of the West, postulating instead that Kearny's "departure" from orders emanated from "a patriotic desire to give to the inhabitants the privileges and immunities so cherished by the people of our own country."[69] Secretary of War William Marcy informed Kearny that his legal code went "in some respects, beyond the line designated by the President" because it conferred constitutional rights on the New Mexico population without congressional approval, and he added that the president had nullified those portions of the document he deemed unlawful.[70]

The code also surfaced during congressional debates that reflected the increasingly sectional political climate of the time. Recognizing that the law did not explicitly establish slavery in New Mexico and did allow "universal suffrage," in the sense that all free adult males could vote, Representative Luther Severance lauded the statutes as a "new feature in democratic progress" that should be emulated throughout the Mexican Cession lands. "I must say," Severance antagonistically declared about the recently adopted Texas state ordinances, "I like Kearny's constitution much better." Noting that the Lone Star State claimed jurisdiction over part of New Mexico, the Maine congressman hoped that Kearny's laws might supersede those of slaveholding Texas in that region.[71] Missouri representative James B. Bowlin stated that the Kearny Code did nothing more than extend "the blessings of our free institutions" to the people of New Mexico, in effect codifying the democratic ideologies that had been flowing into the territory since the Santa Fe trade opened more than two decades earlier.[72] Falsely believing that the mandate precluded slavery from the Southwest, Kentucky representative Garrett Davis thought that Kearny had egregiously transcended his authority. Sarcastically referring to the general as a "law-giving warrior," Davis rebuked his northern counterparts and compared Kearny to a totalitarian dictator, proclaiming that "no absolute autocrat in Europe could have done more."[73] While these controversies surrounding New Mexico's new legal apparatus erupted in the national capital, U.S. soldiers in Santa Fe and the surrounding villages also acted in ways that jeopardized American control over the region.

Despite his promises of an amicable occupation, Kearny and his men behaved condescendingly in their interactions with Nuevomexicanos. Conciliation toward

Mexican civilians was an important wartime strategy of American military leaders, and many commanding officers (including Scott, Taylor, and Wool) pursued that approach to varying degrees. Because Mexico suffered from a bankrupt treasury, lacked foreign support, and had a weak standing army, U.S. troops feared mass civilian uprisings and mob violence as much as they did professional Mexican soldiers. Passing through Santa Fe just weeks before Kearny's troops arrived, Dr. Wislizenus recognized the importance of mollifying native inhabitants during the war. "The official leeches who consider themselves privileged to rule will, of course, make some opposition—if not openly, at least by intrigue," the doctor wrote, criticizing New Mexico's elite aristocracy and the extreme imbalance of power in that society.[74] He understood that careful attention to the peoples' cultural, social, and religious sensibilities might help to avert future problems associated with the occupation.

In New Mexico the strategy of conciliation fell far short of its intent. Irreverent behavior among the occupying American forces began at the uppermost reaches of the military chain of command and trickled down to the enlisted men. U.S. officers in Santa Fe frequently attended fandangos "and even less reputable places of dissipation," setting a poor example for the men under their command.[75] On August 27, as on many other nights, noisy and rowdy partiers frolicked, smoked, and drank into the early morning hours.[76] "Instead of being the strong arm on which the civil authority can depend to enforce order and law and administer justice to all," one anonymous observer complained, "the soldiery have degenerated into a military mob, are the most open violators of law and order, and daily heap insult and injury upon the people of the territory."[77] The failure of the officers to enforce discipline among their troops ranked among the reasons why New Mexicans became so upset over the occupation.

As the months passed the U.S. regulars living at Fort Marcy and the Missouri volunteers who bivouacked near town exacerbated this trend with unruly behavior of their own. In an ominous portent of things to come, a riot broke out among a group of soldiers the day after they entered Santa Fe.[78] Describing the army campsites just south of the capital, Lieutenant Elliott wrote, "Their quarters are but little better in condition than pig-sties, and their officers pay no attention to them." Entering the makeshift lodgings, Elliott "found the rooms so filthy that he could scarcely endure the noisome smell and sights of untold dirtiness."[79] At nighttime, according to Lieutenant Abert, these filthy, foul-mouthed soldiers made their way into town, where they could be found at all hours "mingling with the motley groups of Mexicans and Pueblo Indians."[80] As he traveled through the territorial capital shortly after the occupation, Englishman George Ruxton quipped that "crowds of drunken volunteers filled the streets, brawling and boasting" while "Mexicans, wrapped in sarape, scowled upon them as they passed." American troops appeared to Ruxton as "the dirtiest, rowdiest crew I have ever seen collected together."[81] With this in mind, Donaciano Vigil informed Secretary of State James Buchanan that all volunteers in New Mexico should be replaced with professional soldiers for reasons of "economy, expediency, and efficiency" and claimed that "both the interests of the United States and this Territory clearly demand it."[82]

Reports from Kearny and his successor, Colonel Sterling Price, were replete with descriptions of aberrant behavior, the suppression of which occupied a considerable amount of time and attention and distracted from other important duties. On September 17, 1846, Private William Bray drunkenly pulled a knife on an officer, who then shot and killed him. A week later an altercation between two enlisted men ended when one soldier threw a hatchet at the other, nearly severing his hand. Dozens of courts martial convened to investigate soldiers for a variety of charges, including "habitual drunkenness," "disobedience of orders," "highly unsoldierlike conduct," and even "worthlessness"—a catchall term used when nothing more specific could be decided. For his part, Kearny "regretted to see such a want of discipline and subordination" among his army and ordered all company commanders to exercise greater vigilance in the prosecution of their duties.[83]

To reduce tension Governor Bent declared a civilian curfew, and the military forbade troops from being out past 10:00 P.M., at which time a sentinel's gunshot signaled that all men must return to quarters.[84] Colonel Edward W. Newby issued an order banning civilians from selling liquor without a license and levying a five-dollar fee on all fandangos, citing "a woeful want of sobriety and good order" among the troops as justification for such requirements.[85] Throughout New Mexico, Ruxton wrote, "the most bitter and most determined hostility existed against the Americans."[86] The lifestyle and behavior of some U.S. troops—along with the grandiose proclamations of conquest and coerced pledges of loyalty that officers demanded—added insult to injury to inhabitants of the province and pushed them closer to rebellious action.

The soldiers themselves noticed very few signs of discontent, and indeed some community leaders strategically lured the Americans into a false sense of security. Lewis Garrard, who arrived at Taos in January 1847, wrote that "designing men— artful & learned natives—were busily, insidiously sowing the seeds of discontent among the more ignorant class of the community, more especially the Pueblo Indians."[87] According to James Madison Cutts, the uncontested occupation of Santa Fe turned out to be as much a curse as a blessing, because it "lulled all into the belief of a quiet submission," and many of the American officers failed to detect nonchalant hints of disgruntlement.[88] Just days after Kearny entered Santa Fe, Lieutenant Emory watched as groups of people from Taos arrived to profess allegiance and ask for protection from the Indians. He believed residents of the Rio Arriba region to be "the best disposed toward the United States" in the entire territory.[89]

Despite these public displays of fidelity, rumors of impending armed resistance began to swirl among the locals, and many people believed that Armijo was raising a force in Chihuahua to reclaim possession of New Mexico. Kearny's officers summarily dismissed such reports, however, and did not foresee any tangible threat from the former governor.[90] Because of their military training and disdainful opinion of the largely illiterate Hispanic population, many American officers did not believe that the citizens posed any danger. One officer speculated that mischievous individuals purposely spread rumors of approaching Mexican armies and mass uprisings to induce the War Department to dispatch additional troops to Santa Fe. Some of these people would accrue handsome profits in their stores and saloons if more soldiers garrisoned the town. Of one rumored revolt at Santa Fe in October 1846, Lieutenant George R. Gibson wrote that "the best informed lay it at the doors of a few men who have been reaping a rich harvest from the soldiers, and who adopt this plan to retain a large force at this point."[91]

At least one soldier under Kearny's command did notice hints of discontent among the population, but he concluded that "I cannot be made to believe that these people are either so hardy or foolish to attempt anything in the shape of a revolt." All rumors of potential violence, the informant believed, could be attributed to "the broad head of Mexican braggadocio."[92] A handful of other American officers also noticed signs of displeasure and unrest among New Mexico's people. As Lieutenant Abert approached the town of Manzano in November, inhabitants there greeted him with guns drawn, although they eventually shouldered their weapons. "These people still have a lingering inclination for the old [Mexican] government," Abert wrote after this eye-opening experience, postulating that "it will be some time before they will regard the entrance of the Americans otherwise than as an intrusion."[93] Lieutenant Cooke noted that American merchants in the Rio Abajo entertained strong suspicions of their Hispanic neighbors, believing them to be hatching "a conspiracy to rise and throw off the American rule in this territory."[94] Lieutenant Elliott similarly explained that "there prevails, among many of the New Mexicans, a very bitter feeling towards our Government and people." The wealthier landholding class, he noticed, seemed especially averse to American democracy, largely because they suspected that their political and economic power might be wrested from them as a result of the conquest.[95] Lieutenant A. B. Dyer likewise perceived that the clergy as well as the "wealthy men"—or as Cooke phrased it, "a few of the millionaires"—of New Mexico remained inimical to political transformation for reasons of personal interest.[96]

Influenced by favorable reports from field commanders, President Polk delivered an address to Congress on December 8, 1846, in which he proclaimed that "little if any further resistance is apprehended from the inhabitants" of New Mexico.[97] Had the president delivered his speech a couple of weeks later, he might have taken a different tone. Even as Polk spoke, suspicious American officers in Santa Fe had begun keeping "a sharp eye" on a number of individuals rumored to be contemplating some sort of uprising.[98] On December 17, Governor Bent met with an unnamed Mexican confidante and learned of a conspiracy among residents of the four northernmost counties to expel all U.S. troops and civil authorities through a "far and wide" insurrection.[99] Bent took quick and decisive action to ascertain the names of those involved and had them detained and questioned by military personnel.[100] U.S. officials arrested Miguel Quintana, Francisco Gutiérrez, Juan Ortega, Matías Alire, and Pablo Domínguez for plotting a rebellion, although four of them were released due to insufficient evidence. Only Domínguez, who carried a muster roll bearing the names of former Mexican soldiers in Santa Fe, was held under suspicion of intrigue. Shortly thereafter, authorities jailed five more men—Manuel Piño, Nicholas Piño, Manuel Chaves, José María Sánchez, and José Francisco Baca y Torres—who purportedly concocted an ambitious scheme to storm Santa Fe, capture Governor Bent and Colonel Price, occupy Fort Marcy, seize the cannons there, and "kill off the whole army." The two ringleaders, Tomás Ortíz and Diego Archuleta, remained at large, supposedly somewhere in Chihuahua.[101] A complete investigation of the conspiracy revealed that a number of the most influential citizens in northern New Mexico had actively planned the revolt.[102] According to trader Benjamin Franklin Coons, some local women, "whose hearts our caballeros have won," were to be credited as the informants who notified authorities of the plot and prevented the rebellion from materializing.[103]

Of the two plot leaders, Archuleta boasted an accomplished military background while Ortíz, whose brother served as vicar of New Mexico, represented the powerful ecclesiastical element of the Catholic society in which they lived. Politically, both the army and the church tended to fall on the conservative anti-American side, while their liberal opponents—the ones that Kearny appointed to office after the occupation—usually wedded themselves to the United States cause. As prominent men with large followings, Archuleta and Ortíz had grown accustomed to active participation in local affairs, and the impetus to rebel found inspiration in their omission from Kearny's newly instituted government of American sympathizers. This budding political factionalism, with roots in the Santa Fe trade and Mexico's self-destructive issuance of land grants to foreigners, long predated Kearny's arrival but did not fully blossom until this wartime climax. New Mexico's unstable governmental structure—one in which multiple administrations held office in the two years prior to the war—emanated from factionalized political, economic, and ecclesiastic elites with varying levels of nationalistic dedication to Mexico. Kearny's arrival and subsequent appointment of pro-American liberals like Donaciano Vigil and Antonio José Otero to positions of political control pushed this power struggle to the point of conflagration.[104]

The paranoia emanating from these clandestine activities did not dampen the officers' Christmas spirits. Just one week after arresting the alleged participants, and with the masterminds yet to be apprehended, leaders in Santa Fe organized lavish fandangos and feasts to mark the occasion. Troops paraded through the plaza during the day while their commanders prepared for the evening festivities. Governor Bent hosted an elegant supper at the Palace of the Governors, complete with fine wines, champagne, and imported delicacies that spoiled the attendees with "all the luxuries of an eastern table."[105] Christmas offered the perfect occasion to celebrate the suppression of the uprising. Unbeknownst to Bent, he had just twenty-five days to live.

As holiday hangovers and rumors of intrigue cooled in the days after Christmas, Bent delivered a powerful proclamation on January 5, 1847, outlining steps taken to counteract the unrest. Echoing Kearny's earlier speeches, he informed New Mexicans that they now, one and all, "compose a part of the Union, the cradle of liberty," and he encouraged them to embrace their new political and national identity. Bent condemned Ortíz and Archuleta as "anarchists" and "old revolutionists," portraying them as metaphorically blind men who were unwilling to embrace the benefits of American democracy and liberty. To reiterate the futility of resistance, the governor spoke of Colonel Doniphan's recent Christmas Day victory over Mexican troops at Brazito, describing the ease with which the Missouri volunteers achieved total victory in that battle. He assured his audience that no help would ever come from Chihuahua and warned them that they would be well served to "remain quiet in [their] domestic occupations."[106] Americans believed that their discovery of the scheme, coupled with Doniphan's military triumph, would be "sufficient to nip the plot in the bud," and Lieutenants Elliott and Cooke both thought the conspiracy had ended.[107] Satisfied that all threats had dissipated, Governor Bent left Santa Fe on January 14 and returned to his home and family in Taos without noticing the shifting fortunes around him.

In the months since the Army of the West entered New Mexico, deaths by illness and transfers to alternative theatres of war had sapped military strength and manpower. A force that had originally numbered almost 1,600 men had been depleted to fewer than 1,000 by the time the New Year rolled around. Kearny took 100 dragoons with him to California in September, and Doniphan led some 500 men of the Missouri volunteers toward Chihuahua in December. Still other soldiers remained on detached service in neighboring towns or were manning remote grazing camps, and a significant number of those stationed in Santa Fe were bedridden with measles and various fevers.[108] One observer estimated that only 500 healthy troops garrisoned Santa Fe, and in Taos there was no military presence at all.[109] As U.S. manpower diminished, would-be rebels took note, recognizing that their chances of success increased with each detachment that marched out of the territory and with every sick soldier who died. Psychologically, the decreasing numbers of Americans not only empowered those plotting rebellion but also influenced undecided locals who at first might have seen the ploy as hopeless. The fact that no troops occupied the Rio Arriba helps to explain why, when an insurrection finally materialized, it occurred in the northernmost reaches of the territory and not in Santa Fe or Albuquerque.

On the morning of January 19, Taos became "the culminating point of all the differences between the Americans and the New Mexicans."[110] Although it seemed at the time like a spontaneous uprising, the groundwork for the rebellion had been developing for months, and the outbreak of violence in 1847 signified a climax to the rising action. From the moment U.S troops arrived, the behavior of the rank-and-file and their commanding officers provoked disdain and bitterness among many New Mexico residents who resented the onslaughts of Anglo-Americans. Kearny's insistence that every Hispanic official take a public oath of allegiance to the United States humiliated and embarrassed many people, making them increasingly averse to the American presence. The pomp and show that the Army of the West displayed when entering Santa Fe—parading triumphantly through the streets, firing deafening cannon salutes, taking up residency in the Governor's Palace, and building a fortress directly overlooking the town—irked the native Hispanos as they looked on in muffled contempt. While Kearny's initial occupation of New Mexico transpired without bloodshed, this particular winter night in Taos would be anything but tranquil.

Governor Charles Bent.
Courtesy Palace of the Governors Photo Archives,
New Mexico History Museum/DCA, Santa Fe (negative no. 007004).

A violent crowd of Pueblo Indians and Hispanos—which one American observer called "as merciless a band of savages as ever went on the war path"—made their way to Governor Bent's home near the center of town, where they broke down doors and climbed atop the roof to gain entry.[111] Hearing the commotion, Bent sprung from his bed in time to grab a pistol, while his wife and children, wearing only their nightgowns, used small utensils to dig their way out of the besieged home through a soft adobe wall.[112] Although his terrified spouse and the couple's four children made it to safety after a harrowing escape and a two-week hideout at a friend's house, the governor was not so lucky. Outside the front door, angry men shouted to Bent that "they did not intend to leave an American alive in New Mexico; and as he was Governor, they would kill him first."[113] He yelled out for help, but the only response portended the inevitable: "That they could do nothing—that he must die."[114] And a martyr's death it would be. The assailants tortured Bent, shooting him with arrows and scalping him alive before nailing both the hairy trophy and the writhing body to a wooden plank, whereupon they "carried it in triumph through the streets."[115] Unbeknownst to Bent and other American transplants in New Mexico, the U.S. conquest had altered their social and political status. Despite their family ties and standing in the community, they had become conquerors living among the conquered, and Bent's new role as governor made him the foremost target of an ambitious rebellion intended to oust every American from the territory.[116]

Alongside Bent, prefect Cornelio Vigil, Sheriff Stephen Lee, and circuit attorney James Leal were among the first to die when an angry crowd stormed the town jail, freed two Pueblo Indian prisoners, and burned most of the Taos County records stored there.[117] Despite being a native New Mexican, Vigil had contributed to the American takeover by approving land grants to non-Hispanics, and in so doing he invoked the ire of his surrounding community and made himself a target during the uprising. Nor, for that matter, did Lee's marriage to María Luz Tafoya in 1829 save him from his fate as an American outsider.[118] As the sheriff lay dying, the insurgents "cut his body to pieces, severing all the limbs from it." Nearby, Leal suffered a similar fate: "They shot arrows into his body for some time, not sufficiently deep to destroy life, and, after that, they shot them into his face and eyes, and then scalped him alive." The perpetrators then tossed his naked corpse into the street for stray hogs to feast on. Veteran fur trapper Jim Beckwourth recalled "barbarities [that] exceeded in brutality all my previous experience with the Indians." In a scene reminiscent of the Pueblo Revolt in 1680, the leaders dispatched runners to nearby towns and villages to spread the word: it was time to expel the unwelcome American invaders.[119]

Narciso Beaubien, the son of Judge Charles Beaubien and María Paula Lobato, was the next to perish as he and an Indian slave hid in an outhouse.[120] The attackers killed both, mistaking Narciso for his father, who, as an American judicial appointee, was the intended target.[121] The elder Beaubien, along with Attorney General Hugh N. Smith, had left Taos the day before, and their fortuitous absence on January 19 saved them from the same fate as their colleagues. While the assailants' gruesome torture, murder, and dismemberment of the victims seemed motivated by a spontaneous fit of rage, they had in fact been carefully selected in advance. The objective of the rebellion was not merely to kill Americans but to eliminate all who supported their cause, including native New Mexicans of Hispanic ancestry who had accepted official appointments from Kearny.[122] The rebels targeted those directly associated with the new government, including Anglos like Bent and Hispanics like Vigil. Because they had supported the conquest and accepted political appointments in the new regime, these men were viewed as traitors to the adoptive communities in which they had lived for almost two decades. As a New York newspaper reported, "The Mexicans slew not only the Americans there, but all the Spaniards supposed to be favorable to the American cause."[123] From the rebels' perspective, Bent's role as governor and Beaubien's position as both a judge and co-owner of the immense Beaubien-Miranda Land Grant—which impinged on ancestral Taos Pueblo land—trumped community connections derived from longtime residency and intermarriage.[124]

That same night nine Americans died at nearby Rio Colorado and Arroyo Hondo, and a separate attack on Turley's Mill claimed the lives of seven more men.[125] These deeds accomplished, "most of the lower order of Mexicans . . . rose *en masse* and joined the Pueblo Indians in the work of pillage and murder," Donaciano Vigil recalled. He estimated the total number of insurgents at between 1,500 and 2,000, far from a complete citizen uprising, but an impressive showing nonetheless.[126] Near Santa Fe vigilant troops intercepted couriers as they rode south into the Rio Abajo to disseminate news of the revolt, thus preventing the vitriol from spreading even further.[127] To quell those dissidents already involved in the scheme, Price frantically marched his troops toward Taos.

Before leaving Santa Fe the colonel recalled Major D. B. Edmonson's Missouri volunteers and Captain John Burgwin's U.S. Dragoons from their station at Albuquerque to reinforce his command. Edmonson's troops would remain at the capital to keep the peace, while Price and Burgwin trekked to Taos with 353 soldiers and four howitzers. On January 24 an advance guard under Captain Ceran St. Vrain struck the rebels' position outside of La Cañada, whereupon Price ordered a double-quick march in preparation for an attack. Many of the Nuevomexicanos occupied high ground outside the village, and others fortified themselves in mud huts overlooking the valley. All four cannons began shelling the insurgents' position, but many of the missiles sailed over the enemy's heads and exploded harmlessly beyond. "In a few minutes," Price later reported, "my troops had dislodged the enemy at all points, and they were flying in every direction." As an estimated 1,500 New Mexicans retreated into the surrounding hills, U.S. officers counted 36 enemy fatalities and at least 45 wounded.[128] When newspaper editors in New York learned of the incident two months later, they hailed the routing as just punishment "for the sanguinary massacres which they [the New Mexicans] effected."[129]

Price's column reached Taos on February 3 and found their opponents holed up in the heavily fortified Taos Pueblo for "a last desperate struggle."[130] With two multistory residential towers and an imposing mission church built of two-foot-thick adobe walls, the complex was "admirably calculated for defense."[131] Considered the strongest fortress in the Southwest, Taos Pueblo had "always been regarded by the Mexicans as impregnable," and the ensuing two-day assault on the compound proved to be a difficult and deadly undertaking.[132] When the troops arrived they encountered the grisly murder sites, and, according to Beckwourth, hogs and other

Colonel Sterling Price, c. 1860s.
Courtesy National Archives and Records Administration, Washington, D.C.

animals continued to feast on corpses. "Such scenes of unexampled barbarity filled our soldiers' breasts with abhorrence," the fur trapper recalled, noting that this fueled a "craving for revenge" among the Americans.[133]

Lieutenant A. B. Dyer positioned his artillery within range of the Taos Pueblo church and commenced a fusillade that lasted into the evening. Although the shells "busted handsomely," the explosions failed to penetrate the thick adobe walls. Early the next morning the soldiers resumed their attack, fully expecting a "hard and bloody fight." Two hours of incessant artillery fire once again failed to breach the church walls, whereupon frustrated U.S. troops stormed the building in a desperate charge akin to the American attack on Chapultepec Castle later that year.[134] At Price's order the infantry and dragoons swept like a wave across the battlefield, crashing into the exterior walls while the enemy, fortified within, unleashed a "galling fire" of musketry into the crowd of American soldiers.[135] Those who reached the building unhurt began pounding at the adobe bricks with axes and eventually knocked a hole in the edifice. Dyer repositioned his cannons within thirty yards of the breach and began firing grapeshot into the church interior, effecting devastation on the Hispanos and Indians inside. After twenty minutes the soldiers set the church roof ablaze, causing it to collapse on those within.[136] Captain Burgwin fell mortally wounded, shot through the chest as he charged the compound.[137] When news of his death reached Fort Leavenworth several weeks later, it "cast a gloom over the hearts of all at this post who ever knew him professionally or personally," and when the army built a permanent post at Taos in 1852, they named it Cantonment Burgwin in his honor.[138] American forces lost seven men killed and forty-five wounded. Estimates of enemy losses varied, but out of a total force numbering just over 600 men, between 150 and 200 rebels died, and at least that many more were hurt, leaving an astonishing 65 to 70 percent casualty rate.[139] "They never had so severe a chastising," Lieutenant Elliott wrote with undisguised pride.[140]

American authorities prevented the rebellion from spreading into the Rio Abajo, but they were unable to stop its flow to the villages lining the eastern fringe of the Sangre de Cristos. At Las Vegas the alcalde received the rebel manifesto on January 20 but advised the townspeople against participating because more than two hundred U.S. troops garrisoned the town. Three days later residents of nearby Mora joined the rebellion and shot four Americans who lived there. Despite being desperately short on ammunition, Captain Israel Hendley collected eighty troops at Las Vegas and marched toward the scene. Before embarking he wrote to headquarters in Santa Fe and requested two cannons and "plenty of ammunition" for his soldiers so that he might "subdue and keep in check every town this side of the mountains."[141] At Mora, Hendley's men clashed with 150 Nuevomexicanos, who had fortified themselves in anticipation of the looming fight.[142] Hendley himself died, and three other soldiers sustained wounds during the course of a three-hour affair in which the Americans "slew a number of the insurgents, and utterly destroyed the town."[143] With the leading officer dead and supplies running low, the second in command, Lieutenant T. C. McKarney, ordered the Americans back to Las Vegas. "If we had one or two pieces of artillery to scare them out of their dens," the lieutenant later reported, "we could whip all the Mexicans this side of the ridge." Less than one week later, Captain Jesse I. Morin and a force of Missouri volunteers returned to Mora, where they torched houses, burned cornfields, and killed several Hispanos in retaliation.[144]

Back at Taos, Colonel Price demanded that the vanquished Pueblo Indians turn over their leader, Tomás, for prosecution as a treasonous rebel.[145] After Tomás was arrested, an "exasperated soldier" murdered the prisoner in cold blood, an act that the guards enabled through their salutary negligence.[146] An apathetic Dick Wootton later wrote that "the Indian deserved to be killed and would have been hanged anyhow."[147] President Polk praised "the prompt, spirited, and energetic action, on the part of the officers and men, in putting down the insurrection" and commended them for valor and bravery.[148] Having dampened the insurrectionary spirit, Price made arrangements at Taos "for the security and tranquility of New Mexico" and then returned to Santa Fe.[149] Those preparations amounted to military tribunals for the men accused of treason. "If any man supposes that this people are contented with the change in their political relations, he is most egregiously mistaken," Lieutenant Elliott wrote as these events transpired. "They have no love, but, on the contrary, a large majority of them entertain a very cordial hate, for Americans and American rule."[150]

The trials that occurred after the revolt contributed to this hatred toward Americans and their government. District Attorney Francis P. Blair Jr. served as prosecutor and Charles Beaubien, whose son was killed in the uprising, sat alongside Joab Houghton as a presiding judge.[151] If the manner in which American occupiers had coercively administered oaths of allegiance, if the soldiers' unruly behavior had offended the citizenry, and if the destructive use of force to crush the rebellion had provided impetus for dissent among many New Mexicans, then the trials of the Taos rebels and the public hangings that followed served only to exacerbate political and cultural tensions. Of the several alleged masterminds, Jesús Tafoya and Pablo Chávez died during the fighting at the Taos church; Pablo Montoya had been executed—or, in the words of Beckwourth, "was swung in the wind"—after the surrender; Tomás was shot while sitting in jail (as described above); and two others, Diego Archuleta and Manuel Cortés, had escaped and their whereabouts remained unknown. Cortés eluded capture for more than a year and led a number of raids on American grazing camps before eventually escaping into Chihuahua.[152] Montoya, who "styled himself the Santa Anna of the North," had been one of the principal instigators of the 1837 Chimayó Rebellion and received no sympathy from Governor Donaciano Vigil (Bent's successor), who referred to him as both insane and brutal in his revolutionist exertions.[153] Lacking sufficient evidence, American officials also released twenty-four other accused rebels before holding trials for the remaining culprits.[154]

Six prisoners sauntered into a courtroom at 9 A.M. on the appointed day to meet a fate that they must have known was coming. The judges and prosecutor all came from the United States, and the room stood under the guard of American soldiers. "It certainly did appear to be a great assumption on the part of the Americans to conquer a country and then arraign the revolting inhabitants for treason," Garrard wrote, noting that the militaristic atmosphere of the tribunals ensured a preconceived outcome while dissuading local spectators from further opposition. Beaubien sentenced the rebels to be hung until "*muerto, muerto, muerto*" (dead, dead, dead), whereupon "the poor wretches sat with immovable figures" in the courtroom.[155] The court decided to move forward with the executions as soon as possible lest federal authorities intervene. The following Friday would be "hangman's day" in Taos, and Garrard watched as the last chapter of the Taos Revolt unfolded before him. "*Los Yankees* at *El Casa Americano* drank their juleps and puffed their cigarillos in silence" as they awaited the impending spectacle. Lacking ropes to hang the condemned, the sheriff improvised nooses from borrowed rawhide lariats. A military escort led the six condemned men from their jail cells to the gallows. With heads shaven and arms tied behind their backs, the convicts marched through the streets as women and children gathered to watch the procession. "A death-like stillness reigned" throughout the town as they spoke their last words; one of the men "showed a spirit of martyrdom" and yelled, "*Caraho, Los Americanos!*" or "Fuck the Americans!"[156]

As the trapdoors fell below the men's feet, their bodies swung from the improvised lariat nooses while "convulsive shudders shook their frames [and] the bodies writhed most horribly."[157] Remembering the gruesome deaths of Bent and Burgwin, the U.S. soldiers felt little remorse as they looked on. The men dangled for forty minutes before the ropes were cut, whereupon the sheriff returned the bodies to their weeping families. "A more merited doom was never visited on any scoundrels in the world," Elliott concluded unrepentantly.[158] With the execution complete, many of the Americans headed for the local tavern, where they spent the remainder of the day in "drunken merriment," consuming brandy and Taos Lightning in the company of "handsome señoras."[159] As the liquor wore off over the ensuing days, one soldier wrote that "everything appears to be quiet here at this time."[160]

One of the men convicted of treason, Antonio María Trujillo, had his sentence remitted through an unlikely bureaucratic process that actually reached President Polk's desk. A petition for his pardon based on old age and infirmity was sent to Washington, D.C., soon after the trial, but Polk declined to interfere with civil affairs in the territory. Realizing the shaky legal ground on which the accusations of treason stood, and hoping that clemency in this case might calm heated passions in Taos, Polk recommended that Trujillo's life be spared, but he deferred official judgment to Colonel Price as the leading authority in New Mexico.[161] Price's commutation of Trujillo's death sentence confirmed that a treason charge could not justifiably be levied on an enemy combatant holding citizenship in an opposing nation. During their trial, in fact, the accused had insisted in vain that they could not be guilty of treason against the United States because of their Mexican citizenship. Describing the incident from a Hispanic perspective, George I. Sánchez wrote in 1940 that "Trujillo and his followers were Mexican patriots who made a belated attempt to repel an invader; they were guilty of armed revolt but not of treason."[162]

Secretary of War Marcy believed that the legal error lay in the use of the word 'treason' to describe the crime and determine the punishment. As citizens of an occupied territory, Marcy wrote, the inhabitants owed allegiance to the United States and became subject to its laws, but they could not be accused of treason until the territory in question had been officially transferred to American sovereignty by act of Congress.[163] Senator Benton also called the convictions absurd, stating that the men had been "tried by some sort of a court which had no jurisdiction of treason."[164] The Treaty of Guadalupe Hidalgo included a clause outlining the conditions of citizenship for former residents of the Mexican Republic; the pact aimed to avoid future resistance by allowing any person wishing to remain a citizen of Mexico one year to migrate south of the new international boundary line.[165] The treaty, however, was not signed until February 2, 1848, nearly a year after the Taos executions. President Polk, aware of the legal problem but seemingly ambivalent to the outcome, wrote that "the offenders deserved the punishment inflicted upon them." He admitted the initial error in charging them with treason and acknowledged that their Mexican citizenship should have prohibited their execution as traitors, but he took no action beyond this basic admission of wrongdoing.[166]

After the trials Governor Donaciano Vigil understood the precarious nature of the peace and knew that strong undercurrents of dissent remained. Realizing that terms of enlistment for volunteer troops would soon expire, he requested that Secretary of State Buchanan muster 2,000 more soldiers to occupy New Mexico. "Late events and present circumstances, I think, prove the necessity of that force," the governor concluded, hoping to avoid the same fate as his predecessor by saturating the territory with military might.[167] When the volunteers began mustering out in June 1847, Secretary of War Marcy assured Colonel Price that replacements were being sent in an amount "sufficient to hold that country."[168] While these requisitions for reinforcements seemed to emanate from wartime necessity and civil unrest, the officials who advocated such a strong military presence did so realizing the economic stimulus that so many salaried men would bring to the region.[169]

In the summer of 1847 American control over New Mexico remained tenuous, and another uprising threatened to materialize when a group of Hispanos attacked and killed an army lieutenant and two enlisted men near Las Vegas. Troops immediately arrested seven men implicated in the murders and marched them to Santa Fe, where, in a scene reminiscent of that in Taos, a military tribunal found six of them guilty and sentenced them to be hanged for murder. "They were immediately executed," wrote Lieutenant Dyer, who served as judge advocate during the hearing. Notably, the court forewent the accusation of treason, realizing now the appropriate

Governor Donaciano Vigil.
Courtesy Palace of the Governors Photo Archives,
New Mexico History Museum/DCA, Santa Fe (negative no. #011405).

parameters of prosecution for such a crime. Based on the evidence, Dyer believed that the alcalde at Las Vegas had ordered the men to kill the soldiers, citing this as further evidence of the power and control that a small proportion of politically and socially empowered men exercised over the general population. "The miserable, ignorant, deluded wretches dared not disobey his order," Dyer wrote with an air of nativism, adding that "the mass of the people are so degraded, and have been so long under that kind of despotism, that they are wholly unfit to be citizens of a free government."[170]

Having quelled the January rebellion and executed the primary masterminds, American officers became much more adept at recognizing public perception and worked to preempt future outbreaks of violence. In response Hispano rebels shifted their activities to more-remote locations, where military force could not immediately reach them. Major Robert Walker, commanding a battalion of soldiers at Socorro, once again attributed leadership of this resistance movement to Manuel Cortés, now a captain in the Mexican army's Batallón Activo de Chihuahua, who rode at the helm of thirty men and at one point skirmished with a detachment of U.S. troops near the Pecos River.[171] "A body of Mexicans and Indians, embodied for predatory purposes, have been very annoying," Price grumbled, noting that people in northeastern New Mexico continually harassed government authorities and army grazing camps, sometimes with deadly consequences. On May 20, 1847, armed bandits attacked soldiers near Wagon Mound, inflicting three casualties and driving off two hundred horses and mules. A detachment of seventy-seven troops from Las Vegas overtook the raiders in a canyon of the Canadian River, and an intense skirmish ensued during which soldiers killed forty-one Hispano combatants.[172] One month later, a group of Missouri volunteers pursued another band of rustlers who had stolen horses from the post at Las Vegas. When the overmatched soldiers confronted the thieves, all four were killed and the culprits made off with their loot. An incensed Major D. B. Edmonson marched back into town, where his men shot several people and took at least forty others prisoner. Less than two weeks later Hispanos ambushed yet another grazing camp in an attack that claimed the lives of five more soldiers. Clearly many New Mexicans "entertain[ed] deadly hatred against the Americans," and Price noted with grave concern that the local population had adopted an effective strategy of hit-and-run attacks on secluded campsites.[173] In these three raids alone, Nuevomexicanos slew over a dozen troops and stole hundreds of horses and mules.

Despite these difficulties, President Polk recommended in August 1848 that the country's military force be reduced to the prewar size of approximately ten thousand men, a number that he believed "sufficient" for peacetime purposes. His order not only conformed to public sentiment during a time when many American citizens distrusted a large standing army but also reflected the philosophy of a government commitment to fiscal conservatism. With the Mexican-American War over and no additional violence expected, Polk based his recommendation for cutting military strength on reports from Secretary of War Marcy and Commissioner of Indian Affairs William Medill. Marcy conservatively estimated that only three or four military posts, garrisoned by 1,200 soldiers, would be needed to control New Mexico's Indians and Hispanos and to maintain American control over the territory.[174]

General Kearny died less than two years after the Army of the West captured Santa Fe, and thus he never witnessed the controversies that arose over the nation's retention of that Hispanic and Indian frontier. From a tactical standpoint, Kearny played an important part in New Mexico's inception into the American union of states and territories. The proclamations that he delivered to the Spanish-speaking inhabitants triggered the nation's military obligation to the regional population; he promised locals that U.S. troops could protect them from Indian raids, and in so doing would reverse the prior twenty-five years of neglect shown them by the chronically insolvent and unstable Mexican government. Recognizing that New Mexicans owed allegiance to a foreign nation and had been reared under laws and customs that differed widely from those about to be imposed on them, Kearny also ordered his troops to exercise conciliatory measures when interacting with the civilian population so as to foster amity and goodwill, although many of the men failed to uphold a high standard, and their behavior instead fostered deep resentment among Hispanos.[175]

Ultimately, Kearny's military colleagues were tasked with administering the new civil government, quelling civilian and Indian uprisings, and laying the groundwork for American settlement and infrastructural development. As the editors of the *Santa Fe Republican* wrote, echoing the nationalistic jargon of the times, the United States hoped that New Mexico would emerge "from the blood-stained wave of war that dashes its fearful torrent around us, arising the fairer and lovelier form of the Goddess of Freedom."[176] Establishing political, economic, and legal stability in New Mexico would be crucial to sustaining it as an American possession over the decades to come, although U.S. officials soon realized that the ease with which Kearny's Army of the West wrested the territory from Mexico, and the supposed simplicity of democratic enlightenment reflected in the Santa Fe newspaper, had both been misleading. By February 1847 Lieutenant Dyer understood that the unimpeded occupation of Santa Fe had led everyone to believe that the political transformation "would be hailed with delight by the people." General Kearny, he mused, departed "in the full belief that no effort would be made to wrest the government from us," a fatal assumption for some of the U.S. troops who remained in New Mexico.[177]

Although rumors of intrigue would circulate throughout the region over the ensuing years, much of the impetus to rebel dissipated by 1848.[178] As memories of the Taos Revolt faded, native New Mexicans became increasingly reconciled to the new government, and some residents recognized potential benefits in American citizenship. This was especially true regarding Kearny's promise that U.S. troops would protect them from the deadly and unrelenting Indian raids that had plagued Rio Grande settlements since the Spanish colonial era. In October 1848, after the Mexican-American War ended and civil unrest subsided, a contingent of Nuevomexicanos under the leadership of Taos priest Antonio José Martínez joined with a handful of American officials to memorialize Congress, requesting the organization of a government "purely civil in its character" to replace the wartime military regime. They explained that the Kearny Code, with a few minor alterations, could form the basis of an acceptable territorial administration and asked only that a ban on "domestic slavery" be added to it—a topic that the original doctrine purposely sidestepped—before Congress took official action.[179] The petitioners must have known that any request relative to slavery would be incredibly controversial. U.S. politicians spent the next two years debating the expansion of slavery and popular sovereignty in the West, placing New Mexico in the center of the tensest sectional controversy yet faced by the republic.[180] Now the task of political incorporation, either with or without slavery, would become a pressing concern for Americans wishing to exert power and control over the southwestern domain. For their part, the local memorialists understood that the new government offered a chance to quell Indian raids and pacify a New Mexico frontier that had been enveloped by violence for generations. These two issues—slavery and Indian conflict—would occupy American soldiers and politicians for years to come.

≡ 3 ≡

INDIAN WARS AND THE
CONTEST FOR THE SOUTHWESTERN FRONTIER

Colonel Edwin V. Sumner never really liked New Mexico. The officer first visited in 1846, when he and his company of dragoons escorted General Stephen W. Kearny from Santa Fe to southern California. In July 1851 the fifty-four-year-old Sumner—who received the moniker "Bull Head" during the Mexican-American War—returned to the Southwest, this time to serve as commander of the Ninth Military Department.[1] Secretary of War Charles M. Conrad specifically assigned Sumner to the task, recognizing him as a no-nonsense administrator who would implement controversial new policies without hesitation. In compliance with orders, the colonel promptly removed the troops from New Mexico's towns—where they had been stationed since the conquest five years earlier—and reassigned them to new forts in isolated locations. The soldiers, he said, had become demoralized from their residency in places like Santa Fe, which he called a "sink of vice and extravagance," and needed to be distanced from injurious social influences.[2] Although the military command lauded Sumner's action, many civilians detested the move because it deprived them of soldiers' business at local stores and saloons and left towns vulnerable to Indian raids. Sumner also imposed tighter regulations on army expenditures, reducing the high costs of sustaining over one thousand troops in the remote territory while simultaneously eliminating many of the lucrative government supply contracts that residents previously fulfilled.[3] By December 1852, however, the frustrated colonel had requested a transfer elsewhere, and even his successor as

Colonel Edwin V. Sumner, c. 1855.
Courtesy MOLLUS Mass Photo Collection,
United States Army Heritage and Education Center, Carlisle, Pennsylvania.

department commander, General John Garland, wrote soon after his arrival that "there is undoubtedly a strong disinclination to serve in New Mexico."[4]

As an authoritarian fiscal conservative who viewed New Mexico through the lens of economic rationality, Sumner despised almost everything about it. After less than one year in Santa Fe and Albuquerque, he wrote to War Department officials outlining the difficulties of maintaining an operational military force in the Southwest borderlands. The colonel implored his superiors to abandon the region for the Mexicans and Indians to fight over amongst themselves, as they already had been doing "for over 200 years."[5] Sumner advised Conrad that the government ought to "withdraw all the troops and federal officers," leaving only a supervisory commission to oversee political activities and prevent any rebellion like that at Taos five years earlier. "With regard to their protection from the Indians," Sumner wryly remarked, "they would have the same that was extended to them by the Mexican government—that is to say, permission to defend themselves."[6] The abandonment of New Mexico turned out to be among the few things that Sumner and his civilian counterpart, Governor James S. Calhoun, agreed on during their tenures in office. An irritated Calhoun, in fact, had once explained to the commissioner of Indian affairs that "the military officers and the executive cannot harmonize, and I am not certain that the public interest would not be promoted by relieving us all from duty in this territory."[7]

The department quartermaster seemed to echo Sumner and Calhoun when opining in 1851 that "the inhabitants of the towns and large settlements should be taught to depend upon themselves" for protection from the Indians, noting that civilian militias might become "valuable partisan soldiers" who could contribute to their own defense.[8] The secretary of war concurred, positing that all Anglo-Americans residing in New Mexico should be relocated and remunerated for any property lost or abandoned during the transition. "Even if the government paid for the property quintuple its value," Conrad mused, "it would still, merely on the score of economy, be largely the gainer by the transaction," because the soldiers could be reassigned to places where their services might be of greater immediate benefit to the United States. As far as Sumner and Conrad were concerned, protecting a population of Hispanics—who just half a decade earlier revolted against the U.S. government and threatened to do so again at the time these men wrote—did not warrant the effort and expenses involved.[9] A team of federal commissioners later reported that "since we acquired New Mexico [in 1846] the military expenditures connected with Indian affairs have probably exceeded $4,000,000 annually in that territory alone." They alluded to Sumner's recommendation that New Mexico be abandoned, postulating that "upon the score of economy it would doubtless have been a great saving to the government."[10]

Many New Mexicans did not particularly like Colonel Sumner either. Upon learning of his correspondence with the secretary of war, a Santa Fe newspaper editor obtained copies of the letters and published them for all to read. Derogatorily nicknaming Sumner "The Big Bug of Albuquerque," the writer believed that citizens had been "gratuitously and maliciously assailed." According to the editors, removal of troops from Santa Fe had exacted a heavy toll on the capital and thrust local merchants into an economic downturn. Comparing the colonel to a dictatorial Caesar and sarcastically christening him "High Constable," the journalist William Kephart accused him of acting with preordained malice toward New Mexicans and believed him unfit to serve as department commander.[11] When Indian agent John Greiner asked the colonel to reconsider transferring troops to frontier posts, Sumner's response—that he would do as he wished—did not endear him to either civil authorities or the general public.[12] Perhaps the most heated rivalry, however, occurred when William Carr Lane arrived in 1852 to assume the governorship. Sumner, who sat temporarily in the Palace of the Governors during the four-month interim between Calhoun's and Lane's tenures, promptly removed his headquarters from Santa Fe to Albuquerque just prior to the latter's arrival, distancing himself from civil authority and personally offending the new head of state.[13] The unfriendly relationship between the two, according to congressional delegate Richard Weightman, was "a renewal of the contest for power in New Mexico between the civil and military" branches of government.[14] Richard Kern, an artist who accompanied the colonel to Navajo country in 1851, confided to his brother that "everybody hates old Sumner and all are afraid of him," a sentiment that many shared but few dared to express in public.[15]

Sumner and Conrad epitomized the frustration that many government officials experienced when attempting to administer public affairs in New Mexico, and they were not alone in their opinions about abandoning the region and diverting money and manpower to other areas of the West. The fact that federal bureaucrats ignored such suggestions and continued to pump significant resources into the territory—maintaining a standing army of well over one thousand troops there throughout the antebellum period—indicates just how much importance congressional leaders placed on the region as a geographic and commercial link between Texas and California. If they hoped to establish national infrastructure there, however, Americans would first have to pacify half a dozen nomadic Indian tribes whose homelands overlapped the geopolitical boundaries of the newly established U.S. territory.

The fiscal strategies that Conrad and Sumner espoused in reorganizing the territorial military department came in response to an inspection of New Mexico's posts that Quartermaster Thomas Swords conducted in 1851. Aware of skyrocketing War Department expenditures and wondering what could be done to lessen operating costs in the West, Swords and other officers assessed the regions acquired from Mexico and reported extensively on adverse conditions. Their findings corroborated what Major General Thomas Jesup had already reported to the secretary of war: America's rapid acquisition of Texas, Oregon, California, Utah, and New Mexico between 1845 and 1848 carried unforeseen costs for the nation, especially in the way of military spending. Prior to the annexation of Texas, the War Department maintained 63 military posts in frontier regions that included today's Upper Midwest and many of the states astride the Mississippi River. After 1848 the army added 46 forts in Oregon, California, New Mexico, and Texas, nearly doubling the number of outposts to be equipped and maintained. By 1857 troops manned 138 stations across three million square miles.[16] Furthermore, since the new states and territories were so far removed from preexisting U.S. boundaries, operating costs proved much higher in those areas. The War Department bore the brunt of the expense, because enforcing Indian policy cost more money and required greater manpower than administrating the Bureau of Indian Affairs (BIA).[17]

The federal acquisition of vast territories pushed the military frontier westward from the Mississippi River's north-south axis all the way to the Pacific Ocean in less than four years, practically doubling the distance that troops and supplies had to be transported.[18] "When it is recollected that large accessions have, within a few years past, been made to our territory; that an extensive seaboard will require fortifications, and an enlarged inland frontier needs protection against the Indians, it will appear manifest that the present military establishment of the country is entirely inadequate for its wants," Secretary of War Conrad told the president in 1850.[19] Over the preceding four decades, Congress had failed to increase the size of the federal army in proportion with the annexation of new territory, creating a glaring weakness in national defense. In 1808 the legislated size of the regular army was 9,991 men. After Mexican-American War discharges and downsizing in 1848, the military counted 13,821 soldiers—despite the national population having grown by eighteen million people over the preceding forty years and the incorporation of more than one million square miles of additional territory. An army roughly the same size as it had been at the turn of the century, then, had to patrol a vastly larger geographic area and protect far greater numbers of American citizens, and by the 1850s those responsibilities stretched the military to its limits. Secretary of War Jefferson Davis estimated in 1854 that 400,000 Indians occupied the western domain, but only 11,000 troops patrolled the countryside.[20]

One reason for the lackadaisical support of the military involved a pervasive American perception of true warfare in the nineteenth century. Enamored with Manifest Destiny ideology and empowered by a sense of racial superiority, most citizens did not view Indians as worthy opponents, and thus Congress never officially declared war on any of New Mexico's tribes.[21] Despite Chief Justice John Marshall's reasoning in 1831 that Native Americans constituted "domestic dependent nations"—a legal principle that insinuated tribal sovereignty—federal lawmakers did not see Indians as political entities in the same way that they viewed European countries like England or France.[22] Despite the fact that the treaty-making process implicitly acknowledged tribes as sovereignties, this designation did not influence the popular perception of formal warfare as a conflict between civilized nations.[23] Instead, Americans viewed the standing army as a peacetime establishment—a constabulary body to maintain order and protect settlers—and did not therefore support greater troop levels or monetary expenditures.[24] As Secretary of War John Floyd pointed out, "Whilst appropriations have been made to sustain our Army upon a peace footing, it has been called upon to prosecute an active and sanguinary war" against many different tribes inhabiting half a continent.[25] Herein lay one of the primary dilemmas of Indian warfare in the nineteenth-century American West. Congress did not recognize frontier conflicts with American Indians as real warfare and refused to raise enough troops or provide ample funding to sustain military operations during "peacetime." The Indian Wars—which lasted for decades and involved dozens of tribes—were just as expensive and logistically challenging as any traditional war with a foreign country, yet the army fought them with the bare minimum of resources and manpower. Nowhere did this discrepancy prove more problematic than in the antebellum Southwest.

During the 1850s War Department officials viewed Texas and New Mexico as the most critical regions for military protection and stationed more than half of the entire standing army in those two departments. To bring each company to its full legislated strength, federal personnel intensified recruitment in eastern cities and practically begged Congress to increase the size of the army.[26] Conrad repeatedly asked politicians to approve the formation of at least one new regiment because until they had more troops at their disposal, field officers could not effectively patrol and protect the western frontier. Severe limitations in troops and supplies dictated that officers in New Mexico would chase Indians only if they had an extremely high likelihood of overtaking them.[27] When Jefferson Davis took office as secretary of war in 1853, he remarked that even if Congress enlisted three times the number of troops currently employed for service, his agency could not properly defend the western states and territories, much less the entire nation. In January 1855 President Franklin Pierce finally recommended an enlargement of the army, whereupon lawmakers authorized the recruitment of four additional regiments. Even so, America's standing army never exceeded 16,000 soldiers in the decade prior to the Civil War.[28]

Whereas provisions could be shipped via steamboat or railroad to army outposts in Louisiana, Arkansas, Indian Territory, and Missouri, those same supplies had to be carted overland across great distances to faraway forts and encampments in the Southwest. This required much more money and took a lot more time, causing military expenses to increase more than ninefold and transportation costs for troops and supplies to rise by 1,500 percent between 1844 and 1851.[29] Protecting the landlocked New Mexico frontier proved particularly problematic because of its exposure to multiple Indian tribes and its incredibly isolated location compared to Oregon, California, and Texas—all of which had coastlines and harbors. Large numbers of troops needed to be stationed in New Mexico, and at greater cost than anywhere else in the country. The army paid high rent for privately owned barracks and storehouses in the towns that they garrisoned: the post at Las Vegas cost over $5,000 per year, the one at Doña Ana nearly $4,500, and the remaining locations were not much cheaper. At department headquarters in Santa Fe, leases for officers' quarters totaled $1,800 annually, and the quartermaster department employed 134 people at wages reaching $60 per month. As of April 1851 the Ninth Military Department was paying 377 civilian employees in addition to over 1,000 military personnel. Thomas Swords estimated the cost of feeding and maintaining a single mule at $310 per year, noting that many posts had at least six mule teams with an equal number of teamsters on the payroll. By his calculations, the War Department paid over $190,000 each year just to feed and maintain mules in New Mexico, and with expenses for sustaining the dragoons' horses added to the equation, fees in 1851 came to $308,000 for animals alone. Considering the costs of horses and mules, rent at eleven locations, salaries for over 1,000 soldiers and officers, wages for hundreds of civilian workers, daily rations, and other contingent expenses, New Mexico truly was a drain on federal coffers.[30] In addition, graft only added to the War Department's headaches: for example, the army quartermaster in Santa Fe, Captain Alexander W. Reynolds, used his position to issue fraudulent supply contracts and embezzled an estimated $122,000 between 1849 and 1851.[31]

Even removing troops from their urban posts and stationing them at frontier forts would not significantly cut the army's costs, because the arid countryside could not support the irrigation systems necessary to grow food and forage for so many troops and animals. The only way that reliance on civilian grain and grass contracts could be eliminated, Major General Jesup said, would be to construct extensive dams and aqueducts and create a sophisticated system of irrigation. He also recommended that turnpikes be built to connect the Mississippi River with New Mexico and hoped that the Rio Grande might be dredged and channelized to make it navigable farther inland from the Gulf of Mexico, but none of those fanciful schemes came to fruition. Although he advocated these internal improvements for the sake of national defense, the quartermaster general also understood that such projects would incur astronomical costs that hardly justified the slight savings on military subsistence.[32] The primary means of supply would continue to be civilian contracts and goods shipped over the Santa Fe Trail.

Even if military operations in New Mexico were made more affordable through government-financed improvements, another major obstacle hindered fiscal solvency. "From the experience of the past," Jesup wrote, "I entertain not the slightest hope that the expenses for transportation, forage, and several of the items under the

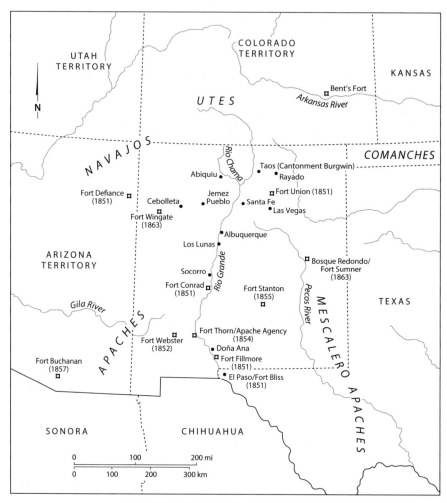

Map 2. New Mexico Military Posts, c. 1850s.

incidental head, can be much reduced unless an entire change be made in our Indian as well as military policy." Before an effective Indian policy could be formulated, he believed that the new international boundary separating the United States from Mexico must be secured, and he advocated militarization of the border to curb illicit Apache and Comanche slave raiding across a geopolitical boundary that indigenous groups did not recognize within their own cultures.[33] Once the military secured the border, Jesup suggested that smaller forts be abandoned and their garrisons consolidated with those at larger posts. Major concentrations of soldiers would then occupy sizable frontier forts with reservations at or near those compounds; the Indians would be dismounted, demobilized, and forced into permanent settlement at remote locations under direct army supervision. Once the Indians were taught a sedentary agrarian lifestyle, they would sustain themselves, rendering military campaigns unnecessary—the so-called "Indian problem" thus mitigated forever. Through this wishfulness, Jesup predicted a 75 percent reduction in War Department expenditures while opening the region for settlement and development.[34] In many ways, his ideas on Indian policy anticipated those that the government followed throughout much of the late nineteenth century, although the outcomes rarely equaled the expectations, and terrible demographic and cultural tolls beset many tribes as a result.

In 1866 Governor William F. M. Arny estimated that New Mexico's nomadic groups had plundered 2,407 horses, 1,155 mules, 13,473 head of cattle, and 294,740 sheep—valued at almost $1.4 million in total—in the twenty years since Kearny's conquest. The human cost came to at least ninety U.S. citizens killed and many more wounded or taken captive, to say nothing of Indian casualties during that same period.[35] As astonishing as they sound, Arny's numbers seem to have been on the conservative side. Boundary Commissioner John Russell Bartlett claimed that half a million animals had been stolen between 1846 and 1850 alone, although he included stock taken from below the U.S.-Mexican border in that estimation.[36] During the first eight years of American sovereignty, territorial residents filed 244 indemnity claims for Indian raids with the Department of the Interior totaling over $500,000.[37] Although these figures represented only civilian losses and did not include animals stolen from the military, Colonel John Munroe—Sumner's predecessor as department commander—suggested that the government honor all requests for remuneration and dole out hundreds of thousands of dollars in payments, despite strong suspicions that some of the claims were either nefarious or exaggerated. Colonel Thomas Fauntleroy expressed his frustration that New Mexicans concocted stories of raids and thefts in hopes of being paid for their losses and to ensure a strong military presence in the territory. As far as Fauntleroy was concerned, crafty civilians had discovered a way to use the government, vis-à-vis the army, to personal advantage for profit and protection.[38] Additionally, some Hispanos abetted the theft of livestock by purchasing stolen animals directly from the Indians. In one such instance, an infuriated Captain Henry Judd accused civic leaders in the Rio Arriba of complicity in contraband trafficking and swore that the culprits would be apprehended and punished.[39] Munroe stressed the need to regulate commerce between New Mexicans and Indians, pointing out that Hispanic and Anglo opportunists illicitly traded guns and ammunition that warriors in turn used to kill residents.[40] The War Department, however, continued to handle these conflicts with vigor and resolve, placing a high level of importance on the pacification of the Southwest.

Just as controlling government spending and maintaining some modicum of fiscal solvency vexed military administrators, so too did formulating and enforcing viable policy prove difficult. Throughout the 1850s and 1860s, officials from the War Department and the BIA continually argued over the proper course of action toward New Mexico's indigenous tribes. This should have come as no surprise to the Indians themselves; since the 1700s Spanish and Mexican authorities had similarly oscillated between policies of total warfare and cautious peace—and confusing combinations of the two.[41] From the moment that responsibility for Indian affairs shifted from the War Department to the newly created Department of the Interior in 1849, tension arose between the civil and military branches regarding the appropriate disposition of western tribes, and within a decade the secretary of war began pressuring Congress to return the BIA to his agency's purview.[42] Fundamentally, however, both bureaucracies sought an end to conflict with American Indians in order to promote settlement, facilitate economic development, and create safe avenues for multidirectional travel and commerce.

For the most part, BIA officials pursued an agenda that involved feeding and caring for Indians at agencies on or near reservations, although this approach proved financially draining and politically untenable until after the Civil War.[43] New Mexico's first superintendent of Indian affairs, James S. Calhoun (soon to be territorial governor), advocated four reservations: one each for the Apaches, Comanches, Navajos, and Utes. If those major tribes could be induced (or forced) to remain on secluded reservations and provided with enough food to prevent starvation, Calhoun believed that raiding would decline and permanent peace might ensue. Hugh Smith, New Mexico's congressional representative, supported the plan and suggested that reserves be set aside and indigenous groups removed to those locations.[44] With the Pueblo Indians, who numbered over 10,000 souls and occupied twenty-two permanent compounds, Calhoun worked to cultivate friendship and cooperation. Already struggling to contain the four nomadic tribes within his jurisdiction, he negotiated treaties with numerous Pueblos and even enlisted some of their men as paid auxiliaries. Calhoun placed so much importance on sustaining friendly relations with the Pueblos that he used funds from his personal salary for that purpose when the treasury ran low. His constituents approved of these measures, writing in a petition to the president that the Pueblo Indians "should be constantly watched and cared for" because "their affections towards us, must not be alienated."[45]

Had it been implemented, Calhoun's reservation strategy would have been problematic, as it did not account for the complexities of tribal structure and internal strife between subgroups and bands. The Apaches, for instance, would have been grouped simply by virtue of their name, despite the fact that the Chiricahuas, Mescaleros, and Jicarillas lived great distances from one another and constituted distinct peoples who rarely coalesced for any reason besides barter.[46] Others with knowledge of the situation pointed out that reservations simply fulfilled a temporary humanitarian agenda that would assuage the guilty consciences of American conquerors. Indian Agent Edmund Graves, posted in southern New Mexico to oversee the Gila Apaches, offered a pessimistic view in 1854. "All that can be expected from an enlightened and Christian government, such as ours is, is to graduate and smooth the pass-way of their final exit from the stage of human existence," Graves wrote, alluding to the reservation and rationing policy as the most compassionate means toward that end.[47]

James L. Collins, who edited Santa Fe's only newspaper and served as superintendent of Indian affairs in the 1850s, outlined the civilian perspective on Indian policy clearly and concisely. The Chiricahua Apaches, he wrote, should be confined to a reservation along the Gila River (in what is today southeastern Arizona), an area at that time uninhabited. After a campaign through there in 1857, Colonel Benjamin Bonneville reported it ideal for the Apaches, explaining that its remoteness would discourage Americans from settling in the region and disturbing the tribe. This idea would ultimately come to fruition, but not until the creation of the San Carlos Reservation in 1872. The Utes, Collins continued, should have their own reserve on the San Juan River of northwestern New Mexico, another area in which few settlers resided. As for the Navajos, the superintendent believed that their own homelands near Canyon de Chelly were sufficiently distant from the settled Rio Grande towns, and he deemed that region could serve as their reservation if enforcement measures could be put in place. Collins left the Southern Comanches out of the equation, hoping that Texas officials would address their fates. These proposed locations might plausibly receive congressional approval, he remarked, because rough terrain excluded them from consideration for railroads. If the Indians did not wish to comply with the policy, he declared, "they should be compelled to submit to it." Collins insisted that the government had an obligation to protect its non-native citizens through whatever means necessary, be they humanitarian, militaristic, or some combination of the two.[48]

Another problem with the reservation strategy involved geographic location. Despite the territory's immense size—stretching horizontally from Texas to California and vertically from Mexico to Utah—neither New Mexicans nor federal lawmakers could agree on specific areas for permanent Indian settlement. For one thing, to limit raiding most civilians insisted that reservations be located a tremendous distance from their homes. Nor could the four reservations be placed near one another, because the tribes might commit hostilities against their Indian neighbors. At the federal level, the primary concern involved the unforeseeable future. Lawmakers worried about creating permanent Indian settlements in areas through which they might one day wish to construct a transcontinental railroad or where valuable mineral deposits might be discovered.[49] These causes for unease precluded almost the entire territory of New Mexico from the establishment of reservations and made Calhoun's preferred policy a difficult sell in Congress, but leading BIA officials continued to press for this outcome by requesting appropriations and soliciting legislative support.[50] Should these ideas fail, Commissioner Bartlett advised Secretary of the Interior Alexander Stuart that the Apaches ought to be "annihilated or removed" deep into southern Mexico. Placing the tribe a thousand miles away on foreign soil, he projected, would prevent raids on American citizens and shift responsibility for the Indians' care onto another government. This unworkable scheme would have been a direct violation of the Treaty of Guadalupe Hidalgo, and it never made it beyond the secretary's desk.[51]

Civil administrators knew that reservations would be difficult to create and sustain, so they began with small steps toward that end. William Carr Lane tried to address the problem during his one-year term as governor and head of Indian affairs in 1852. He negotiated preliminary peace pacts with some tribes and established agencies near military posts, including one at Fort Webster in southwestern New Mexico. Ostensibly bound by unratified treaties, Indian groups were intended to live permanently near their agencies, receive rations from the field agent in charge, and learn how to farm in the Jeffersonian image of republican yeomanry. This was essentially a civilizing project that sought to avert violence and demographic decline while ensuring that American settlers enjoyed unhindered access to the land they wanted. Santa Fe's newspaper at first lauded Lane's policy as an economical one, gushing that it provided "security to our citizens, and [is] humanist towards the Indians themselves." Within a year, however, the strategy had failed. Most nomadic groups could not be forced to remain in one location. Many of them loathed the agricultural lifestyle and continued to commit depredations, and agents overissued rations at great expense to the government. By the time Lane left New Mexico in 1853, his program had created a large deficit in the territorial treasury with little to show in the way of results. Local journalists quickly retreated from their praise, calling Lane's policy "ruinous" and claiming that its broken promises and inadequate oversight actually drove agency Indians to the warpath.[52] Shortly thereafter, acting Commissioner of Indian Affairs Charles Mix opined that the policy of issuing rations and supplies amounted to a counterproductive welfare program that fostered dependency on the government and discouraged tribes from becoming self-sufficient agriculturists. Secretary of the Interior Jacob Thompson called this approach "expensive and radically defective."[53]

Of all the Indian agents who passed through New Mexico's revolving door of civil officials in the 1850s, none upheld the humanitarian agenda more consistently than Michael Steck. Originally a medical doctor from Pennsylvania, Steck reached the territory in 1852 with his ailing wife, hoping that the salubrious climate would improve her declining health. After a brief stint as an agent for the Utes in north-central New Mexico, he accepted an assignment to oversee the Chiricahua and Mescalero Apaches. In 1854 he established the Southern Apache Agency near Fort Thorn, where he administered policy and monitored the Indians over the next five years.[54] Steck believed in providing food as a matter of humanity as well as feasibility, explaining that "self-preservation is the first law of nature" and insisting that any man, regardless of race or creed, would steal before he would starve. "Human nature exhibits itself as well in the Indian as in the Anglo-Saxon," he wrote. "Supply the wants of either, and the disposition to revolt is suppressed or materially weakened." Annual ration allotments of a few thousand dollars, he believed, would prevent most tribes from raiding during the bleak winter months. In Steck's view, which mirrored that of Commissioner George Manypenny, carefully measured BIA expenditures were a preemptive strategy to avoid much costlier military campaigns and higher troop enlistments. Should the government fail to provide for the Indians, Steck warned Governor David Meriwether, "they will again be reduced to the extremity of choosing between stealing or starvation." Federal authorities eventually granted the governor permission and funds to negotiate treaties, and in 1855 he met with several tribes for that purpose.[55] However, during the antebellum era officials in the War Department viewed Indian conflict much differently than their counterparts in the Interior Department, and army personnel continually advocated heavy-handed approaches that called for violent military action to precede peace negotiations.

Colonel Sumner had formulated the military strategy of unlimited warfare toward Indian tribes soon after he assumed command of New Mexico's military department in 1851. His proposed tactics—targeting noncombatants, destroying homes and food stores, and using indiscriminate violence to crush Indian enemies into submission—originated during the colonial era and represented what historian John Grenier calls America's "first way of war."[56] Secretary of War Conrad, who hoped that a humane outcome might ultimately be achieved, supported Sumner's approach and believed that "the most effectual way to protect our settlements is to overawe the Indians by a constant display of military force in their immediate neighborhood." Conrad's successor, Jefferson Davis, echoed that opinion when he reported to Congress that peace could be attained only by stationing massive numbers of troops on the frontier "to restrain aggression by the exhibition of a power adequate to punish."[57]

Taking a cue from Major Enoch Steen, who in 1850 recommended large military campaigns as punishment for unrelenting raids, Sumner planned to dispatch numerous expeditions into Indian country and establish permanent posts in their homelands. With troops near watering holes and camping spots, Sumner reasoned, the Indians "will never venture to make distant hostile expeditions, and have their families and property within striking distance of vigilant garrisons." Building forts was only the beginning. From those installations, mounted soldiers could more easily embark on destructive operations against the Indians, razing their crops and making no distinction "between the friendly and unfriendly."[58] The commander's new administrative plan transformed the military from a defensive body, whose troops garrisoned and protected civilian settlements, to an offensive force that occupied Indians' homelands and actively campaigned in their midst.

Whereas Colonel Sumner articulated the policy of unlimited warfare, his successors perpetuated it and even elaborated on it. After taking command of New Mexico's military department in 1853, General John Garland explicated his own approach to Indian affairs. "The marauding propensities of these half-starved vagabonds will have to be checked by the strong arm of the military," he declared, reiterating the army's continued commitment to controlling and defending New Mexico. Like Sumner before him, Garland's policy relied on overt violence. Outlining for a junior officer the objectives of a Ute campaign in 1855, Garland's office urged the use of force over diplomacy, explaining that the military "does not recognize the principle urged by peace establishment men, that we can wage war upon one part and not the whole of a nation."[59] In 1857, during Colonel Benjamin Bonneville's command of the department, the policy remained unchanged, and the military that year embarked on the largest Indian campaign New Mexico had yet seen. Three years later, when a full-fledged war broke out with the Navajos, Colonel Thomas Fauntleroy pursued the same outcome as each of his predecessors. "If a war against the Navajos becomes necessary, I desire to make it as decisive as possible, by striking a blow that they will never forget," he exclaimed.[60] By the time the Civil War began, more than a decade of campaigning had failed to subdue any of the region's major tribes, and Commissioner of Indian Affairs William Dole criticized unlimited warfare as "nothing more than the killing or capture of a few Indians, and the destruction of some of their villages, leaving the power of the Indians almost unimpaired."[61]

Disagreements over policy came into stark relief when Superintendent of Indian Affairs James Collins and his subagents squared off against the department commander, Colonel Fauntleroy, over the prosecution of war with the Navajos. Collins felt confident that BIA personnel had faithfully executed their duties to care for the Navajo people, whereas War Department authorities continually failed to enforce treaty stipulations. Collins believed that "humanity demands that we should deal with them in such a manner as will prevent their destruction," a mindset fundamentally at odds with that of Fauntleroy, who was planning a military expedition to Canyon de Chelly. "I care nothing about Colonel Fauntleroy or his opinions, except so far as a misunderstanding with him may affect the public service," Collins wrote in a missive to Commissioner of Indian Affairs Alfred Greenwood.[62] Agency officials also quarreled with the commanding officer at Fort Defiance, Major Oliver Shepherd, whom Collins characterized as contemptible. Navajo Indian agent Silas Kendrick found Shepherd to be an impossible colleague who blocked all efforts to treat with the Navajos on peaceful terms while refusing to take decisive action when the Indians broke treaty stipulations.[63] Meanwhile, Secretary of War John B. Floyd warned Fauntleroy that he must not allow BIA officials to hamstring military plans, and Floyd empowered him to punish the Navajos outside the parameters of civil policy should the need for prompt and judicious action arise.[64] Hamstrung by dichotomous bureaucratic objectives, the federal government struggled to devise a workable plan for the southwestern tribes.

Excessive expenditures and quibbles over policy were only two of the problems with which military and civil officials had to contend. High costs drained the federal treasury and siphoned off taxpayer dollars, and interagency disagreements tested men's patience, but neither of those aspects incurred any human toll. The same could not be said for the living conditions at most of the territory's forts, where soldiers suffered from a slew of painful and debilitating illnesses that at best left them bedridden for weeks and at worst sent them to the cemetery in a coffin. Kearny's Army of the West had suffered many illness-related casualties in the months following the occupation of Santa Fe in 1846, and that trend continued until post–Civil War sanitation improvements and medical advancements remedied certain maladies and lessened the severity of others. In an 1855 report on sickness and mortality in the frontier army, Assistant Surgeon General Richard H. Coolidge described New Mexico as "little else than a great sterile mountainous desert, not calculated for the residence of man in a state of civilization." He concluded even more pessimistically that "New Mexico can boast of nothing on a very extensive scale, unless it be . . . actual worthlessness."[65] From a medical standpoint as well as an economic one, many Americans thought it absurd to continue the costly occupation of the Southwest.

Testimony from the field seemed to substantiate Coolidge's report. Doctor J. F. Hammond, an army medical technician stationed in New Mexico, had little positive to say about either the territory or its Hispanic inhabitants, whom he derogatorily described as impotent, pandering, and lacking any "spark of culture." In the first eighteen months of Fort Conrad's existence, from 1851 to 1853, the doctor treated 562 patients, whose most severe afflictions derived from alcohol abuse and sexually transmitted diseases. Between 1849 and 1854, army medics in New Mexico treated 11,867 cases, or an average of nearly 2,000 per year. Approximately 1,000 troops were stationed in the territory throughout that six-year period, so the probability of each man being treated averaged twice per year. Rudimentary medical treatments and poor hygiene, coupled with the seclusion of forts and their lack of adequate hospital facilities, posed serious threats to enlisted men and officers alike, as disease did not discriminate based on rank or status. During the same six-year time frame, 173 men succumbed to illness, their deaths almost invariably attributable to common fevers or other ailments that in today's world rarely claim the life of a patient.[66]

The problem of soldier mortality in antebellum New Mexico was exacerbated by unsanitary living conditions. To quench the thirst of horses and mules, irrigate crops, and sustain the men, the army built most posts near perennial water sources, which often meant swampy lowlands plagued by swarms of malarial mosquitoes. Fort Thorn, established in 1854 along the Rio Grande in south-central New Mexico, provides a case in point. The post surgeon, P. A. Quinan, wrote a scathing report describing the installation. "The buildings constituting the fort are placed within a stone's throw of the swampiest portion of this flat or bottom," he explained, "and in the most admirable manner, if the object be that the garrison shall inhale . . . the pestilential alluvia arising therefrom." For at least six months of every year the lowlands skirting the fort's walls were nothing more than "a surface of oozy mud, covered with green slime, and interspersed with pools of stagnating water [and] a rank vegetation of weeds and grasses." Given these conditions, Quinan wrote, "scarcely a man of this command can be considered fit for the performance of ordinary garrison duty, so debilitated are they by disease." More than two hundred miles to the southwest, Fort Buchanan was equally deplorable. The barracks sat on a low bluff overlooking a swampland, and the doctor reported that malaria afflicted "every person at the post during the last year, except the sutler's employees and an old negro woman." In 1858 alone he treated 769 cases of disease among a garrison numbering only 151 men, meaning that on average each soldier at Fort Buchanan was sick five times that year.[67]

Between 1849 and 1860 New Mexico's military doctors treated an astonishing 34,823 cases among a territorial garrison averaging fewer than 2,000 annually. During that time, 289 troops died from their ailments—far more than the number of army regulars who perished while fighting Indians over those same years.[68] For soldiers at most forts, New Mexico was a miserable and dangerous place to live. In 1849 Captain William Grier of the First Dragoons notified headquarters that a dozen men under his command suffered long-term debilitation stemming from arduous winter campaigning and "the vices of this country." Roughly a quarter of his troops had become "worthless to the company" and needed to be discharged.[69] At Cebolleta the post commander complained that the adobe quarters "are old, cramped, and inconvenient, and *filled* with bed bugs . . . of a larger class and greater numbers than you could easily conceive."[70] Small wonder that so many soldiers detested living in New Mexico and spoke so maliciously of the region. Nonetheless, the number of men dispatched to the territory increased throughout the 1850s; the War Department was fully willing to put enlistees in harm's way to advance the American nation-building project.[71]

In addition to poor living conditions and illness, warfare between Indians and Americans claimed many lives in a seemingly endless and at times desperately violent conflict. By prosecuting warfare with the territory's tribes, the federal government sought not only to secure unchallenged possession of the region for settlement and development but also to fulfill an obligation to protect civilians already living there. When Kearny entered New Mexico, he had declared that the United States would address the issue of Indian raiding and ensure that all Nuevomexicanos could live in safety.[72] His promise would prove difficult to keep because reciprocal hostility had characterized relations between Indians and Hispanics for generations. "It has from time immemorial been the custom of the Indians to steal from the New Mexicans and then the Mexicans to steal from them," agent Steck explained. "This system of thievery and retaliation has been kept up, and under the Mexican rule organized parties were permitted to make campaigns for the avowed purpose of stealing Indian stock."[73] Superintendent of Indian Affairs Collins criticized Kearny for having "considered it an easy matter to relieve them from the war, and to protect them against all further depredations from this formidable foe." Collins specifically mentioned the interminable Navajo wars, noting that annual military campaigns and numerous treaties had all failed to prevent raids on Rio Grande villages. "These murderers have at no time since they have been under the control of the United States ceased their depredations," the superintendent admonished, "and the Mexicans inform us that it has been the same for the last forty years."[74] In a candid confession, the commissioner of Indian affairs wrote in 1863 that "it is now fifteen years since we acquired possession of the Territory, and, so far as I can judge, the security and protection afforded by government to the lives and property of our citizens is but little if any better than at the outset."[75]

Less than a year after Kearny assured New Mexicans that they need not fear the hostile inroads of neighboring tribes, Governor Donaciano Vigil could already sense impending difficulties in upholding those guarantees. Even some enlisted men under Kearny's command perceived the folly in such promises. "General Kearny has taken the treacherous population of New Mexico under his fatherly care and protection," Private Marcellus Edwards quipped, lamenting that he might be among the troops ordered into Indian country.[76] Claiming that American proclamations had "been shamefully violated and disregarded," Vigil prophetically informed Secretary of State James Buchanan that residents would justifiably complain about continuing Indian raids.[77] Just as the governor predicted, Congress began receiving petitions from New Mexicans begging for protection and reminding the government of its obligation to defend them. In 1851 Superintendent Calhoun informed his superiors that murderous raids would continue to occur "until the powers at Washington shall accord to the people of this Territory ample protection." If the government failed to do this, he stressed, then the people would be forced either to abandon New Mexico altogether "or consent to be murdered" by Indians.[78]

In an 1850 memorial to federal lawmakers, citizens criticized the government for failing to protect their "rights in person and property" and reminded congress-men once again of Kearny's pledge. "Barbarous invaders drive off our flocks and herds by thousands," they wailed, "and men women and children are murdered or carried into captivity." New Mexico, the petitioners believed, was in a worse condition than before Americans took control, a bold and perhaps exaggerated claim considering the ruinous neglect that Mexico had shown toward its northernmost province prior to 1846.[79] When rumors abounded in the 1850s that some California tribes might be relocated to reservations in western New Mexico (now Arizona),

panicked citizens again protested the management of Indian affairs, submitting
a petition directly to President Pierce outlining the innumerable problems they
already endured with nearby Indian groups.[80] The territorial legislature submitted
a formal complaint to Congress claiming that Navajos, Apaches, and Utes had
destroyed every vestige of mining and agriculture and "rendered industry of no
avail."[81] Sounding like a broken record, New Mexicans petitioned Congress again
in 1857, grumbling that "our Indians are not under proper control, nor awed into
submission by the power of the general government."[82] Throughout the 1850s and
into the 1860s, similar appeals arrived at the doorstep of the Capitol Building almost
annually. The entreaties invariably criticized the military for failing to control the
Indians, demanded that all tribes be removed to faraway places, and insisted that
more soldiers be assigned to the territory. Coupled with the nation's objective of
retaining control over the Southwest for imperial and commercial purposes, these
constant petitions placed added pressure on federal officials to devise and enforce
Indian policy in New Mexico.

Military campaigns against Indians commenced just weeks after Kearny's
occupation of Santa Fe. At least 30,000 Indians (12,000 Comanches; 4,000–5,000
Utes; 7,000–14,000 Navajos; and 6,000–7,000 Apaches) occupied quadrants of
the Southwest, and the outnumbered U.S. troops were overtasked trying to protect
residents and punish raiders. Each of the four tribes could muster hundreds of
skilled warriors at almost any time to resist enemy encroachment.[83] In October 1846
Colonel Alexander Doniphan led his First Regiment of Missouri Volunteers into
Navajo country, where he met Zarcillos Largos and other leaders at Ojo del Oso.
Attempting to fulfill Kearny's promises, the Missourians avoided hostilities with
their Indian counterparts and negotiated the first treaty between that tribe and the
United States. The colonel explained the circumstances of the American conquest
to Navajo leaders, informing them that future raids along the Rio Grande would
result in warfare not with Mexico but with the more powerful U.S. government.[84]
Expeditions against and treaties with the formidable Navajos would become a
common theme over the next two decades. Having lived in New Mexico for almost
twenty years before the cession, Governor Bent understood the superficiality of
Doniphan's agreement and informed Secretary of State Buchanan that "I have but
little ground to hope that it will be permanent."[85] Doniphan's treaty—like previous
pacts between the Navajos and their Spanish and Mexican neighbors—proved a
failure, and hostilities recommenced shortly thereafter.

A group of confused Navajos ventured to Santa Fe in March 1847, where they
informed Colonel Sterling Price that "they cannot understand the conduct of the

Americans, who came here to *fight* Mexicans, and are now so friendly that they *protect* them." The headmen offered to ally with Americans to fight and kill Hispanic residents, a proposal that Price refused.[86] Matters devolved so rapidly that Colonel Edward Newby brokered a second agreement with Zarcillos Largos, Narbona, and José Largo on May 20, 1848. Almost a carbon copy of Doniphan's treaty, the contract between Newby and the Navajos mandated an exchange of stolen property and captives along with a permanent end to hostilities.[87] The stipulations of this latest pact once again unraveled in the face of ongoing conflict between the tribe and their New Mexican enemies, who were criticized by many U.S. officers as cowards for their lackluster efforts at resisting Navajo inroads.[88]

The first incident of overt violence between Navajos and Americans occurred in 1849, when Colonel John M. Washington led several companies of infantry, dragoons, and artillery into Dinétah. Accompanied by Superintendent Calhoun, the colonel held a council with Narbona, José Largo, and Archuleta, during which the Indians renewed their commitment to Newby's treaty. The diplomatic mission quickly devolved into conflict, however, when a disagreement over a stolen horse erupted into musketry and artillery fire. Armed with four cannons, Washington's forces unleashed deadly volleys at the Indians as they fled, killing the eighty-year-old Narbona and six others. Unfazed, the troops marched onward to Canyon de Chelly. In early September they met with another Navajo delegation, members of which "regretted that, for so trifling a thing as a horse, so much damage had been done." Despite the violent encounter, Chiefs Mariano Martínez and Chapitone promised that their people would respect the agreement and refrain from further raiding. Satisfied with the results, Washington countermarched to Santa Fe, where he learned just one day after his arrival that Navajos had already broken the treaty and killed five Mexicans in a raid near Sandía Pueblo.[89] "It is as natural for them to war against all men, and to take the property of others, as it is for the sun to give light by day," Calhoun joked after learning of the incident.[90]

Even though Doniphan, Newby, and Washington had all failed to exact meaningful commitments to peace, the characteristically confident Sumner believed that he could succeed. In September 1851 he took a break from his controversial reorganization of the Ninth Military Department to lead troops back into Navajo country, retracing Washington's route westward from Santa Fe in what would become the first manifestation of his unlimited warfare approach. His men entered the seemingly impregnable Canyon de Chelly, where they ate from the Navajos' watermelon patches, cornfields, and peach orchards until, according to Private James Bennett of the First Dragoons, bullets began to "fall thickly" from the muskets of angry Indians standing atop adjacent cliffs.[91] When the column returned to headquarters a month later, an exasperated Sumner grumbled that his foes "never forced us, or gave us an opportunity to inflict upon them any signal chastisement." The Navajos had been wise to avoid the colonel, who had no intentions of negotiating peace. "My object was to attack the Indians . . . and to destroy their crops," an embittered and dispassionate Sumner confessed following the unproductive excursion.[92] Unbeknownst to the dragoons, bands of Navajos used the campaign as an opportunity to raid along the Rio Grande, where the withdrawal of troops for the expedition left some settlements unprotected and vulnerable. "They have so successfully committed murders and depredations," Calhoun wrote while Sumner was in the field, "that they do not fear the possibility of being caught by the troops."[93]

Before returning to headquarters Sumner ordered Major Electus Backus and several companies of soldiers to remain behind and establish Fort Defiance in the heart of Navajo lands. "I believe a large post at the Cañon Bonito will in a short time effectually restrain these Indians," he optimistically reported. "If this post does not put a stop to the Navajo depredations, nothing will do it but their entire extermination."[94] The psychological effect seemed immediate: Backus reported just two months later that a party of Navajos came to the fort seeking peace, "as they seem to dread the idea of our establishing new posts" in their country.[95] Although Sumner's active campaigning produced even fewer meaningful results than those of his predecessors, his decision to construct Fort Defiance at one of the tribe's favorite camping and grazing grounds would have significant ramifications.

While Doniphan held council with the Navajos at Ojo del Oso in 1846, General Kearny was marching through southwestern New Mexico on his way to California, a trek that brought him into contact with the Chiricahua Apaches. After the column met with Chief Mangas Coloradas near the Gila River, Captain Henry Smith Turner predicted that "should this country ever get in the possession of the U.S. there will be much difficulty in keeping these Indians in order." He ominously but accurately foresaw the impending difficulties that would plague the next four decades of interaction between Americans and Apaches. Turner postulated that the federal government would have to "buy them up with annuities" in order to purchase good behavior; otherwise "a war with them would be almost as endless as the Florida war with the Seminoles."[96] On his tour through New Mexico and Chihuahua that same year, Dr. Adolph Wislizenus observed that none of the region's agricultural, pastoral, or mining resources could be developed profitably until "the wild Indians . . . have first been subdued."[97] In southern New Mexico, the initial responsibility for achieving this outcome fell to Major Enoch Steen and his dragoons at Doña Ana, from whence the military launched numerous campaigns against the Chiricahua and Mescalero Apaches in the early 1850s.

Already frustrated by relations with the Navajos, Superintendent of Indian Affairs Calhoun complained in February 1850 that Apaches in southern New Mexico "are becoming more troublesome and impudent." During several recent raids near Doña Ana, warriors had murdered Hispanic herders, stolen their livestock, and carried away women and children as captives.[98] In one of their most brazen strikes, a small band of Apaches decoyed Steen's dragoons away from the town, enabling a larger group to raid at will. Embarrassed and irate, Steen wrote to Santa Fe asking for permission to lead a campaign into the Apaches' homelands and destroy their camps. Calhoun liked the idea, proclaiming that "a just and severe chastisement awaits these people for their numerous butcheries." During the two years that U.S. troops occupied Doña Ana, they embarked on no fewer than seven expeditions into Chiricahua and Mescalero Apache country, with little to show in the way of positive results. Following one reconnaissance of the Mimbres River valley, Steen recommended that a satellite post be established in that vicinity, and in January 1852 the department built Fort Webster at the Santa Rita copper mines to monitor the Chiricahuas and dissuade them from further depredations.[99]

Meaning to achieve a permanent end to the Apache conflict, Colonel Sumner traveled to Acoma Pueblo on July 1, 1852, to negotiate a treaty with numerous tribal chiefs, including Mangas Coloradas and Cuchillo Negro. The accord disallowed raiding in both Mexico and the United States, forcing the Indians to submit unequivocally to American rule. The tribe also agreed that forts could be built wherever the army pleased, settlers could pass freely through any portion of their homelands, and all captives would be surrendered to U.S. authorities. In exchange for these concessions, the Apaches would receive gifts and supplies in an amount that the federal government "may deem proper" at a future date. The lopsided pact marked Sumner's only real attempt at nonviolent Indian diplomacy during his tenure as military commander.[100] The colonel afterwards satisfied himself that "if I can keep the Mexicans from committing depredations on them, I have no doubt but the peace will be lasting."[101] Although the Senate ratified the treaty, its provisions went widely ignored and hostilities recommenced in short order.

In August 1853 Sumner transferred command of New Mexico's military department to General John Garland, who would spend the next four years grappling with the same difficulties as his predecessors. Governor David Meriwether informed the general in January 1855 that the Indians "are every day becoming more bold in their attacks."[102] With violence continuing mostly unabated throughout the southern half of the territory, Garland dispatched a large winter campaign against the Mescalero Apaches, aiming to force the tribe into permanent submission. Captain Richard Ewell led a contingent of dragoons and infantry into the Sacramento Mountains of southeastern New Mexico, where he rendezvoused with a second column from Fort Fillmore under Colonel Dixon Miles. Plagued by heavy snows and sparse forage, the troops and animals suffered for the duration of the campaign, and Private James Bennett named one of their nightly stopping places "Camp Starvation."[103] In the expedition's only armed engagement, Captain Henry Stanton, a revered officer, fell dead from a gunshot to the head. Two other dragoons also perished, including Private Thomas Dwyer, who was "dismounted, surrounded, and lanced" after he killed one of the Indians.[104] The loss of Stanton infuriated military leaders throughout the department and heightened their resolve to punish the Mescalero Apaches. Within three months, Garland had selected the site for Fort Stanton, a post that, like Fort Defiance in Navajo country, situated troops permanently within tribal homelands.[105] Less than two months after the fort's construction, humbled Mescalero leaders traveled to Fort Thorn and accepted Governor Meriwether's terms for peace, an outcome that reaffirmed the propriety of building posts on the Indian frontier.[106]

The largest military campaign yet assembled in New Mexico took the field in May 1857 and targeted Apaches who, seven months earlier, had murdered Navajo agent Henry L. Dodge. The unprovoked execution of Dodge sparked a fury throughout the department that exceeded even the ire surrounding Captain Stanton's combat death two years earlier. After identifying the Mogollon subgroup of Chiricahua Apaches as the culprits, the assistant adjutant general fumed that "these Indians may be thoroughly chastised, and their band so broken up that they will not be heard from again as a distinct people." Colonel Bonneville swore to avenge Dodge's murder and began planning an operation in which nearly 1,000 troops would converge on Apache territory from three different directions. In a transnational effort, U.S. authorities contacted the Mexican governors of Chihuahua and Sonora, enlisting their support in defeating "a common enemy" should the Apaches flee south of the border.[107]

From May through July the commanding officers—Bonneville, Miles, Ewell, and William Loring—scoured southwestern New Mexico with detachments of dragoons, infantry, and mounted riflemen, but the troops encountered Apaches on only two occasions. In the first incident, Colonel Loring attacked a camp near the Mimbres River; the headman, Cuchillo Negro, and six others were killed, all of them members of the Gila Apache subgroup, which had not been implicated in Dodge's death.[108] Two months later, the entire command probed westward, traversing the Gila River into today's southeastern Arizona, where they stumbled on a large Coyotero Apache *ranchería*. Catching the Indians by surprise, the attackers killed twenty-four men and women and took twenty-six others prisoner. Bonneville's command suffered just eight troopers wounded in the lopsided affair. "It was a sad sight," Lieutenant John DuBois confided to his diary. "I could not avoid asking myself why we had killed these poor harmless savages," he pondered, noting that the Coyoteros had committed no acts of hostility on American settlements and previously had directed their raids only toward Sonora.[109] Back in Santa Fe, General Garland had a different take on the incident. "The chastisement they have received will be long remembered by them," he gleamed. "The effect . . . will doubtless prove most salutary."[110]

Ignominiously dubbed the "Campaign of Clowns" by one disenchanted junior officer, the expedition came to a close on July 26, 1857, when Bonneville abandoned his makeshift headquarters at the Gila Depot and ordered all troops back to their posts after three grueling months in the field. Colonel Miles called the excursion "the most fatiguing march I ever experienced," and Loring complained of mountains so steep and rugged that "many of the strongest mules fell backwards with their packs." Agent Steck later noted that the Apaches "have never recovered from the effects of the campaign made into their country two years ago," estimating that half of their warriors had since perished. The tribe, he remarked, had been "compelled to scatter in every direction for safety," and the majority fled into northern Mexico seeking asylum.[111] For its part, the military did not emerge unblemished either. The campaign consumed vast resources and, because of the number of troops involved, sapped the department of much-needed manpower. Lieutenant Henry Lazelle offered the pithiest description of Bonneville's campaign, figuring that 800 men had traveled over one thousand miles and expended half a million dollars' worth of supplies for "the recovery of 500 sheep and 10 Indians."[112] The lieutenant's calculation simplified the messy details and contingencies of field operations into the pertinent categories of money, manpower, and distance—the three things that most confounded federal officials in their prosecution of the Indian Wars.[113]

As these events transpired in the southern half of the territory, Utes and Jicarilla Apaches in the northernmost regions also posed problems for civil and military commanders, who responded to dozens of reported raids, kidnappings, and murders throughout the antebellum period. One of the most infamous killings occurred in 1849 when an allied force of Utes and Jicarillas massacred the civilian wagon train of J. M. White and family on the Santa Fe Trail. The Indians slew the men and rode away with Mrs. White, her young daughter, and a black female slave as captives. Superintendent Calhoun immediately dispatched scouting parties to search for the women and even authorized the payment of ransoms if necessary. The elder Mrs. White was killed during an attack on her Jicarilla captors, but the whereabouts of the other two women remained a mystery for two more years. Congress appropriated $1,500 to locate and recover the two missing girls, and bureaucrats at the highest level of government collaborated in a feverish but futile attempt to save their lives. In a petition to President Zachary Taylor, New Mexicans declared that "the savage butchery of poor White and the male part of his party . . . and the yet more horrible fate of Mrs. White, call for a vengeance that there is not power enough in this territory to inflict."[114] Although thousands of Hispanics and Indians lived in a state of captive slavery at the time of Kearny's conquest, it took the abduction of two Anglo women to finally spur U.S. officials to action.

While the death and capture of the Whites directed increased military attention toward the Utes and Jicarillas, a much deadlier encounter incited open warfare with the two tribes. When sixty troops of the First Dragoons marched out of Cantonment Burgwin on March 29, 1854, their commander, Lieutenant John Davidson, had no idea that most of his men would be dead or wounded by the following evening. As the soldiers trekked southward from Taos, they discovered an Indian camp at a site known as Cieneguilla. Motivated by a skirmish earlier that month during which soldiers had killed the Jicarilla chief Lobo and four others, the Indians mounted an offensive that overwhelmed the dragoons. After a fierce three-hour battle against an estimated 300 Jicarillas, Davidson—himself wounded in action—ordered his beleaguered combatants to retreat. Twenty-two soldiers died, twenty-three more sustained injuries, and forty-five horses lay dead on the battlefield. Only a handful of men emerged unhurt from the deadliest firefight yet to occur between federal troops and Indians in New Mexico, an engagement that also claimed the lives of many Jicarilla warriors.[115]

Revenge would be swift, unrelenting, and decisive. Interim Governor William S. Messervy declared war on the Jicarillas—whom he designated an enemy of the state—and threatened the death penalty for anybody who aided or abetted the tribe in any way.[116] For the Indians, the hostile feelings were mutual: while raiding on the upper Arkansas River, Jicarillas and Utes told survivors that "they would murder every American and Mexican they met" so long as a state of hostility existed.[117] In the days following the Battle of Cieneguilla, General Garland dispatched Lieutenant Colonel Philip St. George Cooke with two hundred dragoons and a company of artillery to comb the mountains of northern New Mexico in search of Indians. The column engaged a band of Utes, killing at least six warriors, and soon afterward Garland proclaimed that Messervy's so-called enemies of the state had been "thoroughly humbled" and would beg for peace.[118] In reality, the war between allied Utes and Jicarillas and their American foes had just begun, and army officers spent the next year scouring the countryside. Throughout 1854 military operations claimed the lives of dozens of Indians, resulting in the complete destruction of numerous camps and crushing the tribes' will to fight.[119] Even civilians participated in the assaults, with hundreds of New Mexicans filling the ranks of four militia companies under the command of Ceran St. Vrain. In 1855, with more than 1,000 soldiers and hundreds of armed residents actively campaigning, the Jicarilla Apaches and Muache Utes met with the governor to discuss terms for peace.[120]

As violence between Utes, Jicarillas, and Americans escalated, a member of the Navajo tribe committed an act that very nearly catapulted his kinsmen into a war of their own. In an unprovoked attack, a Navajo man killed Private Nicholas Hefbiner of the Third Infantry—who was cutting hay for the animals at Fort Defiance—and then fled to safety in the nearby mountains. Major Henry Lane Kendrick called the incident an atrocity and lamented that it "threatens very serious consequences," although he acknowledged the murder as an independent act of a miscreant and not a tribal declaration of hostility. An Indian agent subsequently met with several Navajo leaders and stressed the gravity of the situation. If they failed to surrender the killer to U.S. officials, then "war of the most stringent character would be the inevitable result." The agent also reminded Navajos that the coming winter months would provide troops with the perfect opportunity to wage war against the tribe, as cold temperatures and snowfall immobilized women and children and limited the provisions on which their people could draw for subsistence. In November the tribe averted further violence by turning over the murderer at Fort Defiance. Kendrick gathered as many Navajos as he could find, strung a noose around the man's neck, and hung him in plain view for all to see.[121]

The major planned the execution as a warning to the Indians, but the impression faded and the lesson was soon forgotten. In 1858 a similar incident occurred at Fort Defiance, with deadlier consequences for both sides. The commanding officer at that time, Major William Brooks of the Third Infantry, owned a twenty-year-old African American slave named Jim, who had accompanied the major when he transferred to New Mexico several years earlier. On July 12 a Navajo man who had been loitering at the fort shot Jim as he walked across the grounds; the killer then fled astride his horse into the adjacent mountains. A doctor tried to extract the metal arrow point from Jim's lungs, but to no avail; Jim died of the wounds four days later. Furious about the loss of his slave, Brooks demanded that Chief Zarcillos Largos reimburse him for Jim's pecuniary value as human property, promising that any failure to pay for the boy and surrender the escaped murderer "will be considered cause for war." A group of Navajo headmen eventually rode to Fort Defiance and dropped off a corpse that they claimed to be that of Jim's killer. Post surgeon James Cooper McKee determined through an autopsy that the body in fact was that of a young Hispanic man, most likely a captive who was being held as a servant among the tribe. In killing one of their own slaves, Navajos sought to atone for Brooks's loss in the most equitable way they could devise, hoping to bring closure to the issue and avert war with American troops.[122]

Rather than calming the situation, the deceptive gesture infuriated military officials, who felt that the tribe had attempted to shield the culprit from execution. The murder of Jim at Fort Defiance sparked five years of continuous fighting between Americans and Navajos, a conflict that Senator Charles Sumner called "a war of the most bloody nature."[123] Secretary of War John B. Floyd acknowledged that the Navajos constituted "an extremely formidable force" and estimated that they could muster over 3,000 warriors at any time, meaning that prolonged conflict would be deadly for everybody involved.[124] Matters climaxed in 1860, when Navajos perpetrated a number of daring attacks on soldiers near Fort Defiance. In January of that year, 300 Indians executed a hit-and-run assault on the army's beef herd, ambushing a 35-man detachment at a grazing camp just eight miles from the fort. Before the soldiers could grab their guns and gather their thoughts, three troopers lay dead and the Navajos had retreated safely into their mountainous strongholds. A month later Chief Huero led 500 tribesmen in another raid, targeting troops assigned to monitor a herd of cattle seven miles from the post. This time, however, the soldiers repulsed the attack without sustaining any casualties, while the Navajos suffered at least ten warriors injured.[125]

When he learned of these incidents, Superintendent James Collins felt simultaneously enraged and saddened. The Navajos and the U.S. government had affixed their marks and signatures to six treaties over the previous twelve years, he fumed in a letter to Governor Abraham Rencher, "not one of which seems to have been thought of, either by the Indians or ourselves, after they were signed and agreed to." He called the disingenuous treaty-making process a farce, the result being that "the Indians have really learned to believe that the signing of a treaty places them under no obligations." The blame for this, he understood, rested as much with lackadaisical administration and enforcement on the part of American officials as it did on any

Navajo intransigence or dishonesty.[126] As he reflected further over coming days, Collins lamented that "a war with the tribe is now beyond the possibility of prevention." Relations had devolved to the point of unmitigated violence, "not only on account of the heavy cost in which it will involve to the government, but it will most likely destroy the means which the tribe now possesses for self-support." With a downcast tone, he concluded that "I seriously dread the consequences for the Navajos."[127]

In response to these hostile encounters, headquarters ordered troops at every installation to be prepared to take the field at a moment's notice. Colonel Fauntleroy hoped to enlist 300 Ute warriors as auxiliaries, pointing out that these longtime Navajo enemies would accept the plunder taken during armed engagements in lieu of the cash salaries that conventional militiamen demanded. He also collaborated with Kit Carson to formulate a plan for invading Navajo country.[128] Before any troops took the field, however, the tribe launched one of the boldest Indian attacks in the annals of western history. In the predawn hours of April 30, 1860, an estimated 1,000 warriors descended on Fort Defiance from three different directions, catching 206 infantrymen completely by surprise. Fighting lasted past sunrise, when the Indians fled the scene after failing to overwhelm the better-armed soldiers. Twenty-eight-year-old Private Sylvester Johnson died of an arrow wound to the chest, and at least a dozen Navajos also perished in the melee. Given the intensity of combat and the number of men involved, the casualty count was remarkably low. But the brazen premeditated assault on U.S. regulars at a federal post would have a tremendous impact on Americans' resolve to crush the tribe into submission.[129]

Within months of the attack, Colonel Edward Canby gathered fourteen companies of troops in preparation for a massive punitive expedition into Navajo country. Marching in several columns, the men rendezvoused at Fort Defiance before probing deeper into tribal homelands. Throughout September and October hundreds of troops scoured the Chuska Mountains, Pueblo Colorado Wash, and Canyon de Chelly regions. The elderly chief and medicine man Zarcillos Largos, born in the late 1700s and widely regarded among Americans as a levelheaded man of peace and diplomacy, was killed during the relentless campaigning. Skirmishes between soldiers and Indians claimed the lives of dozens more, and weeks of intense marches so severely broke down the dragoons' horses that many of the mounts would never again be serviceable.[130]

Meanwhile, in southwestern New Mexico a deadly and treacherous incident with the Chiricahua Apaches set the stage for more violence in that quarter. After members of the tribe raided John Ward's ranch near the Sonora border on January 27, 1861, Lieutenant George Bascom and a detachment of dragoons rode out of nearby Fort Buchanan in pursuit. When the troops arrived at Apache Pass, they encountered

Cochise and his followers. The two respective leaders met inside an army tent, and Bascom informed Cochise that he would detain his family as prisoners until the tribe returned a captive boy taken during the raid on Ward's ranch. Cochise escaped only after drawing a large bowie knife and slicing his way through the canvas and out of the tent, leaving behind his brother and two nephews. In the days that followed, Apaches ambushed a civilian wagon train and took four prisoners, hoping to exchange them for those whom Bascom held, but to no avail. On the morning of February 8, a tense skirmish broke out near the Apache Pass mail station, during which at least three Indians died and Bascom lost dozens of mules and horses. Before retreating, Cochise and his followers tortured and mutilated the four American prisoners and left their bodies for the troops to bury. Not to be outdone, the soldiers hanged Cochise's family members and three other captives in retaliation, thus concluding the so-called Bascom Affair and initiating more than two decades of unremitting warfare between American troops and Apache warriors.[131]

Colonel Canby's Navajo offensive wrought a severe toll on all involved, and Lieutenant Bascom's betrayal of Cochise sealed the fates of many American troops and settlers over coming years. Before any decisive outcomes could be reached in either case, however, a far graver conflict erupted off the coast of South Carolina. By 1861 New Mexico was poised to serve as a backdrop for multiple theatres of warfare. Not only would federal troops face a Confederate invasion at the dawn of the Civil War, but in the coming months and years they also would be called on to prosecute violent conflicts with Navajos, Apaches, and Comanches. Once again the U.S. government would be tested in its resolve to hold the Southwest, this time from the dual threats of Indian raids and Rebel attack.

When read individually, most antebellum military campaigns in New Mexico appear to have produced mixed results at best. Troops suffered immeasurably from the hardships of illness, warfare, and isolation, while taxpayers footed the enormous bill for ceaseless military maneuvers. Relations between Americans and Indians grew steadily worse, erupting in open warfare with the Apaches and Navajos in the early 1860s. Implementing reservation policy failed to produce the desired results, leading many government officials to adopt Colonel Sumner's unlimited warfare approach as a precursor to peace. Ultimately, few Indians died as a direct result of intensive army operations, and even fewer combat engagements occurred. But when the military campaigns are read together in the broader context of westward expansion, the impact becomes clearer. Short-term goals went unmet as troops attempted to contain the Indians and exact lasting commitments to peace. However, achievements that were not immediately apparent would become more obvious as time wore on.

With limited populations, tribes could not easily replace warriors lost in battle, nor could they weather the demographic decline propagated by fierce tactics that destroyed all means of subsistence and forced them into a lifestyle of constant motion to avoid soldiers.[132] As agent Steck warned the Chiricahua Apaches in 1854, the United States "has more soldiers than you can count, they are like the grass on the prairie or the leaves on the trees—you might kill all that are here but [we] would send ten times as many."[133] He not only cautioned the Indians against future resistance but also alluded to America's determination to control the Southwest. Frontier warfare in North America differed drastically from conventional conflict between nation-states: large, decisive battles rarely occurred, and the results usually remained uncertain. Throughout the antebellum era, private citizens and government agents came to appreciate the protection afforded by a strong military as they attempted to develop mines, farm fertile valleys, graze cattle on open ranges, and survey railroads in advancement of a Manifest Destiny that no longer seemed so simple. The full consequences of antebellum military campaigns were not immediately apparent, but in the years following the Civil War little doubt remained that the soldiers were indispensable to nation-building enterprises. While U.S. troops waged relentless warfare against the Southwest Indian tribes to assert physical dominance over the land and its people, Americans 2,000 miles away undertook a difficult conflict of their own, as lawmakers from the North and South grappled to control the political ideology of New Mexico in relation to slavery and free soil.

= 4 =

POPULAR SOVEREIGNTY
AND PECULIAR INSTITUTIONS

The Missouri Compromise of 1820, which marked the beginning of fervent sectionalist politics in the United States, ranked among the most important pieces of slavery legislation in the antebellum era. The act stipulated that Missouri be admitted as a slave state and Maine as a free state, thus maintaining a balance of representation in the Senate and establishing a precedent for the admission of new states in pairs or groups to avoid lopsided shifts in sectional power. A second component of the law banned slavery in any future U.S. territory or state situated above the 36°30' line of north latitude, from Missouri's southern border to the shores of the Pacific.[1] Wittingly or not, congressional leaders had established clear geographic parameters for the boundary of a southern domain that might one day stretch uninterrupted from ocean to ocean. Lawmakers all but preordained a vast empire of slavery spanning the lower half of the continent, laying the groundwork for the increasingly virulent agitation over that issue that would characterize the nation's next forty-five years. Most Hispanics living in New Mexico—which remained a province of New Spain at that time—probably heard nothing of this new American law, and those who did catch wind of it could scarcely have imagined the political implications that it would one day have for them.

In January 1861—with southern states rapidly seceding in response to Abraham Lincoln's election as president—Ohio representative Thomas Corwin spoke specifically in the context of the Missouri Compromise when he called New Mexico "the great battlefield on which the South and North meet in wicked, foolish, fratricidal strife."[2]

Another Ohioan, Representative John Sherman, echoed that sentiment when he declared, in clear frustration, "Shall New Mexico be free or slave? This is the question upon which this government is to be disrupted, our flag dishonored, and upon which state after state goes out of the Union."[3] Both men echoed Richard Weightman, who had served as a territorial representative to Congress in the early 1850s. The New Mexican people, Weightman had once complained, "have suffered too much already, by having our soil made use of by others as a political battlefield over which to settle the slavery question."[4] Given the territory's ongoing role as a controversial pawn in the slavery debates, these comments were less hyperbolic than some might have imagined. Numerous events over many decades combined to bring about the Civil War, but territorial New Mexico played an important role in the eleventh-hour arguments that ripped the nation apart and sparked a long and bloody conflict.

When it came to supporting the interests of slave owners in the decades leading up to the Civil War, Senator John C. Calhoun never minced words. Many southerners, in fact, held the South Carolinian expansionist in high regard as their foremost political philosopher: the fire-eating Virginia author George Fitzhugh christened Calhoun as the South's own reincarnation of Aristotle.[5] During and after the war with Mexico, the former war hawk spoke frequently and passionately about land that the United States had acquired from its defeated foe, stressing the importance of a perceived Constitutional right to slave property in newly appended territories and states. A lifelong politician, Calhoun abhorred the efforts of abolitionists and Free-Soilers—the radical Northern counterparts to his own Southern extremism—to prohibit slavery in New Mexico and California. If adopted, that course would deprive his native South of critical votes in Congress and further upset the balance of political power in a way that the Missouri Compromise had sought to avoid. The North, Calhoun roared in one speech, was making "the most strenuous effort to appropriate the whole [Mexican Cession] to herself, by excluding the South from every foot of it."[6] He demanded that the new western domain be accessible to all Americans, not merely those of one or the other section, and insisted that every free white male citizen be able to enjoy equal rights should they choose to emigrate there. Speaking of New Mexico and California specifically, Calhoun contended that "they are as much the territories of one state as another. . . . They are the territories of all, because they are the territories of each."[7] In the years following the Mexican-American War, federal leaders, as well as New Mexicans themselves, would have much to say about the ideologies that undergirded Calhoun's proclamations, as New Mexico was thrust headlong into the intense sectional disputes that would plague Congress and the nation throughout the next decade.

The Mexican-American War brought divergent American perspectives on Manifest Destiny into sharp relief, as citizens and legislators debated vigorously over the political disposition of immense tracts of land acquired from Mexico. Once a treaty of peace brought the conflict to an end, congressional leaders considered the conditions under which new western territories and states would be admitted into the Union. By the late 1840s the South and the North had drastically differing visions for the future of the western half of the continent, and those ideas revolved primarily around slavery. When Henry Clay and the Senate Committee of Thirteen convened in April 1850 to review possible conditions for the admittance of California and New Mexico, they did so knowing that "out of our recent territorial acquisitions, and in connection with the institution of slavery, questions most grave have sprung, which . . . endanger the safety of the Union."[8] New Mexico came to represent America's sectional contentions in microcosm, as northern Free-Soilers vied with southern radicals over the ultimate disposition of the Southwest. As with the Kansas-Nebraska Act of 1854, the debate surrounding New Mexico's entry into the Union as either a territory or a state—with or without slavery—incited tremendous discord and portended of greater conflicts to come. As it had since the beginning of the Santa Fe trade in 1821, New Mexico would continue to play an important role in American expansion—both geographic and ideological—during the crisis-ridden 1850s. This time, however, not all U.S. citizens found themselves united in their respective desires for New Mexico's future.

Arriving at an agreement over popular sovereignty for the western territories proved difficult given the sectional turmoil arising from Texas's annexation and the Mexican-American War.[9] Politicians spent months debating the issue of slavery in the vast lands that Mexico's diplomats ceded in 1848, and New Mexico became a subject of heated exchanges in the two houses of Congress, in newspaper editorials, and during everyday conversations throughout eastern cities and backwater towns. The editors of a Santa Fe newspaper hinted at the coming unrest in January 1848—before the Treaty of Guadalupe Hidalgo had even been signed—when they informed readers that "the slave question is of incalculable importance" and predicted that southerners would work assiduously to expand slavery westward from Texas.[10] That forecast proved accurate, as Americans spent the next two and a half years arguing about the future role of the peculiar institution in the Southwest.

One of the first meaningful congressional debates over slavery in New Mexico occurred during the summer of 1848, just weeks after the Senate ratified the Treaty of Guadalupe Hidalgo and officially incorporated the Mexican Cession lands as U.S. possessions. North Carolina representative Richard Donnell offered his thoughts in a speech that must have reminded some listeners of the Wilmot Proviso arguments just eighteen months earlier. "New Mexico and California are the apples of discord," he said, lamenting that "we are already reaping the bitter fruit of national cupidity" over the issue. The United States, he believed, would have been better off had it never acquired territory from Mexico, because the resulting political division might well prove irreparable. Despite being a southerner himself, Donnell opined that slavery could not exist in New Mexico without special congressional action along the same lines as the Missouri Compromise three decades earlier. He noted that previous Mexican laws already abolished African slavery but astutely pointed out that the existence of "peon slavery" precluded New Mexico from any legitimate claim to free-soil status. The North Carolinian concluded by admitting that discussions over slavery in the Southwest had much more to do with political ideology and congressional representation than any desire on the part of southerners to transport large numbers of African American bondsmen there.[11]

Northern radicals also had plenty to say about slavery in the territories. Representative George Marsh of New Hampshire responded to Donnell's comments with a diatribe that addressed everything from the laws of Mexico to the laws of nature. Regarding the former, he noted that the preexisting codes of another country did not apply in New Mexico once that territory shifted to U.S. jurisdiction. Marsh also questioned whether the Mexican congress had a right to abolish slavery as it did in 1837 (the third time that country had outlawed slavery since gaining independence in 1821), opining that Mexico's national constitution left that issue to each state and province to decide individually. The New Hampshire representative was shrewdly applying the American notion of states' rights, as specifically outlined in the U.S. Constitution, to another country's laws and government. However fallacious or misapplied his logic, the purpose was to demonstrate that Congress needed to take concrete action of its own relative to involuntary servitude in the land acquired from Mexico. Marsh insisted that a definitive law—passed by the U.S. Congress, not the Mexican congress—would be necessary to prohibit the peculiar institution in New Mexico. He recommended that the example of the New England states, many of which had independently outlawed slavery years earlier, be followed in the Southwest.[12]

Pennsylvanian David Wilmot rose to his feet after Marsh finished and added his own thoughts to the debate. "The law of slavery is the law of violence and aggression," he provocatively asserted, noting that slavery already had a strong foothold in Texas and that it would soon exist in an unbroken swath across North America unless the government acted to prevent its spread. Wilmot accused slaveholders of conspiring to push their peculiar institution all the way to the Pacific Ocean in order to "insure the ultimate subjugation of the whole southern half of this continent" to southern control. In the eyes of antislavery activists like Marsh and Wilmot, New Mexico formed the last geographic bulwark against the westward spread of slavery. If southerners had their way in New Mexico and California, Wilmot feared, it would represent "the certain triumph of slavery, and the last struggle of freedom." Reiterating the provisions of his infamous Wilmot Proviso of 1846, the Pennsylvanian advocated a policy of nonintervention and containment whereby slavery would be left alone where it already existed, and forever prohibited in any new land incorporated into the United States, including New Mexico. He felt certain that anything other than this course would lead directly to national division and civil war. The topic of slavery in New Mexico therefore bore tremendous importance for the future of the federal union.[13]

A group of New Mexicans injected additional tension into these debates when they petitioned Congress in October 1848, requesting incorporation as a territory without slavery. Several state legislatures in the North advocated this path by passing resolutions in favor of a federal law to prohibit slavery in New Mexico.[14] Missouri senator Thomas Hart Benton sponsored the territorial bill, while his rival John C. Calhoun complained vehemently against any "insolent" action that would outlaw slavery in the Southwest. Texas senator Thomas Rusk also objected, because the petition did not recognize his own state's claim to eastern New Mexico.[15] The request for territorial status fell flat in the prevailing environment of sectional dispute, and the issue remained temporarily undecided. In arguing against New Mexico's admission on the premises of popular sovereignty and the Texas boundary claim, however, Calhoun and Rusk presaged the negotiations that would ultimately result in sectional compromise.

Congressional leaders rekindled the issue two years later in a series of heated discussions that lasted for months. Senators John Berrien of Georgia and Jefferson Davis of Mississippi were among the many outspoken southerners who fought hard to make New Mexico a bastion for slavery. In February 1850 Berrien revisited the Mexican antislavery laws, announcing that the United States could never "subject ourselves to the laws of a foreign nation" and that another country's legal mandates should not dictate American jurisprudence or politics. He also claimed that the only reason racial slavery remained unpopular and unnecessary in New Mexico was because it had been "easily substituted by the system of peonage." The fact that involuntary servitude existed there in the alternative forms of Indian captivity and debt bondage demonstrated to Berrien that Mexico's antislavery edicts had little basis in the lived reality of its citizens.[16] The following day Davis added his own invective to the debate. "Did we admit territory from Mexico subject to the constitution and laws of Mexico?" he asked rhetorically. "Did we pay fifteen millions of dollars for jurisdiction over California and New Mexico, that it might be held subordinate to the law of Mexico?" The fiery Mississippian also pointed out that Nicholas Trist, the American agent who negotiated the Treaty of Guadalupe Hidalgo, explicitly told Mexican diplomats that a prohibition of slavery could not, under any circumstances, be included in the treaty of cession because of the political firestorm it would incite. All of this, Davis proclaimed, meant that slavery could, and indeed should, exist in New Mexico—if not in practice, then at least in political and legal principle.[17]

Connecticut senator Truman Smith led the rebuttal for free-soil northerners, laying out a complex argument that named national legal issues, regional social concerns, and the physical environment of the Southwest as three obstacles to slavery's expansion. Mexico's prior abolition of racial slavery, Smith believed, posed a major hurdle to southerners wishing to implant the chattel system in any land acquired through the Mexican Cession. The senator predicted that ambiguity about the right to own slaves in New Mexico would discourage most masters from taking their human property there in the first place. Equally important, Smith continued, were uncertainties revolving around Hispanic sentiment toward slavery. The local population "are all opposed to negro bondage," he stated, claiming that Nuevomexicanos did not entertain the same prejudices against blacks as did many white Americans. "The negro laborer would find himself on a footing of equality with the white, Indian, or mixed laborer" in New Mexico, Smith asserted, postulating that the racial hierarchy that sustained chattel slavery in the South would never materialize in the multiethnic Southwest. Furthermore, an arid climate, high altitude, infertile soil, and lack of navigable waterways or other sources of transportation would also hamper efforts to make slavery a profitable institution in New Mexico. Citing numerous reports from topographical engineers as supporting evidence, the senator insisted that the natural features of the Southwest conspired against the existence of mass slavery in a region where subsistence agriculture and a largely localized economy predominated. When one considered the presence of thousands of Indian captives and Mexican peons who already filled the demand for labor, it became clear—in Smith's mind, at least—that the southern system would not proliferate to any significant degree in the region. Chattel slavery could not, the Connecticut statesman concluded, "be advantageously used in competition with the cheap peon labor of New Mexico," and any person planning to migrate there would be better off first to sell their slaves and then use the proceeds to reinvest in the "native labor of that country." Although most of Smith's claims were accurate, he seemed to miss the overarching fact that the debates about New Mexico revolved around ideology and politics rather than experiential reality.[18]

Smith was not the only senator who struggled to grasp the true ideological underpinnings of these deliberations. The veteran Whig Daniel Webster of Massachusetts supposed that the climate and geography of the Southwest were so antithetical to slavery that he did not think the arguments were even worth having. Believing that God had created the entire American West in such a fashion as to preclude the existence of plantation-style agriculture, he spoke adamantly about "the impossibility of the existence of African slavery in New Mexico." Webster proposed a laissez faire approach, hoping that the nation could avoid sectional tension if his fellow congressmen would leave the matter alone and allow providential design to dictate the slavery question. Once again, however, a prominent northern politician was overlooking the bigger picture. Topography and environment did not limit or even dictate the flow of ideas, and indeed it was precisely that—the political ideology of slavery—that most southerners sought to nurture in New Mexico.[19]

As deliberations continued into the summer of 1850, another possibility arose that troubled antislavery radicals. In July Senator James Cooper of Pennsylvania expressed the pervasive fear among abolitionists that "Texas may swallow up New Mexico, and plant slavery upon the soil of the Territories."[20] Cooper saw this as the most likely scenario whereby Southern interests might gain political control over New Mexico, even though President Zachary Taylor thought that "there is no reason for seriously apprehending that Texas will practically interfere with [a] possession of the United States."[21] The Texan–Santa Fe Expedition a decade earlier, coupled with Texas's claim to the Rio Grande as its western boundary, supported Cooper's assertion that the nation's newest slave state had cast a fixed gaze on New Mexico for future expansion. Senator Rusk, whose experiences in the Texas borderlands gave him some familiarity with local institutions, discerned a path in 1850 for the legal establishment of slavery in New Mexico. Realizing that the territory's powerful landholding class relied on involuntary servitude in the forms of captivity and peonage, he espoused the popular sovereignty approach, stating that "the best plan that we can adopt is to leave this matter to the regulation of the people among whom it exists." Rusk cared little about peonage and captivity in practice, but he knew that New Mexican policymakers would legalize both systems if allowed the opportunity. Local authorization of involuntary servitude could then be ideologically expanded to include chattel slavery, thus placing New Mexico within the orbit of the Southern cause.[22] Based on Rusk's comments, the perceptive Senator Cooper pointed out that even if Congress banned slavery per se in the Southwest, it would not be enough. The existence of peonage offered ample pretext for southerners to implant their peculiar institution under that guise, and a separate law forbidding debt bondage would therefore be necessary to supplement any abolition measures that Congress might pursue. The slavery situation in New Mexico, Cooper understood, was far more complex than most of his colleagues realized.[23]

Texan antagonism over the boundary dispute, mingled with the state's involvement in the combustible slavery issue, created increasing tension as the year wore on. Texas commissioner Robert S. Neighbors directly intervened in New Mexico politics when he demanded that Colonel John Munroe, commander of the regional military department, put a stop to statehood conventions in light of the unsettled boundary claim.[24] In August 1850 Secretary of War Winfield Scott dispatched 750 troops to Santa Fe in anticipation of hostilities, ordering Munroe to "repel force by force" if necessary.[25] The fact that the War Department assigned so many men for a task that would put them in direct conflict with fellow Americans from Texas—and possibly incite a civil war—indicates the importance that some federal leaders placed on the retention of New Mexico as a free-soil territory. A Texan takeover of New Mexico would have empowered slavery's political base and expanded Southern geography much closer to California and the Pacific coast. The reassignment of federal soldiers to New Mexico served as a preemptive measure to block the South from gaining a stronger foothold in the region and to prevent the extension of slavery westward.

The unexpected death of President Taylor on July 9, 1850, further complicated these matters. Despite being a slave-owning Kentuckian, Taylor had expressed support for the admission of both California and New Mexico to statehood and would have lent his backing to the antislavery constitution that local citizens submitted to Congress.[26] Nonetheless, Taylor's brash handling of the Texas boundary dispute seemed to fuel, rather than stifle, sectional strife in the months preceding his death. His successor, Millard Fillmore, proved more adroit at managing the delicate political situation and helped to bring about the conciliatory legislation that resolved the main issues.[27] The compromise measure that ultimately passed on September 9, 1850, admitted California as a free-soil state, added New Mexico and Utah as popular sovereignty territories, solved the Texas–New Mexico boundary dispute through the federal assumption of $10 million in debt that the Texas Republic had accrued prior to 1845, abolished the slave trade in Washington, D.C., and enacted a strict fugitive slave law in the North. The secretary of war immediately wrote to Colonel Munroe in Santa Fe, informing him that no aggression from Texas was forthcoming and that the military should "abstain from all further interference in the civil or political affairs" of the region.[28] If New Mexicans felt any sense of relief over this peaceful outcome and their new territorial status, however, it would prove short-lived.

Hints of looming unrest emerged as early as 1852, when James Gadsden attempted to establish a slave colony in California under the pretense that southerners had been unfairly excluded from the new state because of its free-soil standing. Gadsden echoed Senator Calhoun's arguments when he pointed out that men from the South had shed blood alongside their northern brethren in the Mexican-American War, that funds from the common federal treasury paid for the Mexican Cession, and that people from the South therefore had as much of a right to settle in California and New Mexico as did those from the North. California's admission as a free state, Gadsden and Calhoun griped, had cheated the South out of equal access to that land because they could not migrate there with slave property.[29] Southern radicals intended to fight for California in spite of agreements outlined in the Compromise of 1850, and residents of New Mexico might have experienced similar intervention had the territorial legislature not taken numerous actions throughout the 1850s that explicitly supported institutions of slavery in both principle and practice.

The first indication of a proslavery swing in 1850s New Mexico was a mere tremor compared to the seismic shifts in territorial policy that came toward the end of that decade. In July 1851 the legislature passed a "Master-Servant Act" to protect the traditional system of debt peonage that had characterized regional labor relations for multiple generations. The new law was enacted in part as a response to the antislavery provisions attached to New Mexico's admittance into the Union as a territory, as influential Hispanic policymakers and landholders perceived a threat to their own institution of involuntary servitude and sought to implement firm legal measures to shield it from meddling abolitionists. The year before, New York newspaperman Horace Greeley—one of the nation's most outspoken critics of slavery—had featured a damning editorial describing New Mexico's system of debtor servitude and demanding that Congress act to eradicate it. Hoping to spark public outrage in the North, Greeley called peonage "much more repugnant" than the race-based chattel system.[30] Other journalists picked up the story, and within days articles about the purported horrors of peonage were being widely disseminated via several newspapers. "If peonage is not slavery, we should like to know what it is," wrote an editor for the *New York Herald* in July 1850. "The creditor has as much command over the labor of the debtor, as the Southern slaveholder has over that of the negro."[31] Headlines simultaneously appeared in an Albany periodical

Newspaper editor and abolitionist Horace Greeley, c. 1860s.
Courtesy National Archives and Records Administration, Washington, D.C.

that informed readers about "peon slavery" in New Mexico and warned of the possibility that sly southerners might use that type of labor as a surrogate for their own chattel system.[32] Influenced by these developments, one U.S. senator proposed an amendment to the 1850 compromise bills that would have "forever abolished and prohibited" peonage, but the suggestion failed to pass when it came to a vote.[33]

The system of debt peonage that U.S. congressmen debated and journalists wrote about appeared in New Mexico during the late Spanish colonial era and proliferated throughout the first half of the nineteenth century. By the time U.S. troops occupied Santa Fe in 1846, large numbers of destitute Hispanics labored as peons on the haciendas and farms of their creditors and benefactors. Through unspoken agreements between masters and servants, many indigent Nuevomexicanos took out small loans from landowners and political elites to pay for baptismal ceremonies, weddings, funerals, and even to purchase everyday items like clothing and food. Debtors would repay what they owed through manual labor, but manipulative masters often used accruing interest to extend the term of servitude for a lifetime. This form of coerced labor, coupled with the enslavement of Indian captives abducted during violent raids on surrounding tribes, thrust thousands of people into a condition of harsh servitude.[34]

American perceptions of peonage were largely derived from the published memoirs and reports of travelers who visited New Mexico, many of whom drew direct comparisons to Southern slavery. James Josiah Webb, a Santa Fe merchant, noted that peons earned just enough in monthly wages to buy overpriced food and clothing from their master's store, meaning that they could never repay the amount of their initial loan plus compounding interest. In most cases, such persons would remain in bondage until death.[35] John Reid, a military officer, wrote that peons constituted the most numerous socioeconomic class in the territory. He specifically blamed the 1851 Master-Servant Act for ensuring that "generation after generation" of New Mexicans remained in a degrading state of servitude and dependency. "The provisions of this system result in enslaving thousands during their health and manhood," Reid observed with disdain.[36] Territorial Secretary William Davis similarly described peonage as a dreadfully oppressive system and referred to it as nothing more than a "charming name for a species of slavery."[37] These were just three of the many witnesses who described New Mexico's alternative systems of involuntary servitude during the antebellum period, and the majority of those portrayals highlighted unmistakable similarities between captivity and peonage in the Southwest and chattel slavery in the South.[38]

These unfamiliar methods of bondage in the Southwest presented one of the most complex cases in the entire decades-long dilemma over American slavery and westward expansion. New Mexican lawmakers understood this, and they took concrete action in 1851 with the Master-Servant Act, which represented a thinly disguised ideological shift toward a Southern brand of politics that would predominate in the territory until the Civil War. Although the law said nothing about racial slavery, it protected the right of a creditor to exercise ownership over a debtor's labor through verbal agreements that sufficed as legally binding contracts. The law outlined the conditions of servitude for laborers, who would be required to toil in the pastures or fields "from sunrise until sunset" until they repaid their debts plus interest—a nearly impossible feat, given the skillful ways masters manipulated account books. Parents were barred from contracting children under twenty-one years to work in their stead, although this provision went widely ignored. A subsection sought to disallow inheritable peon status by forbidding the transfer of a deceased person's debt to family members, but that too was seldom enforced. Local justices of the peace had a legal obligation to hunt down and capture runaway servants, much like law enforcement officials in the East were tasked with pursuing runaway slaves following passage of the Fugitive Slave Act. Taken as a whole, the 1851 edict unequivocally protected the rights of masters to hold servants and force them to work under oppressive conditions, stripping thousands of indigent men and women of their basic freedoms.[39] Through this codification of peonage, New Mexico had taken its first official step toward becoming a slave territory.

Six years later legislators took a more pronounced stride toward proslavery ideology when they approved an "Act Concerning Free Negroes." Although it did not specifically promote racial slavery in the territory, the new law established tight regulations on free blacks who either lived in New Mexico or passed through on their way somewhere else. The territory's 1857 law—the first of two so-called black codes that would appear on its books prior to the Civil War—prohibited "free negroes" from making the territory their permanent home and levied hefty fines and at least one year of hard labor for those who stayed longer than thirty days.[40] The idea and purpose behind the mandate closely resembled the system of convict leasing that emerged decades later in the Jim Crow South.[41] Given that only a couple dozen African Americans resided in all of New Mexico in 1857, the law had little discernable impact on daily life and was almost purely symbolic, coinciding with the infamous Dred Scott decision, which Chief Justice Roger Taney rendered that same year. Primarily segregationist in its intent, New Mexico's 1857 act served as an ideological stepping stone toward a far more pervasive slave code two years later.

On February 3, 1859, legislators passed a bill entitled "An Act to provide for the protection of property in Slaves in this Territory." Modeled on similar slave codes in the southern states, New Mexico's law contained thirty-one sections that regulated master-slave relations. The act dictated the terms of social interaction by prohibiting interracial marriages, forbidding citizens from selling any type of goods to slaves, and banning people from playing cards or other games with servants. Sheriffs were to pursue and detain runaways, advertise their arrest in the newspaper, and auction off any recaptured slaves who went unclaimed. Anybody convicted of aiding or abetting an escape, providing weapons or falsified documents, or inciting rebellion among slaves faced stiff fines and a lengthy prison sentence. If a slave used "insolent language" of any kind, they could expect thirty-nine lashes with the whip. Conviction of a misdemeanor would result in "corporal punishment by branding or with stripes," and slaves were not permitted to testify in court against their accusers. Finally, the code absolutely forbade the emancipation of any black slave within New Mexico's boundaries.[42] The legislature enacted these measures despite the fact that the census enumerated just sixty-four African Americans in the entire territory, only a handful of whom were actually enslaved.[43] Lawmakers had gone to great lengths to devise and pass a slave code with no practical purpose aside from political symbolism, casting an unmistakable ideological gesture toward the Southern platform. Fire-eaters did indeed take notice, with one prominent New Orleans editor exalting New Mexico legislators for their "undeniable legal recognition of slaveholding there."[44]

According to some observers, New Mexico's newly enacted laws derived from the machinations of proslavery ideologues who exerted their influence on territorial policymakers and citizens. Sergeant Major William Need estimated, with some exaggeration, that 80 percent of the regional population "are utterly opposed to the incorporation of the Slave Code in the statutes."[45] New Mexico's U.S. representative had to assure Hispanic lawmakers that such a code would not interfere with the longstanding systems of captivity and peonage before they would vote favorably on the measure.[46] The law passed, Need claimed, because of the resounding sway of Southern sympathizers like territorial secretary Alexander Jackson and congressional representative Miguel Otero. Jackson, a native Mississippian and an outspoken Southern radical, worked closely with Otero—who married into a slave-owning South Carolina family—to concoct the 1859 slave code and ensure that legislators approved it. Mindful of this, Major Need espoused a conspiracy theory that originated with Jefferson Davis himself. While serving as secretary of war during the 1850s, Davis had stationed secessionist military officers in New Mexico, and Democratic presidents Franklin Pierce and James Buchanan reputedly buttressed those assignments by appointing men from the South to serve as territorial governors. All of this, according to Need, transformed New Mexico into a slave territory, and the enactment of the two codes represented the culmination of a decade of Southern intrigue.[47]

Northern journalists, paranoid of Southern conspiracies, embraced this line of reasoning. A Vermont newspaper informant described the circumstances surrounding the 1859 law, writing that Otero hoped to curry personal favor for himself and gain political perks for New Mexico. Horace Greeley's *New-York Daily Tribune* claimed that the slave code served no real purpose and that Otero and Jackson ushered it into law as a propagandist initiative to achieve "political capital" with the southern states.[48] In the ten years since the Compromise of 1850, Greeley wrote, slavery had been implanted in New Mexico "both in the abstract and the concrete—in the form of the slave law and in that of slaves." The controversy over slavery, he explained to his readers, did not depend on the number of slaves in any given state or territory but rather on the legality and the political ideology of the institution.[49] Throughout 1861 Greeley continued to print editorials in which he denounced New Mexico's slave code as "one of the most atrocious slave laws ever known" and condemned Otero as "an avowed secessionist" who had no business representing New Mexicans in Congress.[50]

While the legislature tightened restrictions on African American freedom and legalized chattel slavery, the territorial supreme court pursued a course of judicial activism that worked as a counterbalance against the codes. Judges in Santa Fe heard two cases in 1857 involving debt peonage, and in both they ruled in favor of the servants. Thus, while policymakers worked to validate racial slavery as a symbolic gesture, their peers on the bench endeavored to undermine peonage; the resulting legal decisions would have deep ramifications in a territory that counted thousands of debtor servants among its population. The two court rulings in New Mexico occurred just weeks before the Dred Scott decision, so Taney's federal court was producing proslavery decisions and stripping black bondsmen of their legal rights at almost the same time that Kirby Benedict's territorial court was liberating peons and expanding their legal privileges.[51]

Both New Mexico cases pertained to young women held as peons, and in each instance the judges liberated the aggrieved party from her state of servile bondage. The first hearing dealt with the issues of gifting a child to a master, a servant mother's fitness for custody of her offspring, and the status of children conceived through extramarital relationships between masters and servants. The ruling revolved primarily around the 1851 Master-Servant Act, which prohibited adults from holding minors in servitude. The enslaved mother, Juana Analla, sued for the freedom of her daughter, Catalina Bustamento, on grounds that the child was detained unlawfully "as a peon or a servant," in violation of habeas corpus. Their masters, Marcellina and Carpio Bustamento of Santa Fe, claimed ownership of young Catalina, who had been born through an illicit sexual liaison between the *patrón* Carpio and the slave Juana. Judge C. J. Deavenport ruled in favor of the biological mother despite her peon status, declaring Marcellina's claim to ownership of the girl as her surrogate mother and matriarch to be nefarious. The court returned Catalina to her true mother's custody and chastised Marcellina Bustamento for having "restrained [the] child of her liberty as a peon." In so doing, Deavenport undermined the notion of inheritable servant status in New Mexico and marked a shift toward emancipatory ideology in the territory's judicial branch.[52]

The second trial—also in January 1857—involved contracts between masters and servants and, like the Bustamento case, addressed the legality of servitude for minors. In this instance, Mariana Jaremillo had been bound to labor as a peon in repayment of her father's fifty-one-dollar debt. The girl eventually ran away from her master, José de la Cruz Romero, whereupon he sued to have her remanded to his service. Chief Justice Benedict heard the case on appeal in his Santa Fe courtroom. Realizing that the system of debt peonage lacked a clear legal definition,

Benedict—a former colleague and lifelong friend of Abraham Lincoln—researched the institution to identify its origins and characteristics, with specific emphasis on its comparability to the South's chattel system. Given the ongoing national debates over involuntary servitude, the judge seemed acutely aware of the potential impact of his ruling on the future of free labor in the United States. Benedict traced the evolution of master-servant law through colonial, provincial, and territorial New Mexico before crafting his own concise definition. "The term peon is now used in this country as synonymous with servant," he concluded, noting that legislators carefully regulated the system to the benefit of the master class while officials and judges colluded to subjugate the poorer masses. He called peonage "a system of service between masters and servants" and likened it to the peculiar institution prevailing in the Slave South. Jaremillo was released from bondage because she had not received due process of law at the magistrate level. The judge criticized local authorities for their blatant oversight, lamenting "the unscrupulous disregard which too often prevails in justices' courts in this country as to the legal rights of the unfortunate, the peon and the feeble, when contesting with the influential and more wealthy." As additional supporting evidence, Benedict stressed that Jaremillo's servitude clearly violated a provision of the Master-Servant Act that forbade parents from contracting out their children as peons.[53] In a reversal of judicial fortunes that stunned Hispanic elites, both Catalina Bustamento and Mariana Jaremillo received their freedom at the hands of American judges whose commitment to democracy foreshadowed the demise of coerced labor systems during the Civil War and Reconstruction eras.

New Mexico's 1859 slave code would be the first item addressed at the federal level, although abolitionists and Radical Republicans eventually dealt with peonage and Indian captivity as well. In 1860 the U.S. House of Representatives formed a special committee to investigate the controversial law. The final report, entitled "Slavery in the Territory of New Mexico," recommended that Congress repeal the code in its entirety. A group of ardent Southerners submitted a dissenting minority report, claiming that the provision for popular sovereignty in the Compromise of 1850 allowed New Mexico to pass any laws it wished regarding slavery within territorial borders. In attempting to supersede that mandate by disapproving the slave code, Congress was contradicting the fundamental premise behind popular sovereignty. To rescind the slave law, the minority contingent insisted, would be nothing less than "a palpable disregard of the rights of the people" and a "usurpation of power by Congress." Southern radicals also pointed to the Master-Servant Act and its guarantee of "the right on the part of one to whom labor or service is due" as equally applicable to black slaves, and therefore they claimed that New Mexico had sanctioned all forms of slavery in 1851, shortly after its incorporation as a territory.

The congressional report about slavery in New Mexico revealed a major deficiency in the concept of popular sovereignty. In theory, territories could decide on slavery for themselves. In reality, Congress retained the right to approve or disapprove all territorial legislation, so federal politicians ultimately had the last word, as exemplified in debates surrounding the unsuccessful effort to repeal New Mexico's slave code in 1860.[54] As a strong proponent of popular sovereignty, Democratic Senator Stephen A. Douglas of Illinois was satisfied with New Mexico's law upholding slavery. "The people of Kansas have had their own way, and the people of New Mexico have had their own way," he stated in reference to the residents of those two territories exercising the fundamental tenets of popular sovereignty. "Kansas has adopted a free state; New Mexico has established a slave territory. I am content with both. If the people of New Mexico want slavery, let them have it." Basing his opinion on the premise of popular sovereignty, Douglas believed that only New Mexicans had the right to repeal a slave code of their own creation. "Nonintervention by Congress with slavery in the territories is the platform on which I stand," the elder statesman concluded.[55]

Across the aisle a fellow Democrat, Senator John Reagan of Texas, also took a hardline stance, insisting that the Dred Scott decision legalized the right to transport slaves into U.S. territories. New Mexico's slave code, he contended, aligned with Chief Justice Taney's decision in that landmark case and provided a commonsense protection of the right to own slave property.[56] Debates over a largely symbolic slave law in a remote, sparsely populated western territory revealed, once again, the irreparable damage that sectional politics and slavery had wrought on the American republic. As the year 1860 drew to a close, the ideological tenets undergirding the Compromise of 1850 no longer placated sectional interests, as the New Mexico case clearly demonstrated.

The existence of the slave code also impeded those who hoped that New Mexico might be elevated from territorial status to statehood. The prospect for statehood emerged during the 1860–61 session of Congress, but once again the issue of slavery dominated the debates and prevented politicians from taking favorable action on the initiative. New Mexico presented a unique situation in the ongoing sectional discord, inasmuch as the primary topic of discussion—the political ideology of chattel slavery—did not really concern most territorial residents. Because New Mexicans already used their own traditional forms of coerced labor, they had little practical need for the controversial system of racialized slavery as practiced in the South, making the territory's slave code even more confounding to outside observers. Representative John Sherman of Ohio summarized the situation when he told his peers that New Mexico statehood revolved around two similar but distinct issues—chattel slavery and "their system of peonage." Sherman understood the vagaries of involuntary servitude in the Southwest and, like many of his northern colleagues, refused to vote in favor of statehood because of the continuing presence of peonage, captivity, and slave codes.[57]

Free-Soilers and abolitionists lined up behind Sherman to form a united opposition to New Mexico statehood on the eve of the Civil War. Representative Cadwallader Washburn of Wisconsin argued that admission of the territory as a state would amount to nothing more than two additional pro-Southern, pro-slavery votes in the Senate. Anybody who believed that New Mexico would enter the Union as a free state was delusional, Washburn alleged, pointing to the slave code as proof of the territory's stance on that critical issue.[58] Representative John Bingham of Ohio, who led the congressional effort to repeal the slave code, spoke vehemently against New Mexico statehood and alluded to three separate laws—the 1851 Master-Servant Act, the 1857 Act Concerning Free Negroes, and the 1859 slave code—as undeniable evidence that the territory leaned ideologically and politically toward the South.[59] Pennsylvanian Thaddeus Stevens—one of the most vitriolic abolitionists—told listeners that the slave code "established the most cruel" kind of slavery in New Mexico, and he verbally attacked Miguel Otero for sponsoring the law.[60] Representative Mason Tappan of New Hampshire echoed those sentiments when he concluded that if Congress welcomed New Mexico to statehood, it would amount to a tacit approval of the slave code and would "bring her into the Union as a slave State."[61] With much of the South already in the process of secession and the nation on the brink of a bloody war, New Mexico's slave codes, coupled with the preexisting systems of captivity and peonage, had become a severe political liability.

Prior to the Civil War attempts to overturn the slave code at the territorial level had failed—largely because of the influence of Otero and Jackson—and a deeply divided Congress also fell short of overturning the measure, so it remained on the books.[62] But the Southern rebellion that divided the nation in 1861 completely transformed the issue of slavery in New Mexico, which remained in the Union throughout the Civil War. The existence of slave codes in a federal territory whose citizens fought as Bluecoats against the Confederacy was a blatant anomaly, and it demanded immediate political attention.[63] Determined to rid New Mexico of involuntary servitude, northern politicians renewed their efforts to rescind the slave code once the war began. In the summer of 1861, a U.S. Congress composed strictly of Unionists rejected Otero's reappointment as New Mexico representative, largely because of his complicity in enacting the slave code.[64] That Abraham Lincoln sought to retain Otero at all had much to do with his cautious approach to New Mexico, where he appointed loyal Democrats to reach across party lines and assuage local inhabitants. Throughout his time in office, the finesse with which Lincoln approached New Mexico politics resembled the manner in which he treated the four so-called border states—Missouri, Kentucky, Maryland, and Delaware—because he recognized the faraway southwestern territory as an important Union possession that could thwart Confederate expansion while empowering the Union's political and military base.[65]

Territorial Governor Henry Connelly (another Democratic Lincoln appointee) addressed the local legislature in December 1861 and recommended that the slave code be "modified or entirely repealed."[66] With Confederate troops from Texas already occupying the southern portion of New Mexico, policymakers in Santa Fe understood the direness of the situation and reversed course by nullifying the slave code during the 1861–62 legislative term. Facundo Piño, serving as president of the council, declared that "we have condemned, and put slavery from among our laws," proclaiming somewhat disingenuously that "it is not congenial with our history, our feelings, or interests." Seemingly unmindful of the fact that the slave code had been enacted just two years before the war began, he said that the Confederates who invaded the territory had come to "force upon us by the cannon and rifle, slave institutions, against our will, protests, and tastes."[67] The exigencies of war changed the perspective of many New Mexicans, who relied heavily on Union support to prevent a Texan takeover and understood that the slave code forced federal leaders to question their loyalty.

As the Civil War progressed, the federal government enacted a number of measures that directly impacted slavery in New Mexico, helping to hasten the territory's transition to a free-labor model. On August 6, 1861, Congress passed the First Confiscation Act, marking the beginning of legislative emancipation as a federal policy.[68] Lawmakers expanded that mandate less than a year later by banning all forms of involuntary servitude in U.S. territories, including chattel slavery and Indian captivity.[69] The Second Confiscation Act (July 17, 1862) went a step further, codifying military emancipation by enabling officers and soldiers to protect runaway slaves who escaped to Union lines.[70] The confiscation acts demarcated a gradual transition in Lincoln's objectives, as he moved from a course of limited to complete manumission for all American slaves. The Emancipation Proclamation of January 1, 1863—a declaration that granted freedom to slaves in states or parts of states still in rebellion—represented the final shift in that direction.[71] Although Lincoln and his fellow Republicans aimed these landmark initiatives primarily toward southern black

President Andrew Johnson, c. 1860s.
Courtesy National Archives and Records Administration, Washington, D.C.

slaves, the political ideology of free labor also enveloped New Mexico, as the wave
of emancipation swept westward during and after the Civil War. On June 9, 1865,
President Andrew Johnson signed an executive order prohibiting Indian slavery, and
on December 6 of that same year the Thirteenth Amendment to the Constitution
banned slavery and involuntary servitude in all U.S. states and territories.[72] A year
and a half later, on March 2, 1867, Johnson signed a law barring debt peonage in
New Mexico, marking the final legal abolition of coerced labor and bringing the
territory into the orbit of national freedom.[73]

The enforcement of these laws almost invariably met with resistance in the
Southwest, where lawmakers, landowners, and patrones scrambled to retain traditional systems of labor bondage. William Arny, an antislavery Republican who
served intermittently as New Mexico's governor during and after the Civil War,
recognized the difficulties entailed in achieving freedom for the Indian captives and
debt peons living there. When Congress passed the law in 1862 prohibiting slavery
in the territories, Arny explained the implications to the legislature in hopes of
securing its compliance. He informed colleagues in Santa Fe that the new regulations
pertained not only to black slaves but also to Indian captives and urged them to "do
away with *all involuntary servitude.*" Realizing that he would meet with staunch

opposition, the governor proposed a form of compensated emancipation whereby
masters would be paid a fair market value for each captive that they liberated. This
idea had originated more than a decade earlier, when Superintendent of Indian
Affairs James S. Calhoun advocated a program of compensated manumission as
the only plausible approach to liberating the territory's indigenous slaves, but that
suggestion fell flat until its revival in 1862. Arny also implored territorial officials
to amend the Master-Servant Act, which legalized the subjugation of indigent
debtors in a system of "oppressive servitude" that flew in the face of federal law.[74]

Spurred by Arny's comments, territorial legislators sent a message to Congress
asking what exactly they should do with their Indian slaves. Alluding to the 1862
act that guaranteed freedom to all persons in U.S. territories, they claimed that
most captives had no desire to be set free and insinuated that most of them had
become bound to their masters through deep personal feelings of dependency
and fictive kinship. The memorialists believed that separating captives from their
adoptive families and overseers would be a cruel injustice to the slaves themselves,
but they grudgingly agreed to do so if Congress would appropriate money to pay
the owners and transport the slaves back to their respective tribes of origin.[75] Little
was achieved toward this end, and Superintendent of Indian Affairs Michael Steck
admitted two years later that at least two thousand Indians—mostly Navajos, but
also some Apaches, Comanches, Paiutes, and Utes—remained in captivity and that
the traffic in slaves continued "almost daily, without an effort to stop it." Neither
legislated nor compensated emancipation, Steck wrote, would do much to liberate
New Mexico's Indian servants. Much like black slaves in the South, only the strong
arm of the military could effectively force the manumission of captives, and the
superintendent suggested that the War Department issue orders to Brigadier General
James Carleton, commander of the Military District of New Mexico, to that effect.[76]
This approach had already been attempted to a limited extent in September 1862,
when Colonel Edward Canby circulated an order to post commanders throughout
the territory instructing them to harbor and protect any absconded Indian captives
that arrived at their forts.[77] Although that initial mandate proved limited in its overall
impact, Steck—an antislavery Republican from Pennsylvania—believed that it was
worth a second try since the legislature seemed disinclined to take definitive action.

Ultimately, the release of Indian captives required an executive order, which
President Johnson issued shortly after the Civil War ended. The missive came a full
six months before ratification of the Thirteenth Amendment outlawed involuntary
servitude. "Indians in New Mexico have been seized and reduced into slavery,"
Johnson conceded, ordering that executive branch personnel work to ensure "the

effectual suppression" of a mode of enslavement that violated "the rights of the Indians" as well as federal law.[78] Secretary of the Interior James Harlan informed BIA employees that they must "use all lawful means" to inhibit the captivity of Indians in New Mexico, lecturing that such a system "should not be tolerated in a country professing to be free."[79] In Santa Fe, Superintendent Felipe Delgado complained about the executive order and claimed that the abduction of Indians "has not been to reduce them to slavery, but rather from a Christian piety." Nonetheless, he promised to comply with the order and instructed his field agents accordingly.[80] Contemporaneous federal investigations revealed that at least 3,000 captives remained to be liberated in New Mexico alone, meaning that antislavery crusaders had their work cut out for them.[81]

Special Agent Julius Graves reported in 1866 that many Indians, especially Navajos, "are now held as unwilling captives amongst the people of [the] territory—being bought, sold, and compelled to labor in the most menial capacities." He asked the governor for advice on the best strategy to affect "the speedy abolition of this erroneous and inhuman practice."[82] Despite the enormity and complexity of the task, many of those Indians would indeed be freed from bondage in the years immediately following the Civil War, and the system of captive slavery slowly ended under abolitionist pressure and Radical Republican activism. In his annual message to the legislature in 1866, interim governor Arny lamented that at least several hundred Indians remained in captivity and insisted that all such servants be liberated in accordance with Johnson's executive order and the Thirteenth Amendment.[83] Shortly thereafter territorial lawmakers approved an act abolishing "all involuntary servitude" in New Mexico and repealed preexisting laws that conflicted with the Constitution.[84] In so doing, however, they managed to retain the system of debt peonage by cunningly redefining it in the statutes as a form of voluntary, rather than involuntary, labor.[85]

Even with their defiant redefinition of peonage—which came a mere five weeks after ratification of the Thirteenth Amendment—New Mexican policymakers could not easily avoid the issue, especially with Radical Republican reformers and judicial activists taking increasingly sharp aim at any lingering vestiges of slavery in the American republic. The first major blow to debt bondage came when the New Mexico Supreme Court ruled once again in favor of an aggrieved peon. In 1865 Tomás Heredia had run away from his patrón, José María García, and the case came before the territory's highest tribunal the following year. At the district court in Mesilla, Judge Joab Houghton had originally found against the peon Heredia and returned him to the service of his master. When the case reached Santa Fe on appeal, however, a much different decision resulted. The justices concluded that the Master-Servant Act, despite its modification to describe debtor servitude as a voluntary institution, directly violated multiple federal statutes, including the 1862 act of Congress forbidding involuntary servitude in U.S. territories and the recently ratified Thirteenth Amendment. These national laws, the judges explained, superseded territorial codes, and thus Heredia could not be held in bondage based on the stipulations of the 1851 law regulating masters and servants. From the standpoint of legal doctrine, the case overturned that territorial edict and affirmed the illegality of peonage—and all other forms of coerced labor—in New Mexico.[86]

Although the Heredia ruling provided a juridical foundation upon which activists staged an attack on the institution of peonage, government officials would have to take additional steps to liberate those who remained in servitude. Agent Graves, who had also reported on Indian captivity, told Governor Connelly in 1866 that debt bondage needed to be eradicated "by legislative action."[87] He also informed Commissioner of Indian Affairs Dennis Cooley that "this pernicious system [of peonage] still exists to an alarming extent in all parts of the Territory of New Mexico" and recommended that the government "adopt vigorous measures tending to its immediate abolition."[88] U.S. Secretary of the Interior Orville Browning similarly referred to peonage as "the qualified slavery still prevalent in New Mexico, authorized by its laws, and encouraged and practiced by its people," lamenting that his subagents had tried in vain to eliminate it.[89] Given territorial officials' repeated defiance of emancipatory laws and court rulings, neither Graves nor Browning had much faith that they could exact compliance, and the federal lawmakers understood that any truly effective legislation and enforcement initiatives must emanate from Washington, D.C.

When Senator Charles Sumner, a Radical Republican, received a letter from an anonymous group of New Mexicans in 1867 that described peonage and captivity in explicit detail, he took immediate action. As one of the country's foremost abolitionists, the Massachusetts congressman was appalled by what he read in the message. "As for the peonage of Mexicans, neither the military authorities, nor civil authorities, nor the enactments of Congress can reach it except in cases which are brought to the notice of the courts," the informants wrote. The recent revision of territorial statutes to identify peonage as a voluntary form of labor had effectually circumvented the Thirteenth Amendment and severely complicated efforts to abolish the system, they told Sumner.[90] A specific law, expanding on the Constitutional amendment of 1865, would be needed to eliminate debtor servitude in New Mexico.

Senator Sumner was happy to sponsor such a bill, and he did so in January 1867. During preliminary congressional discussions he stressed that peonage continued to exist throughout New Mexico despite multiple federal statutes outlawing slavery and involuntary servitude. Salutary neglect on the part of local officials, he claimed, enabled the retention of servants throughout the territory, and he urged that regional inhabitants be forced into conformity with the law. Senator John Conness of California, who had some familiarity with the issue due to his own state's troubles with lingering modes of involuntary servitude, added that army officers sometimes acted with complicity by capturing and returning runaway peons and captives. "The administration of military affairs in the Territory of New Mexico has been a standing disgrace to this government," Conness exclaimed, lambasting Brigadier General Carleton for his lack of concern as the district's commander.[91] Senator Henry Wilson denounced peonage as a form of "modified servitude" that the U.S. inherited from Mexico, and the Massachusetts lawmaker lamented that the institution "in most cases is forcible." Republican James R. Doolittle, who had previously oversaw extensive investigations on Indian affairs in the West, added that "the peons live upon the lands and cultivate them as serfs" and lent his support to the measure.[92] Congress passed the bill, and on March 2, 1867, President Johnson signed "An Act to abolish and forever prohibit the System of Peonage in the Territory of New Mexico and other Parts of the United States."[93] Debt peonage was thus the last remnant of involuntary servitude to be outlawed in the reunified American republic, and New Mexico represented the final bastion of legalized slavery.

Cognizant of prior difficulties with emancipation, government officials immediately set out to enforce the new laws prohibiting Indian captivity and Hispano peonage. Superintendent of Indian Affairs A. B. Norton and his subagent, John Ward, notified Pueblo Indian leaders that "peonage in New Mexico is abolished and forbidden" and instructed them to ensure compliance with the new regulations.[94] Governor Robert Mitchell issued a proclamation on April 14, 1867, to inform citizens of the peon law, declaring that all persons held in servitude must be unbound and threatening that anybody who defied his order "will be severely dealt with."[95] His gubernatorial successor, Herman Heath, made a similar announcement in which he proclaimed peonage to be "at variance with the principles of a Republican Government and repugnant to the moral, social and political advancement of the victims of this system of slavery." The peon law, he said, had been "inspired by the true republican spirit of the age" and must be strictly upheld. Heath couched his rhetoric in the context of piety and morality, proclaiming that anybody who continued to hold persons in bondage was engaging in a crime not only against mankind but also against God.[96]

Even with these powerful pronouncements and initiatives, the liberation of peons and captives proved to be painstakingly slow. As Reconstruction progressed and the nation moved toward free labor, the occasional retention of peons in servile bondage continued to elicit reports from witnesses throughout the Southwest. The BIA finally dispatched Radical Republican William Griffin to the territory in 1868 with orders to investigate the situation.[97] While touring New Mexico's settlements, he discovered that almost 90 percent of households that formerly harbored captives or peons had liberated most of them, although a significant number of families continued to hold at least one servant.[98] A diligent detective, Griffin eventually prosecuted 363 individuals (70 cases involving peons and 293 pertaining to Indian captives) for retaining slaves in direct violation of the Thirteenth Amendment, the peon law, and President Johnson's executive order. The proceedings were mostly successful, and all but 11 of the 363 servants received their freedom.[99] Griffin informed the newly liberated men, women, and children that they were "free to live where and work for whom they desired" and would henceforth be "at perfect liberty to go where and when they pleased."[100] The masters and servant-holders, among whom could be counted some of the territory's most influential politicians, priests, and landowners, escaped without prison time or fines, as the predominantly Hispanic grand jury failed to return a single indictment against their peers.[101] Although at least a handful of Hispanos and Indians remained in servitude for the rest of their lives, those instances were relatively few after 1868, and the era of Radical Reconstruction marked the veritable demise of New Mexico's longstanding forms of involuntary labor.

Congressmen Thomas Corwin, John Sherman, and Richard Weightman had not exaggerated when they stated prior to the Civil War that New Mexico was a battleground upon which northerners and southerners sparred in sectional discord. The existence of two alternative forms of servitude in the Southwest further complicated matters, and indeed legalized permutations of slavery persisted in New Mexico even longer than on the nation's tobacco fields and cotton plantations. For southern radicals, the desire to implement slavery in New Mexico was mostly ideological, as they saw an opportunity to expand their section's political power and economic clout. But proslavery men also had a second, and equally important, motive when fighting for supremacy over New Mexico. They saw the territory as a natural geographic extension of their slave empire, and the transportation revolution of the mid-nineteenth century created new possibilities for entrepreneurial southern capitalists and nation builders. In the years following the Mexican-American War, the idea of a railroad spanning the entire continent became less far-fetched, and New Mexico emerged as one of the most logical routes for such a line of transportation. Much like the controversy over slavery in the territories, deliberations about the future location of a railway to the Pacific would thrust New Mexico into the middle of the most intense sectional arguments the nation had yet seen.

$$\Longrightarrow 5 \Longleftarrow$$

RAILROAD CAPITALISM
AND THE TRANSCONTINENTAL LINE

In 1864 New Mexico's legislative assembly sent a message to Congress in hopes that federal leaders might consider their territory as a thoroughfare for a transcontinental railroad. If approved, a route traversing either the 32nd or 35th parallel of latitude would pass directly through New Mexico and Arizona on its way to the Pacific coast. Keenly aware of the Union's need to finance the ongoing Civil War, the legislators claimed that such a railway "would open and develop the resources of the gold fields and silver mines of the three territories of Colorado, New Mexico, and Arizona, which are believed to contain more gold and silver . . . than can be found in any other portion of the world." The legislators offered multiple logical arguments in furtherance of their cause. They assured congressional leaders that a railroad could be built and operated at minimal cost because of the region's favorable terrain and mild weather. It would not interfere with the proposed construction of the more northerly Union Pacific and Central Pacific lines, which Congress had approved in 1862, and a southern route would facilitate migration and economic development in the Southwest.[1] Governor William Arny called New Mexico "the most feasible, practicable, and economical route for a Pacific Railway," noting that the territory provided a year-round option with few major obstacles and would be the cheapest of several possible alternatives in terms of overall cost.[2] As Arny understood, New Mexico held a somewhat unique position in the debates over a transcontinental railroad because the territory had not just one but two potential avenues that passed through it. Many New Mexicans therefore saw the construction of a federally financed railway through their territory as a simple matter of common sense, but events over the preceding fifteen years had already proven the issue to be painfully complex.

The Baltimore & Ohio Railroad, one of the earliest lines in the United States, laid its first rails in 1829, and a frenzy of speculation soon followed as investors pumped capital into new corporate enterprises. By 1852, however, the B&O's tracks stretched barely three hundred miles west of Baltimore.[3] That one of the nation's most well-known lines had yet to reach even Ohio in the 1840s indicated the many complications entailed in constructing and operating railroads across long distances and rough terrain. Yet knowledge of these difficulties did not discourage entrepreneurial dreaming. Asa Whitney, a pioneer of railroad development, introduced the concept of a Pacific connection in 1845 when he pitched to Congress his vision of a northern route that would link Lake Michigan to Oregon Territory. Not to be outdone, southerners rallied behind the South Carolina Railroad Company and its president, James Gadsden, to offer competing proposals during a convention at Memphis. Even former Texas president Sam Houston chimed in with an opinion, suggesting a railroad from Galveston to San Diego as a feasible alternative to any northern route. Whitney, Gadsden, and Houston had sectionalized the transcontinental railroad within one year of the original idea, and political tensions arising from the annexation of Texas and the ongoing war with Mexico prevented any of their plans from gaining traction.[4] But the acquisition of California in 1848, coupled with the discovery of gold there, spurred American capitalists from North and South alike to begin plotting anew to build what would come to be known as the Pacific railway.

In 1849 a House of Representatives select committee produced a seven-hundred-page report on the topic, declaring that the nation must have "easy and rapid communication between the two oceans." Congressmen hoped that the acquisition of the Mexican Cession lands and the development of new railroad technology would enable the United States to create the fabled but as yet apocryphal Northwest Passage, and New Mexico presented one of the most obvious possibilities for that route, albeit in a different geographic location. Senator Jefferson Davis emerged as an adamant proponent of a Pacific railroad, submitting a supplementary report in January 1849 that stressed the financial and political imperatives of the project. Laying steel rails to California, the Mississippi statesman declared, would "perpetuate the political union of the Atlantic and Pacific slopes by continuous lines of settlement from ocean to ocean."[5] Later that year Lieutenant James H. Simpson, a topographical engineer, was ordered to map and survey a possible course westward from Santa Fe, which he did while accompanying Colonel John M. Washington's Navajo expedition. Although his report provided no definitive solutions, he concluded that the 35th parallel would be a feasible right-of-way to Los Angeles or San Diego should the government one day choose that path for a road to the Pacific. Simpson thus reasserted New Mexico's importance as a transportation corridor, and his findings would inform future congressional discussions on the matter.[6]

In the East politicians and capitalists easily concluded that a railway connection with the Pacific coast would allow Americans to compete with Europeans for the Asiatic trade, valued at an estimated $250 million per year, and would facilitate rapid migration to the booming California goldfields.[7] The economic possibilities seemed endless, if only the technology could meet the demand. As with the Santa Fe trade in the 1820s and 1830s, Missourians once again led the charge for a new route west. In St. Louis people were "profoundly impressed with the importance of opening a commercial communication from the Mississippi to the Pacific," realizing that if they could centralize hemispheric commerce in their own state, they could thereby reap previously unimagined wealth and prosperity. One newspaper contributor wrote that Missouri, with steamboat ports on the Mississippi and a railroad to the Pacific, might soon become "the Empire State of the Union."[8] The merchant trade with Santa Fe—once so vital to Missouri's interests—suddenly seemed inconsequential in comparison to the commerce that a railroad connecting two oceans could bring. St. Louis hosted a railroad convention in 1849, attended by 835 delegates from fourteen states. Illinois statesman Stephen A. Douglas served as the conference president, and the powerful Missouri senator Thomas Hart Benton made his presence known throughout the meeting. As attendees discussed the prospects for a transcontinental line to California, they relied chiefly on recent reports from western traveler John C. Frémont, who also happened to be Benton's son-in-law.[9]

The convention debates did not revolve around whether such a project was possible or even feasible at that early date, but rather focused on the most practical route for the line. Any railroads through the West would have to surmount enormous geographic obstacles, including the Rocky Mountains and the Sierra Nevada of California, and in many ways the discussions at St. Louis prefigured similar talks in the halls of Congress during the 1850s. Environmental determinism favored the southerners, who knew the only passageways devoid of dense winter snowpack and steep mountain ridges crossed Texas and New Mexico. The choice of St. Louis to host the conference, however, insinuated a possible compromise, since delegates understood that any new railroad would be controversial due to increasingly volatile sectional politics. Its comparatively central geographic location between North and South made Missouri a location that all Americans might ultimately accept as the starting point for a Pacific railroad. In an ominous portent of things to come, however, the delegates left the meeting with little accomplished aside from an agreement that Congress should take up the matter.[10]

The official report of the St. Louis convention, published that same year (1849) and distributed to national leaders, provided an early glimpse into the political struggles that would accompany transcontinental railroad projects. Recognizing a potential controversy in the making, a Missouri lawyer named John Loughborough added a subtitle to the conference treatise declaring that its purpose was "harmonizing all sections and parties of the union, and rendering these great works truly national in their character." He seemed also to have realized the improbability of this, because the pamphlet that he authored concluded with a prophetic statement: "There is great reason to doubt, whether party warfare, sectional jealousy, and personal ambition may not delay [the railroad's] construction for many years to come." Loughborough not only summarized the convention debates but offered his own opinions as well. The Pacific railroad, he wrote, must have its eastern terminus in either Memphis or St. Louis. Anywhere farther North or South "would be unjust, unequal, and impolitic, and calculated to divide instead of bind these States together," unless a private corporation tackled the internal improvement project independently without government financing or endorsement. This was an impossibility, however, because federal land grants would be needed to build a railroad through the West's public domain.[11]

Loughborough disqualified the two potential southern routes through New Mexico, claiming that the 35th parallel option would have to traverse impassable mesas and canyons west of Albuquerque and that the 32nd parallel through El Paso was likewise infeasible because Mexico retained ownership of a portion of that course south of the Gila River. He bluntly criticized U.S. minister plenipotentiary Nicholas Trist for failing to include this region as part of Mexico's cession of territory in the Treaty of Guadalupe Hidalgo. Loughborough instead proposed a central pathway to the Pacific that would cross the Great Plains and follow the Platte River westward, a solution that reflected his own bias as a Missourian. Regardless of the location, however, Loughborough understood that the railroad's importance to American commerce, empire, and nationalism was unprecedented. Couching his analysis in the typical rhetoric of Manifest Destiny, he thought that the Pacific railroad—even if it went through New Mexico and Texas rather than Missouri—would enable "the principles of constitutional liberty . . . [to] be diffused over the whole earth" and bring about "the permanent, uniform, and final condition of human society."[12]

Journalist and secessionist James DeBow.
From an engraving in the June 1867 issue of DeBow's Review.

The St. Louis convention of 1849 had set the tone for many debates to come, and New Mexico, because of its geographic location, would play a prominent role in those discussions.

By the late 1840s James D. B. DeBow of New Orleans had emerged as one of the leading public voices for southern economic development and railroad construction. He began printing a monthly magazine, *DeBow's Review,* just before the Mexican-American War and used his success as a publisher to promote southern interests, featuring mostly scientific articles about slavery, agriculture, transportation, and economic policy. As editor of the South's highest-circulating periodical, DeBow's ultimate goal was to uphold slavery as an institution and facilitate the expansion of a sectional economy that could operate independently of northern factories and financiers. Throughout the 1840s and 1850s, *DeBow's Review* dedicated considerable editorial energy to the development of transcontinental railroads and a direct southern connection to the Pacific, recognizing that such a link would go a long way toward boosting economic power and achieving sectional self-sufficiency.[13]

From 1846 until the first year of the Civil War, *DeBow's Review* editors closely attended to the proposals for a Pacific railway, perceiving the project as an opportunity to excite sectionalized Southern nationalism.[14] In 1847 Asa Whitney used the periodical to publish his conceptualization of a transcontinental line, although his proposal to build it in the North no doubt irked many of the readers.[15] DeBow, however, saw great merit in the idea and undertook a personal crusade to inspire southern capitalists and financiers. Without a railway connection to the Pacific, he argued in 1849, the newly acquired California coast would remain "isolated and alone." He believed that a railroad was important not only for commercial purposes but also to ensure a strong sense of nationalistic unity throughout a country that now spanned an entire continent. An ardent sectional ideologue, DeBow spent years arguing for a route that would originate either in New Orleans or Memphis and pass through Texas and New Mexico before reaching San Diego. "We want the road, finally, to complete for us that commercial empire after which we have sighed . . . which appears to be ours by a manifest and inevitable destiny," he wrote with characteristic rhetorical flourish. "As a Southron," he continued, "we confess a deep and abiding interest in these schemes to connect the two oceans." He foresaw that a railroad binding the slave states to the Pacific coast could stimulate economic prosperity in cities like Richmond, Charleston, Savannah, and Mobile, creating vibrant commercial metropolises comparable to those in the North. According to another ambitious observer, it might also "make a Southern New York of New Orleans." With this broader hope in mind, men like DeBow understood the importance of New Mexico as the geographic solder that could weld these nation-building visions into a reality.[16]

Despite his enthusiasm, however, DeBow was also a pragmatist who grasped that a southern transcontinental railroad would be unlikely to materialize unless his section achieved independence. As early as 1850 he echoed South Carolina senator John C. Calhoun when he complained about the increasingly lopsided political representation in the U.S. House of Representatives, as the industrializing North continued to attract thousands of European immigrants who rapidly bolstered urban populations and added representatives to the House. After hearing of the Compromise of 1850, which named New Mexico a popular sovereignty territory and California a free-soil state, the editors of *DeBow's Review* feared that a southern railway was slipping from their grasp. "If there were all the merit in the world in its favor, the numerical strength of the north is against us," they lamented, adding that prospects for a railroad across the 32nd or 35th parallels "are destined . . . to lie upon the table until doomsday."[17] That comment proved more prophetic than even DeBow could have imagined. In 1869, when the last spike of the transcontinental railroad was driven into the ground at Utah's Promontory Point—connecting Northern California directly to the upper Midwest—the magazine's embittered editors said nothing about the technological and commercial accomplishment, which they saw as yet another Yankee triumph over their beleaguered regional economy and wounded sectional pride.

With the idea of a transcontinental railroad garnering so much interest in the East, the U.S. government began to dispatch exploring and surveying parties westward as early as 1850. The first such expedition in New Mexico emerged out of an oversight in the Treaty of Guadalupe Hidalgo, wherein American and Mexican diplomats used an inaccurate map to delineate the new international boundary. John Russell Bartlett, a New York bookseller with an abiding interest in Indian cultures and the western frontier, accepted an appointment as federal commissioner and was tasked with resolving the dispute. His work would have profound implications for the ongoing debates over a Pacific railway, and it placed New Mexico firmly within those sectional arguments. Following several meetings in December 1850, Bartlett and his counterpart, Mexican commissioner Pedro García Conde, reached an agreement stipulating that the boundary would be drawn westward from the Rio Grande beginning at a point near Doña Ana, some forty miles north of El Paso.[18] In so doing, both men felt that they had achieved a diplomatic victory for their respective countries. García Conde wrote that the accord "is resolved most favorably in the interests of the [Mexican] Nation," and Bartlett took "very great satisfaction" in having secured possession of the Santa Rita del Cobre copper mining region of southwestern New Mexico.[19]

Despite Bartlett's momentary enthusiasm, this outcome deprived the United States of a potential railroad route, and southerners—including his own surveyor, Andrew B. Gray of Virginia—would condemn him as a northern Whig who, they believed, purposely relinquished the region south of the Gila River.[20] Texans were especially perturbed with Bartlett's boundary agreement, recognizing that the cession of the 32nd parallel, or Gila River Route, all but eliminated the possibility of a Pacific railway through their state. Democratic Congressman Volney Howard of Texas complained that the U.S. Boundary Commission had "surrendered the best route for the railroad."[21] Texas senator Thomas Rusk supported a resolution to block congressional funding for the surveying project, declaring that he would not "vote another dollar to this boundary commission."[22] The fact that Bartlett's party continued to waste vast sums of money—Lieutenant William H. Emory referred to the group as "a useless multitude of officers" who proved themselves "worse than useless"—made the decision that much easier for politicians.[23] By July 1852 all appropriations had been withdrawn, the commission was disbanded amid intense controversy, and no definitive solution to the boundary dispute was in sight.

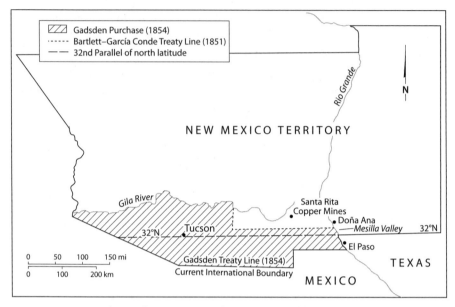

Map 3. The Bartlett–García Conde Agreement and Gadsden Purchase.

Just as the U.S. Boundary Commission was being recalled from New Mexico, businessmen from five southern states met at a railroad convention in Little Rock, Arkansas, to discuss a route from the Mississippi River to "the golden shores of the Pacific Ocean." They focused specifically on the Desert Southwest as the most favorable right-of-way, acknowledging the "worldwide importance" of opening trade between the United States and Asia via what they termed "the Highway of Nations." In support of their argument for a transcontinental railroad, the delegates predicted that the iron horse could generate a profit of $15 million annually through freight revenue and passenger fares, meaning that the estimated $100 million in construction costs could be repaid within a few years. To woo investors they pointed out that the government would also pay enormous sums to transport soldiers, agents, mail, and munitions of war. It was a clever—albeit largely fanciful—sales pitch that looked great on paper, and indeed the American railroad industry would gain widespread renown for scandalous investment schemes rooted in graft and corruption. Dubbing the proposed project "The Mississippi and Pacific Railroad," the conference attendees concluded that the tracks should begin at Memphis and strike westward through Texas and New Mexico before reaching a terminus in southern California.[24] Almost simultaneously, U.S. Representative John D. Freeman of Mississippi proposed a bill calling for a "Southern Atlantic and Pacific Railroad" that would originate at Vicksburg and terminate in San Diego, passing through Louisiana, Texas, and New Mexico on the 1,625-mile journey to California.[25] Even amongst themselves southerners remained deeply divided over which riverside city should host the eastern railhead.

By this time, would-be developers were emerging throughout the country. In 1852 Henry O'Reilly, an Irish-American capitalist whose entrepreneurial experience included a role in the construction of New York's Erie Canal, proposed a telegraph line to the Pacific Coast. Believing that this recently invented technology provided the perfect complement to any transcontinental railway, he heralded "the extraordinary events connected with the sudden colonization of California" and believed that politicians should think seriously about internal improvements in the West. In a message to Congress, O'Reilly stipulated that he neither wanted nor expected direct financial assistance from the government, but he did request that the War Department station soldiers at twenty-mile intervals to protect the cables from Indian attack or enemy sabotage. Although he preferred a geographically central location for this new line of communication—one that began in Missouri and ended at San Francisco—O'Reilly expressed a strong interest in stringing branch wires through New Mexico and acknowledged that the same Gila River Route that southern railroad magnates coveted would also be ideal for a telegraph.[26]

Sensing an opportunity to enhance the territory's role in national politics and economics, members of the New Mexico legislative assembly memorialized Congress on December 31, 1852, regarding recent development proposals. "The citizens of this territory have heard with delight," the petitioners began, "that a project which is worthy of the Great American Republic and of the age is seriously entertained by many enlightened statesmen." They insisted that New Mexico would be an excellent location for steel tracks to the Pacific as well as an electric telegraph line. To support their cause, New Mexicans cited their geographic position between Texas and California, the directness of the route, a mild regional climate with minimal snowfall, the availability of cheap land, and a local abundance of crucial natural resources like stone, timber, and coal.[27] Southerners would repeat these arguments for years to come in hopes that the federal government might lend support to a railroad through the region, and indeed the Pacific Railroad Surveys confirmed most of these claims as early as 1853.

By the end of 1852 Congress had heard six different proposals for a railroad to California, but sectional gridlock prevented any definitive decisions on government support and financing. Across the nation journalists followed the proceedings with obsessive interest, and many newspapers printed daily updates on the congressional deliberations. Writers for the *New York Times* called the transcontinental railroad "one of the greatest problems of the time" and voiced support for a central line terminating at San Francisco. "The telegraph . . . will accompany the rails in their long course," they continued, "and whenever a golden lump of extraordinary size turns up in the morning on the banks of the San Joaquin, it will be known the same day in Wall Street." Editorialists insisted that the federal government promote such a project "at any necessary cost," writing that "it is upon the details alone that any disagreement exists."[28] The pages of *DeBow's Review* revealed where southerners stood on these details, noting that the regional economy would benefit from the trade of Russia, the Indies, and China, to the tune of at least $200 million annually, if only national leaders selected a route along the 32nd parallel.[29]

During the 1852–53 congressional session, Senator William Gwin of California emerged as a leading proponent of a railroad across New Mexico's 35th parallel, a line that would terminate at San Francisco in the west and in Arkansas in the east. Given the political infighting between northerners and southerners, however, Senator Rusk of Texas thought that Congress should gather additional evidence before making any choices.[30] The main purpose of Rusk's suggestion, like other sectional compromises before it, was to delay official action and avert immediate disunion. Betting that objective scientific surveys of the possible routes would support the southern argument for a line through New Mexico and his home state of Texas, Rusk hoped to circumvent sectional ideology and political bias using indisputable science. Although some northerners objected to the idea—the *New York Times* prophetically speculated that a postponement for surveying would "put off, to an indefinite future, the commencement and completion of the work"—congressional leaders approved it and earmarked the army appropriations bill with an addendum granting oversight of the railroad surveys to the War Department.[31] By the end of its 1853 session, Congress had spent a significant amount of time debating railroad routes, the sole outcome being an allowance of a paltry $150,000 for studies of four possible avenues to the Pacific. Secretary of War Jefferson Davis, who bore responsibility for commissioning the surveying parties, scoffed when he learned that such a negligible sum of money was supposed to finance "so gigantic a project," but he quietly relished having authority over such an important issue.[32]

As one of the era's most renowned sectional ideologues, Davis dedicated much of his political career to the promotion of Southern interests before he ultimately assumed the presidency of the Confederate States of America. While serving as secretary of war from 1853–57, the Mississippian was deeply absorbed with economic

U.S. secretary of war and Confederate president Jefferson Davis, c. 1858.
Courtesy National Archives and Records Administration, Washington, D.C.

development and military security on the western frontier. Straying from a strict
constructionist view of the Constitution, he personally believed that the national
government should finance large internal improvements like the transcontinental
railroad, arguing that such infrastructure would promote the common defense of
the American people. In this Davis represented in microcosm the South's new legal
dilemma arising from the idea of a Pacific rail connection. Andrew Jackson had
fought vigorously against federally funded improvements during his two terms as
president, making him a symbolic standard-bearer for southern Democrats who
traditionally opposed such projects. But now, given the enormity of the undertaking,
any entity—public or private—wishing to lay tracks across the continent would need
federal assistance by way of subsidies and land grants. The debates surrounding the
Pacific railroad had resurrected and even exacerbated the old issue of federal dollars
spent on internal improvements, placing men like Davis in an ideological quandary
by pitting their sectional aspirations directly at odds with their interpretations of
the Constitution.[33]

When Congress delegated the Pacific Railroad Surveys to the War Department in 1853, they unwittingly placed the project in the hands of a southerner who
harbored preordained sectional biases. Davis attempted to deflect allegations that

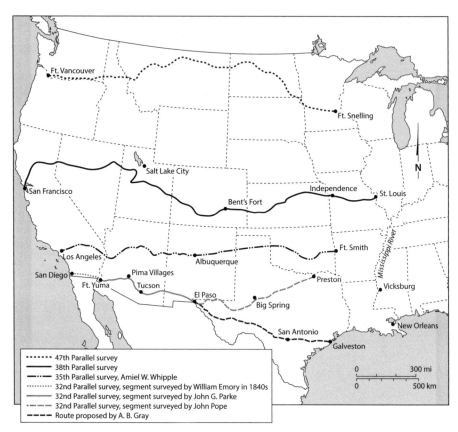

Map 4. Pacific Railroad Surveys, 1853–1854.

he acted with self-interest, insisting in one annual report that scientific fact alone should determine the route of the railway.[34] Much of his enthusiasm for the surveys stemmed from Davis's strong hunch, like Senator Rusk's, that science would rule on the side of the South. Through the Pacific Railroad Surveys, Davis commissioned four major investigations in the West. The northernmost study traversed the 47th parallel of latitude and followed portions of the path that Asa Whitney had proposed several years earlier. A second party examined a Great Plains route that followed the 38th parallel, the most geographically neutral of the four options and a favorite of Missouri's Senator Benton. The final two surveys—which examined the 35th and 32nd parallels of latitude—focused on New Mexico Territory as a connecting thoroughfare.[35] Both corridors had been analyzed and surveyed in the past, but not with specific attention to railroad construction. While working as part of the

U.S. Boundary Commission, John Russell Bartlett and his team had studied and described much of the 32nd parallel from El Paso to San Diego, and some of their work would later be cited in the 1853 reports. In 1851 Captain Lorenzo Sitgreaves had explored the 35th parallel from the Rio Grande to the Colorado River, but his work focused on wagon transportation and the navigability of waterways.[36] The two surveys conducted in 1853 would provide more definitive evidence on these possible southern routes, and both spoke favorably of New Mexico as a pathway to California.

Lieutenant Amiel W. Whipple, a native of Massachusetts who later fought for the Union army, was tasked with surveying the 35th parallel from Fort Smith, Arkansas, to Los Angeles. His party examined a route that traversed the Texas Panhandle, crossed the southern Rocky Mountains at a point twenty miles below Santa Fe, and bridged the Rio Grande at San Felipe Pueblo. This section of New Mexico contained coal deposits that could be mined to provide fuel for locomotives, while an abundance of pine trees in the region might provide timber for the railroad bed. West of the Rio Grande, Whipple reported, "the route was excellent, nearly devoid of hills, with frequent springs and streams of water," and he saw no severe obstacles to construction. Albert H. Campbell, an engineer with the expedition, paid close attention to the steepness of grades and sharpness of curves that would have to be negotiated along the way. Laying the tracks from Fort Smith to the Pecos River would be relatively simple, he believed, because no major geographic barriers blocked the path. Campbell proposed a Rio Grande crossing near Isleta Pueblo south of Albuquerque, enabling the road to follow the established wagon trail to Zuñi Pueblo and beyond. He also predicted that only three points along the entire route—the steep westward descent from the Pecos River, the Rio Grande crossing, and California's Cajon Pass—would pose any difficulty during construction.[37]

Whipple concluded his report with an overview of New Mexico's benefits, reiterating that regional snowfall would rarely inhibit the passage of trains, the natural abundance of wood and coal would provide plenty of fuel, and the relatively level terrain would limit the time, effort, and money required to build the tracks. He acknowledged just one potential drawback, explaining that the Navajos, "a warlike and predatory tribe," might pose a threat to workers along the way. Once completed, the project would span 1,849 miles with an estimated construction cost of $94 million. Despite the price tag, however, Whipple informed Secretary Davis that "a more favorable location for a railway than that described could scarcely be desired."[38] Back in Arkansas editors of one Fort Smith newspaper praised the findings and opined, "Whipple's route is the right road to the land of gold."[39] Four years later, when Lieutenant Joseph C. Ives explored the Colorado River valley and its watershed, he reaffirmed Whipple's findings and told his superiors that the area remained ideal for the Pacific railway.[40]

Equally suitable for a railroad, according to surveyors, was the 32nd parallel of latitude through central Texas and southern New Mexico. This pathway was mapped through a patchwork of expeditions that cobbled together new information from topographical engineers John G. Parke, Andrew B. Gray, and John Pope, as well as incorporating previous scientific reports from William H. Emory and John Russell Bartlett. In his instructions to the respective savants, Davis specifically mentioned that the availability of water to cool locomotive engines would rank among the greatest concerns for the arid desert route, and each of the parties were to investigate the potential for artesian wells to mitigate this shortcoming.[41]

Lieutenant Parke's survey in 1854 required just twenty-seven days to cover a 373-mile stint from the Pima villages of Arizona to the Mesilla Valley of New Mexico, an area that had been acquired through the Gadsden Purchase earlier that year. Much of that distance consisted of "an elevated plain . . . made up of a series of smooth slopes" that would be perfect for laying steel. With little rainfall, however, a railroad through the area would be almost entirely dependent on natural springs and manmade wells for its water supply. He estimated that the 545-mile segment of track from El Paso, on the Rio Grande, to Fort Yuma, on the Colorado River, would cost just $19.6 million but might take eight years to complete. Much like the 35th parallel, the primary benefits of this course were its salubrious climate, hard-packed soil, and an absence of geographic obstructions, although Parke conceded that the dearth of water and fuel would pose logistical problems.[42]

Andrew B. Gray, who had been previously embroiled in the U.S. Boundary Commission controversy, received an appointment to survey a second portion of the 32nd parallel and focused his investigations on the region between El Paso and the Gulf Coast. A southerner, Gray prefaced his report by emphasizing "the practical advantages of the route through the State of Texas," which spanned 783 miles, or roughly half of the entire distance to California. With a clear sense of sectional preference, he predicted that a railroad across the Lone Star State could be completed in under five years and at lower cost than any other section of the line. To minimize labor fees, he recommended the employment of Indians and "Mexican peons," in much the same fashion as Chinese coolies in California.[43] Corporations building railroads in the Old South already used slave labor, and they planned to employ similar tactics on a transcontinental line. James DeBow estimated that the use of bondsmen—in any form—to construct the Pacific railway would reduce employment costs by a factor of seven, proving "how easily and cheaply railroads

may be built with slave labor."[44] Another southern commentator compared railroads
in the North to those in the South and concluded that "the leading element of
the superior success of our roads was their construction by slave labor." Referring
specifically to the transcontinental project, he wrote, "Experience has settled the
wisdom of this policy, and in the future prosecution of the work of the Southern
Pacific Road, the plan of depending on this class of [slave] labor is to be carried into
more perfect execution."[45] In this way, a railway connection along either the 32nd
or 35th parallel would not only benefit the South financially, it would also expand
the institution of slavery westward, which helps to explain some of the vehement
northern objection to these projects. As Gray recognized, however, New Mexico's
preexisting forms of involuntary servitude could fulfill the demand for workers
with Indian captives and Hispanic peons rather than black slaves.

As Gray continued his report, he sounded more like a self-interested promoter
than an objective analyst. He estimated that revenue from day-to-day freighting
operations might reach $15 million annually, while maintenance outlays would
never exceed $6 million per year, netting handsome profits for investors. The only
significant pitfall involved the scarcity of water, although he believed that enough
productive wells could be dug to satisfy the thirst of steam locomotives. Gray
pushed hard for a western terminus in southern rather than northern California,
contending that "there are few harbors, on either coast of North America, superior
to San Diego." Assuming a nationalistic tone, he attempted to assuage any critics
who might accuse him of sectional bias. "The benefits to be derived from the
construction of the railway along the parallel of 32° north latitude, are not alone
confined to the State of Texas," he insisted. "Incalculable as the advantages may be
to her, yet every State in the Union must be deeply interested in it, as likewise the
nations of Europe." In answer to competing proposals for more northerly avenues
through North America, as well as potential passages across Central America's
Panamanian and Tehuantepec isthmuses, he touted his route's "accessibility at all
seasons of the year, free from the drifting snows of the North and malignant diseases
of the tropics." Not only would the railroad bolster global trade between Australia,
Asia, Europe, Mexico, and the United States, but it also would provide substantial
economic benefits to residents of California, New Mexico, and Texas. In Gray's
report, conjecture periodically superseded fact, and empirical data were sometimes
distorted into conformity with sectional stances. But from an engineering standpoint,
he reached the same conclusion as his peers regarding the practicality of the route.[46]

Captain John Pope, also a topographical engineer, conducted a third and final
survey in 1854 that pursued a slightly different course, exploring a possible roadway

from El Paso to Preston, 640 miles to the east on the Texas side of the Red River. About one-third of that route traversed the Llano Estacado, a remarkably flat and featureless plain that Pope described as a "famous desert, without wood or water." The smooth terrain and dense soil were great for railroad construction, Pope wrote, but heavy machinery would be needed to bore artesian wells along much of the route. With this in mind, his crew spent most of their time drilling test shafts to determine just how much water could be brought to the surface in arid West Texas. Despite these challenges, the lieutenant concluded that "the peculiarly favorable character of the ground along the route of the 32nd parallel, the directness of this route over it, and the difficulties to the north and south, would seem to present inducements eminently favorable to the construction of these wells." Like his colleagues Parke and Gray, Pope believed that the greatest obstacle to a Pacific railway along the southern route would be insufficient water, but all three men saw that problem as surmountable.[47]

Pope provided Davis with seven good reasons to build the transcontinental railroad through Texas and New Mexico: easy grades, reasonable construction costs, availability of timber, proximity to navigable rivers, the ease with which artesian wells could be dug, the potential development of agriculture and mining along the corridor, and a mild regional climate.[48] In addition, he reminded the secretary that a railroad could be built through the entire extent of Texas without any controversy over federal land grants, because the state legislature had already pledged to donate the right-of-way. Taken collectively, the Pacific Railroad Surveys provided Davis with scientific evidence to support the viability of a southern route, and he would cite the work of his topographical engineers in furtherance of that objective.[49] The field reports also seemed to justify the purchase from Mexico of additional territory south of the Gila River, which would be needed if the southernmost route was chosen. To accomplish this, Davis dispatched a fellow southerner, the South Carolinian James Gadsden, to negotiate a deal with Mexican president Antonio López de Santa Anna.

In anticipation of impending negotiations, Gadsden was appointed minister to Mexico on May 24, 1853, and received formal instructions from Secretary of State William L. Marcy before departing for Mexico City. Marcy admitted up front that Gadsden would face a difficult task, because "the hostile feelings engendered by the late war with Mexico, embittered by the severe wounds inflicted on her national pride, have not wholly subsided." The secretary referred to the ongoing boundary debacle in southern New Mexico as "a very serious difficulty" and stressed the need to properly adjudicate the international line to the satisfaction of both countries. The touchy situation had been further inflamed when New Mexico governor William Carr Lane traveled to the Mesilla Valley earlier that year and declared American ownership of the contested territory, prompting Mexican officials to threaten military action. In reference to the Pacific railway, Marcy reminded his agent that "a very eligible route for such a road" had been found south of the Gila River—through Mexican territory—and that the acquisition of that land had become a national necessity. Marcy expected Santa Anna to "cede to the United States such a strip of country as may be necessary to bring within our territory a feasible route for such a railroad," and he postulated that a track near the border would benefit Mexican as well as American citizens. "The sole object" in these negotiations, Marcy reiterated, was "an eligible route for a railroad," although Gadsden also hoped to defuse the tensions arising from Governor Lane's actions.[50] President Franklin Pierce alluded to the mission in his first annual message, calling the boundary disagreement an issue of "considerable magnitude" and explaining that the U.S. government was working to ameliorate the situation.[51]

Gadsden reached Mexico City in August 1853 and met with Santa Anna multiple times thereafter. In October special agent Christopher L. Ward visited Gadsden in Mexico and delivered secret verbal instructions from President Pierce. The new orders outlined four acceptable options for the purchase of land and named the price that the government was willing to pay for each. American officials hoped to acquire as much territory as possible, and authorized the agent to dole out as much as $50 million for the largest of the four parcels, which would have included Baja California. At the very least, however, Gadsden was ordered to secure enough land for "an eligible route for a railroad from the Rio Grande to California." He held six conferences with Mexican ministers Manuel Diez de Bonilla and José Salazar Ylarregui, finalized and signed the treaty on December 30, and returned to the United States two weeks later. From New Orleans he sent a telegram to Marcy informing him that "all issues with Mexico [have been] reconciled on conditions honorable and just to both countries."[52]

The treaty that Gadsden and Diez de Bonilla signed in December 1853 delineated very specific latitude and longitude points for a new international line that would originate just north of El Paso and then strike westward to the California coast. The new pact also annulled articles five and eleven of the Treaty of Guadalupe Hidalgo, negating the basis for the boundary dispute and freeing the U.S. government from the burden of repatriating Mexican captives taken during Indian raids. After several rounds of amendments that reduced the purchase price from $15 million to $10 million, the U.S. Senate ratified the treaty on June 29, 1854. Mexican leaders complained that the modified sections were "not reciprocal, but onerous and offensive to the weaker party in all its provisions," and Gadsden returned to Mexico to lobby for Santa Anna's final approval, which came shortly thereafter.[53]

As word of the treaty negotiations and subsequent Senate debates trickled in to eastern newspaper offices, journalists found themselves divided on the issue. In his *New-York Daily Tribune,* abolitionist Horace Greeley railed against the government for spending millions of dollars on a "heaven-forsaken" plot of uninhabitable ground with no purpose other than to provide the South with its thoroughfare for a railroad. "We presume we shall never refuse to buy any land that may be offered to us till after we shall have got all between Terra del Fuego and the North Pole," Greeley exclaimed in a sarcastic critique of American expansionism.[54] In support of this stance, he printed a personal letter from John Russell Bartlett relating his recollections of the region that the United States had just acquired. Southern New Mexico "does not contain one half of one percent of arable land," Bartlett wrote, quipping that "I would consider it a severe punishment to be compelled to live there."[55] Editors at the *New York Times,* a recent upstart that had printed its first edition just three years earlier, also held strong opinions about the latest land-grab scheme. In contrast to Greeley, however, the staff of this fledgling Northern newspaper voiced cautious support for the measure. With an eye toward international diplomacy rather than domestic sectionalism, *New York Times* contributors hoped that the Gadsden Treaty would "restore and perpetuate relations of amity and good will" between the United States and Mexico. The editorialists also expressed measured contentment that so little territory had actually been gained through the purchase, pointing out that the other options Gadsden proposed to Santa Anna would have absorbed far more acreage and cost much more money.[56] The newspapermen voiced a sense of relief that the United States had not bought all of Sonora, predicting that "were it in American hands, no doubt it would be speedily developed into a choice spot for the growth of our most peculiar institution." Somewhat sardonically, they added, "Among those institutions would be a Pacific Railroad."[57]

Few if any men were more excited about the deal than James DeBow, who cooed in his monthly periodical that Gadsden possessed all of the "merits of a pioneer" for securing the southern pathway to the Pacific.[58] With the Gadsden Purchase having expanded New Mexico Territory, it would be up to southern capitalists and promoters to make a reality of DeBow's vision for a transcontinental railroad. Albert Pike, a proslavery author and attorney who would fight for the Confederacy during the Civil War, understood the importance of the project as well as anybody. Wherever the Pacific railroad went, Pike wrote in December 1854, "political and commercial power will go as its inseparable companions." He provocatively raised the specter of secession by declaring, "Much as we need a Southern railroad to the Pacific now, while *in* the Union, we should need it infinitely more, it would be absolutely and literally indispensable, if the North and the South were to separate." A railroad through Texas and New Mexico, Pike concluded, "would bind California to us with hooks of steel," thereby fostering nationwide financial dependency on the Slave South.[59] Such prospects excited southerners, including Francis M. Dimond, president of the Texas Western Railroad Company, who followed these developments with keen interest. After the Gadsden Purchase he republished Gray's railway survey and distributed copies throughout the United States. At the same time, Jefferson Davis issued his first public statements on the matter, announcing that the Pacific Railroad Surveys demonstrated the 32nd parallel to be "the most practical and economical route" westward. This thrilled DeBow, who hailed Davis as an "eminent statesman and honored citizen."[60]

The Atlantic & Pacific Railroad Company (A&P) also reproduced information from Gray's report, and when they released annual stockholder statements, corporate executives expressed strong interest in the southernmost route to California.[61] By 1855 the company had begun negotiations with Texas officials for a right-of-way through that state, recognizing that the Texas Railroad Act of 1854 allowed the legislature "to provide for the construction of the Mississippi and Pacific Railroad."[62] Although this solved part of the problem, the corporation would need federal land grants and congressional backing to push the rails through New Mexico. Basing their conclusions on information from the Pacific Railroad Surveys, A&P executives informed shareholders and potential investors that the 32nd parallel "is shown to be perfectly easy and practicable." They envisioned the New Mexico thoroughfare as "the great ultimate route of the commerce of the world, the route for mails, for passengers, for the gold of California and Australia, for the teas, spices, and other light goods of Asia, and for costly articles and package goods of all the continents." Company officials also postulated, with counterintuitive logic, that "a common road through Texas to the Pacific" would unite the North and South in shared commerce and "render our Union indissoluble." The ultimate effect, they hoped, would be a shift in global trade networks, linking "the triple markets of the Atlantic, the Pacific, and the Mississippi" while giving the United States "command of the exchanges and commerce of the world."[63]

Although the A&P went broke before completing any transcontinental lines, the company's approach to the project set a precedent of dishonesty and corruption that would characterize the nation's transcontinental projects for decades to come. Corporate managers overhyped potential profits and underestimated construction and operating costs to dupe gullible investors through unethical—if not blatantly fraudulent—business techniques. Much of the report relied on fanciful guesswork and outright lies as the basis for financial projections. Because they so egregiously misjudged construction costs at a mere $22,000 per mile (more accurate estimates suggested $75,000 per mile), A&P executives claimed that their profits would dwarf those of "any other railroad on this continent." Like transcontinental investors of the post–Civil War era, stakeholders in the A&P Railroad hoped to derive most of their short-term gains from the sale of checkerboard land grant parcels in Texas and New Mexico. According to the annual report, sponsors could expect the company to sell 6,553,600 acres of land at a starting price of $2.50 per acre, an amount that would purportedly quadruple to $10 per acre once the railway boosted regional economies and carried droves of emigrants into the Southwest. The A&P assured its financiers that land sales alone would produce $85 million in profits. Stockholders could also count on a "perpetual" annual return of 28 percent on their investments, with additional dividends being distributed on an estimated $23 million cash surplus each year. Once land values skyrocketed, an extra $70 million in cash would be dispersed. "In the worst possible aspect of the case," they concluded, "the stockholder . . . would receive twenty-eight per cent, per annum, forever on his investment." This hypothetical scenario was nothing more than a scam—historian Richard White has called these tactics a nineteenth-century Ponzi scheme—and it revolved around the widespread assumption that only one cross-country line would ever be built, meaning that the company would operate free from competition for freight, passenger transit, and government contracts. Fifteen years before the first transcontinental railway was actually completed, the very concept of one was already bringing out the worst in American businessmen.[64]

Robert J. Walker, a Mississippi politician and capitalist with speculative interests in land, cotton, and slaves, served as president of the A&P Railroad Company and had a hand in authoring the misleading reports. A second contributor was Thomas Butler King, a Georgia lawyer and lobbyist who also acted as vice president of the Texas Western Railroad Company. In an ironic twist, these southern men controlled the New York–based A&P Railroad, and they fought hard to convince the rest of the nation that the course through Texas and New Mexico ought to be chosen for the line. Northerners were not so easily fooled, however, and New Yorker Horace Greeley lambasted the entire scheme as ridiculous and foolish. He sarcastically referred to the 32nd parallel as the "Moonshine Route" and called Walker "the great blarney-chief of the Moonshine Railroad."[65] Another New York journalist, C. Glen Peebles, published a pamphlet exposing Walker and King for their fraudulent scams and warning the American people "of the impolicy [sic] of paying any money to the trust branch of this Company." In a scathing indictment of railroad capitalists,

Peebles analyzed the company's finances and discovered that actual investor returns amounted to just one-tenth of one percent—a far cry from the 28 percent that A&P executives advertised. "In organizing the company, it was sought to give it an odor of nationality, and to that end Southern men were brought in," Peebles explained before slandering Walker as an "old flibberty-gibbet." Pointing out that southern men held the managerial positions even though most of the company's capital came from Northern financiers, Peebles saw the entire operation as a scheme "to milk the North as far as possible."[66] Far from unifying the North and South through shared economic interests, as some promoters had claimed it would, the transcontinental railroad continued to drive a wedge between the two sections.

In a further reflection of the growing political and ideological divide, an organization emerged in the 1850s to advance a radical Southern conceptualization of expansion. With sectional turmoil increasing in the wake of the Pacific Railroad Surveys, the Gadsden Purchase, and the Kansas-Nebraska Act, southerners formed the Knights of the Golden Circle (KGC) to promote the idea of a sovereign slave empire extending outward in all directions from the Gulf of Mexico. A railroad along a southerly route of the continental United States would have contributed to the realization of this vision. In theory, the so-called Golden Circle—encompassing, clockwise, the Deep South states, Florida, Cuba, Central America, Mexico, and the gulf coast of Texas—would form the economic core of an independent nation predicated on slavery. Wide-eyed dreamers envisioned an empire stretching as far as the Amazon River basin of South America. The transcontinental line, following either the 35th or 32nd parallel of latitude, would project that ideological and economic influence westward to the Pacific coast and help to complete a powerful hemispheric empire. To this end, the railroad, as well as New Mexico Territory itself, held an important place in the Slave South's globalization and nation-building schemes, to the point that a unique Southern brand of Manifest Destiny developed around these ideas.[67]

Even as organizations like the KGC fueled sectional passions and journalists scrutinized every political move, federal lawmakers still considered new Pacific railroad proposals as the decade wore on. In 1856 Congress reviewed a bill that would have allowed numerous private firms to construct railways through the West, including one from Shreveport, Louisiana, to the Southern California coast. "A railroad across the continent would open up a vast extent of country to settlement," the congressional committee declared in a tired refrain, "and much of what is now believed to be sterile and barren will, no doubt, be found to yield bountifully to the agriculturist." However exciting the prospects, many American statesmen still chafed at the astronomical costs associated with such a venture. Some people questioned whether the commerce of California, valued at $14 million in 1855, justified the expenditure of an estimated $200 million to construct the tracks. Thomas Hart Benton, still deeply enamored with the project, suggested a line across New Mexico's 35th parallel, but he wanted the path to veer northward as it crossed the southern plains, finding a midway point at St. Louis before eventually terminating at Baltimore on the East Coast. As usual, politicians from the slave states objected to Benton's idea because it would deprive their section of the southernmost route.[68] Exasperated with the ongoing uncertainty, editors of the *North American Review* concluded, somewhat wryly, "Whatever may be the ultimate fate of the railroad . . . there can be no doubt as to the great advantages resulting from the explorations themselves" in terms of scientific knowledge.[69] Once again, sectional differences had prevented any decision or even compromise regarding a transcontinental railroad through New Mexico.

The Virginian John B. Floyd, who succeeded Jefferson Davis as secretary of war in 1857, perpetuated bureaucratic support for the southern route during James Buchanan's presidential administration. In his first annual report to Congress, Floyd upheld the 32nd parallel as the best option, but he also opined that at least two additional transcontinental lines should be built.[70] That same year, a new syndicate challenged the Atlantic & Pacific Railroad for access to the 32nd parallel route. Founded in New Orleans, the Southern Pacific Railroad Company aimed to construct a line from Louisiana to California. As its president, George S. Yerger, explained in 1857, "I consider it not only as a great national enterprise, but one that will be especially beneficial to the South, and no city in the Union would derive more lasting benefit from its completion than the city of New Orleans." He proposed to build the line through El Paso, the Mesilla Valley, and the Gadsden Purchase lands south of the Gila River and concluded that "a large part of the immense trade of the Pacific, the Mexican Provinces, western Texas, [and] New Mexico" would thereby be centered in the Deep South. Hopeful of securing congressional approval, the Southern Pacific had already sold half a million dollars in speculative stock certificates and was advertising additional shares at prices ranging from $2.50 to $100 each. Before a single piece of track had even been laid, the Southern Pacific's modus operandi already resembled that of its insolvent and corrupt competitors.[71]

Hoping to make the most of the secretary of war's favorable opinion, lawmakers in Santa Fe sprang to action. The legislature passed a resolution in February 1860 granting the New Mexican Railway Company a right-of-way "to locate, construct, own, and maintain a railway" through the territory. With this local support, the company petitioned Congress to consider their desired route. The memorialists protested government subsidies for more northerly lines, arguing that a thoroughfare through New Mexico offered greater value than any other option. They also contended that "the services to be rendered by a railroad on the southern route will be of much greater value to the United States," citing the need for military defense on the international border as another reason to build the line there. Much as Atlantic & Pacific Railroad executives had done five years earlier, the New Mexican Railway Company's officers insisted that the southwestern territory was the only logical choice for transcontinental rails, and they asked Congress to provide $35 million to kick-start work on the project. Much to the chagrin of the company's benefactors, the Civil War intervened less than a year after their inquiry, ensuring that no route would be chosen that would benefit the South and significantly altering the course of New Mexico's economic future.[72]

In 1858 an engineer named Robert G. Rankin pointed out that the Pacific railroad, if ever completed, would be far more than just a commercial connection for the world. Such a linkage would also be a conduit for ideas and culture, he wrote, because "each line of iron rail is a line or train of thought."[73] Rankin's metaphor goes a long way toward explaining the broader significance of the transcontinental railroad in terms of American politics, economics, society, and democratic ideology. Throughout the antebellum era, congressional speeches, newspaper editorials, engineering surveys, and eyewitness accounts suggested that the Pacific railway was purely an economic enterprise that would benefit either the North or the South depending on the location of the tracks. In reality, however, a railroad connecting one North American coast to the other would irreversibly transform the nation by facilitating the movement of people and their ideas. Although most interested parties never admitted it, the spread of ideology had as much to do with the sectional conflict as did any economic imperatives. A railroad following either of the proposed routes through Texas and New Mexico would not only boost the South's economy to the possible detriment of the North, but it would also propagate the flow of Southern ideas westward, meaning that the railway would be the means whereby proslavery ideology consumed the American West. A railway along a northern route would have a similar but inverse effect, spreading free-labor ideology westward at the potential peril of slavery. A project as transformative as the Pacific railway presented more at stake than money. To some Northern and Southern ideologues, the very future of slavery and free labor—and the perpetuation of American democracy and political union—depended on the route that the steel rails would follow. Thus, when the southern states finally did revolt in 1861, the Confederacy launched an ambitious plot to expand its plantation economy and proslavery ideology through New Mexico and beyond.

= 6 =

THE CIVIL WAR AND THE
FINAL CONTEST FOR NEW MEXICO

Many people contributed to America's decades-long nation-building project in the Southwest, but few understood the region's strategic importance better than Henry Hopkins Sibley. As a military officer in New Mexico during the 1850s, he became closely acquainted with the area's geography, resources, and inhabitants. Sibley resigned his U.S. Army commission on April 28, 1861, and traveled to Virginia for an interview with Jefferson Davis, who was a former Mexican-American War compatriot and fellow West Point graduate. Hopeful that the Confederate president might place him in command of an expeditionary force, Sibley provided detailed information on Union troop strength in New Mexico, noted supplies and provisions upon which an invading army could draw, and described local sentiment toward the Confederacy. With his long-standing interest in the Southwest, Davis hardly needed convincing to adopt the scheme, but Sibley nonetheless reminded him that New Mexico would be the key geographic element in a coast-to-coast Southern empire stretching westward from Texas. Once the Stars and Bars flew above the Santa Fe plaza, the fledgling Confederacy could move on to claim California's goldfields and the rich silver deposits in Colorado and Arizona, all of which would help to fund the war effort. Southern merchants would gain direct access to Pacific commercial networks, and imperial success might attract diplomatic recognition from European countries like England and France. After achieving these objectives, Confederate agents could negotiate with Mexico to acquire northern Chihuahua and Sonora, further expanding the empire and gaining control of ports on the Gulf of California.

It sounded like an ingenious plan—not unlike that of the KGC—especially for two visionaries whose respective military and political careers had revolved around and contributed to American expansion and Manifest Destiny. Transforming the idea into reality, however, proved far more difficult than either man imagined.[1]

When the election of Abraham Lincoln in November 1860 spurred several southern states to secede, the Louisiana-born Sibley, like many federal army officers, made plans to join the Confederacy. Before leaving the Southwest, however, he and fellow secessionist William Loring—who assumed command of New Mexico's military department in March 1861—hatched a plot to lead several companies of federal troops with them into Texas to fight for the Rebel army. Once Sibley reached friendly territory at El Paso, he penned an emotional but incriminatory letter to Loring. "We are at last under the glorious banner of the Confederate States of America," he joyously exclaimed, expressing a strong sense of loyalty to the Southern cause and vaguely describing the clandestine activities in which he and Loring had collaborated before Sibley departed New Mexico.[2] Although the two officers did not follow through with the treasonous scheme, Loring remained in command of New Mexico until June 11, hampering the ability of U.S. personnel to prepare for the war.[3] Loring's extended stay as an imposter in Santa Fe kept him apprised of Union strategy and troop strength during the first three months of the war. It also allowed Texans to seize military equipment at Fort Bliss (El Paso), augmenting the supplies of Confederate forces who had already confiscated federal provisions at San Antonio when General David Twiggs, commander of the Department of Texas, surrendered his command without resistance.[4]

The Confederate government wasted little time in setting the expansionist plan into motion. Sibley left Richmond on July 8 with orders to raise an army in Texas and march toward Santa Fe. Bestowed the rank of brigadier general, Sibley was entrusted "with the important duty of driving the Federal troops" out of New Mexico. In the process, he had the authority to confiscate arms and munitions for the use of his own men and to muster disaffected Union soldiers into the Rebel army. All of this was to be pursued "in the speediest manner possible" to capitalize on any element of surprise that might remain and to achieve the conquest of a western empire at an early stage of the war.[5] Before Sibley returned to San Antonio to raise his army of invasion, however, Lieutenant Colonel John R. Baylor mustered a force of several hundred Texan volunteers and led them to El Paso, where he staged a campaign that preceded Sibley into southern New Mexico by several months.

Federal officers did not lounge idly on the sidelines as their Confederate counterparts plotted the invasion of New Mexico. When Loring departed Santa Fe in June 1861, his successor as department commander, Colonel Edward Canby, made immediate preparations for a looming Confederate attack and developed a multifaceted plan for defending the territory. The same day that he assumed control of New Mexico's military forces, Canby acknowledged the prevailing sentiment in the southern portion of the territory, where Rebel sympathizers congregated in Mesilla and Tucson. Mesilla in particular had become a hotbed of secessionism in the months leading up to the Texan invasion.[6] Speakers at an extralegal Arizona territorial convention held on March 30, 1861, implored all delegates to choose sides in a sectional conflagration that erupted in open warfare less than two weeks later with the shelling of Fort Sumter, South Carolina. Those who cast their lot with the North would find "anarchy, blight, ruin, and neglect," while those favoring the Southern cause might enjoy "freedom, equal rights, and the blessings of a government," according to the unabashedly biased editors of Mesilla's newspaper.[7] The same editorialists claimed that at least 90 percent of the white population in that vicinity favored "a disruption of the Union" and cursed the election of Abraham Lincoln as "disastrous."[8] When Union sympathizer W. W. Mills passed through the town just weeks ahead of Baylor's troops, he sneered that "the Mesilla Times is bitterly disunion, and threatens with death anyone who refuses to acknowledge this usurpation."[9] As for New Mexicans living north of the Mesilla Valley—who composed the bulk of the territorial population—Canby believed that "with few exceptions [they] are loyal, but they are apathetic in disposition," meaning that they may or may not prove reliable if called on to defend the territory.[10]

Predicting that Confederate authorities would try to capitalize on regional sympathies by occupying the Mesilla Valley, the Union commander planned to abandon Forts Buchanan and Breckenridge, transfer the soldiers at both locations to Fort Fillmore, and arrange for strong defensive measures at that position.[11] He also ordered that Forts Craig and Union be heavily reinforced, as those posts would likely be "the initial points both for offensive and defensive operations."[12] Through frantic but vigilant construction efforts, sophisticated earthworks had been completed at both installations by the end of September, well ahead of the Rebel advance up the Rio Grande.[13]

During the pivotal weeks preceding Baylor's invasion, Canby also took a calculated risk to his own reputation and career when he deliberately disobeyed orders to transfer most of New Mexico's federal troops to the eastern theatres of war. Recognizing the veracity of the Texan threat, the colonel stalled in his fulfillment of the instructions. He explained to the adjutant general that the department lacked sufficient modes of transportation for the troops and their equipment and that they

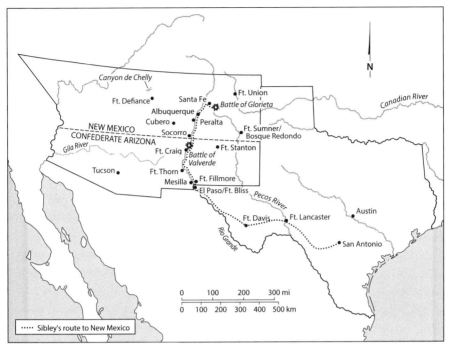

Map 5. New Mexico during the Civil War, 1861–1862.

must therefore remain in New Mexico a while longer. By the time he procured
adequate transportation, Confederates under Baylor had already entered the Mesilla
Valley, and Canby had a viable reason to keep his men in the territory.[14] A commanding officer's decision to disregard orders and stall for time would prove to be among
the deciding factors in the federal government's ability to hold New Mexico for the
duration of the Civil War. From the moment he took charge, Canby was deeply
committed to sustaining control in the Southwest, and his thoughtful planning
and intuitive foresight played a pivotal role in repelling the Confederate advance.

    When Texan forces congregated near El Paso, Union officers felt confident
that the invasion would be carried out "the moment the instigators feel assured
of a probability of success." With the assistance of secessionists in Mesilla, Rebel
troops stood a better than average probability of absorbing southern New Mexico
into the Confederacy.[15] As the Civil War progressed, Canby faced growing threats
from multiple directions, and both Confederates and Indians posed problems
on the southern and eastern peripheries of the territory.[16] To meet these threats,
Canby dispatched scouting parties to monitor New Mexico's Rio Grande, Pecos,

Colonel Edward R. S. Canby, c. 1860s.
Courtesy National Archives and Records Administration, Washington, D.C.

and Canadian River valleys. As late as June 30, 1861, the colonel believed that the invasion would come from the Texas panhandle—by way of the Canadian River—in order to funnel Confederate forces directly toward the supply depot at Fort Union, where enough munitions had been stockpiled to last the territory's federal troops for an entire year of fighting.[17]

Federal officers also organized small groups of Hispanic civilians to pose as Comancheros, "under the ostensible object of trading with the Indians," because such groups would be less likely to attract suspicion while carrying out their undercover operations.[18] Department headquarters authorized the commanding officers at Forts Union and Stanton to hire dozens of Mexicans and Pueblo Indians to serve as spies in the Pecos and Canadian River valleys.[19] The army also employed Kiowa Indians to report any Texan movements that they detected in eastern New Mexico.[20] Within a short time scouts were watching every possible approach to Santa Fe, and no adversarial force of any size could enter the territory unnoticed.[21] As president of New Mexico's legislative assembly, Facundo Piño also implored his fellow Nuevomexicanos to join in the fight against a Texan enemy that threatened their families, property, and honor.[22] Representative Miguel A. Otero likewise pledged his support and assured the secretary of state that his countrymen were "unanimous" in their loyalty to the Union.[23] Canby's clever machinations, coupled with the efforts of influential locals, made the federal defense of New Mexico a collective effort that relied on Union troops, citizen volunteers, Hispanic lookouts, and Indian spies to ensure that no Confederate army maneuvered undetected.

The final element of Canby's defensive strategy involved recruiting and training volunteer forces to buttress federal military power and ensure that Union troops held the numerical advantage in any hostile engagements.[24] Canby began mustering militiamen immediately upon assuming command, and in September 1861 he informed Governor Henry Connelly that four regiments of infantry and cavalry, totaling more than 3,700 men, would be needed to fight alongside the army regulars already stationed throughout the territory. With less than half that number enrolled, Canby contacted Governor William Gilpin of Colorado and requested additional volunteers to fill New Mexico's regiments to capacity.[25] By the end of the year, an impressive 4,755 regulars and volunteers reported themselves for duty in Canby's Union army.[26] The commander hoped that as many as 6,000 soldiers would be in service before Sibley made his way up the Rio Grande, and the ordnance department at Fort Union stockpiled 1.2 million rounds of ammunition in anticipation of impending clashes.[27] Although the Hispanic volunteers endured repeated criticism for mediocre performance in battle, their overall contribution to the federal war effort in the Southwest would prove critical to the retention of New Mexico. Canby himself reflected the varied opinions about volunteers, condemning them as inefficient and ignorant while simultaneously praising their role as "valuable auxiliaries" who remained indispensable to territorial defense.[28] Setting aside the nativist rhetoric that marginalized the role of Nuevomexicanos, Governor Connelly praised the "patriotic outpouring of men" that attended his call to arms, and interim Governor William Arny later praised Hispanics who fought for the Union as devoted Americans and thanked them for their faithful service.[29]

As federal officers undertook these preparatory measures, in July 1861 Baylor led his Texan forces into the Mesilla Valley. Just a few years earlier, editors of a prominent Southern periodical had written that this region—which included the Gadsden Purchase lands—could produce high-quality cotton and could be "adapted to slavery, and hence an angry struggle may be expected."[30] When they wrote these words in the late 1850s, the editors' assumption involved yet another political debacle over slavery in a western territory, but in fact some of the earliest fighting of the Civil War would take place on that very ground to which they referred. Recognizing that Fort Fillmore would be the first point of contact, Canby placed Major Isaac Lynde in command at that post and provided every resource possible for its defense. The hope was that Lynde would be able to "repress any revolutionary movement that may be set on foot" in the region and repel Baylor's outnumbered soldiers.[31] In case Lynde needed even more men, Canby authorized him to raise two companies of volunteers at nearby Las Cruces and Mesilla.[32] The major never pursued that course, hoping instead that four companies of dragoons en route from Fort Buchanan would arrive in time to augment his forces.[33] As the Confederate invasion materialized in the final days of July, Lynde had two straightforward objectives to ensure that New Mexico remained under federal control. His orders directed him to suppress secessionist sentiment in Mesilla and to turn back the Texan assault at all costs. If he could accomplish those tasks, Confederate dreams of conquering New Mexico and planting the Dixie flag on California's coast would dissolve, bringing an end to Sibley's scheme before he even set the larger plan into motion.

Lynde grew increasingly nervous as days passed, and those around him began to sense that New Mexico's fate was in the wrong hands. The major revealed his lack of fortitude three weeks before Baylor's arrival when he informed Canby that "I do not think this post or the valley worth the exertion to hold it."[34] He later described Fort Fillmore as "indefensible against artillery" and too far away from a reliable water source to enable a prolonged stand against an organized and persistent assault.[35] Among the officers serving under Lynde, several were suspected of sympathizing with the Confederacy, and the post sutlers also expressed their proclivities toward the South.[36] When W. W. Mills arrived in Mesilla on June 23, 1861, he reported a scene of anti-Union sentiment, explaining that "a disunion flag is now flying from the house in which I write, and this country is now as much in the possession of the enemy as Charleston [South Carolina] is."[37] Lydia Spencer Lane, the wife of an officer in the Regiment of Mounted Rifles, described the confused state of affairs inside the fort's walls in a scathing indictment of Lynde's leadership and competence. The major "seemed utterly oblivious of the danger, and took no means to strengthen the place," she wrote, concluding that "there could not have been a better man in command to help the Southern cause, nor a worse for the government, than Major Lynde."[38] If Canby made one glaring mistake when preparing for the invasion, it was his decision to place Lynde in command of New Mexico's southernmost military position.

On the morning of July 25—just four days after Confederate soldiers won their first major victory of the Civil War at the Battle of Bull Run (Manassas) in northern Virginia—Baylor's troops bypassed Fort Fillmore unopposed and occupied Mesilla, where secessionists "received [them] with every satisfaction of joy."[39] With his hand now forced, Lynde led 380 troops to meet the Confederates in battle. As the two armies formed skirmish lines in cornfields south of the village, residents climbed atop their houses to watch the spectacle unfold.[40] The brief firefight—the first between Union and Confederate soldiers in New Mexico—resulted in a Rebel victory and induced Lynde's federals to retreat after sustaining ten casualties. Baylor, who opted not to pursue his foe, witnessed the confusion that ensued when the Union riflemen, riding horses, trampled several of their infantry comrades during the chaotic withdrawal from the battlefield.[41]

The following morning, a stunned Baylor stood on an adobe rooftop in Mesilla, peering through binoculars as he observed the entire Union garrison from Fort Fillmore—which outnumbered his troops two to one—retreating over the Organ Mountains on the road to Fort Stanton. Under panicked orders from Lynde, the federals had destroyed the fort's hospital provisions and burned or buried most of the remaining supplies before hastily deserting the post under cover of darkness.[42] Baylor immediately called his men to arms and rode in pursuit, overtaking more than one hundred "fainting, famished soldiers," strung out over more than five miles, most of whom surrendered without incident.[43] Some of the soldiers had filled their canteens with whiskey as they abandoned Fort Fillmore the night before, and the hot summer sun took a brutal toll on the dehydrated men as they stumbled toward San Augustine Springs, which did not emit enough water to resupply so many people and animals. When Baylor confronted him near the springs, Lynde surrendered despite adamant protests from fellow officers.[44] His command had marched more than twenty miles without water, many of the Union men had already been taken prisoner, and 103 women and children—who should have been evacuated from the post long before the Confederates arrived—burdened the command and "paralyzed [them] when in the presence of the enemy."[45] Two days later, the secessionist editors of the *Mesilla Times* celebrated with a front-page headline reading "Arizona Is Free at Last!"[46] Lynde had failed in both of his objectives, and his capitulation would have serious consequences in the months ahead.

With limited supplies and only three hundred men under his command, Baylor could not guard and feed the Union prisoners, so he offered generous terms of surrender by paroling the enlisted men and releasing the civilians.[47] James Cooper McKee, the post surgeon at Fort Fillmore, referred to the surrender as an episode of "cowardice and imbecility" and condemned Lynde as a traitor to his country.[48] Comparing Lynde to the infamous Revolutionary War turncoat Benedict Arnold, editors of a New York newspaper wrote that his timidity was "the most shameful thing ever done by an officer of the United States Army" and expressed fear that New Mexico would be forever lost to the Confederacy.[49] In capitulating his entire

Lieutenant Colonel John R. Baylor, c. 1860s.
Center for Southwest Research, University Libraries, University of New Mexico,
Keleher Collection, ZIM CSWR 000-742-0014.

command without firing a shot, Lynde became the Civil War–era version of Manuel Armijo, and like the former Mexican governor he underwent formal investigation and court martial for his actions. Major Alfred Gibbs of the Regiment of Mounted Rifles pressed charges against Lynde for abandoning his post and violating the Articles of War, Colonel Canby arrested the major when he arrived at Albuquerque, and President Lincoln personally dropped him from the rolls of the Army.[50] "Under the circumstances I considered our case hopeless," Lynde later wrote in an attempt to exonerate himself of wrongdoing, explaining to War Department officials that "it was worse than useless to resist."[51] His surrender of New Mexico's southernmost point of defense left the remainder of the territory vulnerable to attack, imperiled the Union war effort in that region, and reinvigorated the Confederates' expansionist mission.

With Fort Fillmore evacuated, Union troops disarmed and paroled, and local sentiment in his favor, Baylor had achieved the first major Confederate victory in the Southwest. To assert political control over the conquered region, he issued a proclamation establishing the new Confederate Territory of Arizona and named himself governor.[52] He took these actions under the assumption that his superiors would approve them at a later date, recognizing the immediate importance of his accomplishments and fearing that the Confederacy might lose its grasp on the region should he fail to act quickly and decisively. Writing to General Earl Van Dorn, commander of the Department of Texas, Baylor proudly proclaimed that "the vast mineral resources of Arizona, in addition to its affording an outlet to the Pacific, make its acquisition a matter of some importance to our Government."[53] He understood the imperial and economic purposes behind his invasion and appreciated the importance of sustaining the so-called Arizona Strip as a Confederate possession. Ironically, however, Baylor's initial victory would prove more of a curse than a blessing. In addition to justifying Canby's retention of the Union regulars in New Mexico, the surrender of the Fort Fillmore garrison and subsequent occupation of the Mesilla Valley provided federal officials with an early warning of Sibley's impending march from San Antonio. This realization spurred the Union Army to feverish action in recruiting reinforcements and building defensive bulwarks around the territory's most critical forts, and the long delay between Baylor's entrance in July and the arrival of Sibley's second wave of troops in December left ample time for Union soldiers to prepare for conflict.

From his station at Mesilla, Baylor made it clear to Sibley that they needed to act quickly to make the most of the Texans' temporary advantage. Having held the town for two months and desperate for support, an exasperated Baylor informed Sibley in October that Canby had collected more than 2,500 federal soldiers and stationed them at Fort Craig, where they would mount a defensive posture to block the Confederate advance up the Rio Grande. Rumors that General Edwin V. Sumner had landed thousands of additional Union troops at Guaymas on the Mexican coast and was preparing to move eastward toward Baylor's position strained his patience even more. "Hurry up if you want a fight," Baylor cried in a frantic message to Sibley.[54] Infuriated by Sibley's stalled expedition and feeling abandoned on the fringe of enemy territory, Baylor said that he would commence guerrilla attacks on Union scouts and pickets to stall for time, but added that he might have to abandon the entire mission if reinforcements did not arrive.[55] Sibley calmly promised that he would "move very soon" out of San Antonio and offered that, in the meantime, he had faith that Baylor would do "everything of which your small force is capable to hold the enemy in check."[56] It seemed to Baylor as though the man who devised the imperialistic plot had little urgency or motivation in actually executing it.

After three months of recruiting and training at San Antonio, the Sibley Brigade finally marched toward El Paso on November 18, 1861.[57] Aware of Baylor's precarious position and fearful that he would come under intense scrutiny for poor management and slow preparation, Sibley mailed a longwinded letter to Confederate leaders in Richmond offering numerous excuses for the delays. Realizing that the lengthy postponement of the expedition had already diminished his chances for a successful invasion of New Mexico, the general preemptively deflected blame on Texas governor Edward Clark, who, according to Sibley, had shown lackadaisical zeal in helping to raise the two regiments.[58] Not only did Sibley's Army of New Mexico spin its wheels for three months in preparation for the march, but it also suffered from inadequate equipment and supplies, which further hampered the men as they trekked across arid West Texas. They would be forced to live off the land and hoped to capture Union supply depots to sustain the campaign. Sibley was betting on a quick and decisive conquest of New Mexico and expected the cooperation of its civilian population. He failed to devise any contingency plans, so it would be an all-or-nothing expedition.[59]

When Sibley joined Baylor at Mesilla on December 20, 1861, he issued a public announcement outlining the Confederate purposes in mounting the invasion. Hispanic New Mexicans who remembered the proclamations General Kearny made fifteen years earlier must have felt a sense of déjà vu. Sibley confidently announced that his army had "come as friends" to New Mexico "to take possession of it in the name and for the benefit of the Confederate States." He assured inhabitants that resistance would be futile and that his force of 3,000 men was more than sufficient to seize and hold the territory. Parroting Kearny, he informed his listeners that the new government would be composed primarily of native New Mexicans and that their religious, civil, and political liberties would be "maintained sacred and intact." Sibley also implored residents to go peacefully about their daily lives, pledging that they "had nothing to fear" from either him or the troops under his command—a promise that proved baseless once Rebels began confiscating food and supplies from the people. Despite the violent rebellions and individual acts of resistance that had followed Kearny's conquest a decade and a half earlier, Sibley pursued a nearly identical course of action, employing the rhetoric of conciliation and friendship to attract Hispanos to his cause.

Sibley's closing statements revealed the true intent and scope of the invasion. "By geographical position, similarity of institutions, by commercial interests, and by future destinies," he declared, "New Mexico pertains to the Confederacy."[60] To advance this prophecy, Rebel leaders hoped to enlist the support of Mexican statesmen in neighboring Chihuahua and Sonora. Sibley dispatched a diplomatic agent, Colonel James Reily, on a secret mission to visit with the governors of both states. Reily clearly felt the weight of the Southern cause on his shoulders. "We must have Sonora and Chihuahua," he wrote. "With Sonora and Chihuahua we

Brigadier General Henry Hopkins Sibley, c. 1860s.
Courtesy National Archives and Records Administration, Washington, D.C.

gain southern California, and by a railroad to Guaymas render our State of Texas the great highway of nations."[61] Sibley sent letters of introduction to each governor, cryptically explaining that the Confederate government wished to foster relations "not merely of peace, but of amity and good will" with Mexico. In addition to establishing commercial relations, Sibley proposed an agreement in which soldiers from either country could freely cross the international boundary in pursuit of Apaches, a common foe of both nations. The Texan commander was trying to use ongoing Indian warfare as an entree for a military alliance between the Confederacy and Mexico, hoping that such a coalition might evolve into a broader partnership in which Mexico would join in the fight against the Union.[62]

Hoping to take advantage of the political turmoil surrounding the contemporaneous French imperialist project in Mexico, Reily set out on January 2, 1862, to meet with Chihuahua governor Luis Terrazas and Sonora governor Ignacio Pesqueíra. The transparent part of his plan was to arrange for Sibley's army to purchase supplies from Mexico and to establish a depot at the Guaymas port. The more clandestine portion of his assignment, which echoed James Gadsden's mission to Mexico a decade earlier, entailed the prospect of Mexico selling or otherwise ceding its northern frontier states to the Confederacy. Both governors granted the

Confederates permission to buy provisions from Mexican farmers and merchants, but they denied the request for Texas troops to cross the border in pursuit of Apaches and said little about their thoughts on annexation. Their partial support of the Confederacy—which could have jeopardized Mexican neutrality in the Civil War—embraced the economic benefits of supplying Sibley's troops, but Mexican authorities stopped short of any military or political alliance. Because Terrazas and Pesqueíra both received Reily amicably, he lauded this as the first diplomatic recognition of the Confederate States of America by a foreign nation.[63] But by the time Reily had met with both governors, Sibley had already suffered defeat at Glorieta, and his army was retreating to Texas. The entire undertaking in northern Mexico thus became inconsequential.[64]

In the early months of 1862, Canby's army of Union regulars, volunteers, and conscripted militiamen would fight vigorously to ensure that Sibley's mission failed. As the Confederates gradually made their way northward from the Mesilla Valley, Union soldiers dug in at Fort Craig, where the two armies clashed on February 21 in the Southwest's largest Civil War battle. Although the number of men involved and the casualty counts paled in comparison to engagements like Gettysburg, Antietam, and Shiloh, the Battle of Valverde demonstrated the resolve with which both armies would fight for control of New Mexico.[65] Initial reports indicated another Rebel victory as many of the Union combatants retreated to the safety of Fort Craig. Regardless of the final body count, Canby believed that his troops had inflicted enough damage on the poorly equipped and ill-fed invaders to ensure that their mission of conquest would ultimately fail.[66] Focusing on the bigger picture of winning the war, Canby was willing to lose a battle if it meant wearing down his enemies, exhausting their resources, and sapping morale.

As officers filed their reports over the coming days, the human costs and tactical implications of the battle became clearer. An outnumbered Confederate force of about 2,600 men met more than 3,800 Union regulars and volunteers in the wooded bottomlands of the Rio Grande, within earshot of Fort Craig. Canby later claimed that the numerical balance was about the same between the two sides, because more than 1,000 of the Union men were volunteers and unorganized militia who, in the minds of the regular officers, did not count toward their troop strength.[67] Attempting to inflate the laurels of his accomplishment, Sibley submitted an exaggerated report claiming that Union forces numbered over 8,000 men while he himself had only about 1,750 soldiers.[68] The Confederate general, however, was incapacitated—either from illness, intoxication, or a combination of the two—and spent the duration of the battle in a covered wagon.[69] Bedridden and incapable of leading his army,

Sibley temporarily relinquished command to Colonel Tom Green, who directed Confederate operations during the engagement.[70]

The most pivotal moment in the Battle of Valverde occurred when the Rebels charged a Union artillery battery under the command of Captain Alexander McRae, a North Carolinian who remained loyal to the Union throughout the secession crisis. Lieutenant William R. Scurry of the Fourth Texas Cavalry and his men stormed the six-gun battery "unmindful of the driving storm of grape and canister and musket balls hurling around them," and in so doing they had "decided the fortunes of the day."[71] Green praised his soldiers for the desperate assault, noting with admiration that "never were double-barreled shotguns and rifles used to better effect."[72] Captain Rafael Chacón of the New Mexico Volunteers helped to collect the bodies for burial the next day, and he recalled that the "field was covered with blood, horses, torn and dismembered limbs, and heads separated from their bodies."[73] With undisguised anguish, Canby admitted that the defeat of McRae's battery represented the turning point of the battle and wrote of the artillery captain, who perished alongside most of his men, that he "had lived as an example of the best and highest qualities that man can possess."[74] Casualties totaled 111 killed and 160 wounded on the Union side, along with 72 slain and 157 injured for the Confederates—hardly breathtaking numbers when juxtaposed with other Civil War battles, but significant nonetheless for the theatre of action in which they occurred.[75]

After spending two days burying the dead, Sibley ordered his troops north, deciding against an assault on Fort Craig because of his scant provisions and supplies.[76] In choosing this option the Rebel general committed a serious tactical blunder: he left a strong and unvanquished enemy force in his rear while moving toward an equally formidable opposing army ahead of him. The Confederates' strategy of living off the land was already working against them. The Texans did manage to capture some provisions from federal supply stations at Albuquerque and Cubero, but those items would not sustain the large army long enough to complete their mission.[77] Had the Union commander at Albuquerque, Captain Herbert Enos, not burned most of the supplies there before withdrawing toward Fort Union, and had Major James Donaldson not removed 120 wagonloads of provisions from Santa Fe, the Confederates might have gathered enough goods to sustain their expedition.[78] As one member of Sibley's Army of New Mexico later noted, the brigade "would never have experienced any inconvenience" had it not been for the destruction of these crucial supplies.[79] In order to defeat Canby's federals and secure a pathway to the Pacific, Sibley's men needed to capture not only the federal quartermaster depots along the Rio Grande but also the enormous storage facility at Fort Union.

Leaving Fort Craig behind them, the Confederates pushed further into New Mexico and occupied Santa Fe in early March. Although federal troops had abandoned the territorial capital and concentrated themselves at heavily guarded Fort Union, they would not allow Sibley to approach within striking distance of that crucial strategic position. With the fate of New Mexico hanging in the balance, U.S. soldiers had clear instructions "to protect Fort Union at all hazards and leave nothing to chance."[80] On March 26, as the Texans trekked eastward on the Santa Fe Trail, they ran headlong into enemy forces near Apache Pass—the same location where Armijo's Mexicans had planned to meet Kearny's Americans in combat fifteen years earlier. This time, however, neither side intended to retreat without fighting. The Battle of Glorieta would be the climactic scene at which the fate of Confederate imperialism was decided.[81]

As had happened at Valverde, Sibley himself was not present at Glorieta. In the broader context of the Civil War, the Confederate campaign in New Mexico proved singular in that the ranking general never participated in any of his army's major battles, instead relinquishing command to subordinate colonels. One can only imagine the difficulties that Robert E. Lee's Army of Northern Virginia might have faced had he been absent during clashes with the Union's Army of the Potomac, and indeed Sibley's ineffective leadership undermined his own cause in the Southwest. When the fighting at Glorieta subsided, Sibley had little to say about the engagement, informing Adjutant General Samuel Cooper that he had "the honor and pleasure to report another victory" and requesting reinforcements to carry on the campaign. He referred to the battle as a "glorious action" in which the enemy had been driven away "with great loss." As the more detailed reports of field commanders trickled in, however, it became clear that Sibley was wrong in his assessment.[82] The Confederates had in fact suffered a devastating logistical defeat that would force them to abandon their New Mexico campaign and retreat to Texas.

Over the course of two days the opposing armies had clashed numerous times at different locations near Apache Pass. Confederate trooper Theophilus Noel described desperate hand-to-hand combat in which men used their muskets as clubs and shrieked with "demonic yells."[83] At Pigeon's Ranch and Kozlowski's Ranch, fierce firefights claimed the lives of dozens of soldiers on each side. Casualty reports varied, but approximations placed Union losses at or above 48 killed and 70 wounded, while the Confederates suffered roughly identical numbers of dead, wounded, and captured. Each side lost about 10 percent of their forces during the fighting at Glorieta.[84]

The most critical moment of the battle occurred away from combat lines and well behind the Confederate front, when Colonel John M. Chivington led 357

Colorado volunteers in an attack on the Rebel supply train below Apache Pass. There, at Johnson's Ranch, a mere 200 Texans guarded eighty wagons loaded with food, clothing, and ammunition—the main provisions for the entire Rebel army. With the element of surprise in their favor, the Coloradoans surrounded the enemy, forced their surrender, and burned the wagons.[85] Colonel Scurry, who retreated to Santa Fe after Chivington's maneuver, later admitted that "the loss of my supplies so crippled me that after burying my dead I was unable to follow up the victory." The Texans he commanded had not eaten in more than two days—since before the battle even began—and their provisions now lay in ashes at the foot of Apache Pass. As the sun slipped below the western horizon on March 28, Rebel officers raised a flag of truce to collect the wounded and deceased. They then countermarched to Santa Fe and, eventually, out of the territory entirely.[86] Those New Mexicans who had grasped the irony of Sibley's proclamation in December must have again shaken their heads in astonishment: the Confederacy's imperialistic aspirations had dissolved at the exact place where America's expansionist fortunes had been won fifteen years earlier. During the Civil War, as in the Mexican-American War before it, New Mexico had become an important theatre of operations, its control in both instances representing a strategic component of broader goals for the armies involved.

Trapped deep inside enemy territory without a supply line, Sibley's army had no choice but to abandon its mission in New Mexico. By April 12 Union forces retook Santa Fe after thirty-four days of Confederate occupation, and Henry Connelly returned to the Palace of the Governors.[87] Three days later, during a skirmish at Peralta, Connelly's hacienda was ransacked and destroyed as Sibley's beleaguered army retreated toward El Paso.[88] Sharpshooters from both armies periodically "exchanged compliments" across the Rio Grande as the withdrawal continued. By the time they reached Cañada Alamosa—still more than one hundred miles from the safety of Texas soil—starving Rebel soldiers were surviving on small morsels of meat picked from the butchered ribs of their own malnourished horses and oxen. A witness described the column as "weary, tired, sore-footed, more sick than well, and half-starved," noting that some of the men wept from hunger and fatigue.[89] Throughout the campaign, Sergeant Alfred Peticolas and his comrades had to "trudge along day after day with nothing to eat save beans."[90]

From his post at Fort Craig, Colonel Benjamin Roberts wrote that the Texans "have abandoned their sick and wounded everywhere on their line of retreat, and are leaving in a state of demoralization and suffering that has few examples in any war."[91] One Northern sympathizer wrote to Secretary of State William Seward to share news of "the final expulsion of the Texans from our territory, demoralized, disheartened, and evidently much wiser than when a few months ago they entered our territory."[92] As some of the Confederates themselves admitted, Canby could have overtaken them and imprisoned the entire Sibley Brigade had he chosen to do so. But with his own animals worn out and supplies scarce, the Union commander left his vanquished foe to fall back with relatively little pressure, believing that the California Column, approaching from the west, would arrive in time to force Sibley's final surrender. As it turned out, the Californians—numbering nearly 3,000 men—arrived in the Rio Grande valley just after the Confederates slipped back into Texas, and Sibley avoided complete annihilation by a mere stroke of lucky timing.[93]

At the safe haven of Fort Bliss, Sibley sat down on May 4, 1862, to write his final report of the campaign, his despair perhaps equaling what fellow commander Robert E. Lee would feel a year later when defeat at Gettysburg turned back the Confederate invasion of the North. A long list of struggles marked Sibley's expedition. He ranked Indian attacks, illness, and insufficient food and supplies foremost among the reasons for failure. Sibley also complained that his government had neglected to provide funding to purchase articles of subsistence from New Mexico's people and that the reinforcements he requested in February never arrived. The battles at Valverde and Glorieta, along with several smaller engagements, sapped his fighting strength and strained his army's scant provisions. Finally, the numerical strength of Canby's forces, which included thousands of Hispanic volunteers and Army regulars equipped with plenty of supplies and ammunition, made it impossible for Sibley to sustain his mission. The crestfallen Confederate officer admitted, "Except for its political geographical position, the Territory of New Mexico is not worth a quarter of the blood and treasure expended in its conquest." In a stark reversal from the enthusiasm that he had shown Jefferson Davis the previous summer, Sibley concluded rather gloomily: "I cannot speak encouragingly for the future, my troops having manifested a dogged, irreconcilable detestation of the country and the people."[94] In a message to his beleaguered brigade, Sibley attempted to ease the sting of defeat, praising them for participating in "one of the brightest pages in the history of the Second American Revolution." Few, if any, of the starving and vanquished men bought his false declaration of glory.[95]

Casting aside the proclamation as pure nonsense, many of those under Sibley's command struck a different tone, blaming his poor leadership and heavy drinking for the campaign's failure; some wanted to see him court-martialed.[96] Sergeant Peticolas spoke for many of the men when confiding to his diary that "every man in the brigade" hated Sibley for his "poor generalship and cowardice."[97] Hal Hunter, a medical doctor who had accompanied the Rebels into New Mexico, remarked that "the flight of our army . . . will flush with shame the cheek of every Texian when he thinks of [this] unmanly move."[98] Between the commander's periodic inebriation—which seemed to occur at the worst possible moments—and the force's woefully inadequate provisions, the Confederate campaign had little hope for success from the outset. Seeking to exonerate his leader of full blame, Theophilus Noel placed partial responsibility on Baylor's preliminary invasion in the summer of 1861. This, Noel believed, had spurred Union forces to frantic defensive action and afforded them time to prepare for Sibley's arrival. Baylor's advance, he wrote, "was one conceived, concocted, and born . . . in wicked foolishness." Had Baylor and Sibley acted in concert, Noel wrote with the benefit of hindsight, their chances of victory would have drastically improved.[99]

Major Trevanion Teel, a commander of artillery in Sibley's army and a member of the KGC, waited twenty-five years before publishing his thoughts on the doomed Confederate offensive. "The objective aim and design of the campaign was the conquest of California," he wrote matter-of-factly, noting that Utah, Colorado, Arizona, and New Mexico would have provided significant space for the expansion of slavery. He also acknowledged the economic and strategic importance of a Confederacy spanning from Texas to California. Sibley himself had discussed these objectives with Teel at the outset of the campaign in 1861. According to the artillerist, his commander believed that Mexican officials would jump at the chance to sell land because of ongoing political upheavals, the French crisis involving Emperor Maximilian I, and a supposedly amicable relationship between President Benito Juárez and Confederate diplomats. Teel blamed the mission's failure on Sibley, criticizing him as an inept administrator and poor tactician. Had Baylor commanded the invasion instead of Sibley, Teel postulated, "the result might have been different."[100]

Sibley's inability to claim and hold the territory was just one of several major setbacks that the Confederacy faced in the early months of 1862. On February 25, just as the Texans finished burying their dead at Valverde, Union forces occupied Nashville—one of the few industrialized areas in the South—and would hold that city for the remainder of the war. Less than two weeks later Rebels suffered a resounding defeat at the Battle of Pea Ridge in Arkansas, and in April 1862 the U.S. Navy captured New Orleans, one of the most important southern commercial centers. In a matter of weeks the Confederacy surrendered two critical cities to permanent Union occupation, was defeated at a major battle in the trans-Mississippi theater, and lost all hope of capturing New Mexico and California. Had Sibley's fortunes been different, his success in the Southwest might have helped to allay some of Jefferson Davis's other wartime difficulties, but instead the failed New Mexico campaign merely compounded those losses.

Sibley's debacle in New Mexico did not deter other Confederate sympathizers from scheming to reinvade the territory and try the mission a second time. By November 1862 Baylor had begun plotting a new campaign, hoping to raise an army of 6,000 Texas troops for the project. However far-fetched the scheme, rumors of another Rebel attack sent the new department commander, Brigadier General James H. Carleton, into a fit of anxiety. Fresh memories of Colonel Reily's diplomatic mission to Chihuahua and Sonora earlier that year also continued to worry Unionists. Carleton believed that officials in Richmond were still planning either to purchase the northern Mexican states or to somehow prompt their secession from Mexico in order to join the Confederacy. "That there will be a strong effort made to this end, sooner or later, unless we are more successful in the east than we have recently been, is more than probable," Carleton explained to Governor John Evans of Colorado.[101]

With these fears in mind, Carleton asked Colonel Chivington to prepare his volunteers at Denver for a possible repeat of Glorieta, saying that he "had great faith in the fighting qualities of your Colorado boys."[102] The same day he ordered officers stationed in eastern New Mexico to send scouting parties down the Canadian and Pecos Rivers to monitor those approaches to the territory. Hoping to gain the help of local residents, he directed military personnel to inform citizens that they could keep any property captured from the Texans if only they would harass them and delay their march into New Mexico.[103] Local recruiters planned to enlist as many as ten new companies of volunteers, troops at Fort Union returned once more to the task of reinforcing that critical post, and Carleton appealed to Nuevomexicanos to "show their patriotism by volunteering their labor."[104] In southern New Mexico Colonel Joseph R. West received orders to purchase, confiscate, or destroy all of the grain and other provisions in the Mesilla Valley in order to prevent returning Rebels from feeding themselves.[105]

By 1863 Union officers in New Mexico fully expected another armed and bloody Confederate invasion.[106] After visiting El Paso in January and conferring with area residents, however, Carleton's fears subsided as he realized that no such attack was forthcoming.[107] Diplomatic interactions with Mexican statesmen also eased Carleton's concerns. Major David Fergusson, a Union agent sent to Chihuahua City, reported that Governor Terrazas seemed eager to cooperate with U.S. officials.[108] The following year, Governor Pesqueíra granted Carleton permission to transport supplies through the port at Guaymas, Sonora, a clear indication that sentiment south of the border had shifted in favor of the Union government as Confederate fortunes on eastern battlefields flickered and dimmed.[109] Both Carleton and Governor Connelly suggested to Secretary of State Seward that the United States attempt to purchase all of northern Mexico in order to crush any Confederate illusions of acquiring a transcontinental empire, although by that point in the war Richmond officials had abandoned any hope of wresting New Mexico from federal control, and indeed Rebel forces in the East had far more urgent matters to deal with after being defeated at Gettysburg in the summer of 1863.[110] Nevertheless, for the remainder of the Civil War Carleton continued to fear an alliance between Mexico and the Confederacy and to anxiously anticipate the independent actions of Texan bandits who might disrupt Union supply lines. He reminded field commanders to remain vigilant and send out scouts to watch for Confederate "desperadoes" and "mercenaries" who might cause trouble.[111]

Although Union forces prevailed over the most immediate threat of Confederate attack, another pressing issue remained. In New Mexico, contrary to most other Civil War theatres of combat, the federal army faced two distinct enemies, each with vastly different motivations and purposes. While the Sibley Brigade had hoped to conquer New Mexico, incorporate it into the Confederacy, and extend an empire to the Pacific Ocean, the territory's Indian tribes sought to protect the homelands that they had been fighting for centuries to retain. This dynamic, unique to Civil War–era New Mexico, put the military in a precarious position and forced the department to divide its resources, manpower, and attention in multiple directions. Confederate aggression and relentless Indian warfare would occupy most of the territory's federal troops for the duration of the Civil War.

In June 1861—at the very moment when Baylor's first wave of Texans marched into southern New Mexico—Colonel Canby grumbled that "our Indian relations are still unsatisfactory" and lamented that most tribes, aside from the Pueblos, "are openly at war with us."[112] In July, as troops at Fort Fillmore prepared for the approaching Rebels, Apaches struck less than three miles from the post, killing four civilians and driving away more than 2,000 sheep. Just days later a front-page headline in the *Mesilla Times* read: "Another Apache Massacre—The California Mail Destroyed—Seven Men Murdered."[113] Despite protests from local residents, Major Lynde refused to send any soldiers in pursuit because of the looming threat from Confederate invaders.[114] Canby acknowledged that the entire southern half of the territory had been "in a very disturbed condition in consequence of Indian hostilities" and admitted that Apache raiding in that quarter complicated his strategy for thwarting the Rebel onslaught.[115]

Matters only grew worse for Canby and his field commanders as the months wore on. In September a misunderstanding over a horse race between Navajos and Bluecoats at Fort Fauntleroy erupted in violence, claiming the lives of twelve Indians and all but ensuring open warfare between the two groups.[116] With Confederate troops in possession of the Mesilla Valley and Sibley's reinforcements marching westward from San Antonio, Canby anxiously informed War Department officials that "our relations with the Indians in this department are daily becoming more unsatisfactory." In central New Mexico Navajos had begun raiding in retaliation for the deadly horse racing incident. Mescalero and Chiricahua Apaches had also taken to the warpath, filling the power vacuum that resulted from the sudden abandonment of Forts Fillmore, Stanton, Buchanan, Breckenridge, and McLane. To the east of Santa Fe, Kiowas and Comanches added to the mayhem by conducting raids of their own.[117]

These developments were not limited to New Mexico. Throughout the West, according to acting Commissioner of Indian Affairs Charles Mix, the Civil War "afforded an extraordinary occasion for the development of the inherent war spirit among a large number of Indians."[118] Few Civil War commanders, in any theatre of combat, faced more threats from more directions than Colonel Canby in 1861. By December he reached the conclusion that "there is now no choice between [the Indians'] absolute extermination or their removal and colonization at points so remote from the settlements as to isolate them entirely from the inhabitants of the territory."[119] With New Mexico at risk of reverting to Confederate control, Canby feared the logistical hazards of a multifront war with numerous tribes while simultaneously defending against Sibley's invasion from the south. The responsibility for coping with those difficulties, however, would ultimately fall on the shoulders of another military officer.

Having been promoted to the rank of brigadier general, Canby was reassigned to the eastern theatre of combat. On September 18, 1862, the army replaced him as department commander with Brigadier General Carleton, who promptly instituted a program of total warfare against all southwestern tribes.[120] Few commanders in the annals of western history dedicated themselves so adamantly and adhered so rigidly to the doctrine of unlimited and relentless warfare against the Indians. A protégé of Colonel Edwin Sumner, Carleton came to New Mexico as a major with the U.S. Dragoons in the early 1850s. He led numerous campaigns against Jicarilla Apaches and Utes, and by the time he took charge of the territory's military department in 1862 he had a firm understanding of the issues at hand. Carleton attempted to mesh the militaristic ideology of Sumner with the humanitarian approaches of former civil officials like James S. Calhoun and William Carr Lane. He sought to achieve a degree of compatibility between two hardline mindsets on Indian affairs, trying to balance the inherently antithetical strategies of assimilation and extermination. The general saw brutality as a necessary precursor to any lasting peace on a reservation. Carleton reasoned that long-term amity could be reached only by first killing large numbers of tribe members, butchering their animals, and destroying all means of subsistence.[121]

With the Confederate troops already gone when he assumed command of the department, Carleton was free to direct most of his attention toward the defeat and removal of New Mexico's Indians. Multiple factors motivated his determination to bring hostilities with these groups to a permanent end, and the vigor with which Carleton pursued this objective demonstrated his commitment to eliminating any threat that American settlers might face. Nation-building considerations ranked foremost in Carleton's mind. His communications revealed an obsession with New Mexico's potential to yield vast amounts of gold. Indeed, these untapped gold deposits, Carleton believed, had motivated the Confederate invasion in the first place. Writing to General-in-Chief of the Army Henry Halleck in 1863, he described southwestern New Mexico as "one of the richest gold countries in the world" and called it "the new El Dorado," citing this fanciful vision as "one reason why the Rebels want, and why we may not permit them ever to have, a country evidently teeming with millions on millions of wealth." Realizing that most government and military officials continued to look disdainfully upon New Mexico, he reminded Halleck that California had not inspired much American interest either—until the discovery of gold there in 1848—and implored the general "not [to] despise New Mexico as a drain upon the general government. . . . The money will all come back again."[122]

The discovery of gold in 1863 near Prescott, capital of the newly established Arizona Territory, fueled Carleton's resolve, prompting him to request additional troops to facilitate mining operations and ward off Indian attacks.[123] "Providence has indeed blessed us," the giddy officer proclaimed in a letter to the adjutant general. "Now that we need money to pay the expenses of this terrible war, new mines of untold millions are found, and the gold lies here at our feet to be had by the mere picking of it up!" Hyperbolizing the discovery that was made in central Arizona—which never remotely equaled that of California fifteen years earlier— Carleton claimed that the gold at Prescott "can be weighed by the steel yards." A bit more accurately, he predicted that these events would draw waves of settlers into the region. Echoing the imperialistic rhetoric of southerners who had long eyed the region for territorial expansion, the Union officer prophesized that the presence of gold would finally induce the construction of a transcontinental railroad through northern New Mexico and Arizona, "thus uniting the two extremes of the country by bars of steel, until from the Atlantic to the Pacific, we become homogenous in interests as in blood." Carleton worked tirelessly to secure government funding and procure more troops to help dig the gold and protect settlers; at one point, he even mailed a specimen of Arizona gold to President Lincoln. The successful development of mining in the Southwest, he reasoned, would have a twofold importance for the federal government. First, it would provide revenue to fund the Civil War, and second, it would prevent the South from using those mineral resources for the same purpose, as indeed Sibley had hoped to do.[124]

Dreaming of a second great gold rush, Carleton wasted no time in seeking the destruction of the greatest obstacle standing in the path of American expansion. The mineral wealth of Arizona and New Mexico, he lamented, remained "sealed up by dangers from Indians, [and] should *now,* and permanently, be unsealed and open to development by the capitalist as well as by the enterprising poor."[125] With thousands of soldiers at his disposal, the commander saw no reason why the Indians could not be summarily and permanently defeated. Such a large contingent of well-armed troops, Carleton quipped, "ought not to be run over or hooted at by a few naked Indians armed with bows and arrows."[126] Within two weeks of assuming command, Carleton outlined a plan to crush the Navajos, Apaches, and Comanches into submission.[127] He even attempted to make Indian warfare a transnational effort, soliciting the aid of Mexican Minister of Foreign Affairs Sebastián Lerdo de Tejada in defeating Apache groups who used the international border to their strategic advantage in avoiding U.S. troops.[128]

Carleton started with the Mescalero Apaches in southeastern New Mexico, dispatching Colonel Kit Carson to Fort Stanton with orders to subdue the entire tribe and remove them to a new reservation on the Pecos River. In a confidential message, Carleton instructed that "all Indian men of that tribe are to be killed whenever and wherever you can find them." He stripped Carson of any power to negotiate an armistice, reiterating that "you are there to kill them wherever you can find them."[129] Just one month after Carson began his operations, a delegation of Mescalero chiefs rode to Santa Fe and sued for peace. With Governor Connelly sitting at his side, Carleton demanded unconditional surrender and insisted that the headmen settle their people at Bosque Redondo. Carson would remain in the field prosecuting total warfare, the department commander promised, until the tribe relocated to the reservation at Fort Sumner.[130]

While Carson and his volunteers conducted devastating field operations against the Mescaleros, other troops targeted the Chiricahua Apaches west of the Rio Grande. In January 1863 Carleton sent his soldiers to the Gila River headwaters in southwestern New Mexico, hoping to punish groups of Chiricahuas who had been raiding near the Piños Altos mines.[131] Soldiers at nearby Fort McLane took Chief Mangas Coloradas into custody after miners treacherously captured him under a flag of truce. As the venerable headman slept in the fort's prison cell on the night of January 19, 1863, the guardsmen repeatedly poked his bare feet with scorching bayonets heated in their campfire. When the chief cursed his tormentors, they shot him dead, decapitated him, and shipped his head to New York for scientific examination and display in a museum.[132] The execution struck a double blow to the Chiricahuas, for not only did the tribe lose its most respected leader, but the mutilation of his body meant that, according to Apache beliefs, their chief would enter the afterlife in that same desecrated condition.[133] After the murder, an unsympathetic Carleton bragged that his men had "already killed Mangas Coloradas" and more than sixty of his followers, and he promised to continue battling the Chiricahuas "until people can live in that country and explore and work the veins of precious metals which we know about there."[134] The assassination of their leader drove the Apaches to the warpath with greater resolve than ever before. By 1867 BIA personnel could only report that the tribe remained "in open hostility against the people and against the government . . . [and] scarcely a week or a day passes but someone is the victim of their savage ferocity."[135]

As Union soldiers carried out these multifront campaigns against the Apaches, another large detachment marched westward from Albuquerque to Ojo del Gallo, south of present-day Grants, where they constructed Fort Wingate as headquarters for campaigns against the Navajos. Commissioner of Indian Affairs William Dole expressed frustration with the tribe, writing that its members "have been a continual scourge upon the people of New Mexico" and mentioning their "innumerable depredations" as ample justification for definitive action. Dole realized, however, that "the idea of exterminating these Indians is at once so revolting and barbarous that it cannot for a moment be entertained."[136] As New Mexico's military commander, Carleton juggled these contradictory objectives by devising a harsh policy of destructive attrition that stopped short of tribal extermination. To eliminate any future threats—real or imagined—that the Indians might pose to American settlers, while simultaneously placating moralists who opposed genocidal tactics, Carleton decided to gather as many Navajos as possible and move them to the Bosque Redondo reservation, where the majority of Mescalero Apaches had been

Brigadier General James H. Carleton, c. 1860s.
Courtesy National Archives and Records Administration, Washington, D.C.

relocated. "You can feed them cheaper than you can fight them," he believed at that time.[137] Carleton recalled Kit Carson to headquarters and briefed him on the new mission.[138] The famous frontiersman would proceed to Fort Wingate, outfit and equip his troops, and march deep into Navajo homelands on a winter campaign, striking the tribe at precisely the time of year when they would be most vulnerable to attack. "The Navajo Indians have got to be whipped," Carleton instructed. Carson would deliver a stern message to every Navajo that he encountered: "Go to the Bosque Redondo, or we will pursue and destroy you."[139]

Governor Connelly voiced support for this effort to relocate Navajos along the Pecos River.[140] The reservation program, the governor believed, should be pursued with all Southwestern tribes, "peaceably if possible, forcibly if necessary." Connelly complained that the territory's Indians had "roamed lords of the soil over this extensive and valuable tract of country" for far too long. "The white man has an urgent necessity for the lands which have heretofore been thus dedicated to the unprofitable use of the savages," he concluded in his second annual gubernatorial address, stating that relocation of the Apaches, Comanches, Navajos, and Utes would ultimately benefit the tribes and was the only alternative to warfare and extinction. Sylvester Mowry, an Indian agent and mining speculator, was even more succinct.

The Apaches, he ranted, stood as "the great obstacle to the settlement of Arizona, to the transportation of the mails overland to the Pacific, and to the development of the immense mineral wealth of the Territory." For Connelly and Mowry, as for most civil officials, incarceration on remote reservations and continuous government oversight of Indian tribes seemed to be the only option aside from extermination.[141]

With the assistance of Ute scouts, U.S. troops and New Mexico volunteers infiltrated the daunting twin chasms of Canyon de Chelly and Canyon del Muerto in January 1864 to fulfill Carleton's orders. One detachment under Captain Albert Pheiffer traversed the gorges for four days, capturing nineteen Navajo women and children and killing three others.[142] In the months that followed, soldiers destroyed crops, slaughtered sheep, razed peach orchards, and burned wooden hogans to the ground. Leaving behind a path of destruction, Carson's soldiers swept through the Navajo strongholds with devastating ferocity.[143] The campaign of total warfare flushed the Indians from the impregnable canyons, demolished their means of subsistence, and left most of them with little alternative but to lay down their arms. Carson eventually held a council with three tribal spokespersons to demand unconditional surrender and removal.[144] The Navajo Long Walk had begun. Within one month over 3,000 Indians arrived at Bosque Redondo, and thousands more would follow.[145] From his desk in Santa Fe, Carleton praised Carson's "unparalleled success" where so many military commanders had previously failed. "I believe this will be the *last* Navajo war," Carleton concluded in February 1864. Governor Connelly declared April 7 a territorial holiday in celebration of "our happy deliverance from the evils with which we have been so long afflicted."[146]

Seeking to capitalize on their logistical momentum, Carleton's field commanders continued their relentless operations against the Navajos in hopes of interning the entire tribe at Bosque Redondo. Throughout 1864 soldiers marched through tribal strongholds in search of any families who had not yet surrendered. The destruction continued with each successive expedition. In August thirty-five New Mexico volunteers under Captain John Thompson captured Chief Barboncito and his followers, confiscated 1,500 sheep, and felled 4,150 peach trees as they patrolled Canyon de Chelly.[147] The Navajo campaigns claimed an untold number of Indian lives and destroyed nearly every mode of tribal sustenance, leaving some areas deserted and apocalyptic. By September nearly 8,000 Navajos were incarcerated at the Bosque Redondo reservation.[148] "The exodus of this people from the land of their fathers, is not only an interesting but a touching sight," Carleton scribbled in one report, commending the Navajos for what he called a heroic but futile defense of their homelands.[149] For Carleton and his cohorts, the project of Indian removal was off to an auspicious start.

Navajos remembered these proceedings with much less enthusiasm than the U.S. soldiers and commanders who participated in them. Few events, except perhaps the 1930s Navajo Livestock Reduction program, hold such a prominent place in the tribe's oral histories. Of Carson's expedition, Akinabh Burbank recounted that "it was in the fall, when it was about to snow, that a frightened feeling settled among the Navajo people—a feeling of danger from enemies."[150] Not long after this ominous portent, soldiers approached from the eastern horizon. "Word was sent out warning Diné that troops were on the move, destroying property, having no pity on anyone," Howard W. Gorman related.[151] Many Navajos either abandoned their homes and fields and fled the region or hid in caves hoping to elude capture. Those who did surrender, according to Curly Tso, "were herded . . . like bunches of wild cattle, and from there they were moved to Hwééldi [Bosque Redondo]." Many Navajos feared that the government was relocating the tribe for the purpose of "killing them by means of subjecting them to different diseases, starvation, and exposure."[152]

Carson's brutal campaigns took a toll, but the suffering grew worse once the Long Walk commenced. Gorman's grandparents "had to keep walking all the time, day after day," for nearly three weeks until reaching Bosque Redondo three hundred miles away.[153] "It was horrible the way they treated our people," Tso explained. "Some old handicapped people, and children who couldn't make the journey, were shot on the spot, and their bodies were left behind for crows and coyotes to eat."[154] According to Florence Charley, "Women carried their babies on their backs and walked all the way hundreds of miles. They didn't know where they were headed."[155] Traumatized families struggled to comprehend the underlying purposes of the unlimited warfare being directed at them.[156] Some blamed Mexicans and Utes—both traditional enemies with whom the Navajos had quarreled for many generations—for leading the army into Canyon de Chelly and helping to prosecute the removal. Others, like Dugal Tsosie Begay and Eli Gorman, thought that their own Navajo ancestors bore some responsibility. Begay believed that "it was our own fault that we were rounded up and taken to Fort Sumner," while Gorman supposed that "the U.S. government was getting tired of the situation and looked at the Navajos as real potential trouble-makers."[157]

The trauma of the Long Walk paled in comparison to the ordeal that the Navajos would face over the next four years at Hwééldi. From the onset the government failed to appreciate the humanitarian difficulties and astronomical monetary costs entailed in keeping over 8,000 hungry people on an overcrowded reservation. Bosque Redondo sat in a remote area where insufficient food could be grown and where meat and grain had to be shipped overland at great cost, which compounded those logistical problems. "After several years at Fort Sumner, life became very hard for the Navajos," Gorman explained. "There was no wood for fires; there weren't enough seeds to grow their crops, which hardly could grow in the poor ground, anyway; and insects ate what did come up. The White Man used to kill cattle for [the Navajos], but there was not enough meat to go around, just a small piece for each person."[158]

As the first Navajos arrived at Fort Sumner in October 1864, Superintendent of Indian Affairs Michael Steck—an outspoken opponent of Carleton's reservation plan—foresaw the predicament that lay ahead. "I have, from the commencement of the scheme to remove the tribe from their own country, protested against it," he grumbled. The military's plan to detain so many Indians at such a poor location would be a failure unless the War Department dispatched a proportional number of troops to monitor the reservation. Steck also understood that, because of the number of Navajos living there, Bosque Redondo would require "a larger sum of money appropriated than I believe Congress will be willing to appropriate for one tribe of Indians."[159] Whether he appreciated these dilemmas or not, Carleton remained deeply committed to the project. When Steck began pressuring federal administrators to abandon the experiment and send the tribe back to their homelands, Carleton furiously responded that "the Navajos should never leave the Bosque, and never shall if I can prevent it."[160]

As the project commenced Carleton believed that "there is no reason why [the Navajos] will not be the most happy and prosperous and well-provided-for Indians in the United States."[161] He even arranged for "sisters and lay brothers" to provide their pietistic services, thinking that only a proper Christian education could civilize the young generation and ensure a permanent end to the Navajo wars. Foreshadowing Richard Henry Pratt's Indian boarding school experiment at Carlisle, Pennsylvania, Carleton asked Secretary of the Interior John Usher for approval to build a school and dormitories near Fort Sumner. Missionaries could then begin instructing approximately 3,000 Navajo children in reading, writing, and "the truths of Christianity."[162] To occupy the parents while boys and girls attained their enlightenment, Carleton proposed the construction of a gristmill so that Navajos could produce their own flour and feed. The Indians would thereby learn the value of hard work and become accustomed to the stationary and productive lifestyle that Americans wished them to espouse.[163] But reality quickly set in, and the once-enthusiastic Carleton was forced to reckon with Bosque Redondo's many shortcomings. No other issue demanded as much public attention in New Mexico as the controversy surrounding the reservation at Fort Sumner. After arriving in

Navajos under armed guard at the Bosque Redondo Reservation.
Courtesy Palace of the Governors Photo Archives,
New Mexico History Museum/DCA, Santa Fe (negative no. 028534).

Santa Fe in 1865, Interior Department agent Julius Graves found "the Indian question the all absorbing topic of conversation among the entire community," noting
that Carleton's experiment on the Pecos River had become the subject of intense
disagreement throughout the territory.[164]

With so many Navajos having surrendered and the military operations against
them winding down, Carleton confidently assumed that "the great drain upon the
treasury, which has been kept up by these Indian Wars," would come to an end.[165]
As all of this occurred, however, the nation remained embroiled in the Civil War
and federal leaders had far more pressing concerns than the disposition of an Indian
tribe in a remote territory. At first Congress humored Carleton and went along with
his plan, earmarking $100,000 in funding for the reservation in 1864. Hwééldi might
have remained fiscally sustainable if this level of appropriations had sufficed. That
same year, however, the 3,000-acre corn crop at Fort Sumner failed due to a worm
infestation. As maggots feasted on the Navajos' maize, early frosts and hail storms
destroyed fields throughout northern New Mexico, and the entire territory descended
into hunger and hardship. The government would have to feed the Indians, but with
demand for food far outstripping local supply, officials had to obtain those provisions
elsewhere. After just four months of operation, the cost to purchase and import
grain and beef rations reached $400,000, with no end to the expenditures in sight.[166]

In an alarming projection, Superintendent Steck estimated that the recurring annual cost of providing food to all Navajos at the reservation would exceed $1.2 million, while others placed this estimate significantly higher. By 1866 the expense of feeding nearly 9,000 Indians at Fort Sumner had reached $70,000 per month, leading General William T. Sherman to remark nervously that War Department coffers could not sustain such disbursements without additional congressional appropriations. If the entire tribe of 12,000–14,000 souls reached Bosque Redondo—and Carleton insisted that this must happen—Steck predicted that the yearly expense would surpass $2.6 million.[167] Referring specifically to New Mexico, the commissioner of Indian affairs reported that "the care and control of the tribes of this superintendency is enormously expensive to the government."[168]

As Carleton continued to request massive appropriations to keep Bosque Redondo running, he pushed his superiors beyond their limit. In a barrage of letters to Washington, D.C., he asked for money to buy two million pounds of bread, thousands of agricultural implements like hoes and spades, and 4,000 beef cattle. He also wanted a recurring annuity of $150,000 for clothing, along with extra funds to pay the salaries of Indian agents, subagents, bookkeepers, supervisors, and other administrators. Meanwhile, the military department faced the impending discharge of Union troops whose terms of enlistment were due to expire. Fearing that the territory might fall into a "defenseless condition" and that Navajos and Mescaleros would be left unguarded at Fort Sumner, Carleton begged the adjutant general to either extend soldier enlistments or send reinforcements.[169] Politicians cringed at the costs of sustaining Carleton's project and believed that they could find more useful ways to spend treasury money.[170] Carleton had drastically underestimated the expense of relocating the Navajos, and to compensate for that oversight he was asking Congress for a king's ransom. It became far more than federal bureaucrats would—or even could—commit to a single Indian tribe, especially with the Civil War still raging. By 1865 Indian Department personnel had begun pressuring the secretary of the interior to abandon the experiment, recommending that the Navajos be returned to a reservation "in their own country" to reduce annual appropriations and promote "good policy, economy, and humanity."[171] Once again, New Mexico was proving to be very costly for the United States government to manage.

Although Carleton's oversight was eliminated when BIA officials assumed jurisdiction over the reservation in 1867, little was done to allay the problems at Fort Sumner. Superintendent A. B. Norton laid the matter bluntly before the commissioner of Indian affairs. He explained that Navajos relied on mesquite roots for firewood, and they had to walk at least twenty-four miles round-trip to procure the precious commodity. Alkaline water in the Pecos valley sapped the soil's fertility, and an estimated one-quarter of the Indians suffered ailments from drinking the brackish liquid.[172] The hospital at Fort Sumner had been built to accommodate twenty patients, but within one year the post surgeon was turning away many of the approximately four hundred Navajos seeking treatment for the multifarious illnesses that afflicted them. Each month—especially during the bleak winters when food and forage were scarce—dozens of Navajos died.[173] "What a beautiful selection this is for a reservation," Norton wrote with poignant satire. "It has cost the government millions of dollars . . . as I verily believe, from first to last, over $10,000,000." He pointed out that no "white man" would ever live contentedly under such deplorable conditions and demanded that the tribe be returned to their homelands. "The idea of keeping these wild brutes of the forest, if you call them not human beings, subjected to such torture is a disgrace to the age we live in and to the government we support," Norton concluded.[174]

By the time General Sherman and his team of peace commissioners arrived in May 1868, hundreds of Indians had already perished from starvation and sickness. "At Fort Sumner our people spent four years of a miserable life," Navajo elder Yasdesbah Silversmith said in a remarkably measured understatement. "Send us back to Canyon de Chelly!" many Indians cried out as Sherman's officers inspected the woebegone reservation.[175] In light of the extreme costs that the project continued to incur, the U.S. government was finally willing to entertain the possibility of abandoning Bosque Redondo.[176] In reference to the expensive reservation, the general once quipped that it would be cheaper to room and board the entire tribe at the Fifth Avenue Hotel in New York City.[177] With this and other considerations in mind, Sherman helped to arrange the Navajo Treaty of June 1, 1868—the last treaty ratified between the federal government and an Indian tribe—and sent the Diné home by establishing a permanent reservation centered within their four sacred peaks.[178] One relieved Indian agent wrote three months later that the Navajos "are now located upon a reservation in their old country . . . and are living peaceably, happy, and contented."[179] Years of gut-wrenching hardship for the Indians and dizzying expenditures for the federal government had come to an end.

While most of the Navajo tribe sat in confinement at Bosque Redondo, Kit Carson led a third Indian campaign targeting Southern Plains tribes whose recent depredations in the Texas panhandle had roused the military's ire, an anger bolstered by suspicions that they had aided Confederates by providing information on Union troop movements.[180] Carleton initially hoped to send 2,000 soldiers against the Comanches and Kiowas, proposing that the two tribes be "so roughly handled as to make them refrain from these depredations for years to come."[181] Carson had become Carleton's foremost agent of conquest, but his November 1864 encounter with a combined force of Kiowas and Comanches at the Adobe Walls trading post would have a noticeably different outcome than the Mescalero and Navajo campaigns that he previously commanded.[182] Ongoing armed conflicts, coupled with devastating smallpox epidemics during the Civil War years, had cut the Comanche population to just 5,000 souls by the time Carson took the field.[183] Still, the tribe was a formidable fighting force, especially when allied with their Kiowa neighbors.

After a brief rendezvous at Fort Bascom, 335 California cavalrymen and New Mexico volunteers took the field alongside 75 Ute and Jicarilla Apache auxiliaries, hoping to strike the Indians during the difficult winter months. The colonel led his column two hundred miles down the Canadian River before discovering, on the morning of November 25, an Indian village upstream from Adobe Walls. The soldiers impulsively attacked but met staunch resistance. Indian warriors "made several severe charges" before the devastating fire of two mountain howitzers drove them away. After a brief interlude during which a remarkably calm Carson ordered his men to eat breakfast, a reinforced contingent of "at least 1,000 warriors" surrounded the soldiers inside the adobe compound, and their situation suddenly became dire. "The Indians charged so repeatedly and with such desperation that for some time I had serious doubts for the safety" of the troops, Carson reported. Incessant cannon fire ultimately repulsed the onslaught, and troops destroyed an Indian village of 150 lodges before retreating toward safer ground. The campaign suffered two soldiers killed and ten wounded, while Kiowa and Comanche forces lost an estimated sixty men. "I must say they acted with more daring and bravery than I have ever before witnessed," Carson later admitted. He claimed the poor condition of his horses and insufficient ammunition prevented pursuit of the Indians after his troops had torched their village.[184] Taking Carson for his word, Carleton heaped lavish praise on his trusted Indian fighter, calling the engagement at Adobe Walls a "brilliant affair."[185]

A more accurate assessment of the battle emerged in a report that Carson submitted after returning to Fort Bascom. The colonel suggested that a second expedition be outfitted and dispatched, but he implicitly admitted failure by insisting that seven hundred reinforcements and four additional cannons be sent to buttress his manpower. At least one thousand troops would be needed, Carson believed, if he was to have any hope of defeating the Kiowas and Comanches. He also demanded that authorities suppress the Comanchero trade before sending him back afield, pointing out that most of the guns, ammunition, and powder that the Indians used against him had been obtained from Nuevomexicanos bearing passes from Superintendent Steck.[186] The fact that a second expedition was needed, coupled with a request that his force be quadrupled in size, indicated the true extent to which he had vanquished his enemy. The soldiers under Carson's command had in fact been overwhelmed during the confrontation at Adobe Walls, and only the use of heavy artillery had prevented a disaster that might have rivaled that of Custer's Seventh Cavalry at Little Bighorn twelve years later. When Major Edward Bergmann parleyed with several Indian leaders in March 1865, he had orders from Carleton to relay a potent message: "Tell the Comanche chiefs," the department commander instructed him, "that if they attack our trains [on the Santa Fe Trail] we will make a war upon them which they will always remember."[187] Another decade would pass, however, before the Comanches suffered their final military defeats at the Second Battle of Adobe Walls and Palo Duro Canyon in 1874.[188]

As the Civil War drew to a close in March 1865, Congress appointed a special commission to investigate Indian affairs. The voluminous testimony contained in the Doolittle Report contradicted the claims of military officers and BIA agents that efforts to subdue Indian groups had summarily failed. Instead, the evidence unmasked the tremendous toll that decades of warfare had taken on the continent's tribes. With the exception of those living in Indian Territory, all other indigenous groups were "rapidly decreasing in numbers," the commissioners explained, noting that a combination of disease, intemperance, warfare, and immigration had propagated rapid demographic decline.[189] Despite their staunch resistance to conquest and settlement, New Mexico's Indians fell gradually into that same cycle, as American policy initiatives contributed to the battlefield losses that Southwestern tribes sustained during the Civil War era. Although his prosecution of total warfare and implementation of martial law made him one of the most hated men of his time, Carleton accomplished more than any other official in the effort to secure New Mexico for American expansion. When the Civil War ended, the territory remained firmly under Union control, and regional tribes had suffered disastrous defeats that forever altered Anglo-Indian relations, making Carleton one of the most influential agents of empire that New Mexico had ever known.

Just as federal forces asserted an unprecedented aura of authority over territorial Indian affairs, so too did they retain control of New Mexico in the face of Confederate onslaughts. In 1861 Henry Hopkins Sibley had commanded the second large army to invade the region within fifteen years. In terms of imperialistic objectives, military planning, and the number of troops involved, the Confederate expedition bore striking similarities to that of Stephen Watts Kearny in 1846. In execution, however, Kearny and Sibley could hardly have achieved more dichotomous results. In 1846 Missouri volunteers and U.S. dragoons met an untrained, poorly equipped Mexican force under Manuel Armijo, an inept commander who surrendered Santa Fe without resistance. In 1861 the Rebels faced a much more formidable force in Canby's Union regulars and Hispanic volunteers. The Confederate defeat had been a cooperative effort in which Anglos and Hispanos joined for the first time in unified military action against a common enemy. In the face of determined opposition, Sibley failed where Kearny had succeeded, and the Confederate dream of transcontinental empire dissolved in the early months of 1862.

In 1861, as in 1846, New Mexico fell into the sights of imaginative American expansionists who saw the region as a pivotal component of their Manifest Destiny schemes. When the Army of the West approached in August 1846, three decades of merchant capitalism and American trade over the Santa Fe Trail had primed the region for conquest, making Kearny's mission the formal consummation of a long process of indirect geopolitical incorporation. By the time Sibley's Army of New Mexico marched northward from El Paso in the winter of 1861–62, however, social and political conditions had shifted dramatically throughout the Southwest. Fifteen years under the banner of U.S. sovereignty had transformed many Hispanics into loyal American citizens, and thousands of them answered the call to arms at the onset of the Civil War. Even those New Mexicans who did not shoulder a rifle helped to oppose the invasion by refusing to assist the Texans or provide them with food and supplies. Within one year of the shelling of Fort Sumter in South Carolina, Confederate leaders came to realize that Kearny's feat could not be duplicated. Their reliance on the conquest of New Mexico as a means toward an imperial end meant that the Confederacy's odds of winning independence diminished as Sibley's men retreated into Texas. Kearny's successful mission during the Mexican-American War had asserted New Mexico's geopolitical importance to the growing U.S. republic, and Sibley's failed expedition during the Civil War reaffirmed the region's significance to the idea of a transcontinental empire.[190]

CONCLUSION

N ever one to mince words, General William T. Sherman suggested in 1869 that
the federal government do away with the southwestern territories. The cost of
maintaining a standing army in that region was "out of all proportion to its value as
part of the public domain," he remarked, wisecracking that "we had one war with
Mexico to take Arizona, and we should have another to make her take it back."[1]
Despite this influential officer's wishes, the effort to return "undesirable" land to
Mexico never materialized beyond the daydreams of disenchanted men burdened
with the oversight of government affairs in the area. The Desert Southwest was
simply too important to an expansionist nation, and the passage of time would
continue to meld New Mexico's people and political institutions more tightly to
the American republic. Although merchants, soldiers, railroad capitalists, sectional
ideologues, and other newcomers to New Mexico succeeded in drawing the territory
into the United States prior to the Civil War, their efforts did not immediately
Americanize the Hispanic and Indian Southwest. The ensuing decades would be
fraught with additional struggles, as New Mexicans pursued statehood and economic
dynamism while the army continued to wage war on nomadic tribes.

Merchant capitalism, military occupation, political incorporation, economic
expansion, slavery debates, and the fighting that resulted from Southern secession
all exerted strong American influences over New Mexico in the decades after 1821.
Each of these events and processes permanently altered the territory's political,
economic, social, and cultural institutions as it was absorbed into the United States.

Concurrently, however, New Mexico had a reciprocal impact on its adoptive country and played a prominent role in the sectional and secession crises of the mid-nineteenth century. The area's geographic importance as a connection between Texas and California caused the North and South to vie for supremacy over these borderlands. As Americans of different ideological and political persuasions grappled over the future of New Mexico in terms of slavery and the railroad, the territory became enthralled in the sectional debates that tore the nation asunder and drove it into the Civil War.

The Southwest's role in bringing about the nation's second democratic revolution has long been underappreciated. Many events—Texas annexation, the Mexican-American War, the Wilmot Proviso, California statehood, the release of Harriet Beecher Stowe's *Uncle Tom's Cabin,* the Pacific Railroad Surveys, Bleeding Kansas, the Dred Scott case, John Brown's raid on Harper's Ferry, Southern filibustering in Latin America, radical abolitionism and the publication of slave narratives, the breakdown of the Second Party System and the demise of the Whig Party, the rise of the Republican Party and subsequent election of Abraham Lincoln—have been credited with bringing about Southern secession. What has received less attention, however, is the important role that New Mexico played in the nation's sectional conundrum.

For many years leading up to the Civil War, Americans continued to view the Hispanic Southwest as pivotal to their larger nation-building interests despite the extreme costs and hardships entailed in retaining that territory. The large armed force that Kearny led into Santa Fe in 1846, coupled with the remarkable extent to which the federal government dedicated financial resources and military manpower to the region, indicated the nation's intent to hold New Mexico permanently. Tense congressional debates over slavery in the Southwest and the ongoing competition for the railway route in the 1850s demonstrated that Americans not only wanted physical possession of the region but also meant to assert their ideologies and institutions over its people. The bloody contest for control of New Mexico at the outset of the Civil War reaffirmed this strong dedication, as northerners and southerners fought hard to make the territory their own. Both the Union and the Confederacy sought complete hegemony over the Southwest, recognizing its broader importance to the achievement of a coast-to-coast empire. For more than four decades that quest proved more difficult than most American expansionists anticipated, as New Mexico—with its ethnically and culturally diverse population, unforgiving terrain, and geographic isolation—did not lend itself easily to outside control. But despite the associated burdens and costs, the United States and its agents of conquest worked assiduously to realize an outcome favorable to the growing nineteenth-century American nation.

Despite its frequent marginalization (and even condemnation by historical observers), New Mexico played an important role in the sweeping nineteenth-century transformations of American capitalism and democracy. As the United States forged a continental empire, the Southwest borderlands served as a backdrop for economic and demographic expansion and provided a geographic thoroughfare to California and the Pacific coast. New Mexico's southerly location along an international border, its adjacency to both slaveholding Texas and free-soil California, and its predominantly Hispanic and Indian population ensured that the territory would be a politically contentious possession for the American nation. Only after the Civil War did those struggles subside, allowing New Mexico to shed its status as a pawn in the sectional difficulties that defined the country at midcentury. But from 1821 through the immediate postwar years the Southwest proved to be a vexing political and financial concern for the growing United States as its leaders attempted to assert control over the region's land and people in advancement of prevailing expansionist ideology. The fact that many Americans, from North and South alike, exerted so much attention toward the possession and retention of New Mexico demonstrates the territory's overarching importance to national expansion during the era of Manifest Destiny.

Notes

Introduction

1. "Message of William Carr Lane to the Legislative Assembly," Dec. 7, 1852, New Mexico State Records Center and Archives, Territorial Archives of New Mexico (hereafter cited as NMSRCA, TA), Roll 98. For a biographical sketch of Lane, see Calvin Horn, *New Mexico's Troubled Years: The Story of the Early Territorial Governors* (Albuquerque: Horn & Wallace, 1963), 37–49.

2. A. B. Dyer to Col. Talcott, Feb. 17, 1847, NMSRCA, Misc. Letters and Diaries, Box 1, File 5.

3. Edward K. Eckert and Nicholas J. Amato, eds., *Ten Years in the Saddle: The Memoir of William Woods Averell* (San Rafael, CA: Presidio, 1978), 113. A *jacal* was a small residential hut made of mud and sticks.

4. Report of William T. Sherman, Nov. 5, 1866, in *1866 Annual Report of the Secretary of War*, 39th Cong., 2nd Sess., Senate Exec. Doc. No. 1, p. 22. On anti-Hispanic stereotypes, see Raymund A. Paredes, "The Mexican Image in American Travel Literature, 1831–1869," *New Mexico Historical Review* 52 (Jan. 1977): 5–29; David J. Weber, "'Scarce more than apes': Historical Roots of Anglo-American Stereotypes of Mexicans," in *New Spain's Far Northern Frontier: Essays on Spain in the American West, 1540–1821*, ed. David J. Weber (Albuquerque: University of New Mexico Press, 1979), 293–307.

5. "Message of William Carr Lane to the Legislative Assembly," Dec. 7, 1852, NMSRCA, TA, Roll 98.

6. Dr. A. Wislizenus, *Memoir of a Tour to Northern Mexico, Connected with Col. Doniphan's Expedition, in 1846 and 1847* (Washington, D.C.: Tippin & Streeper, 1848), 85–86.

7. Ross Calvin, ed., *Lieutenant Emory Reports: Notes of a Military Reconnaissance* (Albuquerque: University of New Mexico Press, 1951), 61; "Report of Thomas S. Jesup," Oct. 8,

1847, in "Documents from War Department," 30th Cong., 1st Sess., House Exec. Doc. 1, pp. 233–34. On New Mexico's climate and resources, see "Report of Lieut. J. W. Abert of his Examination of New Mexico in the years 1846–47," in "Report of the Secretary of War," Feb. 10, 1848, 30th Cong., 1st Sess., Senate Exec. Doc. 23, p. 1.

8. *1853 Annual Report of the Secretary of War*, 33rd Cong., 1st Sess., Senate Exec. Doc. No. 1, pp. 24–25; *1855 Annual Report of the Secretary of War*, 34th Cong., 1st Sess., Senate Exec. Doc. No. 1, pp. 15–16; "Necessity of a Military Road to the Pacific," *DeBow's Review*, Nov. 1859, pp. 603–5; "Memorial of a Committee Appointed at a Railroad Convention," Dec. 27, 1852, 32nd Cong., 2nd Sess., Senate Misc. Doc. No. 5, p. 3. See also Alvin M. Josephy Jr., *The Civil War in the American West* (New York: Knopf, 1991), 11–12.

9. "Message from the President of the United States," Dec. 5, 1848, 30th Cong., 2nd Sess., House Exec. Doc. No. 1, pp. 9, 13–15.

10. "Message of the President of the United States, New Mexico and California," July 24, 1848, 30th Cong., 1st Sess., House Exec. Doc. 70, pp. 6–7; James Buchanan to William V. Vorhies, Oct. 7, 1848, "Correspondence Relating to Civil Government in California and New Mexico," 30th Cong., 1st Sess., House Exec. Doc. 1, p. 47; James Madison Cutts, *The Conquest of California and New Mexico, by the Forces of the United States, in the Years 1846 and 1847* (Philadelphia: Carey & Hart, 1847), 3.

11. J. D. B. DeBow, "How California Progresses," in *DeBow's Review*, Dec. 1857, pp. 640–44, quotation on 640; John F. Kvach, *DeBow's Review: The Antebellum Vision of a New South* (Lexington: University Press of Kentucky, 2013), 62. On DeBow generally, see ibid., 1–10.

12. On American expansion into Texas, see Andrew J. Torget, *Seeds of Empire: Cotton, Slavery, and the Transformation of the Texas Borderlands, 1800–1850* (Chapel Hill: University of North Carolina Press, 2015), 9–14.

13. Thomas Hart Benton, *Speech of Mr. Benton, of Missouri, on the Oregon Question: Delivered in the Senate of the United States, May 22, 25, & 28, 1846* (Washington, D.C.: Blair & Rives, 1846); "New Year's Address," *Santa Fe Republican*, Jan. 1, 1848. On Manifest Destiny, see Albert K. Weinberg, *Manifest Destiny: A Study of Nationalist Expansionism in American History* (Baltimore: Johns Hopkins University Press, 1935); Gene M. Brack, *Mexico Views Manifest Destiny, 1821–1846: An Essay on the Origins of the Mexican War* (Albuquerque: University of New Mexico Press, 1975); Reginald Horsman, *Race and Manifest Destiny: The Origins of American Racial Anglo-Saxonism* (Cambridge, MA: Harvard University Press, 1981); Thomas R. Hietala, *Manifest Design: Anxious Aggrandizement in Late Jacksonian America* (Ithaca, NY: Cornell University Press, 1985), 173–214; Richard Kluger, *Seizing Destiny: How America Grew from Sea to Shining Sea* (New York: Knopf, 2007); Amy S. Greenberg, *A Wicked War: Polk, Clay, Lincoln, and the 1846 U.S. Invasion of Mexico* (New York: Knopf, 2012). There has been some scholarly dispute on the origins of the phrase "Manifest Destiny." See Daniel Walker Howe, *What Hath God Wrought: The Transformation of America, 1815–1848* (New York: Oxford University Press, 2007), 703.

14. "Message from the President of the United States," March 24, 1846, 29th Cong., 1st Sess., Senate Doc. No. 248; Wislizenus, *Memoir of a Tour to Northern Mexico*, 84–85; Cutts, *Conquest of California and New Mexico*, 16, 23.

15. See Steven Hahn, "The Widest Implications of Disorienting the Civil War Era," in *Civil War Wests: Testing the Limits of the United States*, eds. Adam Arenson and Andrew R. Graybill (Berkeley: University of California Press, 2014), 271. On the impact of these processes in early America, see Howe, *What Hath God Wrought*.

16. Walter Johnson, *River of Dark Dreams: Slavery and Empire in the Cotton Kingdom* (Cambridge, MA: The Belknap Press of Harvard University Press, 2013), 366–94; Calvin Schermerhorn, *The Business of Slavery and the Rise of American Capitalism, 1815–1860* (New Haven, CT: Yale University Press, 2015), 229–32. See also Robert E. May, *Manifest Destiny's Underworld: Filibustering in Antebellum America* (Chapel Hill: University of North Carolina Press, 2002).

17. *1857 Annual Report of the Secretary of War*, 35th Cong., 1st Sess., Senate Exec. Doc. No. 11, pp. 6–9; *1858 Annual Report of the Secretary of War*, 35th Cong., 2nd Sess., Senate Exec. Doc. No. 1, p. 7. On the Mormon conflict, see David L. Bigler and Will Bagley, *The Mormon Rebellion: America's First Civil War, 1857–1858* (Norman: University of Oklahoma Press, 2011); Durwood Ball, *Army Regulars on the Western Frontier, 1848–1861* (Norman: University of Oklahoma Press, 2001), 153–71.

18. Richard White, *Railroaded: The Transcontinentals and the Making of Modern America* (New York: Norton, 2011), 1–38; Howard R. Lamar, *The Far Southwest, 1846–1912: A Territorial History* (Albuquerque: University of New Mexico Press, 2000), 265–306.

19. James F. Brooks, *Captives and Cousins: Slavery, Kinship, and Community in the Southwest Borderlands* (Chapel Hill: University of North Carolina Press, 2002); William S. Kiser, "'A charming name for a species of slavery': Political Debate over Debt Peonage in the Southwest, 1840s–1860s," *Western Historical Quarterly* 45, no. 2 (Summer 2014): 169–89; William S. Kiser, *Borderlands of Slavery: The Struggle over Captivity and Peonage in the American Southwest* (Philadelphia: University of Pennsylvania Press, 2017).

20. David M. Potter, *The Impending Crisis, 1848–1861* (New York: Harper & Row, 1973); Michael F. Holt, *The Political Crisis of the 1850s* (New York: Norton, 1978).

21. William R. Brock, *Parties and Political Conscience: American Dilemmas, 1840–1850* (Millwood, NY: KTO Press, 1979); Christopher Childers, *The Failure of Popular Sovereignty: Slavery, Manifest Destiny, and the Radicalization of Southern Politics* (Lawrence: University Press of Kansas, 2012); William H. Goetzmann, *Army Exploration in the American West, 1803–1863* (Lincoln: University of Nebraska Press, 1979), 209–340.

22. Johnson, *River of Dark Dreams*; Edward E. Baptist, *The Half Has Never Been Told: Slavery and the Making of American Capitalism* (New York: Basic Books, 2014); Schermerhorn, *Business of Slavery*.

23. William G. Robbins, *Colony and Empire: The Capitalist Transformation of the American West* (Lawrence: University Press of Kansas, 1994); Stephen G. Hyslop, *Bound for Santa Fe: The Road to New Mexico and the American Conquest, 1806–1848* (Norman: University of Oklahoma Press, 2002).

24. Megan Kate Nelson, "Death in the Distance: Confederate Manifest Destiny and the Campaign for New Mexico, 1861–1862," in Arenson and Graybill, *Civil War Wests*, 36.

25. Loomis M. Ganaway, *New Mexico and the Sectional Controversy, 1846–1861* (Albuquerque: University of New Mexico Press, 1944); Robert W. Larson, *New Mexico's Quest for*

Statehood, 1846–1912 (Albuquerque: University of New Mexico Press, 1968); Alvin
R. Sunseri, *Seeds of Discord: New Mexico in the Aftermath of the American Conquest,
1846–1861* (Chicago: Nelson-Hall, 1979); Mark J. Stegmaier, *Texas, New Mexico, and
the Compromise of 1850: Boundary Dispute and Sectional Crisis* (Kent, OH: Kent State
University Press, 1996); Lamar, *The Far Southwest.*

26. Jack D. Rittenhouse, *The Constitution of the State of New Mexico, 1850* (Santa Fe: Stagecoach, 1965); Mark Stegmaier, "A Law that Would Make Caligula Blush? New Mexico
Territory's Unique Slave Code, 1859–1861," *New Mexico Historical Review* 87 (Spring
2012): 209–42; Goetzmann, *Army Exploration in the American West;* Josephy, *Civil War
in the American West,* 11–30; Donald S. Frazier, *Blood and Treasure: Confederate Empire
in the Southwest* (College Station: Texas A&M University Press, 1995), 13.

27. David J. Weber, *The Mexican Frontier, 1821–1846: The American Southwest under Mexico*
(Albuquerque: University of New Mexico Press, 1982); David Montejano, *Anglos and
Mexicans in the Making of Texas, 1836–1986* (Austin: University of Texas Press, 1987);
Andrés Reséndez, *Changing National Identities at the Frontier: Texas and New Mexico,
1800–1850* (New York: Cambridge University Press, 2005).

28. See Reséndez, *Changing National Identities,* 93–123.

29. Averam B. Bender, *The March of Empire: Frontier Defense in the Southwest, 1848–1860*
(Lawrence: University of Kansas Press, 1952); William S. Keleher, *Turmoil in New
Mexico, 1846–1868* (Santa Fe: Rydal Press, 1952); Robert M. Utley, *Frontiersmen in Blue:
The United States Army and the Indian, 1848–1865* (New York: MacMillan, 1967); Frank
McNitt, *Navajo Wars: Military Campaigns, Slave Raids, and Reprisals* (Albuquerque:
University of New Mexico Press, 1972); Robert W. Frazer, *Forts and Supplies: The Role
of the Army in the Economy of the Southwest, 1846–1861* (Albuquerque: University of New
Mexico Press, 1983); Ball, *Army Regulars on the Western Frontier;* James M. McCaffrey,
Army of Manifest Destiny: The American Soldier in the Mexican War, 1846–1848 (New
York: New York University Press, 1992); Robert Wooster, *The American Military Frontiers:
The United States Army in the West, 1783–1900* (Albuquerque: University of New Mexico
Press, 2009); William S. Kiser, *Dragoons in Apacheland: Conquest and Resistance in
Southern New Mexico, 1846–1861* (Norman: University of Oklahoma Press, 2012); Jerry D.
Thompson, *A Civil War History of the New Mexico Volunteers and Militia* (Albuquerque:
University of New Mexico Press, 2015).

30. Charles Montgomery, *The Spanish Redemption: Heritage, Power, and Loss on New Mexico's
Upper Rio Grande* (Berkeley: University of California Press, 2002), 39, 52–53, quotations
on 39.

Chapter 1

1. Elliott Coues, ed., *The Expeditions of Zebulon Montgomery Pike,* vol. 2 (1895; reprint,
New York: Dover, 1987), 608–9; Zebulon M. Pike to Nemesio Salcedo, April 4, 1807, in
Donald Jackson, ed., *The Journals of Zebulon Montgomery Pike, with Letters and Related
Documents* (Norman: University of Oklahoma Press, 1966), 2:173–78; Memorandum
of Joaquín del Real Alencaster, April 10, 1807, ibid., 2:193–95. See also Robert Glass

Cleland, *This Reckless Breed of Men: The Trappers and Fur Traders of the Southwest* (New York: Knopf, 1950), 121–22; Max L. Moorhead, *New Mexico's Royal Road: Trade and Travel on the Chihuahua Trail* (Norman: University of Oklahoma Press, 1958), 57–58; Stephen G. Hyslop, *Bound for Santa Fe: The Road to New Mexico and the American Conquest, 1806–1848* (Norman: University of Oklahoma Press, 2002), 3–20.

2. "A Memorial to the Congress relative to the Santa Fe trade," Dec. 27, 1838, in 26th Cong., 1st Sess., Senate Doc. No. 472, p. 5.

3. Alencaster to Nemesio Salcedo, April 15, 1807, in Jackson, *Journals of Zebulon Montgomery Pike*, 2:197–200, quotation on 199–200.

4. Moorhead, *New Mexico's Royal Road*, 85–86, 186–90; James Josiah Webb, *Adventures in the Santa Fe Trade, 1844–1847*, ed. Ralph P. Bieber (Glendale, CA: Arthur H. Clark, 1931), 101. See also "Alphonso Wetmore's Report," Oct. 11, 1831, in "Message from the President of the United States," 22nd Cong., 1st Sess., Senate Doc. No. 90, p. 32.

5. Coues, *Expeditions of Zebulon Montgomery Pike*, 2:738–40. See also W. Eugene Hollon, *The Lost Pathfinder: Zebulon Montgomery Pike* (Norman: University of Oklahoma Press, 1949); George R. Matthews, *Zebulon Pike: Thomas Jefferson's Agent for Empire* (Santa Barbara, CA: Praeger, 2016).

6. *Missouri Gazette,* Oct. 9, 1813.

7. "Message from the President of the United States . . . Relative to the Arrest and Imprisonment of Certain American Citizens at Santa Fe," 15th Cong., 1st Sess., April 15, 1818, House Doc. No. 197, pp. 9–13.

8. A. P. Chouteau and Julius Demun to Henry Clay, May 3, 1825, "Message from the President of the United States," 24th Cong., 1st Sess., Unspecified Doc. No. 400, quotation on 2; "Message from the President of the United States," 15th Cong., 1st Sess., April 15, 1818, House Doc. No. 197, pp. 14–23, quotations on 17, 22; "Relations with Mexico," *Congressional Globe,* 25th Cong., 2nd Sess., April 11, 1838, p. 300; "Internal Trade with Mexico," *Gales and Seaton's Register of Debates in Congress,* 18th Cong., 2nd Sess., Jan. 25, 1825, p. 344; Chouteau to Lewis Cass, Nov. 12, 1831, "Message from the President of the United States," 22nd Cong., 1st Sess., Senate Doc. No. 90, pp. 60–61. See also Cleland, *This Reckless Breed of Men,* 123–26; Anne F. Hyde, *Empires, Nations, and Families: A New History of the North American West, 1800–1860* (Lincoln: University of Nebraska Press, 2011), 6–8, 40–43.

9. David Meriwether, *My Life in the Mountains and on the Plains: The Newly Discovered Autobiography,* ed. Robert A. Griffen (Norman: University of Oklahoma Press, 1965), 82–103, quotations on 87, 90.

10. "Trade and Intercourse between Missouri and the Internal Provinces of Mexico," Jan. 3, 1825, 18th Cong., 2nd Sess., Senate Exec. Doc. No. 7; Moorhead, *New Mexico's Royal Road,* 67.

11. See Marc Simmons, "The Chacón Economic Report of 1803," *New Mexico Historical Review* 60 (Jan. 1985): 81–88; "1812 Exposition of Pedro Bautista Pino," in David J. Weber, *Foreigners in Their Native Land: Historical Roots of the Mexican Americans* (Albuquerque: University of New Mexico Press, 1973), 41. See also Susan Calafate Boyle, *Los Capitalistas: Hispano Merchants and the Santa Fe Trade* (Albuquerque: University of New Mexico Press, 1997), 1–13; Weber, *The Mexican Frontier,* 1–14.

12. See Hyde, *Empires, Nations, and Families,* 6–8.

13. "Treaty of Amity, commerce, and navigation, between the United States of America and the United Mexican States, concluded on the 5th of April, 1831," 22nd Cong., 1st Sess., Senate Exec. Doc. No. 11.

14. See, for example, "Report of Commissioners," Oct. 27, 1827, in Kate L. Gregg, ed., *The Road to Santa Fe: The Journal and Diaries of George Champlin Sibley and Others Pertaining to the Surveying and Marking of a Road from the Missouri Frontier to the Settlements of New Mexico, 1825–1827* (Albuquerque: University of New Mexico Press, 1952), 210.

15. "Trade and Intercourse between Missouri and Mexico," Jan. 3, 1825, 18th Cong., 2nd Sess., Senate Exec. Doc. No. 7, p. 8; "Petition of Sundry Inhabitants of the State of Missouri," Feb. 14, 1825, 18th Cong., 2nd Sess., House Exec. Doc. No. 79.

16. Larry Beachum, *William Becknell: Father of the Santa Fe Trade* (El Paso: Texas Western Press, 1982), 17–19; Cleland, *This Reckless Breed of Men,* 131.

17. Josiah Gregg, *Commerce of the Prairies,* ed. Max L. Moorhead (Norman: University of Oklahoma Press, 1954), 332; "Extending Privilege of Drawback," March 8, 1842, 27th Cong., 2nd Sess., House Report No. 328, p. 17; "A Memorial to the Congress relative to the Santa Fe trade," Dec. 27, 1838, 26th Cong., 1st Sess., Senate Doc. No. 472, p. 6; George C. Sibley to Owen Simpson, May 1, 1825, in K. Gregg, *Road to Santa Fe,* 214–15; "Trade and Intercourse between Missouri and Mexico," Jan. 3, 1825, 18th Cong., 2nd Sess., Senate Exec. Doc. No. 7, p. 3; Wetmore to John Scott, Aug. 19, 1824, in "Petition of Sundry Inhabitants of the State of Missouri," Feb. 14, 1825, 18th Cong., 2nd Sess., House Exec. Doc. No. 79, p. 6. On the experimental nature of the trade, see "Alphonso Wetmore's Report," Oct. 11, 1831, 22nd Cong., 1st Sess., Senate Doc. No. 90, pp. 30–31. For an analysis of an 1820s-era expedition on the trail, see David J. Weber, "Señor Escudero Goes to Washington: Diplomacy, Indians, and the Santa Fe Trade," *Western Historical Quarterly* 43 (Winter 2012): 417–35.

18. "Trade and Intercourse between Missouri and Mexico," Jan. 3, 1825, 18th Cong., 2nd Sess., Senate Exec. Doc. No. 7, p. 7. Josiah Gregg noted in 1844 that "the arrival of a caravan at Santa Fe changes the aspect of the place at once. Instead of the idleness and stagnation which its streets exhibited before, one now sees everywhere the bustle, noise and activity of a lively market town." Gregg, *Commerce of the Prairies,* 80. See also Weber, *The Mexican Frontier,* 125–30.

19. David J. Weber, ed., *Arms, Indians, and the Mismanagement of New Mexico: Donaciano Vigil, 1846* (El Paso: Texas Western Press, 1986), 4.

20. The classic account of the fur trade is Hiram Martin Chittenden, *The American Fur Trade of the Far West,* 2 vols. (Stanford, CA: Academic Reprints, 1954).

21. "Message from the President of the United States," 15th Cong., 1st Sess., April 15, 1818, House Doc. No. 197, p. 18.

22. Cleland, *This Reckless Breed of Men,* 56–57; David J. Weber, *The Taos Trappers: The Fur Trade in the Far Southwest, 1540–1846* (Norman: University of Oklahoma Press, 1971); Weber, *The Mexican Frontier,* 130–34.

23. Cleland, *This Reckless Breed of Men,* 121; Weber, *The Taos Trappers,* 229; Lamar, *The Far Southwest,* 37–41.

24. See Hyde, *Empires, Nations, and Families.*

25. John E. Sunder, ed., *Matt Field on the Santa Fe Trail* (Norman: University of Oklahoma Press, 1960), 213.

26. See Brooks, *Captives and Cousins*, 228–34. For New Mexico marriages, see Ramón A. Gutiérrez, *When Jesus Came the Corn Mothers Went Away: Marriage, Sexuality, and Power in New Mexico, 1500–1846* (Stanford, CA: Stanford University Press, 1991), 271–97.

27. Benton, *Speech of Mr. Benton*, 30.

28. "A Memorial to the Congress relative to the Santa Fe trade," Dec. 27, 1838, in 26th Cong., 1st Sess., Senate Doc. No. 472, p. 7.

29. Gregg, *Commerce of the Prairies,* 78–80; Rebecca McDowell Craver, *The Impact of Intimacy: Mexican-Anglo Intermarriage in New Mexico, 1821–1846* (El Paso: Texas Western Press, 1982), 5–8, 49–57. See also Janet Lecompte, "The Independent Women of Hispanic New Mexico, 1821–1846," *Western Historical Quarterly* 12 (Jan. 1981): 17–35; Reséndez, *Changing National Identities*, 81.

30. Craver, *Impact of Intimacy*, 9–10, 27–29; Weber, *The Taos Trappers*, esp. ch. 11; Cleland, *This Reckless Breed of Men,* 210–11.

31. See George J. Sánchez, *Becoming Mexican-American: Ethnicity, Culture, and Identity in Chicano Los Angeles, 1900–1945* (New York: Oxford University Press, 1993); Anthony Mora, *Border Dilemmas: Racial and National Uncertainties in New Mexico, 1848–1912* (Durham, NC: Duke University Press, 2011).

32. Craver, *Impact of Intimacy*, 31–36; Weber, *The Taos Trappers,* esp. ch. 11; Barton H. Barbour, "Kit Carson and the 'Americanization' of New Mexico," in *New Mexican Lives: Profiles and Historical Stories,* ed. Richard W. Etulain (Albuquerque: University of New Mexico Press, 2002), 163–92.

33. Reséndez, *Changing National Identities,* 248–49.

34. Ibid., 34, 37; Charles Montgomery, *The Spanish Redemption: Heritage, Power, and Loss on New Mexico's Upper Rio Grande* (Berkeley: University of California Press, 2002), 41.

35. Torget, *Seeds of Empire*, 62–66.

36. See Brian DeLay, *War of a Thousand Deserts: Indian Raids and the U.S.-Mexican War* (New Haven, CT: Yale University Press, 2008).

37. Reséndez, *Changing National Identities,* 93, 118, 123; Weber, *The Taos Trappers;* Moorhead, *New Mexico's Royal Road,* 124; Reuben Gold Thwaites, ed., *The Personal Narrative of James O. Pattie of Kentucky* (Cleveland, OH: Arthur H. Clark, 1905), 77. See also Andrés Reséndez, "National Identity on a Shifting Border: Texas and New Mexico in the Age of Transition, 1821–1848," *Journal of American History* 86 (Sept. 1999): 668–88. For economic disparities between the United States and Mexico, see Thomas D. Hall, *Social Change in the Southwest, 1350–1880* (Lawrence: University Press of Kansas, 1989), 181.

38. "Petition of Sundry Inhabitants of the State of Missouri," Feb. 14, 1825, 18th Cong., 2nd Sess., House Exec. Doc. No. 79, p. 5.

39. A. McNair to J. Q. Adams, April 27, 1824, in *Annals of Congress,* May 1824, pp. 2703–4.

40. "Internal Trade with Mexico," *Gales and Seaton's Register of Debates in Congress,* 18th Cong., 2nd Sess., Jan. 25, 1825, p. 344.

41. "Inland Trade between Missouri and Mexico," ibid., Jan. 3, 1825, pp. 109–10.

42. "Inland Trade with Mexico," ibid., Jan. 25, 1825, p. 345.

43. "Petition of Sundry Inhabitants of the State of Missouri," Feb. 14, 1825, 18th Cong., 2nd Sess., House Exec. Doc. No. 79, p. 6.

44. "Trade and Intercourse between Missouri and Mexico," Jan. 3, 1825, 18th Cong., 2nd Sess., Senate Exec. Doc. No. 7, p. 6.

45. Report of Secretary of War Lewis Cass, Feb. 8, 1832, in "Message from the President of the United States," Feb. 9, 1832, 22nd Cong., 1st Sess., Senate Exec. Doc. No. 90, p. 33; Moorhead, *New Mexico's Royal Road*, 187–89.

46. Moorhead, *New Mexico's Royal Road*, 189; Henry Pickering Walker, *The Wagonmasters: High Plains Freighting from the Earliest Days of the Santa Fe Trail to 1880* (Norman: University of Oklahoma Press, 1966), 45; Howe, *What Hath God Wrought*, 502–4.

47. Hall, *Social Change in the Southwest*, 151, 198; Schermerhorn, *Business of Slavery*, 26.

48. "Trade and Intercourse between Missouri and Mexico," Jan. 3, 1825, 18th Cong., 2nd Sess., Senate Exec. Doc. No. 7, p. 6.

49. Richard L. Wilson and Benjamin F. Taylor, *Short Ravelings from a Long Yarn, or, Camp and March Sketches, of the Santa Fe Trail* (Chicago: Geer & Wilson, 1847), 151; Gregg, *Commerce of the Prairies*, 79–80, 159–63, 262.

50. "Trade and Intercourse between Missouri and Mexico," Jan., 1825, 18th Cong., 2nd Sess., Senate Exec. Doc. No. 7, pp. 6–7.

51. Wetmore to Cass, Oct. 22, 1831, in "Message from the President of the United States," Feb. 9, 1832, 22nd Cong., 1st Sess., Senate Exec. Doc. No. 90, p. 33.

52. Gregg, *Commerce of the Prairies*, 336; Webb, *Adventures in the Santa Fe Trade*. On New Mexico trade regulations, see Boyle, *Los Capitalistas*, 19–21; Weber, *The Mexican Frontier*, 147–57.

53. Cleland, *This Reckless Breed of Men*, 212. In 1826 New Mexico issued fifty-nine *guías*, and in 1827 it granted twenty-six. "Notebook of Guías 1826–1827," NMSRCA, Mexican Archives of New Mexico, Roll 6, Frames 472–512.

54. Cleland, *This Reckless Breed of Men*, 218–19.

55. Wilson and Taylor, *Short Ravelings*, 129–30, 140–41, quotation on 141. See also Sunder, *Matt Field on the Santa Fe Trail*, 221–25; Gregg, *Commerce of the Prairies*, 265–68. For scholarly accounts, see Walker, *The Wagonmasters*, 137–40; Moorhead, *New Mexico's Royal Road*, 123–51; Boyle, *Los Capitalistas*, 45–56.

56. Proceedings against Silvester Pratt, Nov. 12, 1826–Aug. 8, 1827, NMSRCA, Mexican Archives of New Mexico, Roll 5, Frames 1321–90; Proceedings re: the legality of beaver pelts, Feb. 23, 1828–April 10, 1828, ibid., Roll 8, Frames 371–437; Proceedings re: trapping of nutria by *extranjeros*, June 4, 1828–June 14, 1828, ibid., Roll 8, Frames 475–503; Proceedings against Ira A. Emmons, April 23, 1827–March 2, 1829, ibid., Roll 7, Frames 204–6; Ewing Young Contraband Proceedings, July 12, 1832–July 25, 1832, ibid., Roll 15, Frames 162–68.

57. "Inland Trade between Missouri and Mexico," *Gales and Seaton's Register of Debates in Congress*, 18th Cong., 2nd Sess., Jan. 3, 1825, pp. 109–10.

58. Hall, *Social Change in the Southwest*, 197.

59. "Inland Trade with Mexico," *Gales and Seaton's Register of Debates in Congress,* 18th Cong., 2nd Sess., Jan. 25, 1825, p. 347.

60. "Report of the Commissioners," Oct. 27, 1827, in Gregg, *Road to Santa Fe,* 204.

61. "Internal Trade with Mexico," *Gales and Seaton's Register of Debates in Congress,* 18th Cong., 2nd Sess., Jan. 25, 1825, pp. 341–44.

62. Ibid., Jan. 26, 1825, p. 356.

63. Ibid., 359.

64. Ibid., 361; Moorhead, *New Mexico's Royal Road,* 67–68; Gregg, *Road to Santa Fe,* 3–7; Walker, *The Wagonmasters,* 19–22.

65. George C. Sibley to Owen Simpson, May 1, 1825, in Gregg, *Road to Santa Fe,* 216.

66. "Alphonso Wetmore's Report," Oct. 11, 1831, 22nd Cong., 1st Sess., Senate Doc. No. 90, p. 32. See also Moorhead, *New Mexico's Royal Road,* 145–46.

67. Henry Clay to Joel Poinsett, Sept. 24, 1825, in *American State Papers, Foreign Relations* (Cornelius Wendell, 1859), 6:581–82.

68. "Report of the Commissioners," Oct. 27, 1827, in Gregg, *Road to Santa Fe,* 8–48, 116, 199.

69. Ibid., 111–18.

70. Ibid., 118, 134–35.

71. Poinsett to Sibley, Dec. 3, 1825, in ibid., 267n.137.

72. "Report of the Commissioners," Oct. 27, 1827, in ibid., 201, 232–33.

73. Ibid., 203–5.

74. Benton to Sibley, June 30, 1825, in Gregg, *Road to Santa Fe,* 213. See also Hyslop, *Bound for Santa Fe,* 48–49.

75. See Frazer, *Forts and Supplies,* 34–36, 40–42; Leo E. Oliva, *Soldiers on the Santa Fe Trail* (Norman: University of Oklahoma Press, 1967).

76. "Internal Trade with Mexico," *Gales and Seaton's Register of Debates in Congress,* 18th Cong., 2nd Sess., Jan. 25, 1825, pp. 344–46.

77. "Report of the Commissioners," Oct. 27, 1827, in Gregg, *Road to Santa Fe,* 206, 210. Emphasis in original.

78. "Treaties with Sundry Indian Tribes," Jan. 11, 1826, 19th Cong., 1st Sess., Treaty and Nomination Reports and Documents; "Treaties with the Kansas and Osage Indians," Jan. 30, 1826, 19th Cong., 1st Sess., Treaty and Nomination Reports and Documents. On the treaties generally, see Hyde, *Empires, Nations, and Families,* 294–98.

79. Senate Report, Dec. 30, 1847, 30th Cong., 1st Sess., Senate Rep. Com. No. 11; Gregg, *Commerce of the Prairies,* 428. For more on Indian depredations on the Santa Fe Trail, see "Alphonso Wetmore's Report," Oct. 11, 1831, 22nd Cong., 1st Sess., Senate Doc. No. 90, pp. 31, 40; Johnathan Dougherty to William Clark, Oct. 25, 1831, in ibid., 52; Oliva, *Soldiers on the Santa Fe Trail,* 93–130; William Y. Chalfant, *Dangerous Passage: The Santa Fe Trail and the Mexican War* (Norman: University of Oklahoma Press, 1994), 21–27; Walker, *The Wagonmasters,* 255–63.

80. Cleland, *This Reckless Breed of Men,* 117–20.

81. Table of men killed or robbed by Indians, in "Message from the President of the United States," 22nd Cong., 1st Sess., Senate Doc. No. 90, pp. 81–86.

82. Gregg, *Commerce of the Prairies,* 19.

83. Forsyth to Cass, Oct. 24, 1831, in "Message from the President of the United States," 22nd Cong., 1st Sess., Senate Doc. No. 90, pp. 75–76.

84. Kiser, *Dragoons in Apacheland,* 20–21.

85. Gregg, *Commerce of the Prairies,* 19–21. On military escorts, see Robert M. Utley, *Fort Union and the Santa Fe Trail* (El Paso: Texas Western Press, 1989), 12–17; Oliva, *Soldiers on the Santa Fe Trail,* 25–54; Walker, *The Wagonmasters,* 230–38; Chalfant, *Dangerous Passage.*

86. "Reorganization of the Army," *Congressional Globe,* 27th Cong., 2nd Sess., Aug. 3, 1842, p. 838.

87. William Gilpin to Roger Jones, Aug. 1, 1848, in "Documents from War Department," 30th Cong., 1st Sess., House Exec. Doc. 1, p. 139.

88. *1850 Annual Report of the Secretary of War,* 31st Cong., 2nd Sess., Senate Exec. Doc. No. 5, p. 4.

89. Collins to A. B. Greenwood, Dec. 5, 1859, in "Indian Hostilities in New Mexico," 36th Cong., 1st Sess., House Exec. Doc. No. 69, pp. 48–49.

90. E. B. Alexander to L. McLaws, May 24, 1850, NA, RG393, M1102, LR, DNM, Roll 2; A. E. Burnside to John Ward, May 23, 1850, ibid.; John Munroe to J. McDowell, May 23, 1850, in Annie H. Abel, ed., *The Official Correspondence of James S. Calhoun* (Washington, D.C.: Government Printing Office, 1915), 207–8.

91. "Message from the President of the United States," Dec. 2, 1850, 31st Cong., 2nd Sess., Senate Exec. Doc. No. 1, p. 11.

92. "Memorial to Congress," Feb. 9, 1857, NA, RG46, Territorial Papers of the U.S. Senate, New Mexico 1840–1854, M200, Roll 14.

93. Kiser, *Dragoons in Apacheland,* 60–62, 89–123. For military activities on the southern plains, see Utley, *Frontiersmen in Blue,* 108–41.

94. "Internal Improvements since 1824," 20th Cong., 2nd Sess., House Doc. No. 7; "Message from the President of the United States," Feb. 10, 1829, 20th Cong., 2nd Sess., Unspecified Doc. No. 69, pp. 7, 14, 21; "Internal Improvements," Jan. 5, 1831, 21st Cong., 2nd Sess., House Exec. Doc. No. 30, p. 17; "Expenditures for Internal Improvements," Dec. 11, 1834, 23rd Cong., 2nd Sess., House Exec. Doc. No. 18, p. 12.

95. "Alphonso Wetmore's Report," Oct. 11, 1831, 22nd Cong., 1st Sess., Senate Doc. No. 90, pp. 32–33; "A Memorial to the Congress relative to the Santa Fe trade," Dec. 27, 1838, in 26th Cong., 1st Sess., Senate Doc. No. 472; "Memorial of the General Assembly of Missouri," Feb. 16, 1839, 25th Cong., 3rd Sess., Senate Doc. No. 225; "Extending Privilege of Drawback," March 8, 1842, 27th Cong., 2nd Sess., House Report No. 328; "Message of the President," *Congressional Globe,* 26th Cong., 2nd Sess., Jan. 5, 1841, p. 6. See also Drawback Bills of Dec. 14, 1840; Dec. 14, 1841; Dec. 14, 1842; Jan. 20, 1843; and Jan. 6, 1845, all in NA, RG46, Territorial Papers of the U.S. Senate, New Mexico 1840–1854, M200, Roll 14.

96. On drawback and debenture as they pertained to the Santa Fe trade, see Moorhead, *New Mexico's Royal Road,* 72–74, 93–94; Thomas E. Chávez, *Manuel Alvarez, 1794–1856: A Southwestern Biography* (Niwot: University Press of Colorado, 1990), 87–88.

97. "A Memorial to the Congress relative to the Santa Fe trade," Dec. 27, 1838, in 26th Cong., 1st Sess., Senate Doc. No. 472, pp. 6–7, quotation on 7.

98. "Extending Privilege of Drawback," March 8, 1842, 27th Cong., 2nd Sess., House Report No. 328, p. 18.

99. Moorhead, *New Mexico's Royal Road,* 75.

100. "Extending Privilege of Drawback," March 8, 1842, 27th Cong., 2nd Sess., House Report No. 328, p. 18.

101. Inaugural Address of Mirabeau B. Lamar, Dec. 19, 1838, in Charles A. Gulick Jr. and Katherine Elliott, *The Papers of Mirabeau Buonapart Lamar* (Austin, TX: J. C. Baldwin & Sons 1922), 2:320.

102. "Santa Fe Expedition," *Congressional Globe,* 27th Cong., 2nd Sess., Jan. 14, 1842, pp. 131–32. The classic account of the expedition is George Wilkins Kendall, *Narrative of the Texan–Santa Fe Expedition* (New York: Harper & Brothers, 1844). See also Thomas Falconer, *Letters and Notes of the Texan Santa Fe Expedition, 1841–1842* (New York: Dauber & Pine, 1930); Noel M. Loomis, *The Texan–Santa Fe Pioneers* (Norman: University of Oklahoma Press, 1958); Fayette Copeland, *Kendall of the Picayune: Being His Adventures in New Orleans, on the Texan Santa Fe Expedition, in the Mexican War, and in the Colonization of the Texas Frontier* (Norman: University of Oklahoma Press, 1943), 57–107. On the role of Texas, see Hall, *Social Change in the Southwest,* 185–89, 199.

103. "General Appropriation Bill," *Congressional Globe,* 27th Cong., 2nd Sess., April 15, 1842, p. 428; "In Senate," ibid., July 14, 1842, p. 752.

104. Gregg, *Commerce of the Prairies,* 344.

105. "Speech of Mr. Benton of Missouri, Annexation of Texas," *Congressional Globe,* 28th Cong., 1st Sess., May 1844, Appendix, 485.

106. Ibid., 475–79. On the Texas boundary claims, see Robert W. Larson, *New Mexico's Quest for Statehood, 1846–1912* (Albuquerque: University of New Mexico Press, 1968), 15–23; Stegmaier, *Texas, New Mexico, and the Compromise of 1850,* 7–62.

107. *Congressional Globe,* 28th Cong., 2nd Sess., Jan. 15, 1845, pp. 367–71; ibid., Jan. 1845, Appendix, 336; ibid., Feb. 25, 1845, p. 347.

108. Ibid., Jan. 1845, Appendix, 108.

109. Daniel H. Usner Jr., *Indians, Settlers, and Slaves in a Frontier Exchange Economy: The Lower Mississippi Valley before 1783* (Chapel Hill: University of North Carolina Press, 1992).

110. See Gregg, *Commerce of the Prairies,* 333–36.

111. Moorhead, *New Mexico's Royal Road,* 28–55, 194; John O. Baxter, *Las Carneradas: Sheep Trade in New Mexico, 1700–1860* (Albuquerque: University of New Mexico Press, 1987), 62–80; Hall, *Social Change in the Southwest,* 146–57; Ross Frank, *From Settler to Citizen: New Mexican Economic Development and the Creation of Vecino Society, 1750–1820* (Berkeley: University of California Press, 2000), 119–75, 226. For an analysis of the New Mexico economy that emphasizes the role of Indians, see Brooks, *Captives and Cousins,* 208–28.

112. See Reséndez, *Changing National Identities,* 123; Hall, *Social Change in the Southwest,* 154–55, 199–200.

113. Boyle, *Los Capitalistas,* 57–72, 89–99; Reséndez, *Changing National Identities,* 101.
114. "A Memorial to the Congress relative to the Santa Fe trade," Dec. 27, 1838, in 26th Cong., 1st Sess., Senate Doc. No. 472, pp. 7–8.
115. McNitt, *Navajo Wars,* 52–91; Brooks, *Captives and Cousins,* 250–54.
116. Gregg, *Commerce of the Prairies,* 332; Reséndez, *Changing National Identities,* 249; Montgomery, *The Spanish Redemption,* 40–41; Walker, *The Wagonmasters,* 294. For the impact of capitalism in New Mexico, see Deena J. González, *Refusing the Favor: The Spanish-Mexican Women of Santa Fe, 1820–1880* (New York: Oxford University Press, 1999), 41–43.
117. See Hall, *Social Change in the Southwest,* 167–200.

Chapter 2

1. George Croghan, *Army Life on the Western Frontier: Selections from the Official Reports Made between 1826 and 1845,* ed. Francis Paul Prucha (Norman: University of Oklahoma Press, 1958), 43nn.140–43; Susan Shelby Magoffin, *Down the Santa Fe Trail and into Mexico: The Diary of Susan Shelby Magoffin, 1846–1847,* ed. Stella M. Drumm (New Haven, CT: Yale University Press, 1926), 106. See also Cutts, *Conquest of California and New Mexico,* 33–35. For a biographical account, see Dwight L. Clarke, *Stephen Watts Kearny: Soldier of the West* (Norman: University of Oklahoma Press, 1961).
2. Calvin, *Lieutenant Emory Reports,* 30–31; Keleher, *Turmoil in New Mexico,* 3–35; Oliva, *Soldiers on the Santa Fe Trail,* 55–76; Chalfant, *Dangerous Passage,* 3–20; Hyslop, *Bound for Santa Fe,* 325–69; Hyde, *Empires, Nations, and Families,* 378–88.
3. "Messages of the President of the United States," 30th Cong., 1st Sess., House Exec. Doc. 60, p. 155.
4. Ibid., 153–55. See also Milo Milton Quaife, ed., *The Diary of James K. Polk during His Presidency, 1845 to 1849* (Chicago: A. C. McClung, 1910), 1:443.
5. On the antiwar movement, see Amy S. Greenberg, *A Wicked War: Polk, Clay, Lincoln, and the 1846 U.S. Invasion of Mexico* (New York: Knopf, 2012).
6. Quaife, *Diary of James K. Polk,* 2:289; John J. Farrell, ed., *James K. Polk, 1795–1849: Chronology-Documents-Bibliographic Aides* (Dobbs Ferry, NY: Oceana, 1970), 32.
7. *Congressional Globe,* 29th Cong., 2nd Sess., Appendix, Feb. 10, 1847, p. 337.
8. Ibid., Feb. 13, 1847, p. 204.
9. Ibid., 368.
10. Clarke, *Stephen Watts Kearny,* 3–10, 57, 69, 101–45; Lamar, *The Far Southwest,* 52; "Messages of the President of the United States," 30th Cong., 1st Sess., House Exec. Doc. 60, p. 170. On the Army of the West, see John T. Hughes, *Doniphan's Expedition: Containing an Account of the Conquest of New Mexico; General Kearny's Overland Expedition to California; Doniphan's Campaign against the Navajos; His Unparalleled March upon Chihuahua and Durango; and the Operations of General Price at Santa Fe* (Cincinnati: J. A. and U. P. James, 1848), 35; George Rutledge Gibson, *Journal of a Soldier under Kearny and Doniphan, 1846–1847,* ed. Ralph P. Bieber (Glendale, CA: Arthur H. Clark, 1935), 125–26; Ralph Emerson Twitchell, *Leading Facts of New Mexican History* (Cedar

Rapids, IA: Torch Press, 1912), 2:213n.150. For a transnational history of the occupation, see Reséndez, *Changing National Identities*, 237–63.

11. Scott to Kearny, Nov. 3, 1846, in "Messages of the President of the United States," 30th Cong., 1st Sess., House Exec. Doc. 60, p. 164.

12. "Message from the President of the United States to the Two Houses of Congress," Dec. 8, 1846, 29th Cong., 2nd Sess., House Exec. Doc. No. 4, pp. 21–22. See also Quaife, *Diary of James K. Polk*, 2:169–70.

13. Kearny to Armijo, Aug. 1, 1846, in Max L. Moorhead, ed., "Notes and Documents," *New Mexico Historical Review* 26 (Jan. 1951), 80.

14. William L. Marcy to Kearny, June 18, 1846, in "California and New Mexico," 31st Cong., 1st Sess., House Exec. Doc. 17, pp. 240–41; Quaife, *Diary of James K. Polk*, 1:472, 474–75.

15. Thomas Hart Benton, *Thirty Years' View, or, A History of the Working of the American Government for Thirty Years, from 1820 to 1850* (New York: D. Appleton, 1856), 2:683–84; James W. Magoffin to William H. Crawford, April 4, 1849, NMSRCA, Ralph Emerson Twitchell Collection (hereafter Twitchell Collection), Serial #8472, Folder 65.

16. George F. Ruxton, *Adventures in Mexico and the Rocky Mountains* (New York: Harper & Brothers, 1848), 110; Magoffin to Marcy, Aug. 26, 1846, NMSRCA, Twitchell Collection, Serial #8472, Folder 65; Philip St. George Cooke to Magoffin, Feb. 21, 1849, ibid.

17. Philip St. George Cooke, *The Conquest of New Mexico and California: An Historical and Personal Narrative* (New York: G. P. Putnam's Sons, 1878), 28–32.

18. Armijo to Kearny, Aug. 12, 1846, in Moorhead, "Notes and Documents," 81–82. Italics in original. See also Bieber, *Marching with the Army of the West*, 98; Reséndez, *Changing National Identities*, 250–51.

19. Magoffin to Marcy, Aug. 26, 1846, NMSRCA, Twitchell Collection, Serial #8472, Folder 65; Cooke to Magoffin, Feb. 21, 1849, ibid.; Magoffin to Crawford, April 4, 1849, ibid.; Claim of James W. Magoffin, undated, ibid.

20. Thomas E. Chávez, *Manuel Alvarez, 1794–1856: A Southwestern Biography* (Niwot: University Press of Colorado, 1990), 107–8; Moorhead, *New Mexico's Royal Road*, 157–61, 183.

21. See Daniel Tyler, "Governor Armijo's Moment of Truth," *Journal of the West* 11 (April 1972): 313; Frances Leon Swadesh, *Los Primeros Pobladores: Hispanic Americans of the Ute Frontier* (Notre Dame, IN: University of Notre Dame Press, 1974), 64; Reséndez, *Changing National Identities*, 250–51, 252n.49. On Magoffin, see "Later from New Mexico," *New-York Daily Tribune*, March 9, 1847; Claim of James W. Magoffin, NMSRCA, Twitchell Collection, Serial #8472, Folder 65.

22. "Messages of the President of the United States," 30th Cong., 1st Sess., House Exec. Doc. 60, p. 168

23. Manuel Armijo Proclamation, Aug. 8, 1846, NMSRCA, Benjamin Read Collection, Box 1, Folder 20. For Armijo's activities, see Lansing B. Bloom, "New Mexico under Mexican Administration: Part 3—New Mexico as a Department, 1837–1846," *Old Santa Fe* 2 (April 1915): 351–65.

24. Manuel Armijo circular to the Prefects of the Northern Districts, Jan. 10, 1846, NMSRCA, María G. Duran Collection, Folder 10.

25. Mariano Paredes y Arrillaga to Armijo, March 25, 1846, NMSRCA, Donaciano Vigil Collection, Box 3, Folder 109.

26. Manuel Armijo Proclamation, June 6, 1846, NMSRCA, Mexican Archives of New Mexico, Roll 41, Frames 277–78.

27. Wislizenus, *Memoir of a Tour to Northern Mexico*, 20. See also Antonio Serna Proclamation, July 19, 1846, NMSRCA, Donaciano Vigil Collection, Box 3, Folder 121.

28. Bloom, "New Mexico under Mexican Administration," 356, 361.

29. Minutes of the Legislative Assembly, Aug. 10, 1846, quoted in Bloom, "New Mexico under Mexican Administration," 364–65.

30. Dwight L. Clarke, ed., *The Original Journals of Henry Smith Turner: With Stephen Watts Kearny to New Mexico and California, 1846–1847* (Norman: University of Oklahoma Press, 1966), 70–71; Calvin, *Lieutenant Emory Reports*, 46, 47–49; Gibson, *Journal of a Soldier under Kearny*, 193, 199; Bieber, *Marching with the Army of the West*, 153.

31. Clarke, *Journals of Henry Smith Turner*, 71–72; Cooke, *Conquest of New Mexico and California*, 34, 37; Gibson, *Journal of a Soldier under Kearny*, 193–94; "Diary of an Officer of the Army of the West," *New-York Daily Tribune*, Oct. 3, 1846; Calvin, *Lieutenant Emory Reports*, 49–52. For Robidoux's involvement, see Keleher, *Turmoil in New Mexico*, 122n.36.

32. Clarke, *Journals of Henry Smith Turner*, 71–72; Cooke, *Conquest of New Mexico and California*, 34, 37; Calvin, *Lieutenant Emory Reports*, 49–52; Jacob S. Robinson, *A Journal of the Santa Fe Expedition under Colonel Doniphan* (1848; reprint, Princeton, NJ: Princeton University Press, 1932), 23; "Diary of an Officer of the Army of the West," *New-York Daily Tribune*, Oct. 3, 1846.

33. Cooke, *Conquest of New Mexico and California*, 34–35, 40. For congressional discussion of Kearny's citizenship oaths, see "House of Representatives," *Congressional Globe,* 29th Cong., 2nd Sess., Dec. 9, 1846, p. 14; "Constitution of Iowa," ibid., Dec. 15, 1846, p. 39.

34. Unidentified soldier to Dearest Wife, Aug. 22, 1846, NMSRCA, Getty Family Collection, Box 1, Folder 1.

35. Magoffin, *Down the Santa Fe Trail*, 110.

36. Gregg, *Commerce of the Prairies*, 95.

37. Gibson, *Journal of a Soldier under Kearny*, 201, 210. Armijo collected annual import duties between $50,000 and $60,000 and charged a fee of $500 per wagonload. Calvin, *Lieutenant Emory Reports*, 61. For Armijo's treatment of New Mexicans, see Gregg, *Commerce of the Prairies*, 79–80, 262; Ruxton, *Adventures in Mexico and the Rocky Mountains*, 157; Cooke, *Conquest of New Mexico and California*, 32–33; W. W. H. Davis, *El Gringo, or, New Mexico and Her People* (Santa Fe: Rydal Press, 1938), 115, 202–3; Wilson and Taylor, *Short Ravelings*, 140, 151; "Diary of an Officer of the Army of the West," *New-York Daily Tribune*, Oct. 3, 1846. On administrative corruption, see Moorhead, *New Mexico's Royal Road*, 127–28, 185; Weber, *Arms, Indians, and the Mismanagement of New Mexico*, 26. For secondary accounts, see Daniel Tyler, "Gringo Views of Governor Manuel Armijo," *New Mexico Historical Review* 45 (Jan. 1970), 23–46; Tyler, "Governor Armijo's Moment of Truth," 309–10; Chávez, *Manuel Alvarez*, 57–58; DeLay, *War of a Thousand Deserts*, 255.

38. Tyler, "Gringo Views of Governor Armijo," 24–25. See also Kendall, *Narrative of the Texan–Santa Fe Expedition,* 1:295–98, 359–60.

39. Cooke, *Conquest of New Mexico and California,* 32, 38; Mark L. Gardner, ed., *Brothers on the Santa Fe and Chihuahua Trails: Edward James Glasgow and William Henry Glasgow, 1846–1848* (Niwot: University Press of Colorado, 1993), 91; Calvin, *Lieutenant Emory Reports,* 53, 67, 70, 79.

40. "Report of Lieut. J. W. Abert," 30th Cong., 1st Sess., Senate Exec. Doc. 23, p. 3. See also Ruxton, *Adventures in Mexico and the Rocky Mountains,* 119; Clarke, *Original Journals of Henry Smith Turner,* 73, 142; Cooke, *Conquest of New Mexico and California,* 50–51; Calvin, *Lieutenant Emory Reports,* 58.

41. Armijo to Ugarte, Aug. 20, 1846, in *Diario Oficial de la Federación,* Sept. 10, 1846; "Report of Gov. Manuel Armijo to the Minister of Foreign Relations," Sept. 8, 1846, in Moorhead, "Notes and Documents," 78.

42. Armijo to Ugarte, Aug. 20, 1846, in *Diario Oficial de la Federación,* Sept. 10, 1846.

43. Moorhead, "Notes and Documents," 79; Tyler, "Governor Armijo's Moment of Truth," 314.

44. "Report of Gov. Manuel Armijo to the Minister of Foreign Relations," Sept. 8, 1846, in Moorhead, "Notes and Documents," 76–78; Henry Connelly to Magoffin, Sept. 20, 1848, NMSRCA, Twitchell Collection, Serial #8472, Folder 65; Magoffin to Marcy, Aug. 26, 1846, ibid.

45. "Report of the Citizens of New Mexico to the President of Mexico," Sept. 26, 1846, in Moorhead, "Notes and Documents," 69–74. See also Tyler, "Governor Armijo's Moment of Truth," 309.

46. Moorhead, "Notes and Documents," 73–75. Italics in original. See also D. Carlos Ma. De Bustamante, *El Nuevo Bernal Diaz del Castillo, ó sea, Historia de la invasion de los anglo-americanos en México* (1847; reprint, Mexico: Secretaría de Educación Pública, 1949), 223–24.

47. "Proceedings against Manuel Armijo," March 1847, Archivo de la Defensa Nacional, Expediente 2588, Roll 11, at Bancroft Library. I thank Andrés Reséndez for providing his copies and annotations of these documents.

48. Armijo to Minister of War and Navy, March 30, 1847, ibid.; José Antonio Heredia to Minister of War and Navy, Jan. 26, 1847, ibid.

49. Gibson, *Journal of a Soldier under Kearny,* 212–13.

50. Calvin, *Lieutenant Emory Reports,* 57; Kearny to Roger Jones, Sept. 16, 1846, NMSRCA, Albert H. Schroeder Papers, Serial #10787, Folder 1143; J. F. Gilmer to Richard S. Elliott, Nov. 1, 1846, in *The Mexican War Correspondence of Richard Smith Elliott,* eds. Mark L. Gardner and Marc Simmons (Norman: University of Oklahoma Press, 1997), 95–96; Hughes, *Doniphan's Expedition,* 122–23.

51. "Report of Lieut. J. W. Abert," 30th Cong., 1st Sess., Senate Exec. Doc. 23, p. 38.

52. Hughes, *Doniphan's Expedition,* 78; Clarke, *Journals of Henry Smith Turner,* 72–73; Gibson, *Journal of a Soldier under Kearny,* 235. The cannons had been loaded with empty cartridges as the army entered the town, in preparation for this ceremony. Bieber, *Marching with the Army of the West,* 159.

53. Gardner and Simmons, *Mexican War Correspondence of Richard Smith Elliott,* 71.

54. Ibid., 74–76; Gibson, *Journal of a Soldier under Kearny*, 216. See also González, *Refusing the Favor*, 41.

55. "Report of Lieut. J. W. Abert," 30th Cong., 1st Sess., Senate Exec. Doc. 23, p. 32. See also Magoffin, *Down the Santa Fe Trail*, 103.

56. Lewis H. Garrard, *Wah-To-Yah and the Taos Trail* (Palo Alto, CA: American West, 1968), 175.

57. General Kearny Order of Sept. 3, 1846, NMSRCA, Donaciano Vigil Collection, Box 3, Folder 123.

58. Calvin, *Lieutenant Emory Reports*, 56–57.

59. Gardner and Simmons, *Mexican War Correspondence of Richard Smith Elliott*, 73. Emphasis in original.

60. "Messages of the President of the United States," 30th Cong., 1st Sess., House Exec. Doc. 60, pp. 150, 170–71. See also Kearny Proclamation, Aug. 19, 1846, NMSRCA, Bloom-McFie Collection, Folder 1; "Diary of an Officer of the Army of the West," *New-York Daily Tribune*, Oct. 3, 1846; Hughes, *Doniphan's Expedition*, 85–87. On New Mexican citizenship, see John M. Nieto-Phillips, *The Language of Blood: The Making of Spanish-American Identity in New Mexico, 1880s–1930s* (Albuquerque: University of New Mexico Press, 2004), 51–57.

61. Cutts, *Conquest of California and New Mexico*, 39.

62. "Excerpt from William H. Glasgow's 'Memorandums,'" Aug. 1846, in Gardner, *Brothers on the Santa Fe and Chihuahua Trails*, 165; "The Government of New Mexico," *Santa Fe Republican*, Oct. 30, 1847.

63. Kearny to Jones, Sept. 22, 1846, in "Messages of the President of the United States," 30th Cong., 1st Sess., House Exec. Doc. 60, p. 176; Cooke, *Conquest of New Mexico and California*, 63; Hughes, *Doniphan's Expedition*, 120. See also Joseph G. Dawson III, *Doniphan's Epic March: The 1st Missouri Volunteers in the Mexican War* (Lawrence: University Press of Kansas, 1999), 85–87.

64. Polk Message of Dec. 22, 1846, in "Messages of the President of the United States," 30th Cong., 1st Sess., House Exec. Doc. 60, p. 150; Hughes, *Doniphan's Expedition*, 121. On the role of Hispanics in territorial government, see Montgomery, *The Spanish Redemption*, 42–43.

65. Kearny to Jones, Sept. 22, 1846, in "Messages of the President of the United States," 30th Cong., 1st Sess., House Exec. Doc. 60, p. 176. On Bent's marriage, see Craver, *Impact of Intimacy*, 11, 21–22.

66. Receipt dated Oct. 20, 1846, NMSRCA, L. B. Prince Personal Papers, Serial #14023, Folder 29; "Report of the Committee on Territories," Jan. 10, 1857, 34th Cong., 3rd Sess., House Report No. 60.

67. For the full text of the code, see "Organic Law of the Territory of New Mexico," Nov. 23, 1846, 30th Cong., 1st Sess., House Exec. Doc. No. 60, pp. 177–229. On Indian affairs, see Lamar, *The Far Southwest*, 86.

68. Marcy to Polk, Dec. 21, 1846, in "Messages of the President of the United States," 30th Cong., 1st Sess., House Exec. Doc. 60, p. 151.

69. Polk Message of Dec. 22, 1846, in "Messages of the President of the United States," 30th Cong., 1st Sess., House Exec. Doc. 60, p. 150; "Occupation of Mexican Territory," Dec. 22, 1846, 29th Cong., 2nd Sess., House Exec. Doc. No. 19, pp. 1–3; Quaife, *Diary of James K. Polk*, 2:282.

70. Marcy to Kearny, Jan. 11, 1847, in "Message of the President of the United States, New Mexico and California," 30th Cong., 1st Sess., House Exec. Doc. 70, pp. 13–14; Chávez, *Manuel Alvarez*, 117–19.

71. *Congressional Globe*, 29th Cong., 2nd Sess., Feb. 4, 1847, p. 285.

72. Ibid., Appendix, Dec. 24, 1846, p. 75.

73. *Congressional Globe*, 29th Cong., 2nd Sess., Feb. 26, 1847, p. 520. For congressional debate on the Kearny Code, see ibid., Dec. 9, 1846, p. 16; Appendix, Dec. 22, 1846, p. 200; Appendix, Feb. 8, 1847, p. 316; Feb. 9, 1847, p. 354; *Congressional Globe*, 30th Cong., 1st Sess., July 10, 1848, p. 912.

74. Wislizenus, *Memoir of a Tour to Northern Mexico,* 85.

75. Anonymous letter published in *Niles Weekly Register* 72, June 19, 1847, p. 252.

76. Clarke, *Journals of Henry Smith Turner,* 74.

77. Anonymous letter published in *Niles Weekly Register,* June 19, 1847, p. 252.

78. Kearny Report, Aug. 19, 1846, NA, RG94, T-1115, Roll 1.

79. Gardner and Simmons, *Mexican War Correspondence of Richard Smith Elliott,* 174.

80. "Report of Lieut. J. W. Abert," 30th Cong., 1st Sess., Senate Exec. Doc. 23, p. 32.

81. Ruxton, *Adventures in Mexico and the Rocky Mountains,* 190.

82. Vigil to Buchanan, March 26, 1847, "Insurrection against the Military Government in New Mexico and California, 1847 and 1848," 56th Cong., 1st Sess., Senate Doc. No. 442, p. 32. For a biographical sketch of Vigil, see Manuel G. Gonzales, *The Hispanic Elite of the Southwest* (El Paso: Texas Western Press, 1989), 12–15.

83. General Orders No. 28, Sept. 19, 1846, NA, RG94, T-1115, Roll 1; General Orders No. 31, Sept. 24, 1846, ibid.; General Orders No. 1, Nov. 1, 1848, ibid.

84. Governor Bent Proclamation, Oct. 21, 1846, NMSRCA, Donaciano Vigil Collection, Box 3, Folder 124; Gardner and Simmons, *Mexican War Correspondence of Richard Smith Elliott,* 94.

85. *Santa Fe Republican,* Sept. 24, 1847.

86. Ruxton, *Adventures in Mexico and the Rocky Mountains,* 197.

87. Garrard, *Wah-To-Yah and the Taos Trail,* 175. On Garrard generally, see Roy W. Meyer, "New Light on Lewis Garrard," *Western Historical Quarterly* 6 (July 1975): 261–78.

88. Cutts, *Conquest of California and New Mexico,* 217.

89. Calvin, *Lieutenant Emory Reports,* 58; Clarke, *Journals of Henry Smith Turner,* 74.

90. Clarke, *Journals of Henry Smith Turner,* 75; Hughes, *Doniphan's Expedition,* 35; Gibson, *Journal of a Soldier under Kearny,* 99.

91. Gibson, *Journal of a Soldier under Kearny,* 259.

92. "Later from New Mexico," *New-York Daily Tribune,* March 3, 1847.

93. "Report of Lieut. J. W. Abert," 30th Cong., 1st Sess., Senate Exec. Doc. 23, pp. 67, 69.

94. Ralph P. Bieber, ed., *Exploring Southwestern Trails, 1846–1854* (Glendale, CA: Arthur H. Clark, 1938), 88; "Later from New Mexico," *New-York Daily Tribune,* March 3, 1847.

95. Gardner and Simmons, *Mexican War Correspondence of Richard Smith Elliott*, 106. See also Brooks, *Captives and Cousins*, 282.

96. Dyer to Col. Talcott, Feb. 17, 1847, NMSRCA, Misc. Letters and Diaries, Box 1, File 5; Bieber, *Exploring Southwestern Trails,* 88. See also Ralph Emerson Twitchell, *The History of the Military Occupation of the Territory of New Mexico from 1846 to 1851 by the Government of the United States* (Chicago: Rio Grande Press, 1963), 330–31; George I. Sánchez, *Forgotten People: A Study of New Mexicans* (Albuquerque: University of New Mexico Press, 1940), 15–16.

97. "Message from the President of the United States to the Two Houses of Congress," Dec. 8, 1846, 29th Cong., 2nd Sess., House Exec. Doc. No. 4, p. 23.

98. Gardner and Simmons, *Mexican War Correspondence of Richard Smith Elliott*, 131; Cooke, *Conquest of New Mexico and California*, 111.

99. Charles Bent to Buchanan, Dec. 26, 1846, in "New Mexico and California," 30th Cong., 1st Sess., House Exec. Doc. No. 70, p. 17; Dyer to Talcott, Feb. 17, 1847, NMSRCA, Misc. Letters and Diaries, Box 1, File 5.

100. Bent to Buchanan, Dec. 26, 1846, in "New Mexico and California," 30th Cong., 1st Sess., House Exec. Doc. No. 70, p. 17.

101. Gardner and Simmons, *Mexican War Correspondence of Richard Smith Elliott*, 131–35; Magoffin, *Down the Santa Fe Trail*, 188; Sterling Price to Roger Jones, Feb. 15, 1847, in "Report of the Secretary of War," 30th Cong., 1st Sess., Senate Exec. Doc. No. 1, p. 520; "Report of Lieut. J. W. Abert," Feb. 10, 1848, 30th Cong., 1st Sess., Senate Exec. Doc. 23, p. 95.

102. Price to Jones, Feb. 15, 1847, in "Report of the Secretary of War," 30th Cong., 1st Sess., Senate Exec. Doc. No. 1, p. 520.

103. "Further Particulars from Santa Fe," *New-York Daily Tribune*, March 10, 1847. There was speculation that the infamous Santa Fe gambler and saloonkeeper Doña Gertrudis Barceló acted as one of the informants. See Deena J. González, "La Tules of Image and Reality: Euro-American Attitudes and Legend Formation on a Spanish-Mexican Frontier," in *Building with Our Hands: New Directions in Chicana Studies,* eds. Adela de la Torre and Beatríz M. Pesquera (Berkeley: University of California Press, 1993), 75–90; Mary J. Straw Cook, *Doña Tules: Santa Fe's Courtesan and Gambler* (Albuquerque: University of New Mexico Press, 2007), 37–49; Twitchell, *Leading Facts of New Mexican History*, 2:233n.168.

104. Reséndez, *Changing National Identities,* 244–46, 255–56; Brooks, *Captives and Cousins*, 282. See also Benton, *Thirty Years' View,* 2:683.

105. Gardner and Simmons, *Mexican War Correspondence of Richard Smith Elliott*, 137; "Report of Lieut. J. W. Abert," Feb. 10, 1848, 30th Cong., 1st Sess., Senate Exec. Doc. 23, pp. 97–98.

106. Proclamation of Charles Bent, Jan. 5, 1847, NMSRCA, Ina Sizer Cassidy Collection, Folder 5.

107. Dyer to Talcott, Feb. 17, 1847, NMSRCA, Misc. Letters and Diaries, Box 1, File 5; Gardner and Simmons, *Mexican War Correspondence of Richard Smith Elliott*, 138; Cooke, *Conquest of New Mexico and California*, 111.

108. Cutts, *Conquest of California and New Mexico,* 220; Gibson, *Journal of a Soldier under Kearny,* 270; Gardner and Simmons, *Mexican War Correspondence of Richard Smith Elliott,* 83, 92–93, 107–10, 157; George Rutland Gibson, *Over the Chihuahua and Santa Fe Trails, 1847–1848: George Rutledge Gibson's Journal,* ed. Robert W. Frazer (Albuquerque: University of New Mexico Press, 1981), 39.

109. Price to Jones, Feb. 15, 1847, 30th Cong., 1st Sess., Senate Exec. Doc. No. 1, p. 521; Cutts, *Conquest of California and New Mexico,* 222.

110. Garrard, *Wah-to-Yah and the Taos Trail,* 174.

111. Howard Louis Conard, *Uncle Dick Wootton: The Pioneer Frontiersman of the Rocky Mountain Region,* ed. Milo Milton Quaife (Chicago: R. R. Donnelley, 1957), 156; "The Story of Governor Bent's Massacre as Told by His Daughter Teresina Bent Scheurich Who Was a Witness," NMSRCA, Jaramillo-Bent-Scheurich Family Papers, Folder 13.

112. Cutts, *Conquest of California and New Mexico,* 222–23. See also Hyde, *Empires, Nations, and Families,* 385–86.

113. Gardner and Simmons, *Mexican War Correspondence of Richard Smith Elliott,* 139. See also "Story of Governor Bent's Massacre," NMSRCA, Jaramillo-Bent-Scheurich Family Papers, Folder 13.

114. Cutts, *Conquest of California and New Mexico,* 222.

115. Gardner and Simmons, *Mexican War Correspondence of Richard Smith Elliott,* 139; Cutts, *Conquest of California and New Mexico,* 222–23. For firsthand accounts of Charles Bent, see James Hobbs, *Wild Life in the Far West: Personal Adventures of a Border Mountain Man* (Hartford, CT: Wiley, Waterman & Eaton, 1874), 18; "Report of Lieut. J. W. Abert," 30th Cong., 1st Sess., Senate Exec. Doc. 23, pp. 32, 125; Cooke, *Conquest of New Mexico and California,* 111–12; Ruxton, *Adventures in Mexico and the Rocky Mountains,* 200.

116. Hyde, *Empires, Nations, and Families,* 385–88. On the Taos Revolt, see "Late Insurrection and Atrocities in New Mexico," *New-York Daily Tribune,* April 19, 1847; L. Bradford Prince, *Historical Sketches of New Mexico from the Earliest Records to the American Occupation* (Kansas City, MO: Ramsey, Millett & Hudson, 1883), 313–25; Twitchell, *History of the Military Occupation,* 124–32; E. Bennett Burton, "The Taos Rebellion," *Old Santa Fe* 1 (Oct. 1913), 176–209; David Lavender, *Bent's Fort: A Historical Account of the Adobe Empire that Shaped the Destiny of the American Southwest* (Garden City, NY: Doubleday, 1954), 277–93; M. Morgan Estergreen, *Kit Carson: A Portrait in Courage* (Norman: University of Oklahoma Press, 1962), 172–79; Chris Emmett, *Fort Union and the Winning of the Southwest* (Norman: University of Oklahoma Press, 1965), 48–70; Michael McNierney, ed., *Taos 1847: The Revolt in Contemporary Accounts* (Boulder, CO: Johnson Publishing, 1980); James A. Crutchfield, *Revolt at Taos: The New Mexican and Indian Insurrection of 1847* (Yardley, PA: Westholme, 2015), 61–113; Hyslop, *Bound for Santa Fe,* 381–403; Brooks, *Captives and Cousins,* 281–86.

117. Cutts, *Conquest of California and New Mexico,* 222; "March Term 1847," NMSRCA, Dorothy Woodward Penitente Collection, Box 4, Folder 88; Vigil to Buchanan, Feb. 16, 1847, in "New Mexico and California," 30th Cong., 1st Sess., House Exec. Doc. No. 70, p. 18–19.

118. Lamar, *The Far Southwest,* 43–44; Craver, *Impact of Intimacy,* 11, 41–45.

119. Cutts, *Conquest of California and New Mexico,* 222–23; Gardner and Simmons, *Mexican War Correspondence of Richard Smith Elliott,* 139–43, quotation on 143; Garrard, *Wah-to-Yah and the Taos Trail,* 166–67; James P. Beckwourth, *The Life and Adventures of James P. Beckwourth, Mountaineer, Scout, and Pioneer, and Chief of the Crow Nation of Indians, Written from His Own Dictation by T. D. Bonner* (London: Sampson Low & Son, 1856), 485–86, quotation on 485; "Late Insurrection and Atrocities," *New-York Daily Tribune,* April 19, 1847.

120. Narciso was of French-Canadian and Hispanic lineage; his father, Charles Beaubien, married María Paula Lobato at Taos in 1827. Craver, *Impact of Intimacy,* 11.

121. Garrard, *Wah-to-Yah and the Taos Trail,* 167; Conard, *Uncle Dick Wootton,* 159.

122. Price to Jones, Feb. 15, 1847, in Report of the Secretary of War, 30th Cong., 1st Sess., Senate Exec. Doc. No. 1, p. 520.

123. "From Santa Fe," *New-York Daily Tribune,* March 19, 1847.

124. Craver, *Impact of Intimacy,* 11, 41–45; Lamar, *The Far Southwest,* 44.

125. Price to Jones, Feb. 15, 1847, in "Report of the Secretary of War," 30th Cong., 1st Sess., Senate Exec. Doc. No. 1, p. 520; Ruxton, *Adventures in Mexico and the Rocky Mountains,* 226–30.

126. Vigil to Buchanan, Feb. 16, 1847, in "New Mexico and California," 30th Cong., 1st Sess., House Exec. Doc. No. 70, p. 18. For a biographical sketch of Vigil, see Twitchell, *History of the Military Occupation,* 207–13.

127. Price to Jones, Feb. 15, 1847, in "Report of the Secretary of War," 30th Cong., 1st Sess., Senate Exec. Doc. No. 1, p. 521; Beckwourth, *Life and Adventures,* 484–85.

128. Price to Jones, Feb. 15, 1847, in "Report of the Secretary of War," 30th Cong., 1st Sess., Senate Exec. Doc. No. 1, pp. 521–22, 527; Gardner and Simmons, *Mexican War Correspondence of Richard Smith Elliott,* 148; Dyer to Talcott, Feb. 17, 1847, NMSRCA, Misc. Letters and Diaries, Box 1, Folder 5; Vigil to Buchanan, Feb. 16, 1847, in "New Mexico and California," 30th Cong., 1st Sess., House Exec. Doc. No. 70, p. 18; Cooke, *Conquest of New Mexico and California,* 113–14.

129. "Battle in Santa Fe: Mexicans Completely Routed," *New-York Daily Tribune,* April 7, 1847; "From Santa Fe," *New-York Daily Tribune,* April 8, 1847.

130. Vigil to Buchanan, Feb. 16, 1847, in "New Mexico and California," 30th Cong., 1st Sess., House Exec. Doc. No. 70, p. 18–19; Dyer to Talcott, Feb. 17, 1847, NMSRCA, Misc. Letters and Diaries, Box 1, Folder 5. On the Battle of Embudo, see Price to Jones, Feb. 15, 1847, in "Report of the Secretary of War," 30th Cong., 1st Sess., Senate Exec. Doc. No. 1, pp. 523–24; 527; Rufus Ingalls to C. Wharton, Feb. 16, 1847, in "Insurrection against the Military Government," 56th Cong., 1st Sess., Senate Doc. No. 442, pp. 16–17; Gardner and Simmons, *Mexican War Correspondence of Richard Smith Elliott,* 149; Cooke, *Conquest of New Mexico and California,* 114–15.

131. Price to Jones, Feb. 15, 1847, in "Report of the Secretary of War," 30th Cong., 1st Sess., Senate Exec. Doc. No. 1, pp. 523–24; Garrard, *Wah-to-Yah and the Taos Trail,* 176.

132. Dyer to Talcott, Feb. 17, 1847, NMSRCA, Misc. Letters and Diaries, Box 1, Folder 5; Gardner and Simmons, *Mexican War Correspondence of Richard Smith Elliott,* 180; "The Troops of New Mexico," *Santa Fe Republican,* Aug. 31, 1848.

133. Beckwourth, *Life and Adventures*, 486.

134. Price to Jones, Feb. 15, 1847, in "Report of the Secretary of War," 30th Cong., 1st Sess., Senate Exec. Doc. No. 1, p. 524–25; Dyer to Talcott, Feb. 17, 1847, NMSRCA, Misc. Letters and Diaries, Box 1, Folder 5; Gardner and Simmons, *Mexican War Correspondence of Richard Smith Elliott*, 150.

135. Ingalls to Wharton, Feb. 16, 1847, in "Insurrection against the Military Government," 56th Cong., 1st Sess., Senate Doc. No. 442, p. 17.

136. Dyer to Talcott, Feb. 17, 1847, NMSRCA, Misc. Letters and Diaries, Box 1, Folder 5; Price to Jones, Feb. 15, 1847, in "Report of the Secretary of War," 30th Cong., 1st Sess., Senate Exec. Doc. No. 1, p. 524–25; Gardner and Simmons, *Mexican War Correspondence of Richard Smith Elliott*, 152; Garrard, *Wah-to-Yah and the Taos Trail*, 176–78; Conard, *Uncle Dick Wootton*, 165–66; Beckwourth, *Life and Adventures*, 487–88.

137. Gardner and Simmons, *Mexican War Correspondence of Richard Smith Elliott*, 153–54, quotation on 176; Cooke, *Conquest of New Mexico and California*, 121; William N. Grier to H. W. Staunton, Feb. 15, 1847, in "Insurrection against the Military Government," 56th Cong., 1st Sess., Senate Doc. No. 442, pp. 15–16.

138. C. Wharton to Jones, April 1, 1847, in "Insurrection against the Military Government," 56th Cong., 1st Sess., Senate Doc. No. 442, p. 17. For military activities at Taos, see Lawrence R. Murphy, "The United States Army in Taos, 1847–1852," *New Mexico Historical Review* 47 (Jan. 1972): 33–48.

139. Price to Jones, Feb. 15, 1847, in "Report of the Secretary of War," 30th Cong., 1st Sess., Senate Exec. Doc. No. 1, p. 525, 528–29; Dyer to Talcott, Feb. 17, 1847, NMSRCA, Misc. Letters and Diaries, Box 1, Folder 5; Donaciano Vigil Circular, Feb. 12, 1847, in "New Mexico and California," 30th Cong., 1st Sess., House Exec. Doc. No. 70, p. 24; Gardner and Simmons, *Mexican War Correspondence of Richard Smith Elliott*, 154–55; "Battle of Pueblo de Taos," *New-York Daily Tribune*, April 19, 1847.

140. Gardner and Simmons, *Mexican War Correspondence of Richard Smith Elliott*, 152.

141. I. R. Hendley to Price, Jan. 23, 1847, in "Report of the Secretary of War," 30th Cong., 1st Sess., Senate Exec. Doc. No. 1, p. 531–32; W. S. Murphy to Headquarters, Jan. 25, 1847, in "Insurrection against the Military Government," 56th Cong., 1st Sess., Senate Doc. No. 442, p. 20; Gardner and Simmons, *Mexican War Correspondence of Richard Smith Elliott*, 145. For events at Mora, see Prince, *Historical Sketches of New Mexico*, 325–27; James W. Goodrich, "Revolt at Mora, 1847," *New Mexico Historical Review* 47 (Jan. 1972): 49–60.

142. Price to Jones, Feb. 15, 1847, in "Report of the Secretary of War," 30th Cong., 1st Sess., Senate Exec. Doc. No. 1, p. 530. On Captain Hendley, see Francis B. Heitman, *Historical Register and Dictionary of the United States Army* (Washington, D.C.: Government Printing Office, 1903), 2:55.

143. T. C. McKarney to Price, Jan. 25, 1847, in "Report of the Secretary of War," 30th Cong., 1st Sess., Senate Exec. Doc. No. 1, pp. 532–33; Murphy to Price, Jan. 25, 1847, in ibid., 533; Vigil to Buchanan, Feb. 16, 1847, in "New Mexico and California," 30th Cong., 1st Sess., House Exec. Doc. No. 70, pp. 18–19.

144. "Insurrection against the Military Government," 56th Cong., 1st Sess., Senate Doc. No. 442, p. 26; Goodrich, "Revolt at Mora," 56.

145. Price to Jones, Feb. 15, 1847, in "Report of the Secretary of War," 30th Cong., 1st Sess., Senate Exec. Doc. No. 1, p. 525

146. Garrard, *Wah-to-Yah and the Taos Trail*, 147; Dyer to Talcott, Feb. 17, 1847, NMSRCA, Misc. Letters and Diaries, Box 1, Folder 5; Conard, *Uncle Dick Wootton*, 169.

147. Conard, *Uncle Dick Wootton*, 169.

148. William L. Marcy to Price, June 11, 1847, in "New Mexico and California," 30th Cong., 1st Sess., House Exec. Doc. No. 70, p. 32–33.

149. Price to Jones, March 31, 1848, in "Report of the Secretary of War," 30th Cong., 1st Sess., House Exec. Doc. 1, p. 113.

150. Gardner and Simmons, *Mexican War Correspondence of Richard Smith Elliott*, 156.

151. Frank P. Blair to John Y. Mason, April 1, 1847, in "New Mexico and California," 30th Cong., 1st Sess., House Exec. Doc. No. 70, p. 27; Chávez, *Manuel Alvarez*, 101.

152. Brooks, *Captives and Cousins*, 286–87.

153. Beckwourth, *Life and Adventures*, 486–87; Circular of Donaciano Vigil, Jan. 22, 1847, in "New Mexico and California," 30th Cong., 1st Sess., House Exec. Doc. No. 70, p. 22. For the 1837 uprising, see Janet Lecompte, *Rebellion in Rio Arriba, 1837* (Albuquerque: University of New Mexico Press, 1985).

154. Donaciano Vigil Circular, Feb. 12, 1847, in "New Mexico and California," 30th Cong., 1st Sess., House Exec. Doc. No. 70, pp. 23–24; Price to Jones, Feb. 15, 1847, in "Report of the Secretary of War," 30th Cong., 1st Sess., Senate Exec. Doc. No. 1, p. 525.

155. Garrard, *Wah-to-Yah and the Taos Trail*, 162–63.

156. Ibid., 163, 181–89. See also Garrard to Dear Mother, May 15, 1847, in Meyer, "New Light on Lewis Garrard," 271; Lewis Garrard to Kenner Garrard, Sept. 10, 1847, ibid., 274–75.

157. Garrard, *Wah-to-Yah and the Taos Trail*, 189.

158. Gardner and Simmons, *Mexican War Correspondence of Richard Smith Elliott*, 164, 181.

159. Garrard, *Wah-to-Yah and the Taos Trail*, 189–91.

160. Dyer to Talcott, Feb. 17, 1847, NMSRCA, Misc. Letters and Diaries, Box 1, Folder 5.

161. Marcy to Price, June 11, 1847, in "New Mexico and California," 30th Cong., 1st Sess., House Exec. Doc. No. 70, p. 32. On the Trujillo proceedings, see Emmett, *Fort Union*, 62–64; Chávez, *Manuel Alvarez*, 113–14.

162. Sánchez, *Forgotten People*, 48.

163. Marcy to Polk, July 19, 1848, in "New Mexico and California," 30th Cong., 1st Sess., House Exec. Doc. No. 70, p. 12; Marcy to Price, June 26, 1847, ibid., 33–34.

164. Benton, *Thirty Years' View*, 2:683. See also "Resolutions," *Congressional Globe*, 30th Cong., 1st Sess., Dec. 20, 1847, p. 58.

165. Hunter Miller, ed., *Treaties and Other International Acts of the United States of America* (Washington, D.C.: Government Printing Office, 1931–48), 5:219–22.

166. "New Mexico and California," 30th Cong., 1st Sess., House Exec. Doc. No. 70, p. 5. See also Gardner and Simmons, *Mexican War Correspondence of Richard Smith Elliott*, 156.

167. Vigil to Buchanan, Feb. 16, 1847, in "New Mexico and California," 30th Cong., 1st Sess., House Exec. Doc. No. 70, p. 19; Bent to Buchanan, Dec. 26, 1846, ibid., 17; Antonio José Martínez to Price, April 12, 1947, NMSRCA, Papers of Governors Kearny, Bent, and Price, Serial #13888, Folder 6. An army inspector reported in 1850 that at least 2,200

soldiers were needed in New Mexico. Colonel George Archibald McCall, *New Mexico in 1850: A Military View,* ed. Robert W. Frazer (Norman: University of Oklahoma Press, 1968), 181.

168. Marcy to Price, June 26, 1847, in "New Mexico and California," 30th Cong., 1st Sess., House Exec. Doc. No. 70, pp. 27–28, 34; *Santa Fe Republican*, Sept. 10, 1847. See also Robert E. Shalhope, *Sterling Price: Portrait of a Southerner* (Columbia: University of Missouri Press, 1971), 61–62; Chalfant, *Dangerous Passage*, 103–18.

169. Wooster, *American Military Frontiers*, 119–21.

170. Dyer to Talcott, Aug. 11, 1847, NMSRCA, Misc. Letters and Diaries, Box 1, File 5.

171. Robert Walker to W. E. Prince, Dec. 29, 1847, NA, RG94, AGO, LR 1805–89, File P-94–1848, Entry 12, with enclosed muster rolls of the Chihuahua Battalion. I thank John P. Wilson for bringing this document to my attention.

172. Price to Jones, July 20, 1847, in "Report of the Secretary of War," 30th Cong., 1st Sess., Senate Exec. Doc. No. 1, pp. 534–35; D. B. Edmonson to Price, June 14, 1847, ibid., 535–38; Brooks, *Captives and Cousins*, 286.

173. Price to Jones, July 20, 1847, "Report of the Secretary of War," 30th Cong., 1st Sess., Senate Exec. Doc. No. 1, pp. 534–35; Edmonson to Price, June 14, 1847, ibid., 535.

174. "Message of the President of the United States," Aug. 2, 1848, 30th Cong., 1st Sess., House Exec. Doc. 76, pp. 1–4.

175. Twitchell, *History of the Military Occupation of the Territory of New Mexico,* 65–67.

176. "New Year's Address," *Santa Fe Republican*, Jan. 1, 1848.

177. A. B. Dyer to Col. Talcott, Feb. 17, 1847, NMSRCA, Misc. Letters and Diaries, Box 1, File 5.

178. On rumors of rebellion after 1848, see James S. Calhoun to Luke Lea, June 30, 1851, in *1851 Annual Report of the Commissioner of Indian Affairs*, 197 (hereafter cited as *RCIA*); Calhoun to Lea, July 25, 1851, ibid., 199; Calhoun to Edwin V. Sumner, Aug. 4, 1851, ibid., 203; Calhoun to William Medill, Oct. 14, 1849, in Abel, *Correspondence of James S. Calhoun,* 51–52; Calhoun to W. C. Dawson, April 12, 1852, in ibid., 523–24; John Greiner to Lea, April 30, 1852, NA, RG75, OIA, LR, NMS, M234, Roll 547; Sumner to Daniel Webster, May 8, 1852, NA, RG393, M1072, LS, DNM, Roll 1; Sumner to Charles M. Conrad, Oct. 29, 1852, ibid. See also Ball, *Army Regulars on the Western Frontier*, 21.

179. "Petition of the People of New Mexico," Oct. 14, 1848, 30th Cong., 2nd Sess., Senate Misc. Doc. 5, pp. 1–2.

180. For the debate on the New Mexico petition, see "New Mexico," *Congressional Globe*, 30th Cong., 2nd Sess., Dec. 13, 1848, pp. 33–37.

Chapter 3

1. On Sumner, see Heitman, *Historical Register of the U.S. Army,* 2:936; Ball, *Army Regulars on the Western Frontier,* 20–22, 66; Kiser, *Dragoons in Apacheland,* 95. For praise of Sumner's policy, see Thomas Swords to Thomas S. Jesup, Oct. 25, 1851, in "Report of the Quartermaster General," 32nd Cong., 1st Sess., House Exec. Doc. No. 2, p. 239.

2. Sumner to Roger Jones, Oct. 24, 1851, RG393, M1072, LS, DNM, Roll 1.

3. Conrad to Sumner, April 1, 1851, in Abel, *Correspondence of James S. Calhoun*, 383; Sumner to Jones, Oct. 24, 1851, RG393, M1072, LS, DNM, Roll 1; *1851 Annual Report of the Secretary of War*, 32nd Cong., 1st Sess., Senate Exec. Doc. No. 1, pp. 106, 111–12. For civilian protests, see Petition of El Paso residents to Sumner, Aug. 4, 1851, NA, RG393, M1102, LR, DNM, Roll 4; Petition of Doña Ana residents to Calhoun, Aug. 8, 1851, in Abel, *Correspondence of James S. Calhoun*, 402–3. On Sumner's military reorganization, see Utley, *Frontiersmen in Blue*, 86–89; Frazer, *Forts and Supplies*, 61–85; Wooster, *American Military Frontiers*, 125–27.

4. Sumner to Samuel Cooper, Dec. 19, 1852, RG393, M1072, LS, DNM, Roll 1; John Garland to Lorenzo Thomas, Nov. 27, 1853, ibid.

5. Sumner to Jones, Nov. 20, 1851, ibid.

6. Sumner to Conrad, May 27, 1852, in *1852 Annual Report of the Secretary of War*, 32nd Cong., 2nd Sess., Senate Exec. Doc. No. 1, pp. 23–25.

7. Calhoun to Luke Lea, Oct. 1, 1851, in *1851 RCIA*, 205.

8. Swords to Jesup, Oct. 25, 1851, in "Report of the Quartermaster General," 32nd Cong., 1st Sess., House Exec. Doc. No. 2, p. 239; *1850 Annual Report of the Secretary of War*, 31st Cong., 2nd Sess., Senate Exec. Doc. No. 5, p. 5. Calhoun wanted to raise a militia of one thousand men but did not receive permission to do so. Calhoun to George Crawford, May 22, 1849, in Abel, *Correspondence of James S. Calhoun*, 14–15. A decade later, Secretary of War John Floyd again suggested that civilian militias be incorporated into the territorial defense system. See *1859 Annual Report of the Secretary of War*, 36th Cong., 1st Sess., Senate Exec. Doc. No. 2, p. 4; Croghan Ker to Lafayette McLaws, Jan. 29, 1849, NA, RG393, M1102, LR, DNM, Roll 1.

9. *1852 Annual Report of the Secretary of War*, 32nd Cong., 2nd Sess., Senate Exec. Doc. No. 1, pp. 5–6; Sumner to Conrad, Oct. 29, 1852, NA, RG393, M1072, LS, DNM, Roll 1.

10. "Condition of the Indian Tribes," 39th Cong., 2nd Sess., Senate Report No. 156, p. 7.

11. "Col. Sumner and his Movements," *Santa Fe Weekly Gazette*, Dec. 25, 1852; "Hon. Charles M. Conrad Secretary of War," ibid., Feb. 19, 1853; "The Big Bug of Albuquerque," ibid.; "The Cessation of Indian Hostilities in New Mexico," ibid., Feb. 26, 1853; "Col. Sumner's Letter on New Mexico," ibid., March 5, 1853.

12. Greiner to Sumner, Aug. 30, 1852, and Sumner to Greiner, Aug. 31, 1852, in "Letterbook of Communications sent by the Secretary of the Territory, 1852–1859," NMSRCA, TA, Roll 27.

13. On the feud between Sumner and Lane, see Sumner to Jones, May 8, 1852, RG393, M1072, LS, DNM, Roll 1; Sumner to Cooper, Oct. 25, 1852, ibid.; Sumner to Lane, Oct. 24, 1852, ibid.

14. Weightman to Lane, Oct. 7, 1852; Weightman to Lane, Nov. 18, 1852; Weightman to Lane, Jan. 13, 1853, all from Missouri Historical Society, William Carr Lane Papers. For civil-military disputes, see Sumner to Calhoun, Aug. 8, 1851, in *1851 RCIA*, 204; Calhoun to Lea, Oct. 1, 1851, ibid., 204–5.

15. Richard Kern to Edward Kern, Aug. 24, 1851, in David J. Weber, *Richard H. Kern: Expeditionary Artist in the Far Southwest, 1848–1853* (Albuquerque: University of New Mexico Press, 1985), 145.

16. "Report of the Quartermaster General," Nov. 22, 1851, in 32nd Cong., 1st Sess., House Exec. Doc. No. 2, p. 219; *1857 Annual Report of the Secretary of War*, 35th Cong., 1st Sess., Senate Exec. Doc. No. 11, p. 3.

17. William P. Dole to J. P. Usher, Nov. 15, 1864, in *1864 RCIA*, 17.

18. See Wooster, *American Military Frontiers*.

19. *1850 Annual Report of the Secretary of War*, 31st Cong., 2nd Sess., Senate Exec. Doc. No. 5, p. 3; *1851 Annual Report of the Secretary of War*, 32nd Cong., 1st Sess., Senate Exec. Doc. No. 1, pp. 108–10.

20. *1853 Annual Report of the Secretary of War*, 33rd Cong., 1st Sess., Senate Exec. Doc. No. 1, pp. 11–12; *1854 Annual Report of the Secretary of War*, 33rd Cong., 2nd Sess., Senate Exec. Doc. No. 1, p. 6; "Report of the Secretary of War on the Subject of Indian Hostilities," 33rd Cong., 2nd Sess., Senate Exec. Doc. No. 22. The actual strength of the army was typically 30–40 percent less than the legislated strength. See *1850 Annual Report of the Secretary of War*, 31st Cong., 2nd Sess., Senate Exec. Doc. No. 5, p. 3; *1852 Annual Report of the Secretary of War*, 32nd Cong., 2nd Sess., Senate Exec. Doc. No. 1, p. 3; McCall, *New Mexico in 1850*, 184; Ball, *Army Regulars on the Western Frontier*, xix–xxxi. On the failure of Congress to increase the size of the army, see Utley, *Frontiersmen in Blue*, 10–17.

21. On Americans' views toward southwestern Indians, see DeLay, *War of a Thousand Deserts*, 291–96.

22. On tribal sovereignty, see N. Bruce Duthu, *Shadow Nation: Tribal Sovereignty and the Limits of Legal Pluralism* (New York: Oxford University Press, 2013), 12–16. For Marshall's decision, see Cherokee Nation v. State of Georgia 30 U.S. 1 (1831).

23. On the treaty-making process, see Francis Paul Prucha, *American Indian Treaties: The History of a Political Anomaly* (Berkeley: University of California Press, 1994), 1–21; Colin G. Calloway, *Pen and Ink Witchcraft: Treaties and Treaty Making in American Indian History* (New York: Oxford University Press, 2013), 2–8.

24. Ball, *Army Regulars on the Western Frontier*, xii; Utley, *Frontiersmen in Blue*, 18.

25. *1860 Annual Report of the Secretary of War*, 36th Cong., 2nd Sess., Senate Exec. Doc. No. 1, p. 5.

26. *1850 Annual Report of the Secretary of War*, 31st Cong., 2nd Sess., Senate Exec. Doc. No. 5, p. 3.

27. J. H. Dickinson to O. H. P. Taylor, March 30, 1849, NA, RG393, M1102, LR, DNM, Roll 1. See also Calhoun to Medill, Aug. 15, 1849, in Abel, *Correspondence of James S. Calhoun*, 20.

28. *1850 Annual Report of the Secretary of War*, 31st Cong., 2nd Sess., Senate Exec. Doc. No. 5, p. 5; *1851 Annual Report of the Secretary of War*, 32nd Cong., 1st Sess., Senate Exec. Doc. No. 1, p. 105; *1853 Annual Report of the Secretary of War*, 33rd Cong., 1st Sess., Senate Exec. Doc. No. 1, pp. 5–6; "Report of the Secretary of War on the Subject of Indian

Hostilities," 33rd Cong., 2nd Sess., Senate Exec. Doc. No. 22, p. 1; *1855 Annual Report of the Secretary of War*, 34th Cong., 1st Sess., Senate Exec. Doc. No. 1, p. 3. See also Ball, *Army Regulars on the Western Frontier*, xx–xxii. On the role of Davis in expanding the armed forces, see Matthew Karp, *This Vast Southern Empire: Slaveholders at the Helm of American Foreign Policy* (Cambridge, MA: Harvard University Press), 209–16.

29. "Report of the Quartermaster General," Nov. 22, 1851, in 32nd Cong., 1st Sess., House Exec. Doc. No. 2, pp. 220–21; *1850 Annual Report of the Secretary of War*, 31st Cong., 2nd Sess., Senate Exec. Doc. No. 5, pp. 8–9; *1851 Annual Report of the Secretary of War*, 32nd Cong., 1st Sess., Senate Exec. Doc. No. 1, p. 110. For transportation costs, see Jerry Thompson, ed., *Texas and New Mexico on the Eve of the Civil War: The Mansfield and Johnston Inspections, 1859–1861* (Albuquerque: University of New Mexico Press, 2001), 50. On army expenses, see Frazer, *Forts and Supplies*, 33–163.

30. Swords to Jesup, Oct. 25, 1851, in "Report of the Quartermaster General," 32nd Cong., 1st Sess., House Exec. Doc. No. 2, pp. 235–51; ibid., 220; "Consolidated Report of J.C. McFerran," April 1851, NA, RG393, M1102, LR, DNM, Roll 3; Calhoun to Alexander Stuart, March 31, 1851, in Abel, *Correspondence of James S. Calhoun*, 306. See also Ball, *Army Regulars on the Western Frontier*, 28–29. On rent expenses, see McCall, *New Mexico in 1850*, 111–76.

31. Weymouth T. Jordan Jr., John D. Chapla, and Shan C. Sutton, "'Notorious as the Noonday Sun': Capt. Alexander Welch Reynolds and the New Mexico Territory, 1849–1859," *New Mexico Historical Review* 75 (Oct. 2000): 464.

32. "Report of the Quartermaster General," Nov. 22, 1851, in 32nd Cong., 1st Sess., House Exec. Doc. No. 2, pp. 223, 226.

33. Ibid., 223–25. On the militarized U.S.-Mexico border, see Samuel Truett, *Fugitive Landscapes: The Forgotten History of the U.S.-Mexico Borderlands* (New Haven, CT: Yale University Press, 2006), 13–32; Rachel St. John, *Line in the Sand: A History of the Western U.S.-Mexico Border* (Princeton, NJ: Princeton University Press, 2011), 39–62.

34. "Report of the Quartermaster General," Nov. 22, 1851, in 32nd Cong., 1st Sess., House Exec. Doc. No. 2, pp. 223–25.

35. "Second Annual Message to the Legislative Assembly," William F. M. Arny, Dec. 1866, NMSRCA, TA, Roll 98. For other estimates, see Julius K. Graves to Cooley, Undated Report of Jan. 1866, in *1866 RCIA*, 136.

36. John Russell Bartlett, *Personal Narrative of Explorations and Incidents in Texas, New Mexico, California, Sonora and Chihuahua, 1850–1853* (New York: D. Appleton, 1854), 2:386.

37. "Claims for Depredations by Indians in the Territory of New Mexico," 35th Cong., 1st Sess., Senate Exec. Doc. No. 55; Calhoun to Lea, Feb. 2, 1851, in *1851 RCIA*, 187. See also Kiser, *Dragoons in Apacheland*, 45–46; McCall, *New Mexico in 1850*, 178.

38. Munroe to Jones, March 30, 1851, NA, RG393, M1072, LS, DNM, Roll 1; *1851 Annual Report of the Secretary of War*, 32nd Cong., 1st Sess., Senate Exec. Doc. No. 1, pp. 107–8; Thomas T. Fauntleroy to Lorenzo Thomas, Nov. 6, 1859, in "Indian Hostilities in New Mexico," 36th Cong., 1st Sess., House Exec. Doc. No. 69, pp. 10–11.

39. Circular of Capt. Henry B. Judd, April 3, 1849, NA, RG393, M1102, LR, DNM, Roll 1.

40. Munroe to Jones, June 11, 1850, NA, RG393, M1072, LS, DNM, Roll 1.

41. See McNitt, *Navajo Wars*, 3–91; William B. Griffen, *Utmost Good Faith: Patterns of Apache-Mexican Hostilities in Northern Chihuahua Border Warfare, 1821–1848* (Albuquerque: University of New Mexico Press, 1988); Edwin R. Sweeney, *Mangas Coloradas: Chief of the Chiricahua Apaches* (Norman: University of Oklahoma Press, 1998), 27–136; David J. Weber, *Bárbaros: Spaniards and Their Savages in the Age of Enlightenment* (New Haven, CT: Yale University Press, 2005), 138–77; Ned Blackhawk, *Violence over the Land: Indians and Empires in the Early American West* (Cambridge, MA: Harvard University Press, 2006); Pekka Hämäläinen, *The Comanche Empire* (New Haven, CT: Yale University Press, 2008).

42. *1860 Annual Report of the Secretary of War*, 36th Cong., 2nd Sess., Senate Exec. Doc. No. 1, p. 5. See also Donald L. Fixico, *Bureau of Indian Affairs* (Santa Barbara, CA: Greenwood, 2012), 1–22; Francis Paul Prucha, *The Great Father: The United States Government and the American Indians* (Lincoln: University of Nebraska Press, 1984), 1:319–23; Ball, *Army Regulars on the Western Frontier*, 13–23.

43. On the reservation system, see Robert A. Trennert Jr., *Alternative to Extinction: Federal Indian Policy and the Beginnings of the Reservation System, 1846–1851* (Philadelphia: Temple University Press, 1975), 94–130. For the BIA's policy, see Dole to Usher, Nov. 15, 1864, in *1864 RCIA*, 147–49.

44. Calhoun to Orlando Brown, Feb. 3, 1850, in Abel, *Correspondence of James S. Calhoun*, 141; Calhoun to Medill, July 29, 1849, ibid., 19–20; Calhoun to Medill, Oct. 15, 1849, ibid., 55–57; Hugh N. Smith to Brown, March 9, 1850, in *1850 RCIA*, 142. For Calhoun's orders, see Medill to Calhoun, April 7, 1849, in Abel, *Correspondence of James S. Calhoun*, 3–5.

45. Calhoun to the Indians of the Pueblo of Taos, Feb. 2, 1850, in Abel, *Correspondence of James S. Calhoun*, 136–38; Calhoun to Brown, July 16, 1850, ibid., 227–28. On personal expenses, see Calhoun to Brown, Aug. 30, 1850, ibid., 255. For the petition, see "Petition to the President of the United States," Feb. 27, 1850, ibid., 159.

46. See Morris E. Opler, *An Apache Life-Way: The Economic, Social, and Religious Institutions of the Chiricahua Indians* (New York: Cooper Square, 1965).

47. E. A. Graves to George W. Manypenny, June 8, 1854, in *1854 RCIA*, 181–83, quotation on 181.

48. "The Indians of New Mexico," *Santa Fe Weekly Gazette*, Oct. 18, 1856; Bonneville to Collins, Sept. 22, 1857, in *1857 RCIA*, 295. On proposals for a Navajo reservation, see Michael Steck to Dole, Oct. 10, 1864, in *1864 RCIA*, 184–86.

49. William Pelham to Steck, Oct. 3, 1855, Center for Southwest Research, Inventory of the Michael Steck Papers, Roll 2; Bonneville to Collins, Sept. 22, 1857, in *1857 RCIA*, 295.

50. Denver to Jacob Thompson, Nov. 30, 1857, in *1857 RCIA*, 9; Dole to Caleb B. Smith, Nov. 27, 1861, in *1861 RCIA*, 20.

51. Bartlett to Alexander Stuart, Feb. 19, 1852, NA, OIA, LR, M234, Roll 546.

52. *Santa Fe Weekly Gazette*, Dec. 18, 1852; "The Indians Becoming Troublesome, The Policy of Governor Lane," *Santa Fe Weekly Gazette*, Dec. 31, 1853; Lane to Steck, July 11, 1853, Center for Southwest Research, Inventory of the Michael Steck Papers, Roll 1; Meriwether to Manypenny, Sept. 1, 1854, in *1854 RCIA*, 166–68.

53. Charles E. Mix to Thompson, Nov. 6, 1858, in *1858 RCIA*, 6; Report of Jacob Thompson, in *1860 RCIA*, 5. See also Levi J. Keithly to Steck, Sept. 22, 1863, in *1863 RCIA*, 115.

54. Kiser, *Dragoons in Apacheland*, 149, 152–53.

55. Steck to Dole, Sept. 19, 1863, in *1863 RCIA*, 111; Steck to Meriwether, Oct. 1854, Center for Southwest Research, Inventory of the Michael Steck Papers, Roll 1; Meriwether to Steck, April 28, 1855, ibid.; Manypenny to Meriwether, Aug. 8, 1854, NA, RG75, OIA, NMS, T21, Roll 2; Steck to Collins, Aug. 10, 1858, in *1858 RCIA*, 198. For Indian Department expenses, see Calhoun to Brown, March 30, 1850, in Abel, *Correspondence of James S. Calhoun*, 175–81; Manypenny to R. McClelland, Nov. 25, 1854, in *1854 RCIA*, 14; Meriwether to Manypenny, Sept. 1855, in *1855 RCIA*, 186–90; Collins to Denver, Aug. 30, 1857, in *1857 RCIA*, 278; Collins to Greenwood, Sept. 17, 1859, in *1859 RCIA*, 336. For Meriwether's treaties, see Ball, *Army Regulars on the Western Frontier*, 16; Prucha, *American Indian Treaties*, 241–42.

56. See John Grenier, *The First Way of War: American War Making on the Frontier, 1607–1814* (Cambridge, MA: Cambridge University Press, 2005), 1–12.

57. *1850 Annual Report of the Secretary of War*, 31st Cong., 2nd Sess., Senate Exec. Doc. No. 5, p. 5; *1851 Annual Report of the Secretary of War*, 32nd Cong., 1st Sess., Senate Exec. Doc. No. 1, p. 106; *1853 Annual Report of the Secretary of War*, 33rd Cong., 1st Sess., Senate Exec. Doc. No. 1, p. 6. See also Ball, *Army Regulars on the Western Frontier*, 38–55; Utley, *Frontiersmen in Blue*, 56–57.

58. Sumner to Jones, Jan. 27, 1852, NA, RG393, M1072, LS, DNM, Roll 1.

59. Garland to Thomas, Nov. 27, 1853, ibid.; Nichols to Fauntleroy, Feb. 6, 1855, ibid. On Garland as department commander, see Frazer, *Forts and Supplies*, 87–115.

60. Fauntleroy to Thomas, Jan. 29, 1860, in "Indian Hostilities in New Mexico," 36th Cong., 1st Sess., House Exec. Doc. No. 69, pp. 29–30; Collins to Greenwood, Feb. 10, 1860, ibid., 62–63.

61. Dole to Usher, Oct. 31, 1863, in *1863 RCIA*, 14.

62. Collins to Greenwood, Nov. 27, 1859, in "Indian Hostilities in New Mexico," 36th Cong., 1st Sess., House Exec. Doc. No. 69, p. 47; Collins to Greenwood, Jan. 7, 1860, ibid., 51–52; Collins to Greenwood, Feb. 4, 1860, ibid., 56.

63. Collins to Greenwood, Feb. 5, 1860, ibid., 59; Silas F. Kendrick to O. L. Shepherd, Oct. 25, 1859, ibid., 48; Kendrick to Shepherd, Jan. 20, 1860, ibid., 60; Kendrick to Collins, Jan. 23, 1860, ibid., 61.

64. Floyd to Fauntleroy, Jan. 10, 1860, in "Indian Hostilities in New Mexico," 36th Cong., 1st Sess., House Exec. Doc. No. 69, p. 27.

65. "Statistical Report on the Sickness and Mortality in the Army of the United States . . . From January 1849 to January 1855," prepared by Richard H. Coolidge, 34th Cong., 1st Sess., Senate Exec. Doc. No. 96, pp. 415, 417.

66. Ibid., 415, 417, 423, 432–35. On medical facilities, see W. G. Freeman to Munroe, May 27, 1850, NA, RG393, M1102, LR, DNM, Roll 2; Electus Backus to John C. McFerran, Feb. 13, 1852, ibid., Roll 4.

67. "Statistical Report on the Sickness and Mortality in the U.S. Army," 36th Cong., 1st Sess., Senate Exec. Doc. No. 52, pp. 214–16, 224; Thompson, *Texas and New Mexico on the Eve of the Civil War*, 64. See also E. H. Abadie to Nichols, Dec. 9, 1855, NA, RG393, M1120, LR, DNM, Roll 4.

68. "Statistical Report on the Sickness and Mortality in the U.S. Army," 36th Cong., 1st Sess., Senate Exec. Doc. No. 52, p. 225.

69. Grier to McLaws, Dec. 3, 1849, NA, RG393, M1102, LR, DNM, Roll 1.

70. John Buford to McLaws, June 1, 1850, ibid., Roll 2. Emphasis in original.

71. On military health, see Paul Kraemer, "Sickliest Post in the Territory of New Mexico: Fort Thorn and Malaria, 1853–1860," *New Mexico Historical Review* 71 (July 1996): 221–35.

72. Calvin, *Lieutenant Emory Reports*, 50.

73. Steck to Manypenny, May 1853, Center for Southwest Research, Inventory of the Michael Steck Papers, Roll 2.

74. Collins to Mix, Sept. 27, 1858, in *1858 RCIA*, 188–90.

75. Dole to Usher, Oct. 31, 1863, in *1863 RCIA*, 14.

76. Bieber, *Marching with the Army of the West*, 177.

77. Donaciano Vigil to James Buchanan, March 26, 1847, in "New Mexico and California," 30th Cong., 1st Sess., House Exec. Doc. 70, pp. 25–26.

78. Calhoun to Lea, Feb. 16, 1851, in *1851 RCIA*, 191.

79. 1850 Memorial to Congress, NA, RG46, Territorial Papers of the U.S. Senate, New Mexico 1840–1854, M200, Roll 14. See also Calhoun to Medill, Oct. 1, 1849, in Abel, *Correspondence of James S. Calhoun*, 32; "Petition to President Millard Fillmore," June 30, 1851, ibid., 366–68.

80. *Santa Fe Weekly Gazette*, June 4, 1853.

81. Undated Memorial to Congress (1850s), NA, RG46, Territorial Papers of the U.S. Senate, New Mexico 1840–1854, M200, Roll 14.

82. Memorial to Congress, Feb. 9, 1857, ibid.

83. For population estimates, see "Message of the President of the United States," Aug. 2, 1848, 30th Cong., 1st Sess., House Exec. Doc. 76, p. 11; Charles Bent to Medill, Nov. 10, 1846, in Abel, *Correspondence of James S. Calhoun*, 6–9.

84. For the 1846 Navajo treaty, see Doniphan to Jones, March 4, 1847, 30th Cong., 1st Sess., Senate Exec. Doc. No. 1, p. 496; Hughes, *Doniphan's Expedition*, 188–89. See also McNitt, *Navajo Wars*, 117–20.

85. Bent to Buchanan, Dec. 26, 1846, in "New Mexico and California," 30th Cong., 1st Sess., House Exec. Doc. No. 70, p. 17.

86. Gardner and Simmons, *Mexican War Correspondence of Richard Smith Elliott*, 156. Emphasis in original.

87. McNitt, *Navajo Wars*, 127–31. For the treaty, see Frank McNitt, ed. *Navaho Expedition: Journal of a Military Reconnaissance from Santa Fe, New Mexico, to the Navaho Country,*

Made in 1849 by Lieutenant James H. Simpson (Norman: University of Oklahoma Press, 1964), 253–57.

88. "Report of Lieut. J. W. Abert," 30th Cong., 1st Sess., Senate Exec. Doc. 23, p. 46; Alfred Pleasonton to J. W. Alley, March 28, 1851, NA, RG393, M1102, LR, DNM, Roll 3.

89. McNitt, *Navaho Expedition*, 65–69, 88–95, 165, quotation on 73; Calhoun to Medill, Oct. 1, 1849, in Abel, *Correspondence of James S. Calhoun*, 26–37. For Washington's treaty, see Charles J. Kappler, *Indian Affairs: Laws and Treaties* (Washington, D.C.: Government Printing Office, 1904), 2:583–85. For overviews of the campaign, see McNitt, *Navajo Wars*, 137–54; Weber, *Richard H. Kern*, 67–113. On antebellum Navajo relations, see Peter Iverson, *Diné: A History of the Navajos* (Albuquerque: University of New Mexico Press, 2002), 35–56.

90. Calhoun to Medill, Oct. 1, 1849, in Abel, *Correspondence of James S. Calhoun*, 33.

91. James A. Bennett, *Forts and Forays: A Dragoon in New Mexico, 1850–1856* (Albuquerque: University of New Mexico Press, 1948), 28–31, quotation on 31. For a similar account, see Eckert and Amato, *Ten Years in the Saddle*, 177–82.

92. Sumner to Jones, Jan. 27, 1852, NA, RG393, M1072, LS, DNM, Roll 1.

93. Calhoun to Conrad, Aug. 31, 1851, in Abel, *Correspondence of James S. Calhoun*, 413; Calhoun to Lea, Aug. 31, 1851, ibid., 414.

94. Sumner to Jones, Jan. 27, 1852, NA, RG393, M1072, LS, DNM, Roll 1; Sumner to Lane, June 15, 1853, ibid.; Sumner to Jones, Oct. 24, 1851, ibid. On the Sumner campaign, see McNitt, *Navajo Wars*, 193–99.

95. Backus to AAAG, NA, RG393, M1102, LR, DNM, Roll 4. On Fort Defiance, see Henry L. Kendrick to Nichols, Nov. 13, 1853, ibid., Roll 7; 1851 Annual Report of the Secretary of War, 32nd Cong., 1st Sess., Senate Exec. Doc. No. 1, p. 106.

96. Clarke, *Journals of Henry Smith Turner*, 85, quotations on 103. On the meeting between Kearny and Mangas Coloradas, see Sweeney, *Mangas Coloradas,* 143–44; Kiser, *Dragoons in Apacheland*, 16–17.

97. Wislizenus, *Memoir of a Tour to Northern Mexico*, 83.

98. Calhoun to Brown, Feb. 28, 1850, in Abel, *Correspondence of James S. Calhoun*, 155.

99. Steen to McLaws, Feb. 5, 1850, NA, RG393, M1102, LR, DNM, Roll 1; Calhoun to Brown, June 12, 1850, in Abel, *Correspondence of James S. Calhoun*, 209. On Fort Webster, see Buford to McFerran, Dec. 19, 1851, NA, RG393, M1102, LR, DNM, Roll 4. For military activities at Doña Ana, see Kiser, *Dragoons in Apacheland*, 66–73, 112–13, 235–37; William S. Kiser, "Louis Geck," in *Soldiers in the Southwest Borderlands, 1848–1886*, ed. Janne Lahti (Norman: University of Oklahoma Press, 2017), 35–56.

100. For the treaty, see Kappler, *Indian Affairs*, 2:598–600. See also Annie H. Abel, ed., "The Journal of John Greiner," *Old Santa Fe* 3 (July 1916): 220–22; Richard Weightman to Lane, Oct. 7, 1852, Missouri Historical Society, William Carr Lane Papers; *Santa Fe Weekly Gazette,* Nov. 20, 1852.

101. Sumner to Jones, July 21, 1852, NA, RG393, M1072, LS, DNM, Roll 1.

102. Meriwether to Garland, Jan. 24, 1855, NA, RG393, M1120, LR, DNM, Roll 4.

103. Garland to Miles, Dec. 26, 1854, NA, RG393, M1072, LS, DNM, Roll 1; Bennett, *Forts and Forays*, 59–63, quotation on 62.

104. Ewell to Nichols, Feb. 10, 1855, NA, RG393, M1120, LR, DNM, Roll 4.
105. Garland to Thomas, Feb. 28, 1855, NA, RG393, M1072, LS, DNM, Roll 1. On Stanton's death, see Miles to Nichols, Feb. 5, 1855, ibid.; Garland to Cooper, Feb. 2, 1855, NA, RG393, M1072, LS, DNM, Roll 1; Bennett, *Forts and Forays*, 61–63. On the establishment of Fort Stanton, see Miles to Garland, April 28, 1855, NA, RG393, M1120, LR, DNM, Roll 4; Garland to Thomas, May 31, 1855, NA, RG393, M1072, LS, DNM, Roll 1. See also C. L. Sonnichsen, *The Mescalero Apaches* (Norman: University of Oklahoma Press, 1958), 74–81; John P. Ryan, *Fort Stanton and Its Community, 1855–1896* (Las Cruces, NM: Yucca Tree, 1998), 1–32.
106. Treaty with the Apaches at Fort Thorn, June 9, 1855, Center for Southwest Research, Inventory of the Michael Steck Papers, Roll 1. See also Steck to Garland, March 6, 1855, NA, RG393, M1120, LR, DNM, Roll 4.
107. Nichols to Steen, Feb. 17, 1857, NA, RG393, M1072, LS, DNM, Roll 2; Bonneville to Thomas, Jan. 31, 1857, ibid.; Nichols to Thomas, April 28, 1857, ibid.
108. Loring to Bonneville, May 1857, NA, RG393, M1120, LR, DNM, Roll 6; Bonneville to Nichols, May 1857, ibid.
109. George P. Hammond, ed., *Campaigns in the West, 1856–1861: The Original Journal and Letters of Colonel John Van Deusen DuBois* (Tucson: Arizona Pioneers Historical Society, 1949), 30.
110. Garland to Thomas, Aug. 1, 1857, NA, RG393, M1072, LS, DNM, Roll 2.
111. Nichols to Bonneville, July 26, 1857, ibid.; Miles to Bonneville, May 30, 1857, NA, RG393, M1120, LR, DNM, Roll 6; Loring to Bonneville, May 1857, ibid.; Steck to Collins, Aug. 12, 1859, in *1859 RCIA*, 345. For the "campaign of clowns" quote, see Dan L. Thrapp, *Victorio and the Mimbres Apaches* (Norman: University of Oklahoma Press, 1974), 54.
112. Frank D. Reeve, ed., "Puritan and Apache," *New Mexico Historical Review* 24 (Jan. 1949): 50–51.
113. For the Gila Campaign, see Kiser, *Dragoons in Apacheland*, 203–31; Sweeney, *Mangas Coloradas*, 352–56.
114. In Abel, *Correspondence of James S. Calhoun,* see: Calhoun to Medill, Oct. 29, 1849, pp. 63–66; Calhoun to Brown, Nov. 2, 1849, pp. 68–69; Calhoun to Brown, Nov. 30, 1849, p. 88; Brown to Calhoun, Dec. 28, 1849, pp. 94–95; Auguste Lacome to Calhoun, March 16, 1850, p. 170; Calhoun to Brown, March 25, 1850, pp. 170–72; Lea to Calhoun, Nov. 18, 1850, pp. 269–70; "Petition to the President of the United States," Feb. 27, 1850, p. 158. See also McLaws to Grier, Oct. 29, 1849, NA, RG393, M1072, LS, DNM, Roll 1; Meriwether to Manypenny, Sept. 1, 1854, in *1854 RCIA*, 170.
115. J. W. Davidson to George A. H. Blake, April 1, 1854, NA, RG393, M1120, LR, DNM, Roll 4; Garland to Thomas, April 1, 1854, NA, RG393, M1072, LS, DNM, Roll 1; Bennett, *Forts and Forays*, 54. On the death of Chief Lobo, see Garland to Thomas, March 29, 1854, ibid. For the Battle of Cieneguilla, see Will Gorenfeld and David M. Johnson, "The Battle of Cieneguilla," in *Battles and Massacres on the Southwestern Frontier: Historical and Archaeological Perspectives,* eds. Ronald K. Wetherington and Frances Levine (Norman: University of Oklahoma Press, 2014), 9–76. This analysis of

the battle criticizes Davidson's leadership and postulates, without substantial supporting evidence, that the soldiers were all intoxicated.

116. Proclamation of William S. Messervy, April 10, 1854, NMSRCA, TA, Roll 98.

117. Blake to Nichols, Jan. 24, 1855, NA, RG393, M1120, LR, DNM, Roll 4.

118. Garland to Thomas, April 20, 1854, NA, RG393, M1072, LS, DNM, Roll 1; Garland to Thomas, June 30, 1854, ibid.; Garland to Thomas, July 30, 1854, ibid.

119. For reports of the campaigns, see Philip St. George Cooke to Nichols, May 24, 1854, NA, RG393, M1120, LR, DNM, Roll 3; Carleton to Cooke, June 5, 1854, ibid.; George Sykes to Cooke, July 2, 1854, ibid.; Fauntleroy to Samuel D. Sturgis, March 28, 1855, ibid., Roll 4; Fauntleroy to Sturgis, May 5, 1855, ibid.; St. Vrain to W. Magruder, June 17, 1855, ibid.; Fauntleroy to L. C. Easton, July 15, 1855, ibid.; Nichols to Carleton, Jan. 13, 1855, NA, RG393, M1072, LS, DNM, Roll 1; Garland to Meriwether, Jan. 22, 1855, ibid.; Garland to Thomas, Jan. 31, 1855, ibid.; Meriwether to Manypenny, Sept. 1855, in *1855 RCIA*, 187; Jacqueline Dorgan Meketa, ed., *Legacy of Honor: The Life of Rafael Chacón, A Nineteenth-Century New Mexican* (Albuquerque: University of New Mexico Press, 1986), 100–4. See also Blackhawk, *Violence over the Land*, 198–200.

120. Garland to Thomas, March 31, 1855, NA, RG393, M1072, LS, DNM, Roll 1. On militias, see Meriwether to Garland, Jan. 30, 1855, NA, RG393, M1120, LR, DNM, Roll 4. On Indians seeking peace, see Fauntleroy to Easton, July 28, 1855, ibid.; Meriwether to Garland, Sept. 14, 1855, ibid.

121. Henry Lane Kendrick to Nichols, Oct. 23, 1854, NA, RG393, M1120, LR, DNM, Roll 3; Kendrick to Nichols, Nov. 11, 1854, ibid. See also McNitt, *Navajo Wars*, 251–54.

122. William T. H. Brooks to Nichols, July 15, 1858, NA, RG393, M1120, LR, DNM, Roll 7; Samuel M. Yost to Collins, Aug. 31, 1858, RG75, OIA, T21, LR, NMS, Roll 3; Yost to Collins, Sept. 9, 1858, ibid.; Garland to William Brooks, July 26, 1858, RG393, M1072, LS, DNM, Roll 2; James C. McKee to Yost, Sept. 9, 1858, in J. Lee Correll, ed., *Through White Men's Eyes: A Contribution to Navajo History* (Window Rock, AZ: Navajo Heritage Center, 1979), 2:156; *Santa Fe Weekly Gazette*, July 24 and Aug. 21, 1858; Brooks to AAG, Nov. 30, 1857, NA, RG393, M1120, LR, DNM, Roll 6. Additional correspondence relating to the incident is in Correll, *Through White Men's Eyes* 2:133–56. For scholarly accounts, see Brooks, *Captives and Cousins*, 310–14; McNitt, *Navajo Wars*, 325–28, 358.

123. "Peonage in New Mexico," *Santa Fe Weekly Gazette*, Feb. 2, 1867. On Jim's death as a cause of war with the Navajos, see Collins to Mix, Sept. 27, 1858, in *1858 RCIA*, 190–91; and statements by Kirby Benedict, John Greiner, and James L. Collins, July 4, 1865, in "Condition of the Indian Tribes," 39th Cong., 2nd Sess., Senate Report No. 156, pp. 325, 328, 331.

124. *1858 Annual Report of the Secretary of War*, 35th Cong., 2nd Sess., Senate Exec. Doc. No. 1, p. 4.

125. Shepherd to J. D. Wilkins, Jan. 17, 1860, in "Indian Hostilities in New Mexico," 36th Cong., 1st Sess., House Exec. Doc. No. 69, pp. 30–32; Shepherd to Wilkins, Feb. 14, 1860, ibid., 42–44. See also McNitt, *Navajo Wars*, 380–81.

126. Collins to Abraham Rencher, Jan. 21, 1860, in "Indian Hostilities in New Mexico," 36th Cong., 1st Sess., House Exec. Doc. No. 69, pp. 57–59, quotations on 58.

127. Collins to Greenwood, Jan. 29, 1860, ibid., 54; Collins to Greenwood, Feb. 4, 1860, ibid., 56.

128. General Orders No. 2, Feb. 18, 1860, "Indian Hostilities in New Mexico," 36th Cong., 1st Sess., House Exec. Doc. No. 69, pp. 39–40; Fauntleroy to Thomas, Jan. 29, 1860, ibid., 29–30; Collins to Greenwood, Feb. 10, 1860, ibid., 62–63.

129. McNitt, *Navajo Wars*, 382–84; Maurice Frink, *Fort Defiance and the Navajos* (Boulder, CO: Fred Pruett, 1968), 51–61. For an analysis that emphasizes Indian slavery, see Andrés Reséndez, *The Other Slavery: The Uncovered Story of Indian Enslavement in America* (New York: Houghton Mifflin Harcourt, 2016), 278–93.

130. McNitt, *Navajo Wars*, 391–407. For correspondence related to the campaign, see Correll, *Through White Men's Eyes*, 3:54–132.

131. George N. Bascom to Dabney H. Maury, Feb. 14, 1861, NA, RG393, M1120, LR, DNM, Roll 13; Bascom to Pitcairn Morrison, Feb. 25, 1861, ibid.; Isaiah N. Moore to Maury, Feb. 25, 1861, ibid. On the Bascom Affair generally, see Edwin R. Sweeney, *Cochise: Chiricahua Apache Chief* (Norman: University of Oklahoma Press, 1991), 142–65.

132. See, for example, Michael Steck Monthly Report, July 30, 1855, in which Steck reported that the Apaches "cannot bring into the field over half the number of warriors that they could have 20 years ago." Center for Southwest Research, Inventory of the Michael Steck Papers, Series 2, Roll 1.

133. Michael Steck Personal Notes, Aug. 1854, ibid.

Chapter 4

1. Childers, *Failure of Popular Sovereignty*, 40–73.

2. Speech of Thomas Corwin, *Congressional Globe,* 36th Cong., 2nd Sess., Jan. 21, 1861, Appendix, 74–75.

3. "Army Appropriation Bill," ibid., Jan. 18, 1861, p. 455.

4. R. H. Weightman to H. S. Foote, Dec. 15, 1851, in "Contested Election from New Mexico," *Congressional Globe,* 32nd Cong., 1st Sess., March 17, 1852, p. 755. See also "Mr. Weightman and New Mexico," *National Era,* Jan. 1, 1852. For Weightman's views on slavery in New Mexico, see "Speech of Hon. Richard H. Weightman of New Mexico," March 15, 1852 (Washington, D.C.: Congressional Globe Office, 1852).

5. George Fitzhugh, "The Politics and Economies of Aristotle and Mr. Calhoun," *DeBow's Review,* Aug. 1857, pp. 163–72.

6. Quoted in Richard K. Crallé, ed., *Speeches of John C. Calhoun, Delivered in the House of Representatives and in the Senate of the United States* (New York: Russell & Russell, 1968), 4:548.

7. Ibid., 497. See also "The Slavery Question," *Congressional Globe,* 29th Cong., 2nd Sess., Feb. 19, 1847, pp. 453–55; "New Mexico," *Congressional Globe,* 30th Cong., 2nd Sess., Dec. 19, 1848, pp. 33–34; "Slavery in the New Territories," *DeBow's Review,* July 1849, pp. 62–73.

8. Senate Select Committee Report, May 8, 1850, 31st Cong., 1st Sess., Senate Rep. Com. No. 123, p. 1.

9. See Stegmaier, *Texas, New Mexico, and the Compromise of 1850*.

10. "The Slave Question," *Santa Fe Republican*, Jan. 29, 1848.

11. "Slavery in the Territories," *Congressional Globe*, 30th Cong., 1st Sess., Appendix, July 29, 1848, pp. 1060–61.

12. Ibid., Aug. 3, 1848, pp. 1072–74.

13. Ibid., Aug. 3, 1848, p. 1078.

14. "Relations of States," *Congressional Globe*, 36th Cong., 1st Sess., May 24, 1860, pp. 2311–12.

15. "New Mexico," *Congressional Globe*, 30th Cong., 2nd Sess., Dec. 19, 1848, pp. 33–37, quotation on 33. For Benton's views on the Compromise of 1850, see Benton, *Thirty Years' View*, 2:749–65.

16. "Slavery in the Territories, Speech of Mr. Berrien," *Congressional Globe*, 31st Cong., 1st Sess., Appendix, Feb. 12, 1850, pp. 207–8

17. "Slavery in the Territories, Speech of Mr. Davis," ibid., Feb. 13, 1850, pp. 151–53, quotation on 151.

18. Speech of Truman Smith, ibid., 31st Cong., 1st Sess., July 8, 1850, pp. 1180–86, quotations on 1180.

19. Daniel Webster to R. H. Gardiner, June 17, 1850, in Daniel Webster, *The Works of Daniel Webster* (Boston: C. Little & Jas. Brown, 1851), 6:568–75, quotation on 571.

20. Speech of James Cooper, *Congressional Globe*, 31st Cong., 1st Sess., July 1, 1850, pp. 1010–12.

21. "Message from the President of the United States," 31st Cong., 1st Sess., June 17, 1850, Senate Exec. Doc. No. 56, p. 1.

22. Speech of Thomas Rusk, *Congressional Globe*, 31st Cong., 1st Sess., June 6, 1850, p. 1144.

23. Speech of Samuel Cooper, ibid., July 1, 1850, pp. 1010–12. On the congressional debates, see Kiser, *Borderlands of Slavery*, 23–56.

24. Robert S. Neighbors to John Munroe, April 15, 1850, in "Message from the President of the United States," 31st Cong., 1st Sess., June 17, 1850, Senate Exec. Doc. No. 56, p. 15. See also "Message from the President of the United States, relative to the claim of Texas to jurisdiction over part of New Mexico," Aug. 6, 1850, 31st Cong., 1st Sess., Senate Exec. Doc. No. 67.

25. Winfield Scott to John Munroe, Aug. 6, 1850, in Abel, *Correspondence of James S. Calhoun*, 164–65.

26. For Taylor's views, see "California and New Mexico," Feb. 6, 1850, 31st Cong., 1st Sess., House Exec. Doc. No. 17, pp. 1–4. For New Mexico's statehood constitution, see Rittenhouse, *Constitution of the State of New Mexico*. See also "Proclamation of John Munroe," May 28, 1850, in Abel, *Correspondence of James S. Calhoun*, 219–20. On the 1850 debates, see Larson, *New Mexico's Quest for Statehood*, 13–61; Stegmaier, *Texas, New Mexico, and the Compromise of 1850*, 115–33; Lamar, *The Far Southwest*, 61–70.

27. Stegmaier, *Texas, New Mexico, and the Compromise of 1850*, 167–200, 317–19.

28. Charles Conrad to Munroe, Sept. 10, 1850, in Abel, *Correspondence of James S. Calhoun*, 220–21.

29. Stacey L. Smith, *Freedom's Frontier: California and the Struggle over Unfree Labor, Emancipation, and Reconstruction* (Chapel Hill: University of North Carolina Press, 2013), 48.

30. "Peon Slavery on the Rio Grande—Letter from the Border," *New-York Daily Tribune,* July 15, 1850.

31. "Important from New Mexico—Slavery and Peonage," *New York Herald,* July 18, 1850.

32. "New Mexico—Slavery Recognized in Her Constitution," *Daily Albany Argus,* July 24, 1850; "The New Mexican Delegate," ibid., July 26, 1850.

33. *Congressional Globe,* 31st Cong., 1st Sess., June 5, 1850, p. 1135, and June 6, 1850, p. 1144.

34. On debt peonage, see Charles H. Harris III, *A Mexican Family Empire: The Latifundio of the Sánchez Navarros, 1765–1867* (Austin: University of Texas Press, 1975), 218–20; Weber, *The Mexican Frontier,* 211–12; Howard Lamar, "From Bondage to Contract: Ethnic Labor in the American West, 1600–1890," in *The Countryside in the Age of Capitalist Transformation,* eds. Steven Hahn and Jonathan Prude (Chapel Hill: University of North Carolina Press, 1985), 299–300; Montejano, *Anglos and Mexicans in the Making of Texas,* 76–82; Kiser, "'A charming name for a species of slavery,'" 169–89; Reséndez, *The Other Slavery,* 238–40, 245–46; Kiser, *Borderlands of Slavery,* 11–14, 16–17, 88–111.

35. Webb, *Adventures in the Santa Fe Trade,* 101–2.

36. John C. Reid, *Reid's Tramp, or a Journal of the Incidents of Ten Months Travel through Texas, New Mexico, Arizona, Sonora, and California* (Austin, TX: Steck, 1935), 143–45.

37. Davis, *El Gringo,* 98–99.

38. For firsthand accounts of peonage in New Mexico, see Fabiola Cabeza de Baca, *We Fed Them Cactus* (Albuquerque: University of New Mexico Press, 1954), 6; Wislizenus, *Memoir of a Tour to Northern Mexico,* 23–24; Ruxton, *Adventures in Mexico and the Rocky Mountains,* 116; Brantz Mayer, *Mexico, As It Was and As It Is* (Philadelphia: G. B. Zieber, 1847), 201–2; Gregg, *Commerce of the Prairies,* 182–84; James F. Meline, *Two Thousand Miles on Horseback: Santa Fe and Back* (Albuquerque, NM: Horn & Wallace, 1966), 120–21; John Ayers, "A Soldier's Experience in New Mexico," *New Mexico Historical Review* 24 (Oct. 1949), 261; Cooke, *Conquest of New Mexico and California,* 34–35; McCall, *New Mexico in 1850,* 85; Irving Howbert, *Memories of a Lifetime in the Pikes Peak Region* (Glorieta, NM: Rio Grande Press, 1970), 169; Henry Inman, *The Old Santa Fe Trail: The Story of a Great Highway* (Topeka, KS: Crane, 1916), 374; Calvin, *Lieutenant Emory Reports,* 87; Garrard, *Wah-To-Yah and the Taos Trail,* 138–39.

39. "Law regulating contracts between masters and servants," NA, RG46, Territorial Papers of the U.S. Senate, Roll 14 (New Mexico, 1840–1854).

40. "An Act Concerning Free Negroes," in *Laws of the Territory of New Mexico, Sixth Legislative Assembly, 1856–1857* (Santa Fe: Office of the Democrat, 1857), 48–50.

41. On convict labor in the New South, see Alex Lichtenstein, *Twice the Work of Free Labor: The Political Economy of Convict Labor in the New South* (New York: Verso, 1996); Douglas A. Blackmon, *Slavery by Another Name: The Re-Enslavement of Black Americans from the Civil War to World War II* (New York: Anchor, 2009); Talitha L. LeFlouria, *Chained in Silence: Black Women and Convict Labor in the New South* (Chapel Hill: University of North Carolina Press, 2015).

42. "An Act to provide for the protection of property in Slaves in this Territory," in *Laws of the Territory of New Mexico, Eighth Legislative Assembly, 1858–1859* (Santa Fe: A. DeMarle, 1859), 64–80; Stegmaier, "A Law that Would Make Caligula Blush?," 209–42.

43. Abraham Rencher to William Seward, April 14, 1861, NA, RG59, U.S. State Department, New Mexico Territorial Papers, 1851–1872, Microfilm T17, Roll 2.

44. "Slavery in New-Mexico," *DeBow's Review,* May 1859, p. 601. On New Mexico's slave codes, see Kiser, *Borderlands of Slavery,* 112–41.

45. William Need to Simon Cameron, Sept. 27, 1861, in *The War of the Rebellion: A Compilation of the Official Records of the Union and Confederate Armies* (hereafter cited as *OR*) (Washington, D.C.: Government Printing Office, 1882), ser. 1, vol. 50, part 2, p. 638.

46. "Interesting Letter from New Mexico," *Montpelier Watchman and State Journal,* clipping in E. P. Walton to A. B. Greenwood, June 9, 1859, NA, RG75, OIA, LR, NMS, M234, Roll 549.

47. Need to Cameron, Sept. 27, 1861, in *OR,* ser. 1, vol. 50, part 2, p. 638. See also *New-York Daily Tribune:* "Mr. Robinson's Proposition," Jan. 5, 1861; "Mistakes Corrected," Feb. 22, 1861; and "The Slave Code of New Mexico," April 16, 1861. For a background of Alexander Jackson, see Martin Hardwick Hall, *Sibley's New Mexico Campaign* (Austin: University of Texas Press, 1960), 14–16. For a biographical sketch of Miguel Otero, see Laura E. Gómez, *Manifest Destinies: The Making of the Mexican American Race* (New York: New York University Press, 2007), 98–99. For Otero's political activities, see Mark Stegmaier, "New Mexico's Delegate in the Secession Winter Congress, Part 1: Two Newspaper Accounts of Miguel Otero in 1861," *New Mexico Historical Review* 86 (Summer 2011): 385–92; Mark Stegmaier, "New Mexico's Delegate in the Secession Winter Congress, Part 2: Miguel A. Otero Responds to Horace Greeley, and Greeley takes Revenge," *New Mexico Historical Review* 86 (Fall 2011): 513–23. On Davis's military appointments while serving as secretary of war, see William J. Cooper Jr., *Jefferson Davis, American* (New York: Alfred A. Knopf, 2000), 251–52.

48. "The Slave Code of New Mexico," *New-York Daily Tribune,* April 16, 1861.

49. "Shall We Give Up New-Mexico?," ibid., Feb. 25, 1861.

50. *New-York Daily Tribune:* "Mr. Robinson's Proposition," Jan. 5, 1861; "Governor of New-Mexico," July 15, 1861. For additional Greeley commentary, see ibid., "A Few Questions about New Mexico," Jan. 23, 1861; "Mistakes Corrected," Feb. 22, 1861.

51. Kiser, *Borderlands of Slavery,* 103–10. A handful of court cases involving peonage transpired during the 1850s, although none of them would have the far-reaching legal implications of the 1857 hearings. See José María Gutierres v. Pablo Maldonado et. al., April 5, 1854, NMSRCA, San Miguel County District Court Records, Serial #13533, Folder 1, Case #21; Lorenzo Labadi vs. Vicente Ortega, July 26, 1854, NMSRCA, Records of the District Court of Valencia County; Cruz Marqués v. José Manuel Angel, Oct. 3, 1855, NMSRCA, San Miguel County District Court Records, Serial #13533, Folder 1, Case #24; Manuel Armijo v. Pablo Gamboa, Aug. 25, 1860, NMSRCA, Bernalillo County Probate Court Records, Serial #13734, Folder #51.

52. Marcellina Bustamento v. Juana Analla, Jan. 1857, in Charles H. Gildersleeve, *Reports of Cases Argued and Determined in the Supreme Court of the Territory of New Mexico from*

January term 1852 to January term 1879 (San Francisco: A. L. Bancroft, 1881), 1:255–62, quotations on 257, 259.

53. Mariana Jaremillo v. José de la Cruz Romero, Jan. 1857, in ibid., 190–208, quotations on 193, 206. For Kirby Benedict's career in New Mexico, see Aurora Hunt, *Kirby Benedict: Federal Frontier Judge* (Glendale, CA: Arthur H. Clark, 1961), 109–11; Pete Daniel, *The Shadow of Slavery: Peonage in the South, 1901–1969* (Urbana: University of Illinois Press, 1972), 15–16; Arie W. Poldevaart, *Black-Robed Justice: A History of the Administration of Justice in New Mexico from the American Occupation in 1846 until Statehood in 1912* (Holmes Beach, FL: Gaunt, 1999), 49–66.

54. "Slavery in the Territory of New Mexico," May 10, 1860, 36th Cong., 1st Sess., House Report No. 508, quotations on 8–9, 32, 34.

55. "Admission of Kansas," *Congressional Globe,* 36th Cong., 1st Sess., March 1, 1860, p. 916.

56. "President's Message, ibid., 928.

57. "Army Appropriation Bill," *Congressional Globe,* 36th Cong., 2nd Sess., Jan. 18, 1861, p. 455.

58. "Enrolled Bills," ibid., Jan. 22, 1861, pp. 514–15.

59. "State of the Union, Speech of Hon. J. A. Bingham," ibid., Jan. 22, 1861, Appendix, 83.

60. "State of the Union," *Congressional Globe,* 36th Cong., 2nd Sess., Jan. 29, 1861, p. 623.

61. "Evening Session," ibid., Feb. 5, 1861, p. 761.

62. "Report of the Special Committee . . . upon the Bill to repeal the Act of Feb. 3, 1859 for the protection of property in slaves," NA, RG59, U.S. State Department, New Mexico Territorial Papers, 1851–1872, Microfilm T17, Roll 2.

63. See Mark Stegmaier, "'An Imaginary Negro in an Impossible Place?': The Issue of New Mexico Statehood in the Secession Crisis, 1860–1861," *New Mexico Historical Review* 84 (Spring 2009): 263–90.

64. Otero to Seward, Sept. 1, 1861, NA, RG59, U.S. State Department, New Mexico Territorial Papers, 1851–1872, Microfilm T17, Roll 2.

65. Deren Earl Kellogg, "Lincoln's New Mexico Patronage: Saving the Far Southwest for the Union," *New Mexico Historical Review* 75 (Oct. 2000): 511–29.

66. "First Annual Message of Governor Henry Connelly," Dec. 4, 1861, NA, RG59, U.S. State Department, New Mexico Territorial Papers, 1851–1872, Microfilm T17, Roll 2. Four years later, Connelly attacked the 1857 Act Concerning Free Negroes, which outlived the 1859 slave code and remained on the books even after the Civil War had ended. Connelly said that the law "is equally in discord with the legislation of Congress, and the proclamation of the president abolishing slavery and restoring to civil rights the freedmen of the African race." See "The Fourth Annual Message of Governor Henry Connelly," Dec. 1865, ibid., Roll 3.

67. Facundo Piño, "Address to the Legislative Assembly of New Mexico," Jan. 29, 1862, in NA, RG46, Territorial Papers of the U.S. Senate, New Mexico 1840–1854, M200, Roll 14; "Executive Message of His Excellency William F. M. Arny," Dec. 2, 1862 (Santa Fe: Office of the Santa Fe Gazette, 1862), 11–12.

68. "An Act to confiscate Property used for Insurrectionary Purposes," Aug. 6, 1861, *United States Statutes at Large, Treaties, and Proclamations of the United States of America* (Boston: Little, Brown, 1863), 12:319.

69. "An Act to Secure Freedom to all Persons within the Territories of the United States," *U.S. Statutes at Large*, 36th Cong., 2nd Sess., ch. 112, p. 432.

70. "An Act to suppress Insurrection, to punish Treason and Rebellion, to seize and confiscate the Property of Rebels, and for other Purposes," July 17, 1862, *U.S. Statutes at Large*, 12:589–92.

71. James Oakes, *Freedom National: The Destruction of Slavery in the United States, 1861–1865* (New York: Norton, 2012), 143, 236–42, 344–45; Brooks D. Simpson, *The Reconstruction Presidents* (Lawrence: University Press of Kansas, 1998), 33–35.

72. Executive Order of Andrew Johnson, June 9, 1865, RG75, OIA, T21, LR, NMS, Roll 6. For seminal works on the amendment, see Michael Vorenberg, *Final Freedom: The Civil War, the Abolition of Slavery, and the Thirteenth Amendment* (Cambridge, UK: Cambridge University Press, 2001); Alexander Tsesis, *The Thirteenth Amendment and American Freedom: A Legal History* (New York: New York University Press, 2004).

73. "An Act to abolish and forever prohibit the System of Peonage in the Territory of New Mexico and other Parts of the United States," *U.S. Statutes at Large*, 39th Cong., 2nd Sess., ch. 187, p. 546.

74. "Executive Message of His Excellency William F. M. Arny," Dec. 2, 1862 (Santa Fe: Office of the Santa Fe Gazette, 1862), 13–14, quotation on 12, italics in original; Calhoun to Orlando Brown, March 31, 1850, in Abel, *Correspondence of James S. Calhoun*, 183. Some military officers also suggested compensated emancipation. See, for example, B. L. Beall to J. H. Dickerson, March 12, 1849, NA, RG393, M1102, LR, DNM, Roll 1; Thomas Fitzpatrick to B. L. Beall, Feb. 24, 1849, ibid.

75. "Memorial to Congress," Jan. 29, 1863, NA, RG46, Territorial Papers of the U.S. Senate, New Mexico 1840–54, M200, Roll 14.

76. Michael Steck to William P. Dole, Jan. 13, 1864, NA, RG75, OIA, NMS, LR, 1849–1880, M234, Roll 552.

77. Edward R. S. Canby, General Orders No. 81, Sept. 9, 1862, ibid. See also Thompson, *Civil War History of the New Mexico Volunteers*, 19–20, 225.

78. Executive Order of Andrew Johnson, June 9, 1865, NA, RG75, OIA, NMS, 1849–80, Microfilm T21, Roll 6.

79. James Harlan to Dole, June 12, 1865, ibid.

80. Dole to Felipe Delgado, June 4, 1865, ibid.; Delgado to Dole, July 16, 1865, ibid., M234, Roll 552.

81. Testimony of James H. Carleton and Kirby Benedict, in "Condition of the Indian Tribes," 39th Cong., 2nd Sess., Senate Report No. 156, pp. 325–26. On the abolition of Indian slavery, see Reséndez, *The Other Slavery*, 295–313.

82. Graves to Dennis N. Cooley, Undated Report of Jan. 1866, in *1866 RCIA*, 133–34. See also Reséndez, *The Other Slavery*, 299–300.

83. W. F. M. Arny, Second Annual Message to the Legislative Assembly, Dec. 1866, NMS-RCA, TA, Roll 98.

84. *Laws of the Territory of New Mexico, 1866–1867* (Santa Fe: Manderfield & Tucker, 1867), 44.

85. Journal of the Legislative Assembly, Dec. 4, 1865 to Feb. 1, 1866, NMSRCA, TA, Microfilm Reel 3.

86. Tomás Heredia vs. José María García, Dec. 4, 1865, Third Judicial District Court of New Mexico, at NMSRCA, U.S. Territorial and New Mexico Supreme Court Records, Box 3, No. 36; Tomás Heredia vs. José María García, Jan. 26, 1867, New Mexico Territorial Supreme Court, in ibid.; "The Supreme Court on Peonage," *Santa Fe Weekly Gazette*, Feb. 2, 1867.

87. Graves to Connelly, Jan. 9, 1866, NMSRCA, TA, Roll 98.

88. Graves to Dennis N. Cooley, Undated Report of Jan. 1866, in *1866 Annual Report of the Secretary of the Interior* (Washington, D.C.: Government Printing Office, 1866), 133–34.

89. Ibid., 33.

90. "Peonage in New Mexico," *Santa Fe Weekly Gazette,* Feb. 2, 1867.

91. "Peonage in New Mexico," *Congressional Globe,* 39th Cong., 2nd Sess., Jan. 3, 1867, pp. 239–40, quotation on 240.

92. "Abolition of Peonage," ibid., Feb. 19, 1867, pp. 1571–72.

93. "An Act to abolish and forever prohibit the System of Peonage in the Territory of New Mexico and other Parts of the United States," *U.S. Statutes at Large*, 39th Cong., 2nd Sess., ch. 187, p. 546.

94. A. B. Norton to John Ward, Aug. 6, 1867, NA, RG75, OIA, NMS, T21, Misc. Docs., Roll 8.

95. "Proclamation by the Governor of the Territory of New Mexico," April 14, 1867, NA, RG59, T17, New Mexico Territorial Papers, Roll 3.

96. "Proclamation of Governor Herman M. Heath," June 10, 1868, ibid.

97. Lawrence R. Murphy, "Reconstruction in New Mexico," *New Mexico Historical Review* 43 (April 1968), 106–9.

98. Brooks, *Captives and Cousins,* 240.

99. Ibid., 385–403.

100. Griffin to Stephen B. Elkins, Sept. 28, 1868, NA, RG46, Territorial Papers of the U.S. Senate, Roll 14, New Mexico, 1840–54.

101. Murphy, "Reconstruction in New Mexico," 106; "Additional Evidence," Grand Jury Proceedings, NA, RG46, Territorial Papers of the U.S. Senate, Roll 14, New Mexico, 1840–54. See also Laura E. Gómez, "Off-White in an Age of White Supremacy: Mexican Elites and the Rights of Indians and Blacks in Nineteenth Century New Mexico," in *Colored Men and Hombres Aquí: Hernandez v. Texas and the Emergence of Mexican-American Lawyering*, ed. Michael A. Olivas (Houston: Arte Público Press, 2006), 36; Gómez, *Manifest Destinies*, 89.

Chapter 5

1. "Memorial to Congress," March 4, 1864, 38th Cong., 1st Sess., Senate Misc. Doc. No. 52.

2. "Second Annual Message to the Legislative Assembly," William F. M. Arny, Dec. 1866, NMSRCA, TA, Roll 98.

3. John F. Stover, *History of the Baltimore and Ohio Railroad* (West Lafayette, IN: Purdue University Press, 1987).

4. See *DeBow's Review:* "Intercommunication between the Atlantic and Pacific Oceans," Oct. 1847, pp. 164–76; "Internal Improvements," May 1847, p. 447; "Intercommunication between the Atlantic and Pacific Oceans," July 1849, pp. 18, 20; "Railroad to the Pacific," Sept. 1860, pp. 339–42. See also George Leslie Albright, *Official Explorations for Pacific Railroads, 1853–1855* (Berkeley: University of California Press, 1921), 10–20. On Asa Whitney, see David Haward Bain, *Empire Express: Building the First Transcontinental Railroad* (New York: Viking, 1999), 3–46.

5. "Canal or Railroad between the Atlantic and Pacific Oceans," Feb. 20, 1849, 30th Cong., 2nd Sess., House Report No. 145, pp. 1, 34, 57–58, 413.

6. Abert to Simpson, May 5, 1849, NA, RG393, M1102, LR, DNM, Roll 1; McNitt, *Navaho Expedition*, 160–62. See also "Route from Fort Smith to Santa Fe," Feb. 21, 1850, 31st Cong., 1st Sess., House Exec. Doc. No. 45, pp. 1–25.

7. "Canal or Railroad between the Atlantic and Pacific Oceans," Feb. 20, 1849, 30th Cong., 2nd Sess., House Report No. 145, p. 63.

8. "A Journey to the West," *DeBow's Review,* March 1858, p. 253.

9. John Loughborough, *The Pacific Telegraph and Railway* (St. Louis: Charles & Hammond, 1849), iii, iv. In 1845 Benton presented his own plan for a "national central railway" extending westward from his home state of Missouri. Although retirement from the Senate ended his direct political control over the situation after 1850, he continued to lobby for Missouri's railroad interests after leaving Congress. See "Col. Benton and the Pacific Railroad," *New York Times,* Nov. 25, 1852. On Benton and the railroad, see Albright, *Official Explorations for Pacific Railroads,* 15–20; Bain, *Empire Express,* 37–38.

10. Loughborough, *Pacific Telegraph and Railway,* xii. On the convention generally, see Albright, *Official Explorations for Pacific Railroads,* 22–25.

11. Loughborough, *Pacific Telegraph and Railway,* xix, 12, 31–32.

12. Ibid., xviii, 16, 31, 34, 51.

13. Kvach, *DeBow's Review,* 1–10, 59–62, 95–96.

14. Ibid., 4–6.

15. Asa Whitney, "Intercommunication between the Atlantic and Pacific Oceans," *DeBow's Review,* Oct. 1847, pp. 164–76.

16. J. D. B. DeBow, "Intercommunication between the Atlantic and Pacific Oceans," ibid., July 1849, pp. 1–37, quotations on 5, 32, 36; C. Graham to H. S. Fulkerson, March 6, 1860, in "Atlantic and Pacific Railroad," ibid., Nov. 1860, p. 596.

17. "Pacific Rail-Road," *DeBow's Review,* Dec. 1850, p. 601.

18. See Bartlett, *Personal Narrative of Explorations;* "Report of the Secretary of the Interior, in answer to . . . the boundary between the United States and Mexico," Feb. 28, 1850, 31st Cong., 1st Sess., Senate Exec. Doc. No. 34, parts 1 and 2; "Report of the Secretary of the Interior . . . in relation to the commission appointed to run and mark the boundary between the United States and Mexico," Aug. 31, 1852, 32nd Cong., 1st Sess., Senate Exec. Doc. No. 119. On the International Boundary Commission, see Robert V. Hine, *Bartlett's West: Drawing the Mexican Boundary* (New Haven, CT: Yale University Press, 1968); Goetzmann, *Army Exploration in the American West,* 153–208; Joseph Richard Werne, *The Imaginary Line: A History of the United States and Mexican Boundary Survey, 1848–1857*

(Fort Worth: Texas Christian University Press, 2007); William S. Kiser, *Turmoil on the Rio Grande: The Territorial History of the Mesilla Valley, 1846–1865* (College Station: Texas A&M University Press, 2011), 47–69; St. John, *Line in the Sand,* 25–35.

19. Pedro García Conde to Mexican Minister of Relations, Dec. 24, 1850, quoted in Werne, *The Imaginary Line,* 56; John Russell Bartlett to Alexander Stuart, Dec. 28, 1850, in "Report of the Secretary of the Interior . . . in relation to the boundary between the United States and Mexico," 32nd Cong., 1st Sess., Senate Exec. Doc. No. 119, p. 391; José Salazar Ylarregui, *Datos de los trabajos astronómicos y topográficos . . . por la Comisión de Limites mexicana en la línea que divide esta república de la de los Estados-Unidos* (Mexico City: Imprenta de Juan R. Navarro, 1850), 8–9. See also Oscar J. Martinez, "Surveying and Marking the U.S.-Mexico Boundary: The Mexican Perspective," in *Drawing the Borderline: Artist-Explorers of the U.S.-Mexico Boundary Survey,* ed. Dawn Hall (Albuquerque, NM: Albuquerque Museum, 1996), 13–22. For the boundary conflict as it related to the Mesilla Valley, see Mora, *Border Dilemmas,* 74–78, 82–88.

20. Werne, *The Imaginary Line,* 71–72, 139–42; John Mack Faragher, "North, South, and West: Sectional Controversies and the U.S.-Mexico Boundary Survey," in Hall, *Drawing the Borderline,* 1–11.

21. "The Pacific Railroad," *Congressional Globe,* 32nd Cong., 1st Sess., July 6, 1852, Appendix, 777.

22. "Mexican Boundary Commissioner," *Congressional Globe,* 32nd Cong., 1st Sess., July 6, 1852, p. 1660.

23. "Report of the United States and Mexican Boundary Survey, Made under the Direction of the Secretary of the Interior, by William H. Emory," 34th Cong., 1st Sess., Senate Exec. Doc. No. 108, vol. 1, p. 11. See also William H. Emory to A. D. Bache, Jan. 21, 1852, quoted in Hine, *Bartlett's West,* 71; George Clinton Gardner to his Father, April 9, 1852, in *Fiasco: George Clinton Gardner's Correspondence from the U.S.-Mexico Boundary Survey, 1849–1854,* eds. David J. Weber and Jane Lenz Elder (Dallas: Southern Methodist University Press, 2010), 188. For the itemized expenses through 1849, see "Report of the Secretary of the Interior, in answer to . . . the boundary between the United States and Mexico," 31st Cong., 1st Sess., Senate Exec. Doc. No. 34, Part 1, pp. 49–53.

24. "Memorial of a Committee Appointed at a Railroad Convention," Dec. 27, 1852, 32nd Cong., 2nd Sess., Senate Misc. Doc. No. 5, quotations on 2, 3, 7. On railroad corruption generally, see White, *Railroaded.*

25. "Southern Atlantic and Pacific Railroad," *Congressional Globe,* 32nd Cong., 1st Sess., May 6, 1852, pp. 1271–74.

26. "Memorial of Henry O'Reilly," April 6, 1852, 32nd Cong., 1st Sess., Senate Misc. Doc. No. 67, quotation on 1.

27. "Memorial to Congress," Dec. 31, 1852, NA, RG46, Territorial Papers of the U.S. Senate, New Mexico, 1840–54, Roll 14.

28. "The Atlantic and Pacific Railroad," *New York Times,* Jan. 28, 1853; "The Pacific Railroad," ibid., Feb. 5, 1853.

29. "China and the Indies—Our 'Manifest Destiny' in the East," *DeBow's Review,* Dec. 1853, pp. 568, 571.

30. For congressional deliberations on the railroad, see "Railroad to the Pacific," *Congressional Globe*, 32nd Cong., 2nd Sess., Jan. 13, 1852, pp. 280–84; "Railroad to the Pacific," ibid., Jan. 17, 1852, pp. 314–21; "Railroad to the Pacific," ibid., Jan. 27, 1852, pp. 420–24.

31. "Pacific Railroad Schemes," *New York Times*, Feb. 5, 1853; "Pacific Railroad and Pennsylvania," ibid., Feb. 4, 1853. On the Pacific Railroad Surveys, see Albright, *Official Explorations for Pacific Railroads*, 27–43; Goetzmann, *Army Exploration in the American West*, 262–304; Bain, *Empire Express*, 48–52. Senator Gwin was purportedly an operative for the Knights of the Golden Circle in California. See David C. Keehn, *Knights of the Golden Circle: Secret Empire, Southern Secession, Civil War* (Baton Rouge: Louisiana State University Press, 2013), 129–30.

32. *1853 Annual Report of the Secretary of War*, 33rd Cong., 1st Sess., Senate Exec. Doc. No. 1, p. 23.

33. Cooper, *Jefferson Davis, American*, 256–58; Felicity Allen, *Jefferson Davis: Unconquerable Heart* (Columbia: University of Missouri Press, 1999), 202–24; Nelson, "Death in the Distance," 33.

34. *1853 Annual Report of the Secretary of War*, 33rd Cong., 1st Sess., Senate Exec. Doc. No. 1, pp. 16–27.

35. Albright, *Official Explorations for Pacific Railroads*, 29–43. For Benton's views, see "National Central Highway from the Mississippi River to the Pacific Ocean," *Congressional Globe*, 30th Cong., 2nd Sess., Feb. 7, 1849, pp. 470–74; "Highway to the Pacific," ibid., 31st Cong., 2nd Sess., Dec. 16, 1850, pp. 56–58.

36. On the Sitgreaves expedition, see "Report of an Expedition Down the Zuni and Colorado Rivers," 32nd Cong., 2nd Sess., Senate Exec. Doc. No. 59; S. W. Woodhouse, *From Texas to San Diego in 1851: The Overland Journal of Dr. S. W. Woodhouse, Surgeon-Naturalist of the Sitgreaves Expedition,* eds. Andrew Wallace and Richard H. Hevly (Lubbock: Texas Tech University Press, 2007); and Weber, *Richard H. Kern*, 143–86.

37. "Reports of explorations and surveys, to ascertain the most practicable and economical route for a railroad from the Mississippi River to the Pacific Ocean," 33rd Cong., 2nd Sess., Senate Exec. Doc. No. 78, vol. 3, part 1, pp. 4–31, quotations on 4, 14.

38. Ibid., vol. 3, part 2, pp. 63–76; "The Pacific Railroad: Indian Tribes on Mr. Whipple's Route," *New York Times*, April 27, 1854. See also Grant Foreman, *A Pathfinder in the Southwest: The Itinerary of Lieutenant A. W. Whipple during his Explorations for a Railway Route from Fort Smith to Los Angeles in the Years 1853 and 1854* (Norman: University of Oklahoma Press, 1941); Goetzmann, *Army Exploration in the American West*, 287–89.

39. "Important News from Albuquerque," *Fort Smith Herald* article reprinted in *New York Times*, Dec. 27, 1853.

40. "Report upon the Colorado River of the West, explored in 1857 and 1858 by Lieutenant Joseph C. Ives, Corps of Topographical Engineers," 36th Cong., 1st Sess., House Exec. Doc. No. 90, pp. 6, 96. On the 35th parallel route, see H. Craig Miner, *The St. Louis–San Francisco Transcontinental Railroad: The Thirty-Fifth Parallel Project, 1853–1890* (Lawrence: University Press of Kansas, 1972).

41. "Reports of explorations and surveys, to ascertain the most practicable and economical route for a railroad," 33rd Cong., 2nd Sess., Senate Exec. Doc. No. 78, vol. 7, Introduction,

15; Wislizenus, *Memoir of a Tour to Northern Mexico*, 85–86. See also Albright, *Official Explorations for Pacific Railroads,* 121–22. For histories of the topographical engineers and western surveys, see Edward S. Wallace, *The Great Reconnaissance: Soldiers, Artists, and Scientists on the Frontier, 1848–1861* (Boston: Little, Brown, 1955); William H. Goetzmann, *Exploration and Empire: The Explorer and the Scientist in the Winning of the American West* (New York: Knopf, 1966), 231–354.

42. "Reports of explorations and surveys, to ascertain the most practicable and economical route for a railroad," 33rd Cong., 2nd Sess., Senate Exec. Doc. No. 78, vol. 7, part 1, pp. 19–42, quotation on 19.

43. A. B. Gray, *Survey of a Route for the Southern Pacific R.R., on the 32nd Parallel* (Cincinnati, OH: Wrightson, 1856), 5, 85. On coolie labor, see Stacey L. Smith, *Freedom's Frontier: California and the Struggle over Unfree Labor, Emancipation, and Reconstruction* (Chapel Hill: University of North Carolina Press, 2013), 193–98; White, *Railroaded,* 297–98.

44. "Superiority of Slave Labor in Constructing Railroads," *DeBow's Review,* March 1855, p. 406. See also "Is Slave Labor in the Construction of Southern Railroads to be Preferred to Free Labor?," ibid., Dec. 1855, pp. 728–29.

45. "The Southern Pacific Railroad," *DeBow's Review*, Dec. 1859, p. 725.

46. Gray, *Survey of a Route for the Southern Pacific R.R.,* 79, 89–90.

47. "Reports of explorations and surveys, to ascertain the most practicable and economical route for a railroad," 33rd Cong., 2nd Sess., Senate Exec. Doc. No. 78, vol. 2, report no. 4 (John Pope), 5–12, quotations on 8, 9.

48. Ibid., 47–50.

49. *1856 Annual Report of the Secretary of War*, 34th Cong., 3rd Sess., Senate Exec. Doc. No. 5, pp. 19–22.

50. Marcy to Gadsden, July 15, 1853, in Miller, *Treaties and Other International Acts,* 6:342–46. On Governor Lane's occupation of the Mesilla Valley, see Proclamation of William Carr Lane, March 13, 1853, NA, RG59, U.S. State Department, Dispatches from United States Consuls in Ciudad Juárez, 1850–1906, Microcopy 54, Roll 1; William G. B. Carson, ed., "William Carr Lane Diary," *New Mexico Historical Review* 39 (Oct. 1964): 300; Lane to his Wife, Feb. 15, 1853, in Ralph P. Bieber, ed., "Letters of William Carr Lane, 1852–1854," *New Mexico Historical Review* 3 (April 1928): 192. For Mexican perspectives on Lane's proclamation, see "From Mexico," *New York Times,* July 20, 1853; "Agresión americana en Chihuahua," *El Siglo Diez y Nueve,* April 10, 1853; "Ministerio de Relaciones," ibid., April 27, 1853; "Noticias nacionales: La cuestión de la Mesilla," ibid., May 13, 1853; "La cuestión de la Mesilla," ibid., June 6, 1853; Angel Trías to Lane, March 28, 1853, *Alcance al Centinela,* March 29, 1853.

51. "The President's Message," *New York Times,* Dec. 7, 1853.

52. Marcy to Christopher L. Ward, Oct. 22, 1853, in Miller, *Treaties and Other International Acts,* 6:360–62, quotations on 362, 387.

53. Marcy to Gadsden, Oct. 13, 1854, ibid., 341. See also ibid., 376, 386. For the Gadsden Treaty and related correspondence, see ibid., 293–438. On the Gadsden Purchase generally, see Paul N. Garber, *The Gadsden Treaty* (Philadelphia: University of Pennsylvania Press, 1923); David Devine, *Slavery, Scandal, and Steel Rails: The 1854 Gadsden Purchase*

and the Building of the Second Transcontinental Railroad across Arizona and New Mexico Twenty-Five Years Later (New York: iUniverse, 2004), 44–89.

54. "Gadsden's Treaty," *New-York Daily Tribune,* Jan. 26, 1854.

55. John Russell Bartlett to Horace Greeley, April 25, 1854, in "Gadsden's Attack on Commissioner Bartlett," *New-York Daily Tribune,* April 27, 1854; "The Pacific Railroad: Letter from John R. Bartlett on the Southern Route," *New York Times,* Dec. 29, 1853.

56. See the *New York Times:* "The New Mexican Treaty," Feb. 15, 1854; "The Expected Vote on the Nebraska Bill—The Gadsden Treaty," Feb. 2, 1854; "The Gadsden Treaty," Feb. 28, 1854; "A Few Words on the Treaty," March 27, 1854; "The Gadsden Treaty Ratified," April 26, 1854; "Santa Anna and the Treaty," June 16, 1854.

57. "Sonora," ibid., Jan. 12, 1854.

58. "Some Notes on Mexico and General Jackson," *DeBow's Review,* July 1857, pp. 94–98, quotation on 94.

59. Albert Pike, "Pacific Railroad—Plan of the Southern Convention," ibid., Dec. 1854, pp. 593–99, quotations on 595, 596. Emphasis in original. For a similar perspective that threatened secession, see W. Burwell, "True Policy of the South—Suggestions for the Settlement of our Sectional Differences," ibid., Nov. 1856, pp. 469–90.

60. "On What Route are we to have the Pacific Railroad?," *DeBow's Review,* Sept. 1855, pp. 336–41, quotations on 336, 337. For Jefferson Davis's personal views on the railroad, see *1855 Annual Report of the Secretary of War,* 34th Cong., 1st Sess., Senate Exec. Doc. No. 1, pp. 14–17. For correspondence related to his tenure as secretary of war, see Lynda Lasswell Crist and Mary Seaton Dix, eds., *The Papers of Jefferson Davis, Volume 5: 1853–1855* (Baton Rouge: Louisiana State University Press, 1985).

61. Gray, *Survey of a Route for the Southern Pacific R.R.;* n.a., *Circular to the Stockholders of the Atlantic and Pacific Railroad Company* (New York: Geo. F. Nesbitt, 1855). On the Atlantic & Pacific Railroad Company, see Albright, *Official Explorations,* 26–27.

62. "An act to provide for the construction of the Mississippi and Pacific Railroad," quoted in its entirety in "The Southern Route to the Pacific," *DeBow's Review,* May 1854, pp. 545–49.

63. *Circular to the Stockholders,* 6, 12, 14.

64. Ibid., 6–12, 16; Loughborough, *Pacific Telegraph and Railway,* xvi; "The Pacific Railroad," *DeBow's Review,* May 1854, p. 507. For the Ponzi scheme comparison, see White, *Railroaded,* 201. In 1848 General Land Office commissioner Richard M. Young valued the land in New Mexico and California at just twenty-five cents per acre, and he wrote a letter directly to Robert Walker, president of the Atlantic & Pacific Railroad Company, informing him of that valuation. Young to Robert J. Walker, Nov. 22, 1848, in "Correspondence Relating to Civil Government in California and New Mexico," Oct. 7, 1848, 30th Cong., 1st Sess., House Exec. Doc. No. 1, p. 72.

65. Untitled article on the Gadsden Treaty, *New-York Daily Tribune,* Jan. 30, 1854.

66. C. Glen Peebles, *Exposé of the Atlantic & Pacific Railroad Company* (New York: New York Examiner, 1854), 3, 9, 14.

67. Nelson, "Death in the Distance," 33; Keehn, *Knights of the Golden Circle,* 1–4, 129–31; Johnson, *River of Dark Dreams,* 330–420. On Southern control of Amazonia, see M. F.

Maury, "Direct Foreign Trade of the South," *DeBow's Review,* Feb. 1852, pp. 126–48; for a scholarly analysis, see Karp, *This Vast Southern Empire,* 141–48.

68. "Pacific Railroad and Telegraph," Aug. 16, 1856, 34th Cong., 1st Sess., House Report No. 358, pp. 2, 29–31, 36–37. For Benton's advocacy of the central route, see "The Pacific Railroad: Letter from Col. Benton to the Citizens of Missouri," *New York Times,* Nov. 2, 1853.

69. "The Pacific Railroad," *North American Review* 82 (Jan. 1856): 235.

70. *1857 Annual Report of the Secretary of War,* 35th Cong., 1st Sess., Senate Exec. Doc. No. 11, p. 13.

71. "The Southern Pacific Railroad," *DeBow's Review,* May 1857, pp. 509–13, quotations on 510. This Southern Pacific Railroad Company should not be confused with a later corporation by the same name that constructed its line from California eastward through Arizona, New Mexico, and Texas. That railway connected California to New Orleans in 1883. See Devine, *Slavery, Scandal, and Steel Rails,* 102–214.

72. "Memorial of the New Mexican Railway Company in Relation to the Pacific Railroad," May 21, 1860, 36th Cong., 1st Sess., House Misc. Doc. No. 85, quotation on 1.

73. "The American Railroad System," *DeBow's Review,* May 1858, p. 386. Connecticut senator Truman Smith voiced a similar opinion in 1853, saying that a railroad through New Mexico would civilize the otherwise "wretched" Hispanics living there. See "The Pacific Railroad: Remarks of Truman Smith in favor of the Road," *New York Times,* March 17, 1853.

Chapter 6

1. On Sibley's resignation, see Dabney Maury to Henry Hopkins Sibley, April 30, 1861, NA, RG393, M1072, LS, DNM, M1072, Roll 2; Jerry Thompson, *Henry Hopkins Sibley: Confederate General of the West* (Natchitoches, TX: Northwestern State University Press, 1987), 208–9. For his meeting with Davis, see Frazier, *Blood and Treasure,* 36, 46–50, 75; and Thompson, *Henry Hopkins Sibley,* 216–19. For Sibley's objectives, see T. T. Teel, "Sibley's New Mexican Campaign—Its Objects and the Causes of its Failure," in *Battles and Leaders of the Civil War,* eds. Robert Johnson and Clarence Buel (New York: Century, 1887), 2:700. On the importance of Arizona, see Sibley to Samuel Cooper, Jan. 28, 1862, in *The Civil War in West Texas and New Mexico: The Lost Letterbook of Brigadier General Henry Hopkins Sibley,* eds. John P. Wilson and Jerry Thompson (El Paso: Texas Western Press, 2001), 116. For accusations that Davis participated in secessionist schemes, see William Need to Simon Cameron, Sept. 27, 1861, *OR,* series 1, vol. 50, part 2, pp. 637–41. On the role of Davis in westward expansion, see Josephy, *Civil War in the American West,* 11–12. For Confederate expansion, see Nelson, "Death in the Distance," 33–52.

2. Sibley to Loring, June 12, 1861, *OR,* series 1, vol. 4, pp. 55–56.

3. On the Sibley-Loring plot, see Thompson, *Henry Hopkins Sibley,* 209–12. On Loring's resignation, see Loring to Lorenzo Thomas, March 22, 1861, NA, RG393, M1072, LS, DNM, Roll 2; Edward R. S. Canby to AAG, June 11, 1861, *OR,* series 1, vol. 1, p. 606; Canby to AAG, Aug. 16, 1861, ibid., vol. 4, p. 63.

4. Frazier, *Blood and Treasure,* 28–29.

5. Samuel Cooper to Sibley, July 8, 1861, *OR,* series 1, vol. 4, p. 93.

6. Abraham Rencher to William H. Seward, May 18, 1861, NA, RG59, U.S. State Department, New Mexico Territorial Papers, 1851–72, Microfilm T17, Roll 2.

7. *Mesilla Times,* March 30, 1861.

8. *Mesilla Times* article reprinted in *San Francisco Herald,* Nov. 4, 1860.

9. W. W. Mills to John S. Watts, June 23, 1861, *OR,* series 1, vol. 4, p. 56. See also W. W. Mills, *Forty Years at El Paso, 1858–1898,* ed. Rex W. Strickland (El Paso: Carl Hertzog, 1962), 37–57.

10. Canby to AAG, Aug. 16, 1861, *OR,* series 1, vol. 4, p. 65. On the loyalties of Hispanic New Mexicans, see Mora, *Border Dilemmas,* 88–94.

11. Canby to AAG, June 11, 1861, NA, RG393, M1072, LS, DNM, Roll 2; A. L. Anderson to Isaac Lynde, June 30, 1861, ibid.; Canby to AAG, June 16, 1861, *OR,* series 1, vol. 4, pp. 35–36; Anderson to Lynde, June 16, 1861, ibid., 37–38.

12. Canby to AAG, Aug. 16, 1861, *OR,* series 1, vol. 4, p. 64.

13. Canby to AAG, Sept. 8, 1861, NA, RG393, M1072, LS, DNM, Roll 2.

14. Canby to AAG, June 16, 1861, ibid.; Canby to AAG, July 22, 1861, ibid.; Abraham Rencher to Seward, Aug. 10, 1861, NA, RG 59, U.S. State Department, New Mexico Territorial Papers, 1851–72, Microfilm T17, Roll 2.

15. Anderson to Lynde, June 30, 1861, NA, RG393, M1072, LS, DNM, Roll 2.

16. Canby to Ft. Wise Commanding Officer, June 16, 1861, ibid.; Canby to Rencher, June 20, 1861, ibid.

17. Canby to AAG, June 30, 1861, *OR,* series 1, vol. 4, p. 50; W. R. Shoemaker to J. C. Fremont, Aug. 17, 1861, ibid., 66.

18. Anderson to William Chapman, June 19, 1861, ibid., 40.

19. Anderson to Ft. Stanton Commanding Officer, June 16, 1861, NA, RG393, M1072, LS, DNM, Roll 2; Anderson to Ft. Union Commanding Officer, June 19, 1861, ibid.

20. Elmer Otis to Canby, Aug. 22, 1861, *OR,* series 1, vol. 4, p. 67.

21. Canby to AAG, Jan. 11, 1862, ibid., 84.

22. Facundo Piño, "Address to the Legislative Assembly of New Mexico," Jan. 29, 1862, in NA, RG46, Territorial Papers of the U.S. Senate, New Mexico 1840–54, M200, Roll 14.

23. Miguel A. Otero to Seward, June 20, 1861, NA, RG59, U.S. State Department, New Mexico Territorial Papers, 1851–1872, Microfilm T17, Roll 2.

24. Anderson to R. M. Morris, June 25, 1861, NA, RG393, M1072, LS, DNM, Roll 2; Anderson to N. R. Russell, June 25, 1861, ibid.; Anderson to B. S. Roberts, June 26, 1861, ibid.; Rencher to Seward, Aug. 10, 1861, NA, RG59, U.S. State Department, New Mexico Territorial Papers, 1851–1872, Microfilm T17, Roll 2.

25. Canby to Henry Connelly, Sept. 8, 1861, NA, RG393, M1072, LS, DNM, Roll 2; Proclamation by Governor Abraham Rencher, Aug. 5, 1861, NA, RG59, U.S. State Department, New Mexico Territorial Papers, 1851–1872, Microfilm T17, Roll 2; Proclamation of Governor Henry Connelly, Sept. 9, 1861, NMSRCA, TA, Roll 98; Canby to William Gilpin, Sept. 8, 1861, NA, RG393, M1072, LS, DNM, Roll 2.

26. "Abstract from Field Return," Dec. 31, 1861, *OR*, series 1, vol. 4, p. 81; Jerry D. Thompson, ed., *New Mexico Territory during the Civil War: Wallen and Evans Inspection Reports, 1862–1863* (Albuquerque: University of New Mexico Press, 2008), 79–81. For troop strength in New Mexico, see Thompson, *Civil War History of the New Mexico Volunteers,* 443.

27. William Nicodemus to W. R. Shoemaker, Nov. 22, 1861, NA, RG393, M1072, LS, DNM, Roll 2.

28. Canby to AAG, Dec. 8, 1861, ibid.

29. "First Annual Message of Governor Connelly," Dec. 4, 1861, NA, RG59, U.S. State Department, New Mexico Territorial Papers, 1851–72, Microfilm T17, Roll 2; "Second Annual Message to the Legislative Assembly," William F. M. Arny, Dec. 1866, NMSRCA, TA, Roll 98. For a definitive treatment of the New Mexico volunteers, see Thompson, *Civil War History of the New Mexico Volunteers,* esp. 13–431.

30. "The Cotton Fields of Arizona Territory," *DeBow's Review,* April 1858, p. 320; "The New Territory of Arizona," ibid., Nov. 1857, pp. 543–44.

31. Anderson to Lynde, June 16, 1861, NA, RG393, M1072, LS, DNM, Roll 2; Canby to AAG, June 23, 1861, ibid.

32. Canby to Lynde, June 23, 1861, *OR,* series 1, vol. 4, p. 45.

33. Anderson to Lynde, June 30, 1861, NA, RG393, M1072, LS, DNM, Roll 2; John P. Wilson, "Retreat to the Rio Grande: The Report of Captain Isaiah N. Moore," *Rio Grande History* 2 (1975): 4–8.

34. Lynde to Canby, July 7, 1861, *OR,* series 1, vol. 4, p. 58.

35. Lynde to AAG, Aug. 7, 1861, ibid., 5.

36. John P. Wilson, "Whiskey at Fort Fillmore: A Story of the Civil War," *New Mexico Historical Review* 68 (April 1993): 117.

37. Mills to John S. Watts, June 23, 1861, *OR,* series 1, vol. 4, p. 56.

38. Lydia Spencer Lane, *I Married a Soldier, or, Old Days in the Old Army* (1893; reprint, Albuquerque, NM: Horn & Wallace, 1964), 105–7, 115, quotations on 105, 106; Jerry D. Thompson, *Colonel John Robert Baylor: Texas Indian Fighter and Confederate Soldier* (Hillsboro, TX: Hill Junior College Press, 1971), 31, 37.

39. "Arizona Is Free at Last!" *Mesilla Times,* July 29, 1861.

40. *Mesilla Times,* July 27, 1861, and Oct. 17, 1861.

41. Report of John R. Baylor, Aug. 3, 1861, *OR,* series 1, vol. 4, p. 16; Baylor to T. A. Washington, Sept. 21, 1861, ibid., 17–18; Major Isaac Lynde, "Brief Statement of Facts," undated, in Wilson, *When the Texans Came,* 47–48. For firsthand accounts of the battle, see James Cooper McKee, *Narrative of the Surrender of a Command of U.S. Forces at Fort Fillmore, New Mexico, in July, a.d. 1861* (Houston: Stagecoach, 1960), 17–21; Richard Wadsworth, "The Battle of Mesilla: A Rebel View," *Southern New Mexico Historical Review* (Jan. 2005): 8–9. On the Battle of Mesilla generally, see Kiser, *Turmoil on the Rio Grande,* 161–66.

42. Jerry D. Thompson, ed., *From Desert to Bayou: The Civil War Journal and Sketches of Morgan Wolfe Merrick* (El Paso: Texas Western Press, 1991), 11n.70, 25; Lane, *I Married a Soldier,* 114; Undated Statement of Capt. F. J. Crilly, in Wilson, *When the Texans Came,* 43.

43. Baylor to Washington, Sept. 21, 1861, *OR,* series 1, vol. 4, pp. 18–20; "The Surrender of New Mexico—The Treason of the Officers," Oct. 19, 1861, in Wilson, *When the Texans Came,* 50–51.

44. Baylor to Washington, Sept. 21, 1861, *OR,* series 1, vol. 4, pp. 18–20; Alfred Gibbs to Canby, Aug. 6, 1861, ibid., 7–8; Undated Statement of Alfred Gibbs, ibid., 9–11. See also Wilson, "Whiskey at Fort Fillmore," 109–32.

45. Undated Statement of J. Cooper McKee, *OR,* series 1, vol. 4, pp. 12–13. See also Undated Statement of Capt. C. H. McNally, ibid., 13; "Terms of Surrender," July 27, 1861, ibid., 7.

46. *Mesilla Times,* July 29, 1861. See also "Particulars of the Surrender of the Federal Troops in the Mesilla Valley," *Daily Alta California,* Sept. 3, 1861.

47. "Terms of Surrender," July 27, 1861, *OR,* series 1, vol. 4, p. 7; Report of John R. Baylor, Aug. 3, 1861, ibid., 16–17. A total of 492 men surrendered to Baylor, of which 410 were paroled, 26 deserted, 16 remained in confinement as prisoners of war, and 40 did not receive parole. "Recapitulation of Troops Surrendered," July 27, 1861, ibid., 15; *Mesilla Times,* Aug. 10, 1861.

48. Undated Statement of J. Cooper McKee, *OR,* series 1, vol. 4, pp. 12–13.

49. "New-Mexico," *New-York Daily Tribune,* Sept. 5, 1861.

50. Gibbs to AAG, Nov. 7, 1861, *OR,* series 1, vol. 4, p. 9; Canby to AAG, Sept. 6, 1861, NA, RG393, M1072, LS, DNM, Roll 2; Canby to AAG, March 16, 1866, NA, RG94, File L736, CB1866, Major Isaac Lynde Records; Thomas to Simon Cameron, Dec. 11, 1861, *OR,* series 1, vol. 4, p. 15; General Orders No. 102, Nov. 25, 1861, ibid., 16.

51. Lynde to AAG, Aug. 7, 1861, *OR,* series 1, vol. 4, pp. 5–6. For overviews of Lynde's surrender, see Richard Wadsworth, *Incident at San Augustine Springs: A Hearing for Major Isaac Lynde* (Las Cruces, NM: Yucca Tree, 2002); Kiser, *Turmoil on the Rio Grande,* 166–74.

52. Proclamation of John R. Baylor, Aug. 1, 1861, *OR,* series 1, vol. 4, pp. 20–21.

53. Baylor to Van Dorn, Aug. 14, 1861, ibid., 23.

54. Baylor to Sibley, Oct. 24, 1861, *OR,* series 1, vol. 4, pp. 127–28; Baylor to Sibley, Oct. 25, 1861, ibid., 132–33; Sibley to Cooper, Sept. 2, 1861, in Wilson and Thompson, *Civil War in West Texas and New Mexico,* 40. By December 1861 Rebel officers had reliable information that no Union troops would land at Guaymas. Sibley to Cooper, Dec. 16, 1861, ibid., 81.

55. Baylor to Commander of Dept. of Texas, Oct. 25, 1861, *OR,* series 1, vol. 4, p. 129; Baylor to Simeon Hart, Oct. 24, 1861, ibid., 128.

56. A. M. Jackson to Baylor, Nov. 11, 1861, in Wilson and Thompson, *Civil War in West Texas and New Mexico,* 73.

57. For an accounting of Sibley Brigade enlistees, see Martin Hardwick Hall, *The Confederate Army of New Mexico* (Austin, TX: Presidial, 1978).

58. Sibley to Cooper, Nov. 16, 1861, *OR,* series 1, vol. 4, pp. 141–43; General Orders No. 9, ibid., 143.

59. Thompson, *Henry Hopkins Sibley,* 222–46; Nelson, "Death in the Distance," 33–52. For Sibley's reliance on New Mexicans, see Facundo Piño, "Address to the Legislative Assembly of New Mexico," Jan. 29, 1862, in NA, RG46, Territorial Papers of the U.S.

Senate, New Mexico 1840–1854, M200, Roll 14. For accounts of Sibley's campaign, see Theophilus Noel, *A Campaign from Santa Fe to the Mississippi; Being a History of the Old Sibley Brigade from its First Organization to the Present Time . . .* (Shreveport, LA: Shreveport News, 1865), 5–39; Jerry Thompson, ed., *Civil War in the Southwest: Recollections of the Sibley Brigade* (College Station: Texas A&M University Press, 2001); Don E. Alberts, ed., *Rebels on the Rio Grande: The Civil War Journal of A .B. Peticolas* (Albuquerque, NM: Merit, 1993).

60. Proclamation of Henry H. Sibley, Dec. 20, 1861, *OR,* series 1, vol. 4, pp. 89–90; Frazier, *Blood and Treasure,* 127–36.

61. Reily to John H. Reagan, Jan. 26, 1862, *OR,* series 1, vol. 50, pp. 825–26.

62. Jackson to Reily, Dec. 31, 1861, *OR,* series 1, vol. 4, pp. 167–68; Sibley to Cooper, Jan. 3, 1862, ibid., 167; Sibley to Governors of Chihuahua and Sonora, Dec. 21, 1861, in Wilson and Thompson, *Civil War in West Texas and New Mexico,* 86–88.

63. Reily to Sibley, Jan. 20, 1862, *OR,* series 1, vol. 4, pp. 170–74; Luis Terrazas to Sibley, Jan. 11, 1862, ibid., 171–72.

64. See Thompson, *Henry Hopkins Sibley,* 239–42; Martin Hardwick Hall, "Colonel James Reily's Diplomatic Missions to Chihuahua and Sonora," *New Mexico Historical Review* 31 (July 1956): 232–45.

65. For reports of the Battle of Valverde, see Canby to AG, Feb. 22, 1862, *OR,* series 1, vol. 9, p. 487; Sibley to Cooper, May 4, 1862, ibid., 508–9; Benjamin Roberts to William Nicodemus, Feb. 23, 1862, ibid., 493–97; Henry Connelly to Seward, March 1, 1862, NA, RG 59, U.S. State Department, New Mexico Territorial Papers, 1851–72, Microfilm T17, Roll 2; Noel, *Campaign from Santa Fe,* 19–23; Alberts, *Rebels on the Rio Grande,* 42–52, 63–66; Wilson, *When the Texans Came,* 242–56, 302–3; Thompson, *Civil War in the Southwest,* 27–70; Meketa, *Legacy of Honor,* 166–73. For analyses of the battle, see Hall, *Sibley's New Mexico Campaign,* 83–103; Thompson, *Henry Hopkins Sibley,* 245–68; John Taylor, *Bloody Valverde: A Civil War Battle on the Rio Grande, February 21, 1862* (Albuquerque: University of New Mexico Press, 1995).

66. Canby to AG, Feb. 22, 1862, *OR,* series 1, vol. 9, p. 487; Canby to AG, March 1, 1862, ibid., 492.

67. Canby to AG, March 1, 1862, ibid., 488, 492. On the role of volunteers and militia at Valverde, see Thompson, *Civil War History of the New Mexico Volunteers,* 113–37.

68. Sibley to Cooper, May 4, 1862, *OR,* series 1, vol. 9, pp. 507–9.

69. See Thompson, *Henry Hopkins Sibley,* 252, 261. One individual claiming familiarity with these events refuted the widespread claim that Sibley was drunk during the Battle of Valverde. See Willis L. Robards to Jefferson Davis, Dec. 8, 1862, in Crist, *Papers of Jefferson Davis,* 8:536–37.

70. Sibley to Cooper, May 4, 1862, *OR,* series 1, vol. 9, pp. 507–9; Thomas Green to Jackson, Feb. 22, 1862, ibid., 522.

71. William R. Scurry to Jackson, Feb. 22, 1862, ibid., 513–16, quotations on 515; Henry W. Ragnet to Jackson, Feb. 23, 1862, ibid., 516–18.

72. Green to Jackson, Feb. 22, 1862, ibid., 518–22, quotation on 520. See also Noel, *Campaign from Santa Fe,* 20.

73. Meketa, *Legacy of Honor*, 171.

74. Canby to AG, March 1, 1862, *OR*, series 1, vol. 9, p. 492.

75. Taylor, *Bloody Valverde*, 136, 142; Thompson, *Henry Hopkins Sibley*, 267.

76. Sibley to Cooper, May 4, 1862, *OR*, series 1, vol. 9, pp. 507–9.

77. Ibid.; A. S. Thurmond to Commanding Officer of C.S. Forces, March 3, 1862, ibid., 529–30.

78. J. L. Davidson to G. R. Paul, March 10, 1862, *OR*, series 1, vol. 9, p. 527; Enos to Donaldson, March 11, 1862, ibid., 527–28.

79. Noel, *Campaign from Santa Fe*, 22.

80. John P. Slough to AG, March 30, 1862, *OR*, series 1, vol. 9, pp. 534–35.

81. On the Battle of Glorieta, see Connelly to Seward, March 30, 1862, NA, RG 59, U.S. State Department, New Mexico Territorial Papers, 1851–1872, Microfilm T17, Roll 2; various reports of participants, *OR*, series 1, vol. 9, pp. 532–45; Noel, *Campaign from Santa Fe*, 23–25; Thompson, *Civil War in the Southwest*, 92–98; Alberts, *Rebels on the Rio Grande*, 77–86. For analyses of the battle, see Ray C. Colton, *The Civil War in the Western Territories: Arizona, Colorado, New Mexico, and Utah* (Norman: University of Oklahoma Press, 1959), 49–80; Hall, *Sibley's New Mexico Campaign*, 141–60; Thompson, *Henry Hopkins Sibley*, 269–307; Don E. Alberts, *The Battle of Glorieta: Union Victory in the West* (College Station: Texas A&M University Press, 1998); Thomas S. Edrington and John Taylor, *The Battle of Glorieta Pass: A Gettysburg in the West, March 26–28, 1862* (Albuquerque: University of New Mexico Press, 1998).

82. Sibley to Cooper, March 31, 1862, *OR*, series 1, vol. 9, pp. 540–41; Sibley to Cooper, May 4, 1862, ibid., 509; Scurry to Sibley, March 30, 1862, ibid., 541–42; Scurry to Jackson, March 31, 1862, ibid., 543–45.

83. Noel, *Campaign from Santa Fe*, 23.

84. Alberts, *Battle of Glorieta*, 138; Edrington and Taylor, *Battle of Glorieta Pass*, 130–31, 134–35.

85. J. M. Chivington to AG, March 28, 1862, *OR*, series 1, vol. 9, pp. 538–39; Slough to AG, March 30, 1862, ibid., 534–35.

86. Scurry to Sibley, March 30, 1862, ibid., 541–42; Scurry to Jackson, March 31, 1862, ibid., 543–45.

87. Paul to Connelly, April 12, 1862, NA, RG59, U.S. State Department, New Mexico Territorial Papers, 1851–72, Microfilm T17, Roll 2; Connelly to Seward, April 19, 1862, ibid.

88. Canby to AG, April 23, 1862, *OR*, series 1, vol. 9, p. 551. For the fighting at Peralta, see Alberts, *Rebels on the Rio Grande*, 103–6.

89. Noel, *Campaign from Santa Fe*, 27, 31.

90. Alberts, *Rebels on the Rio Grande*, 56, 61, 67.

91. Roberts to Thomas, April 23, 1862, *OR*, series 1, vol. 9, pp. 553–54; see also Carleton to Thomas, Oct. 10, 1862, NA, RG393, M1072, LS, DNM, Roll 3.

92. Peter Connelly to Seward, May 4, 1862, NA, RG59, U.S. State Department, New Mexico Territorial Papers, 1851–72, Microfilm T17, Roll 2.

93. G. Wright to Carleton, Jan. 31, 1862, *OR*, series 1, vol. 4, p. 91; Nicodemus to AAG, July 20, 1862, NA, RG393, M1072, LS, DNM, Roll 2. On the Confederate retreat, see Thompson,

Henry Hopkins Sibley, 292–307. On the California Column, see Darlis Miller, *The California Column in New Mexico* (Albuquerque: University of New Mexico Press, 1982), 3–30. For firsthand accounts from California Column soldiers, see Neil B. Carmony, ed., *The Civil War in Apacheland: Sergeant George Hand's Diary* (Silver City, NM: High-Lonesome, 1996); John C. Cremony, *Life among the Apaches* (San Francisco: A. Roman, 1868), 144–322.

94. Sibley to Cooper, May 4, 1862, *OR,* vol. 9, pp. 506–12; Sibley to Cooper, June 2, 1862, in Wilson and Thompson, *Civil War in West Texas and New Mexico,* 167–68. Sibley had begged for reinforcements after the Battle of Valverde. See Sibley to Cooper, Feb. 22, 1862, *OR,* series 1, vol. 9, pp. 505–6. On the campaign's failure, see Nelson, "Death in the Distance," 47–48.

95. Sibley to the Soldiers of the Army of New Mexico, May 1862, in Alberts, *Rebels on the Rio Grande,* 135.

96. Thompson, *Henry Hopkins Sibley,* 302.

97. Alberts, *Rebels on the Rio Grande,* 118.

98. Hal Hunter to "Dear Advocate," May 29, 1862, in Jerry Thompson, ed., "'Is This to Be the Glory of Our Brave Men?': The New Mexico Civil War Journal and Letters of Dr. Henry Jacob 'Hal' Hunter," *New Mexico Historical Review* 75 (Oct. 2000): 584.

99. Noel, *Campaign from Santa Fe,* 15.

100. Teel, "Sibley's New Mexican Campaign," 2:700. At least two of the Confederate officers under Sibley's command—Thomas Green and Trevanion Teel—were members of the KGC. See Keehn, *Knights of the Golden Circle,* 154.

101. Carleton to John Evans, Jan. 28, 1863, NA, RG393, M1072, LS, DNM, Roll 3; Carleton to Thomas, Feb. 1, 1863, ibid.; Carleton to Seward, Feb. 20, 1863, ibid.

102. Carleton to Chivington, Dec. 8, 1862, ibid.

103. Carleton to Carson, Dec. 8, 1862, NA, RG393, M1072, LS, DNM, Roll 3; Carleton to Joseph Updegraff, Dec. 8, 1862, ibid.

104. Carleton to Thomas, Oct. 10, 1862, ibid.; Carleton to St. Vrain, Dec. 9, 1862, ibid.

105. Carleton to West, Nov. 18, 1862, ibid.

106. See Arny to Seward, May 28, 1863, NA, RG 59, U.S. State Department, New Mexico Territorial Papers, 1851–72, Microfilm T17, Roll 2.

107. Carleton to John Evans, Jan. 28, 1863, NA, RG393, M1072, LS, DNM, Roll 3; Carleton to Thomas, Feb. 1, 1862, ibid.

108. Carleton to Terrazas, Feb. 20, 1863, ibid.; Carleton to Thomas, Feb. 23, 1863, ibid. See also Arny to Terrazas, Oct. 21, 1862, NA, RG59, U.S. State Department, New Mexico Territorial Papers, 1851–72, Microfilm T17, Roll 2; Arny to Terrazas, March 17, 1863, ibid.; Terrazas to Arny, March 24, 1863, ibid.

109. Carleton to Ignacio Pesqueíra, April 20, 1864, in "Condition of the Indian Tribes," 39th Cong., 2nd Sess., Senate Report No. 156, p. 177.

110. Carleton to Seward, March 8, 1863, NA, RG393, M1072, LS, DNM, Roll 3; Carleton to Seward, Sept. 13, 1863, ibid.; Connelly to Seward, Aug. 23, 1863, NA, RG59, U.S. State Department, New Mexico Territorial Papers, 1851–72, Microfilm T17, Roll 2.

111. Carleton to Reuben Creel, April 23, 1863, NA, RG393, M1072, LS, DNM, Roll 3; Carleton to Joseph Smith, April 27, 1863, ibid.; Carleton to Edward B. Willis, April 28,

1863, ibid.; Carleton to West, May 17, 1863, ibid.; Carleton to Thomas, Oct. 9, 1864, ibid.

112. Canby to AAG, June 23, 1861, *OR,* series 1, vol. 4, p. 44; see also Connelly to Seward, July 27, 1862, NA, RG59, U.S. State Department, New Mexico Territorial Papers, 1851–72, Microfilm T17, Roll 2

113. *Mesilla Times,* July 29, 1861.

114. Lynde to AAG, July 21, 1861, *OR,* series 1, vol. 4, p. 60.

115. Canby to AAG, Aug. 16, 1861, ibid., 63.

116. Canby to AAG, Sept. 22, 1861, ibid., 71. See also McNitt, *Navajo Wars,* 410–29.

117. Canby to AAG, Dec. 1, 1861, *OR,* series 1, vol. 4, p. 77.

118. Charles E. Mix to O. H. Browning, Nov. 15, 1867, in *1867 RCIA,* 2.

119. Canby to AAG, Dec. 1, 1861, *OR,* series 1, vol. 4, p. 77; Carleton to Thomas, Sept. 30, 1862, in Lawrence C. Kelly, ed., *Navajo Roundup: Selected Correspondence of Kit Carson's Expedition against the Navajo, 1863–1865* (Boulder, CO: Pruett, 1970), 10–11.

120. Carleton attained the rank of major on Sept. 7, 1861, and was promoted again on April 28, 1862, to Brigadier General. Heitman, *Historical Register of the U.S. Army,* 1:282.

121. For Carleton's approach to Indian affairs, see Sonnichsen, *The Mescalero Apaches,* 96–119; Gerald Thompson, *The Army and the Navajo: The Bosque Redondo Reservation Experiment, 1863–1868* (Tucson: University of Arizona Press, 1976), 10–27; Wooster, *American Military Frontiers,* 167–72. For a biographical sketch of Carleton, see Aurora Hunt, *Major General James Henry Carleton 1814–1873: Western Frontier Dragoon* (Glendale, CA: Arthur H. Clark, 1958), esp. 235–96.

122. Carleton to Halleck, May 10, 1863, NA, RG393, M1072, LS, DNM, Roll 3.

123. Carleton to Thomas, Aug. 2, 1863, ibid.; Connelly to Seward, Aug. 23, 1863, NA, RG59, U.S. State Department, New Mexico Territorial Papers, 1851–1872, Microfilm T17, Roll 2.

124. Carleton to Thomas, Sept. 13, 1863, NA, RG393, M1072, LS, DNM, Roll 3; Sibley to Cooper, June 2, 1862, in Wilson and Thompson, *Civil War in West Texas and New Mexico,* 167. See also Carleton to James R. Doolittle, Oct. 22, 1865, in "Condition of the Indian Tribes," 39th Cong., 2nd Sess., Senate Report No. 156, p. 98; Carleton to Montgomery Blair, Sept. 13, 1863, in ibid., 136–37; Carleton to Salmon P. Chase, Sept. 20, 1863, in ibid., 140.

125. Carleton to John C. McFerran, May 15, 1865, NA, RG393, M1072, LS, DNM, Roll 3. Emphasis in original.

126. Carleton to Edwin A. Rigg, Aug. 6, 1863, in "Condition of the Indian Tribes," 39th Cong., 2nd Sess., Senate Report No. 156, p. 124.

127. Carleton to Thomas, Sept. 30, 1862, NA, RG393, M1072, LS, DNM, Roll 3. For an overview of Carleton's initiatives in 1862–63, see Thompson, *Civil War History of the New Mexico Volunteers,* 267–98; Andrew E. Masich, *Civil War in the Southwest Borderlands, 1861–1867* (Norman: University of Oklahoma Press, 2017), 106–48. In 1866 Governor William F. M. Arny voiced support for Carleton's approach, informing the territorial legislature that "the mineral resources of New Mexico are scarcely known or appreciated, and will not be until the Indians are subdued and placed upon reservations."

"Second Annual Message to the Legislative Assembly," William F. M. Arny, Dec. 1866, NMSRCA, TA, Roll 98, Frames 351–71.

128. Carleton to Sebastián Lerdo de Tejada, Feb. 22, 1865, NA, RG393, M1072, LS, DNM, Roll 3. The year before, Carleton had made a similar request of Chihuahua governor Luis Terrazas and Sonora governor Ignacio Pesqueíra. See Carleton to Terrazas, April 20, 1864, and Carleton to Pesqueíra, April 20, 1864, both in "Condition of the Indian Tribes," 39th Cong., 2nd Sess., Senate Report No. 156, pp. 177–78.

129. Carleton to Christopher Carson, Oct. 12, 1862, NA, RG393, M1072, LS, DNM, Roll 3.

130. Carleton to Carson, Nov. 25, 1862, ibid.; Carleton to Thomas, March 19, 1863, ibid. See also Lorenzo Labadi to Michael Steck, Oct. 22, 1864, in *1864 RCIA*, 347–48; Labadi to J. K. Graves, Jan. 4, 1866, in *1866 RCIA*, 139–41. For an account of the Mescaleros at Bosque Redondo, see Cremony, *Life Among the Apaches,* 197–309.

131. Carleton to Thomas, Jan. 2, 1863, NA, RG393, M1072, LS, DNM, Roll 3.

132. See Sweeney, *Mangas Coloradas,* 450–65; Paul Andrew Hutton, *The Apache Wars: The Hunt for Geronimo, the Apache Kid, and the Captive Boy Who Started the Longest War in American History* (New York: Crown, 2016), 95–104; Thompson, *Civil War History of the New Mexico Volunteers,* 286–87.

133. Eve Ball, *In the Days of Victorio: Recollections of a Warm Springs Apache* (Tucson: University of Arizona Press, 1970), 48; Eve Ball, *Indeh: An Apache Odyssey* (Provo, UT: Brigham Young University Press, 1980), 20.

134. Carleton to Samuel J. Jones, April 27, 1863, NA, RG393, M1072, LS, DNM, Roll 3. See also Carleton to Thomas, Feb. 1, 1863, ibid.

135. A. B. Norton to N. G. Taylor, Aug. 24, 1867, in *1867 RCIA,* 193.

136. William P. Dole to Caleb B. Smith, Nov. 26, 1862, in *1862 RCIA,* 188.

137. Carleton to Thomas, Sept. 6, 1863, NA, RG393, M1072, LS, DNM, Roll 3; Carleton to Carson, Aug. 18, 1863, in "Condition of the Indian Tribes," 39th Cong., 2nd Sess., Senate Report No. 156, pp. 128–29.

138. Carleton to Carson and J. Francisco Chavez, June 23, 1863, ibid., 116.

139. Carleton to Chavez, Aug. 7, 1863, ibid., 126; Carleton to Carson, Sept. 19, 1863, ibid., 139.

140. Thompson, *The Army and the Navajo,* 17, 71.

141. Second Annual Message of Henry Connelly, Dec. 9, 1863, NA, RG59, U.S. State Department, New Mexico Territorial Papers 1851–1872, Microfilm T-17, Roll 2; Diego Archuleta to J. W. Denver, Sept. 30, 1857, in *1857 RCIA,* 284–87; Sylvester Mowry to Denver, ibid., 298–99; Collins to Dole, Oct. 10, 1862, in *1862 RCIA,* 385.

142. Albert Pheiffer to Lawrence Murphy, Jan. 20, 1864, in Kelly, *Navajo Roundup,* 102–4. On the use of Ute auxiliaries, see Carson to AAG, July 24, 1863, *OR,* series 1, vol. 26, pt. 1, pp. 233–34; Carson to Carleton, July 24, 1863, ibid., 234; Statement of Colonel Kit Carson, in "Condition of the Indian Tribes," 39th Cong., 2nd Sess., Senate Report No. 156, p. 97. See also McNitt, *Navajo Wars,* 442–46; Clifford E. Trafzer, *The Kit Carson Campaign: The Last Great Navajo War* (Norman: University of Oklahoma Press, 1982), 80–82, 140–62; Thompson, *Civil War History of the New Mexico Volunteers,* 299–326; Reséndez, *The Other Slavery,* 284–93.

143. For Carson's recollection of the campaign, see Undated Statement of Kit Carson, in "Condition of the Indian Tribes," 39th Cong., 2nd Sess., Senate Report No. 156, p. 97. For additional correspondence relating to the Canyon de Chelly operations, see Kelly, *Navajo Roundup,* 81–109.

144. Trafzer, *Kit Carson Campaign,* 160–62; Ruth Roessel, ed., *Navajo Stories of the Long Walk Period* (Chinle, AZ: Navajo Community College Press, 1973), 130–31, 202.

145. Carleton to Thomas, Feb. 7, 1864, NA, RG393, M1072, LS, DNM, Roll 3; Carleton to Thomas, Feb. 27, 1864, ibid. For the Long Walk, see Iverson, *Diné,* 51–57; Trafzer, *Kit Carson Campaign,* 169–97.

146. Carleton to Thomas, Feb. 7, 1864, NA, RG393, M1072, LS, DNM, Roll 3; Proclamation of Governor Henry Connelly, March 23, 1864, NA, RG59, U.S. State Department, New Mexico Territorial Papers, 1851–72, Microfilm T17, Roll 2.

147. Stephen C. Jett, ed., "The Destruction of Navajo Orchards in 1864: Captain John Thompson's Report," *Arizona and the West* 16 (Winter 1974): 365–78; Steck to Dole, Oct. 10, 1864, in *1864 RCIA,* 329. See also Thompson, *Civil War History of the New Mexico Volunteers,* 327–44. For correspondence relating to the 1864 campaigns, see Kelly, *Navajo Roundup,* 25–158; Correll, *Through White Men's Eyes,* 4:19–180.

148. For statistics on Bosque Redondo, see Carleton to Thomas, Feb. 7, 1864, NA, RG393, M1072, LS, DNM, Roll 3; Carleton to Thomas, Feb. 27, 1864, ibid.; Carleton to Halleck, March 20, 1864, ibid.; Carleton to Dole, Sept. 19, 1864, ibid.; Felipe Delgado to D. N. Cooley, Sept. 10, 1865, in *1865 RCIA,* 345; Report of William T. Sherman, Nov. 5, 1866, in *1866 Annual Report of the Secretary of War,* 39th Cong., 2nd Sess., Senate Exec. Doc. No. 1, p. 22; Theo. H. Dodd to A. B. Norton, June 30, 1867, in *1867 RCIA,* 203. In 1865 there were also 472 Mescalero Apaches living at the reservation; see Cooley to James Harlan, Oct. 31, 1865, in ibid., 188. All but nine of those fled on Nov. 3, 1865, ending the period of dual tribal occupancy. Dodd to Norton, Aug. 28, 1866, in *1866 RCIA,* 149.

149. Carleton to Thomas, March 12, 1864, NA, RG393, M1072, LS, DNM, Roll 3.

150. Roessel, *Navajo Stories of the Long Walk,* 127.

151. Ibid., 25.

152. Ibid., 103.

153. Ibid., 30.

154. Ibid., 103.

155. Ibid., 149.

156. On unlimited war, see Grenier, *First Way of War,* 1–12.

157. Roessel, *Navajo Stories of the Long Walk,* 213, 200.

158. Ibid., 191. On Bosque Redondo generally, see Ruth M. Underhill, *The Navajos* (Norman: University of Oklahoma Press, 1956), 127–43; James D. Shinkle, *Fort Sumner and the Bosque Redondo Indian Reservation* (Roswell, NM: Hall-Poorbaugh, 1965); Thompson, *The Army and the Navajo;* Katherine M. B. Osburn, "The Navajo at the Bosque Redondo: Cooperation, Resistance, and Initiative, 1864–1868," *New Mexico Historical Review* 60 (Oct. 1985), 399–413; Iverson, *Diné,* 57–63; Brooks, *Captives and Cousins,* 332–34. For correspondence relating to Bosque Redondo, see Correll, *Through White Men's Eyes,* 5:21–498.

159. Steck to Dole, Oct. 10, 1864, in *1864 RCIA,* 330. For disagreements between Steck and Carleton, see Carleton to Thomas, March 19, 1864, in "Condition of the Indian Tribes," 39th Cong., 2nd Sess., Senate Report No. 156, pp. 168–69; Cooley to Harlan, Oct. 31, 1865, in *1865 RCIA,* 188.

160. Carleton to Thomas, Feb. 7, 1864, and March 19, 1864, NA, RG393, M1072, LS, DNM, Roll 3.

161. Carleton to Thomas, Nov. 22, 1863, ibid.

162. Carleton to Thomas, Sept. 6, 1863, NA, RG393, M1072, LS, DNM, Roll 3; Carleton to Usher, Aug. 14, 1864, ibid.; Carleton to Usher, March 30, 1865, ibid.; Carleton to Henry B. Bristol, July 17, 1864, in "Condition of the Indian Tribes," 39th Cong., 2nd Sess., Senate Report No. 156, pp. 187–88.

163. Carleton to John C. McFerran, May 15, 1865, NA, RG393, M1072, LS, DNM, Roll 3.

164. Graves to Cooley, Undated Report, in *1866 RCIA,* 131, 134. Graves sided with Carleton, praising him as an efficient administrator and lauding the Bosque Redondo as the best policy for New Mexico.

165. Carleton to Thomas, April 17, 1864, in "Condition of the Indian Tribes," 39th Cong., 2nd Sess., Senate Report No. 156, p. 176.

166. 38th Cong., 1st Sess., Senate Bill No. 226, April 11, 1864, in NA, RG46, Territorial Papers of the U.S. Senate, New Mexico 1840–54, M200, Roll 14; Carleton to Usher, Aug. 27, 1864, NA, RG393, M1072, LS, DNM, Roll 3; Carleton to Thomas, Oct. 30, 1864, ibid.

167. Report of William T. Sherman, Nov. 5, 1866, in *1866 Annual Report of the Secretary of War,* 39th Cong., 2nd Sess., Senate Exec. Doc. No. 1, p. 22; Steck to Dole, Oct. 10, 1864, in *1864 RCIA,* 327; Dole to Usher, Oct. 31, 1863, in *1863 RCIA,* 14; Dole to Usher, Nov. 15, 1864, in *1864 RCIA,* 19. The actual costs of subsisting the Navajos in 1865 exceeded $1.5 million. For expenditures at Bosque Redondo in 1865 and 1866, see Cooley to Harlan, May 1, 1866, in *1866 RCIA,* 142–44; Norton to Cooley, Sept. 28, 1866, ibid., 146–47; Dodd to Norton, Aug. 28, 1866, ibid., 150.

168. Dole to Usher, Nov. 15, 1864, in *1864 RCIA,* 161.

169. Carleton to Thomas, Feb. 7, 1864; May 31, 1864; and Aug. 27, 1864, all in NA, RG393, M1072, LS, DNM, Roll 3; Thompson, *Civil War History of the New Mexico Volunteers,* 367.

170. Carleton to Thomas, Feb. 7, 1864; March 6, 1864; and March 12, 1864, all in NA, RG393, M1072, LS, DNM, Roll 3.

171. Dole to Usher, Nov. 15, 1864, in *1864 RCIA,* 163–64; Steck to Dole, Oct. 10, 1864, ibid., 327–30.

172. Norton to N. G. Taylor, Aug. 24, 1867, in *1867 RCIA,* 190. On the scarcity of firewood at Fort Sumner, see Cremony, *Life among the Apaches,* 199–200.

173. See Thompson, *The Army and the Navajo,* 47–48, 80–81, 98–99, 128–29. On the Fort Sumner hospital, see Thompson, *New Mexico Territory during the Civil War,* 129.

174. Norton to Taylor, Aug. 24, 1867, in *1867 RCIA,* 190.

175. Roessel, *Navajo Stories of the Long Walk,* 119, 205.

176. See, for example, Taylor to O. H. Browning, Nov. 23, 1868, in *1868 RCIA,* 4.

177. Sherman to John Rawlins, Sept. 21, 1866, in "Protection across the Continent," 39th Cong., 2nd Sess., House Exec. Doc. No. 23, p. 15.

178. For the treaty, see Kappler, *Indian Affairs*, 2:1015–20; Iverson, *Diné*, 63–65. On the treaty negotiations, see John L. Kessell, "General Sherman and the Navajo Treaty of 1868: A Basic and Expedient Misunderstanding," *Western Historical Quarterly* 12 (July 1981): 251–72.

179. N. M. Davis to Taylor, Sept. 15, 1868, in *1868 RCIA*, 161.

180. Carleton to Steck, Oct. 29, 1864, NA, RG393, M1072, LS, DNM, Roll 3.

181. Carleton to Thomas, Aug. 29, 1864, ibid.

182. On Kit Carson as an Indian fighter, see Tom Dunlay, *Kit Carson and the Indians* (Lincoln: University of Nebraska Press, 2000).

183. Hämäläinen, *The Comanche Empire*, 313.

184. Carson to Carleton, Dec. 4, 1864, *OR*, series 1, vol. 41, part 1, pp. 939–42. See also George H. Pettis, *Kit Carson's Fight with the Comanche and Kiowa Indians, at the Adobe Walls on the Canadian River, November 25th, 1864* (Providence, RI: Sidney S. Rider, 1878). On the Battle of Adobe Walls, see Thompson, *Civil War History of the New Mexico Volunteers*, 367–75; Brooks, *Captives and Cousins*, 338–39; James Bailey Blackshear, *Fort Bascom: Soldiers, Comancheros, and Indians in the Canadian River Valley* (Norman: University of Oklahoma Press, 2016), 103–12.

185. Carleton to Carson, Dec. 15, 1864, *OR*, series 1, vol. 41, part 1, p. 944.

186. Carson to Benjamin C. Cutler, Dec. 16, 1864, ibid., 943.

187. Carleton to Bergmann, March 15, 1865, in "Condition of the Indian Tribes," 39th Cong., 2nd Sess., Senate Report No. 156, p. 220.

188. Hämäläinen, *The Comanche Empire,* 313–20, 336–41.

189. "Condition of the Indian Tribes," 39th Cong., 2nd Sess., Senate Report No. 156, p. 3.

190. Thompson, *Henry Hopkins Sibley,* 307.

Conclusion

1. Sherman quoted in Hutton, *The Apache Wars,* 118.

Bibliography

Archival Sources

Bancroft Library. Berkeley, CA.
Archivo de la Defensa Nacional. "Proceedings against Manuel Armijo," March 1847. Expediente 2588, Roll 11.
Center for Southwest Research. University of New Mexico, Albuquerque.
Inventory of the Michael Steck Papers
Missouri Historical Society. St. Louis.
William Carr Lane Papers
U.S. National Archives and Records Administration. Microfilm Publications. Washington, D.C.
Record Group 46. U.S. Senate, New Mexico Territorial Papers, 1840–54. Microcopy 200.
Record Group 59. U.S. State Department, New Mexico Territorial Papers, 1851–72. Microfilm T17.
———. U.S. State Department, Dispatches from U.S. Consuls in Ciudad Juárez, 1850–1906. Microcopy 54.
Record Group 75. U.S. Office of Indian Affairs, Letters Received 1824–80, New Mexico Superintendency, 1849–80. Microcopy 234.
Record Group 94. U.S. War Department, Records of the Adjutant General's Office, Orders Issued by Brigadier General Stephen Watts Kearny and Brigadier General Sterling Price to the Army of the West, 1846–48. Microcopy T1115.
———. U.S. War Department, Records of the Adjutant General's Office, Selected Records from File L736, CB1866, Major Isaac Lynde.
———. U.S. War Department, Records of the Adjutant General's Office, Letters Received 1805–89. File P-94-1848, Entry 12.

Record Group 393. U.S. War Department, Letters Sent, Ninth Military Department, Department of New Mexico, and District of New Mexico, 1849–90. Microcopy 1072.

———. U.S. War Department, Registers of Letters Received by Headquarters, Ninth Military Department, 1849–53. Microcopy 1102.

———. U.S. War Department, Registers of Letters Received by Headquarters, Department of New Mexico, 1854–65. Microcopy 1120.

New Mexico State Records Center and Archives. Santa Fe.

Bloom-McFie Collection

Ina Sizer Cassidy Collection

María G. Duran Collection

Getty Family Collection

Jaramillo-Bent-Scheurich Family Papers

Mexican Archives of New Mexico

Misc. Letters and Diaries

Papers of Governors Kearny, Bent, and Price

L. B. Prince Personal Papers

Benjamin Read Collection

Albert H. Schroeder Papers

Territorial Archives of New Mexico

Ralph Emerson Twitchell Collection

Donaciano Vigil Collection

Dorothy Woodward Penitente Collection

WPA Collection

Congressional Documents

"Alphonso Wetmore's Report," Oct. 11, 1831, in "Message from the President of the United States," 22nd Cong., 1st Sess., Senate Doc. No. 90.

Annals of Congress, 1789–1824.

"California and New Mexico," Feb. 6, 1850, 31st Cong., 1st Sess., House Exec. Doc. No. 17.

"Canal or Railroad between the Atlantic and Pacific Oceans," Feb. 20, 1849, 30th Cong., 2nd Sess., House Report No. 145.

"Claims for Depredations by Indians in the Territory of New Mexico," 35th Cong., 1st Sess., Senate Exec. Doc. 55.

"Condition of the Indian Tribes," 39th Cong., 2nd Sess., Senate Report No. 156.

Congressional Globe, 1846–73.

"Correspondence Relating to Civil Government in California and New Mexico," Oct. 7, 1848, 30th Cong., 1st Sess., House Exec. Doc. No. 1.

"Documents from War Department," 30th Cong., 1st Sess., House Exec. Doc. 1.

"Expenditures for Internal Improvements," Dec. 11, 1834, 23rd Cong., 2nd Sess., House Exec. Doc. No. 18.

"Extending Privilege of Drawback," March 8, 1842, 27th Cong., 2nd Sess., House Report No. 328.

Gales and Seaton's Register of Debates in Congress, 1824–37.

"Indian Hostilities in New Mexico," April 12, 1860, 36th Cong., 1st Sess., House Exec. Doc. No. 69.

"Insurrection against the Military Government in New Mexico and California, 1847 and 1848," 56th Cong., 1st Sess., Senate Doc. No. 442.

"Internal Improvements since 1824," 20th Cong., 2nd Sess., House Doc. No. 7.

"Internal Improvements," Jan. 5, 1831, 21st Cong., 2nd Sess., House Exec. Doc. No. 30.

"Memorial of a Committee Appointed at a Railroad Convention," Dec. 27, 1852, 32nd Cong., 2nd Sess., Senate Misc. Doc. No. 5.

"Memorial of the General Assembly of Missouri," Feb. 16, 1839, 25th Cong., 3rd Sess., Senate Doc. No. 225.

"Memorial of Henry O'Reilly," April 6, 1852, 32nd Cong., 1st Sess., Senate Misc. Doc. No. 67.

"Memorial of the New Mexican Railway Company in Relation to the Pacific Railroad," May 21, 1860, 36th Cong., 1st Sess., House Misc. Doc. No. 85.

"Memorial to Congress," March 4, 1864, 38th Cong., 1st Sess., Senate Misc. Doc. No. 52.

"A Memorial to the Congress of the United States relative to the Santa Fe trade," Dec. 27, 1838, 26th Cong., 1st Sess., Senate Doc. No. 472.

"Message from the President of the United States . . . Relative to the Arrest and Imprisonment of Certain American Citizens at Santa Fe," 15th Cong., 1st Sess., April 15, 1818, House Document No. 197.

"Message from the President of the United States," 20th Cong., 2nd Sess., Feb. 10, 1829, Unspecified Doc. No. 69.

"Message from the President of the United States . . . concerning the Fur Trade, and Inland Trade to Mexico," Feb. 9, 1832, 22nd Cong., 1st Sess., Senate Doc. No. 90.

"Message from the President of the United States," 24th Cong., 1st Sess., Unspecified Document No. 400.

"Message from the President of the United States," March 24, 1846, 29th Cong., 1st Sess., Senate Doc. No. 248.

"Message from the President of the United States to the Two Houses of Congress," Dec. 8, 1846, 29th Cong., 2nd Sess., House Exec. Doc. No. 4.

"Messages of the President of the United States, with the Correspondence, therewith communicated, between the Secretary of War and other officers of the Government, on the Subject of the Mexican War," April 28, 1848, 30th Cong., 1st Sess., House Exec. Doc. No. 60.

"Message of the President of the United States," Aug. 2, 1848, 30th Cong., 1st Sess., House Exec. Doc. 76.

"Message from the President of the United States," Dec. 5, 1848, 30th Cong., 2nd Sess., House Exec. Doc. No. 1.

"Message of the President of the United States, New Mexico and California," July 24, 1848, 30th Cong., 1st Sess., House Exec. Doc. No. 70.

"Message from the President of the United States," June 17, 1850, 31st Cong., 1st Sess., Senate Exec. Doc. No. 56.

"Message from the President of the United States, Relative to the Claim of Texas to Jurisdiction over Part of New Mexico," Aug. 6, 1850, 31st Cong., 1st Sess., Senate Exec. Doc. No. 67.

"Message from the President of the United States," Dec. 2, 1850, 31st Cong., 2nd Sess., Senate Exec. Doc. No. 1.

"New Mexico and California," 30th Cong., 1st Sess., House Exec. Doc. No. 70.

"Occupation of Mexican Territory," Dec. 22, 1846, 29th Cong., 2nd Sess., House Exec. Doc. No. 19.

"Organic Law of the Territory of New Mexico," Nov. 23, 1846, 30th Cong., 1st Sess., House Exec. Doc. No. 60.

"Pacific Railroad and Telegraph," Aug. 16, 1856, 34th Cong., 1st Sess., House Report No. 358.

"Petition of Sundry Inhabitants of the State of Missouri," Feb. 14, 1825, 18th Cong., 2nd Sess., House Exec. Doc. No. 79.

"Protection across the Continent," 39th Cong., 2nd Sess., House Exec. Doc. No. 23.

"Report of the Committee on Territories," Jan. 10, 1857, 34th Cong., 3rd Sess., House Report No. 60.

"Report of an Expedition Down the Zuni and Colorado Rivers," 32nd Cong., 2nd Sess., Senate Exec. Doc. No 59.

"Report of Lieut. J. W. Abert of his Examination of New Mexico in the years 1846–47," in "Report of the Secretary of War," Feb. 10, 1848, 30th Cong., 1st Sess., Senate Exec. Doc. 23.

"Report of the Quartermaster General," Nov. 22, 1851, 32nd Cong., 1st Sess., House Exec. Doc. No. 2.

"Report of the Secretary of the Interior, in answer to a resolution of the Senate calling for information in relation to the operations of the commission appointed to run and mark the boundary between the United States and Mexico," Feb. 28, 1850, 31st Cong., 1st Sess., Senate Exec. Doc. No. 34, Parts 1 and 2.

"Report of the Secretary of the Interior, made in compliance with a resolution of the Senate calling for information in relation to the commission appointed to run and mark the boundary between the United States and Mexico," Aug. 31, 1852, 32nd Cong., 1st Sess., Senate Exec. Doc. No. 119.

"Report of the Secretary of War," 30th Cong., 1st Sess., Senate Exec. Doc. No. 1.

"Report of the Secretary of War on the Subject of Indian Hostilities," 33rd Cong., 2nd Sess., Senate Exec. Doc. No. 22.

"Report of the United States and Mexican Boundary Survey, Made under the Direction of the Secretary of the Interior, by William H. Emory," 34th Cong., 1st Sess., Senate Exec. Doc. No. 108.

"Reports of explorations and surveys, to ascertain the most practicable and economical route for a railroad from the Mississippi River to the Pacific Ocean," vols. 2, 3, 7, 33rd Cong., 2nd Sess., Senate Exec. Doc. No. 78.

"Report upon the Colorado River of the West, Explored in 1857 and 1858 by Lieutenant Joseph C. Ives, Corps of Topographical Engineers," 36th Cong., 1st Sess., House Exec. Doc. No. 90.

"Route from Fort Smith to Santa Fe," Feb. 21, 1850, 31st Cong., 1st Sess., House Exec. Doc. No. 45.

Senate Select Committee Report, May 8, 1850, 31st Cong., 1st Sess., Senate Report Com. No. 123.

"Slavery in the Territory of New Mexico," May 10, 1860, 36th Cong., 1st Sess., House Report No. 508.

"Speech of Hon. Richard H. Weightman of New Mexico," March 15, 1852, Washington, D.C., Congressional Globe Office, 1852.

"Statistical Report on the Sickness and Mortality in the Army of the United States . . . from January 1849 to January 1855," prepared by Richard H. Coolidge, 34th Cong., 1st Sess., Senate Exec. Doc. No. 96.

"Statistical Report on the Sickness and Mortality in the United States Army . . . from January 1855 to January 1860," prepared by Richard H. Coolidge, 36th Cong., 1st Sess., Senate Exec. Doc. No. 52.

"Trade and Intercourse between Missouri and the Internal Provinces of Mexico," Jan. 3, 1825, 18th Cong., 2nd Sess., Senate Exec. Doc. No. 7.

"Treaties with the Kansas and Osage Indians," Jan. 30, 1826, Treaty and Nomination Reports and Documents, 19th Cong., 1st Sess.

"Treaties with Sundry Indian Tribes," Jan. 11, 1826, Treaty and Nomination Reports and Documents, 19th Cong., 1st Sess.

"Treaty of Amity, commerce, and navigation, between the United States of America and the United Mexican States, concluded on the 5th of April, 1831," 22nd Cong., 1st Sess., Senate Exec. Doc. No. 11.

U.S. Government Documents and Publications

Abel, Annie H., ed. *The Official Correspondence of James S. Calhoun while Indian Agent at Santa Fe and Superintendent of Indian Affairs in New Mexico, 1849–1852.* Washington, D.C.: Government Printing Office, 1915.

American State Papers, Foreign Relations, vol. 6. Cornelius Wendell, Printer, 1859.

Annual Reports of the Commissioner of Indian Affairs. Washington, D.C.: Government Printing Office, 1850–68.

Annual Report of the Secretary of the Interior. Washington, D.C.: Government Printing Office, 1866.

Annual Reports of the Secretary of War. Washington, D.C.: Government Printing Office, 1849–66.

Cherokee Nation v. State of Georgia. 30 U.S. 1 (1831).

Heitman, Francis B. *Historical Register and Dictionary of the United States Army, from Its Organization, September 29, 1789, to March 2, 1903.* 2 vols. Washington, D.C.: Government Printing Office, 1903.

Kappler, Charles J. *Indian Affairs: Laws and Treaties.* 7 vols. Washington, D.C.: Government Printing Office, 1904.

Miller, Hunter, ed. *Treaties and Other International Acts of the United States of America.* 8 vols. Washington, D.C.: Government Printing Office, 1931–48.

United States Statutes at Large, Treaties, and Proclamations of the United States of America. 37th Congress, vol. 12, March 1861 to March 1863. Boston: Little, Brown, 1863.

———. 39th Congress, vol. 14, March 1865 to March 1867. Boston: Little, Brown, 1868.

The War of the Rebellion: A Compilation of the Official Records of the Union and Confederate Armies. Series 1. 53 vols. Washington, D.C.: Government Printing Office, 1880–1901.

Published Primary Sources

Alberts, Don E., ed. *Rebels on the Rio Grande: The Civil War Journal of A. B. Peticolas.* Albuquerque, NM: Merit Press, 1993.

Ball, Eve. *In the Days of Victorio: Recollections of a Warm Springs Apache.* Tucson: University of Arizona Press, 1970.

Ball, Eve, with Nora Henn and Lynda Sánchez. *Indeh: An Apache Odyssey.* Provo, UT: Brigham Young University Press, 1980.

Bartlett, John Russell. *Personal Narrative of Explorations and Incidents in Texas, New Mexico, California, Sonora, and Chihuahua, 1850–1853.* 2 vols. New York: D. Appleton, 1854.

Beckwourth, James P. *The Life and Adventures of James P. Beckwourth, Mountaineer, Scout, and Pioneer, and Chief of the Crow Nation of Indians, Written from his own Dictation by T. D. Bonner.* London: Sampson Low & Son, 1856.

Benton, Thomas Hart. *Speech of Mr. Benton, of Missouri, on the Oregon Question: Delivered in the Senate of the United States, May 22, 25, & 28, 1846.* Washington, DC: Blair & Rives, 1846.

———. *Thirty Years' View, or, A History of the Working of the American Government for Thirty Years, from 1820 to 1850.* 2 vols. New York: D. Appleton, 1856.

Bieber, Ralph P., ed. *Marching with the Army of the West: The Journals of Abraham R. Johnston, 1846, Marcellus Ball Edwards, 1847–48, and Philip Gooch Ferguson, 1847–48.* Glendale, CA: Arthur H. Clark, 1936.

———, ed. *Exploring Southwestern Trails, 1846–1854.* Glendale, CA: Arthur H. Clark, 1938.

Calvin, Ross, ed., *Lieutenant Emory Reports: Notes of a Military Reconnaissance.* Albuquerque: University of New Mexico Press, 1951.

Carmony, Neil B., ed. *The Civil War in Apacheland: Sergeant George Hand's Diary.* Silver City, NM: High-Lonesome Books, 1996.

Circular to the Stockholders of the Atlantic and Pacific Railroad Company. New York: Geo. F. Nesbitt, 1855.

Clarke, Dwight L., ed. *The Original Journals of Henry Smith Turner: With Stephen Watts Kearny to New Mexico and California, 1846–1847.* Norman: University of Oklahoma Press, 1966.

Conard, Howard Louis. *Uncle Dick Wootton: The Pioneer Frontiersman of the Rocky Mountain Region.* Edited by Milo Milton Quaife. Chicago: R. R. Donnelley & Sons, 1957.

Cooke, Philip St. George. *The Conquest of New Mexico and California: An Historical and Personal Narrative.* G. P. Putnam's Sons, 1878; reprint, Albuquerque: Horn and Wallace, 1964.

Correll, J. Lee. *Through White Men's Eyes, A Contribution to Navajo History: A Chronological Record of the Navajo People from Earliest Times to the Treaty of June 1, 1868.* 6 vols. Window Rock, AZ: Navajo Heritage Center, 1979.

Coues, Elliott, ed. *The Expeditions of Zebulon Montgomery Pike*. 2 vols. 1895; reprint, New York: Dover, 1987.

Crallé, Richard K., ed. *Speeches of John C. Calhoun, Delivered in the House of Representatives and in the Senate of the United States*. 6 vols. New York: Russell & Russell, 1968.

Cremony, John C. *Life among the Apaches*. San Francisco: A. Roman, 1868.

Crist, Lynda Lasswell, and Mary Seaton Dix, eds. *The Papers of Jefferson Davis. Volume 5: 1853–1855*. Baton Rouge: Louisiana State University Press, 1985.

———. *The Papers of Jefferson Davis. Volume 8: 1862*. Baton Rouge: Louisiana State University Press, 1995.

Croghan, George. *Army Life on the Western Frontier: Selections from the Official Reports Made between 1826 and 1845*. Edited by Francis Paul Prucha. Norman: University of Oklahoma Press, 1958.

Cutts, James Madison. *The Conquest of California and New Mexico, by the Forces of the United States, in the Years 1846 and 1847*. Philadelphia: Carey & Hart, 1847.

Davis, W. W. H. *El Gringo, or, New Mexico and Her People*. Santa Fe: Rydal Press, 1938.

Eckert, Edward K., and Nicholas J. Amato, eds. *Ten Years in the Saddle: The Memoir of William Woods Averell*. San Rafael, CA: Presidio Press, 1978.

Falconer, Thomas. *Letters and Notes on the Texan Santa Fe Expedition, 1841–1842*. New York: Dauber & Pine, 1930.

Farrell, John J., ed. *James K. Polk, 1795–1849: Chronology-Documents-Bibliographic Aides*. Dobbs Ferry, NY: Oceana Publications, 1970.

Gardner, Mark L., ed. *Brothers on the Santa Fe and Chihuahua Trails: Edward James Glasgow and William Henry Glasgow, 1846–1848*. Niwot: University Press of Colorado, 1993.

Gardner, Mark L., and Marc Simmons, eds. *The Mexican War Correspondence of Richard Smith Elliott*. Norman: University of Oklahoma Press, 1997.

Garrard, Lewis H. *Wah-To-Yah and the Taos Trail*. Palo Alto, CA: American West Publishing, 1968.

Gibson, George Rutledge. *Journal of a Soldier under Kearny and Doniphan, 1846–1847*. Edited by Ralph P. Bieber. Glendale, CA: Arthur H. Clark, 1935.

———. *Over the Chihuahua and Santa Fe Trails, 1847–1848: George Rutledge Gibson's Journal*. Edited by Robert W. Frazer. Albuquerque: University of New Mexico Press, 1981.

Gildersleeve, Charles H. *Reports of Cases Argued and Determined in the Supreme Court of the Territory of New Mexico from January term 1852 to January term 1879*. Vol. 1. San Francisco: A. L. Bancroft & Co., 1881.

Gray, A. B. *Survey of a Route for the Southern Pacific R.R., on the 32nd Parallel*. Cincinnati: Wrightson, 1856.

Gregg, Josiah. *Commerce of the Prairies*. Edited by Max L. Moorhead. Norman: University of Oklahoma Press, 1954.

Gregg, Kate L., ed. *The Road to Santa Fe: The Journal and Diaries of George Champlin Sibley and Others Pertaining to the Surveying and Marking of a Road from the Missouri Frontier to the Settlements of New Mexico, 1825–1827*. Albuquerque: University of New Mexico Press, 1952.

Gulick, Charles A., Jr., and Katherine Elliott. *The Papers of Mirabeau Buonapart Lamar*. 2 vols. Austin, TX: J. C. Baldwin & Sons, 1922.

Hammond, George P., ed. *Campaigns in the West, 1856–1861: The Original Journal and Letters of Colonel John Van Deusen DuBois.* Tucson: Arizona Pioneers Historical Society, 1949.

Hobbs, James. *Wild Life in the Far West: Personal Adventures of a Border Mountain Man.* Hartford, CT: Wiley, Waterman & Eaton, 1874.

Howbert, Irving. *Memories of a Lifetime in the Pikes Peak Region.* Glorieta, NM: Rio Grande Press, 1970.

Hughes, John T. *Doniphan's Expedition: Containing an Account of the Conquest of New Mexico; General Kearny's Overland Expedition to California; Doniphan's Campaign against the Navajos; His Unparalleled March upon Chihuahua and Durango; and the Operations of General Price at Santa Fe.* Cincinnati: J. A. and U. P. James, 1848.

Inman, Henry. *The Old Santa Fe Trail: The Story of a Great Highway.* Topeka, KS: Crane & Co., 1916.

Jackson, Donald, ed. *The Journals of Zebulon Montgomery Pike, with Letters and Related Documents.* 2 vols. Norman: University of Oklahoma Press, 1966.

Kelly, Lawrence C., ed. *Navajo Roundup: Selected Correspondence of Kit Carson's Expedition against the Navajo, 1863–1865.* Boulder, CO: Pruett Publishing, 1970.

Kendall, George Wilkins. *Narrative of the Texan–Santa Fe Expedition.* New York: Harper & Brothers, 1844.

Lane, Lydia Spencer. *I Married a Soldier, or, Old Days in the Old Army.* 1893; reprint, Albuquerque, NM: Horn & Wallace, 1964.

Laws of the Territory of New Mexico, Sixth Legislative Assembly, 1856–1857. Santa Fe: Office of the Democrat, 1857.

Laws of the Territory of New Mexico, Eighth Legislative Assembly, 1858–1859. Santa Fe: A. DeMarle, 1859.

Laws of the Territory of New Mexico, 1866–1867. Santa Fe: Manderfield & Tucker, 1867.

Loughborough, John. *The Pacific Telegraph and Railway.* St. Louis: Charles & Hammond, 1849.

Magoffin, Susan Shelby. *Down the Santa Fe Trail and into Mexico: The Diary of Susan Shelby Magoffin, 1846–1847.* Edited by Stella M. Drumm. New Haven, CT: Yale University Press, 1926.

Mayer, Brantz. *Mexico, As It Was and As It Is.* Philadelphia: G. B. Zieber, 1847.

McCall, Colonel George Archibald. *New Mexico in 1850: A Military View.* Edited by Robert W. Frazer. Norman: University of Oklahoma Press, 1968.

McKee, James Cooper. *Narrative of the Surrender of a Command of U.S. Forces at Fort Fillmore, New Mexico, in July, a.d. 1861.* Houston: Stagecoach Press, 1960.

McNierney, Michael, ed., *Taos 1847: The Revolt in Contemporary Accounts.* Boulder, CO: Johnson Publishing, 1980.

McNitt, Frank, ed. *Navaho Expedition: Journal of a Military Reconnaissance from Santa Fe, New Mexico, to the Navaho Country, Made in 1849 by Lieutenant James H. Simpson.* Norman: University of Oklahoma Press, 1964.

Meketa, Jacqueline Dorgan, ed. *Legacy of Honor: The Life of Rafael Chacón, A Nineteenth-Century New Mexican.* Albuquerque: University of New Mexico Press, 1986.

Meline, James F. *Two Thousand Miles on Horseback: Santa Fe and Back.* Albuquerque, NM: Horn & Wallace, 1966.

Meriwether, David. *My Life in the Mountains and on the Plains: The Newly Discovered Autobiography*. Edited by Robert A. Griffen. Norman: University of Oklahoma Press, 1965.

Mills, W. W. *Forty Years at El Paso, 1858–1898*. Edited by Rex W. Strickland. El Paso, TX: Carl Hertzog, 1962.

Noel, Theophilus. *A Campaign from Santa Fe to the Mississippi; Being a History of the Old Sibley Brigade from Its First Organization to the Present Time; Its Campaigns in New Mexico, Arizona, Texas, Louisiana, and Arkansas in the Years 1861–2–3–4*. Shreveport, LA: Shreveport News Printing, 1865.

Peebles, C. Glen. *Exposé of the Atlantic & Pacific Railroad Company*. New York: New York Examiner, 1854.

Pettis, George H. *Kit Carson's Fight with the Comanche and Kiowa Indians, at the Adobe Walls on the Canadian River, November 25th, 1864*. Providence, RI: Sidney S. Rider, 1878.

Quaife, Milo Milton, ed. *The Diary of James K. Polk during His Presidency, 1845 to 1849*. 4 vols. Chicago: A. C. McClung, 1910.

Rittenhouse, Jack D. *The Constitution of the State of New Mexico, 1850*. Santa Fe: Stagecoach Press, 1965.

Robinson, Jacob S. *A Journal of the Santa Fe Expedition under Colonel Doniphan*. 1848; reprint, Princeton, NJ: Princeton University Press, 1932.

Roessel, Ruth, ed. *Navajo Stories of the Long Walk Period*. Chinle, AZ: Navajo Community College Press, 1973.

Ruxton, George F. *Adventures in Mexico and the Rocky Mountains*. New York: Harper & Brothers, 1848.

Salazar Ylarregui, José. *Datos de los trabajos astronómicos y topográficos, dispuestos en forma de diario, practicados durante el año 1849 y principios de 1850 por la Comisión de Limites Mexicana en la línea que divide esta república de la de los Estados-Unidos*. Mexico City: Imprenta de Juan R. Navarro, 1850.

Sunder, John E., ed. *Matt Field on the Santa Fe Trail*. Norman: University of Oklahoma Press, 1960.

Thompson, Jerry D., ed. *From Desert to Bayou: The Civil War Journal and Sketches of Morgan Wolfe Merrick*. El Paso: Texas Western Press, 1991.

———, ed. *Civil War in the Southwest: Recollections of the Sibley Brigade*. College Station: Texas A&M University Press, 2001.

———, ed. *Texas and New Mexico on the Eve of the Civil War: The Mansfield & Johnston Inspections, 1859–1861*. Albuquerque: University of New Mexico Press, 2001.

———, ed. *New Mexico Territory during the Civil War: Wallen and Evans Inspection Reports, 1862–1863*. Albuquerque: University of New Mexico Press, 2008.

Thwaites, Reuben Gold, ed. *The Personal Narrative of James O. Pattie of Kentucky*. Cleveland, OH: Arthur H. Clark, 1905.

Webb, James Josiah. *Adventures in the Santa Fe Trade, 1844–1847*. Edited by Ralph P. Bieber. Glendale, CA: Arthur H. Clark, 1931.

Weber, David J. *Foreigners in their Native Land: Historical Roots of the Mexican Americans*. Albuquerque: University of New Mexico Press, 1973.

———, ed. *Arms, Indians, and the Mismanagement of New Mexico: Donaciano Vigil, 1846*. El Paso: Texas Western Press, 1986.

Weber, David J., and Jane Lenz Elder, eds. *Fiasco: George Clinton Gardner's Correspondence from the U.S.-Mexico Boundary Survey, 1849–1854.* Dallas: Southern Methodist University Press, 2010.

Webster, Daniel. *The Works of Daniel Webster.* 6 vols. Boston: C. Little & Jas. Brown, 1851.

Wilson, John P. *When the Texans Came: Missing Records from the Civil War in the Southwest, 1861–1862.* Albuquerque: University of New Mexico Press, 2001.

Wilson, John P., and Jerry Thompson, eds. *The Civil War in West Texas and New Mexico: The Lost Letterbook of Brigadier General Henry Hopkins Sibley.* El Paso: Texas Western Press, 2001.

Wilson, Richard L., and Benjamin F. Taylor. *Short Ravelings from a Long Yarn, or, Camp and March Sketches, of the Santa Fe Trail.* Chicago: Geer & Wilson, 1847.

Wislizenus, Dr. A., *Memoir of a Tour to Northern Mexico, Connected with Col. Doniphan's Expedition, in 1846 and 1847.* Washington, DC: Tippin & Streeper, 1848.

Woodhouse, S. W. *From Texas to San Diego in 1851: The Overland Journal of Dr. S. W. Woodhouse, Surgeon-Naturalist of the Sitgreaves Expedition.* Edited by Andrew Wallace and Richard H. Hevly. Lubbock: Texas Tech University Press, 2007.

Newspapers and Periodicals

Alcance al Centinela (Chihuahua City, Mex.)

Daily Albany (NY) *Argus*

Daily Alta California (San Francisco)

DeBow's Review (New Orleans)

Diario Oficial de la Federación (Mexico City)

El Siglo Diez y Nueve (Mexico City)

Mesilla (NM) *Times*

Missouri Gazette (St. Louis)

Montpelier (VT) *Watchman & State Journal*

National Era (Washington, DC)

New Orleans Daily Picayune

New-York Daily Tribune

New York Times

Niles Weekly Register (Baltimore)

San Francisco Herald

Santa Fe Republican

Santa Fe Weekly Gazette

Weekly Reveille (St. Louis)

Books

Alberts, Don E. *The Battle of Glorieta: Union Victory in the West.* College Station: Texas A&M University Press, 1998.

Albright, George Leslie. *Official Explorations for Pacific Railroads, 1853–1855.* Berkeley: University of California Press, 1921.

Allen, Felicity. *Jefferson Davis: Unconquerable Heart*. Columbia: University of Missouri Press, 1999.

Arenson, Adam, and Andrew R. Graybill, eds. *Civil War Wests: Testing the Limits of the United States*. Berkeley: University of California Press, 2014.

Bain, David Haward. *Empire Express: Building the First Transcontinental Railroad*. New York: Viking, 1999.

Ball, Durwood. *Army Regulars on the Western Frontier, 1848–1861*. Norman: University of Oklahoma Press, 2001.

Baptist, Edward E. *The Half Has Never Been Told: Slavery and the Making of American Capitalism*. New York: Basic Books, 2014.

Baxter, John O. *Las Carneradas: Sheep Trade in New Mexico, 1700–1860*. Albuquerque: University of New Mexico Press, 1987.

Beachum, Larry. *William Becknell: Father of the Santa Fe Trade*. El Paso: Texas Western Press, 1982.

Bender, Averam B. *The March of Empire: Frontier Defense in the Southwest, 1848–1860*. Lawrence: University of Kansas Press, 1952.

Bigler, David L., and Will Bagley. *The Mormon Rebellion: America's First Civil War, 1857–1858*. Norman: University of Oklahoma Press, 2011.

Blackhawk, Ned. *Violence over the Land: Indians and Empires in the Early American West*. Cambridge, MA: Harvard University Press, 2006.

Blackmon, Douglas A. *Slavery by Another Name: The Re-Enslavement of Black Americans from the Civil War to World War II*. New York: Anchor Books, 2009.

Blackshear, James Bailey. *Fort Bascom: Soldiers, Comancheros, and Indians in the Canadian River Valley*. Norman: University of Oklahoma Press, 2016.

Boyle, Susan Calafate. *Los Capitalistas: Hispano Merchants and the Santa Fe Trade*. Albuquerque: University of New Mexico Press, 1997.

Brack, Gene M. *Mexico Views Manifest Destiny, 1821–1846: An Essay on the Origins of the Mexican War*. Albuquerque: University of New Mexico Press, 1975.

Brock, William R. *Parties and Political Conscience: American Dilemmas, 1840–1850*. Millwood, NY: KTO Press, 1979.

Brooks, James F. *Captives and Cousins: Slavery, Kinship, and Community in the Southwest Borderlands*. Chapel Hill: University of North Carolina Press, 2002.

Bustamante, D. Carlos Ma. de. *El Nuevo Bernal Diaz del Castillo, ó sea, Historia de la invasion de los anglo-americanos en México*. 1847; reprint, Mexico: Secretaría de Educación Pública, 1949.

Cabeza de Baca, Fabiola. *We Fed Them Cactus*. Albuquerque: University of New Mexico Press, 1954.

Calloway, Colin G. *Pen and Ink Witchcraft: Treaties and Treaty Making in American Indian History*. New York: Oxford University Press, 2013.

Chalfant, William Y. *Dangerous Passage: The Santa Fe Trail and the Mexican War*. Norman: University of Oklahoma Press, 1994.

Chávez, Thomas E. *Manuel Alvarez, 1794–1856: A Southwestern Biography*. Niwot: University Press of Colorado, 1990.

Childers, Christopher. *The Failure of Popular Sovereignty: Slavery, Manifest Destiny, and the Radicalization of Southern Politics*. Lawrence: University Press of Kansas, 2012.

Chittenden, Hiram Martin. *The American Fur Trade of the Far West*. 2 vols. Stanford, CA: Academic Reprints, 1954.

Clarke, Dwight L. *Stephen Watts Kearny: Soldier of the West*. Norman: University of Oklahoma Press, 1961.

Cleland, Robert Glass. *This Reckless Breed of Men: The Trappers and Fur Traders of the Southwest*. New York: Knopf, 1950.

Colton, Ray C. *The Civil War in the Western Territories: Arizona, Colorado, New Mexico, and Utah*. Norman: University of Oklahoma Press, 1959.

Cook, Mary J. Straw. *Doña Tules: Santa Fe's Courtesan and Gambler*. Albuquerque: University of New Mexico Press, 2007.

Cooper, William J., Jr. *Jefferson Davis, American*. New York: Alfred A. Knopf, 2000.

Copeland, Fayette. *Kendall of the Picayune: Being His Adventures in New Orleans, on the Texan Santa Fe Expedition, in the Mexican War, and in the Colonization of the Texas Frontier*. Norman: University of Oklahoma Press, 1943.

Craver, Rebecca McDowell. *The Impact of Intimacy: Mexican-Anglo Intermarriage in New Mexico, 1821–1846*. El Paso: Texas Western Press, 1982.

Crutchfield, James A. *Revolt at Taos: The New Mexican and Indian Insurrection of 1847*. Yardley, PA: Westholme Publishing, 2015.

Daniel, Pete. *The Shadow of Slavery: Peonage in the South, 1901–1969*. Urbana: University of Illinois Press, 1972.

Dawson, Joseph G., III. *Doniphan's Epic March: The 1st Missouri Volunteers in the Mexican War*. Lawrence: University Press of Kansas, 1999.

DeLay, Brian. *War of a Thousand Deserts: Indian Raids and the U.S.-Mexican War*. New Haven, CT: Yale University Press, 2008.

Devine, David. *Slavery, Scandal, and Steel Rails: The 1854 Gadsden Purchase and the Building of the Second Transcontinental Railroad across Arizona and New Mexico Twenty-Five Years Later*. New York: iUniverse, 2004.

Dunlay, Tom. *Kit Carson and the Indians*. Lincoln: University of Nebraska Press, 2000.

Duthu, N. Bruce. *Shadow Nation: Tribal Sovereignty and the Limits of Legal Pluralism*. New York: Oxford University Press, 2013.

Edrington, Thomas S., and John Taylor. *The Battle of Glorieta Pass: A Gettysburg in the West, March 26–28, 1862*. Albuquerque: University of New Mexico Press, 1998.

Emmett, Chris. *Fort Union and the Winning of the Southwest*. Norman: University of Oklahoma Press, 1965.

Estergreen, M. Morgan. *Kit Carson: A Portrait in Courage*. Norman: University of Oklahoma Press, 1962.

Fixico, Donald L. *Bureau of Indian Affairs*. Santa Barbara, CA: Greenwood, 2012.

Foreman, Grant. *A Pathfinder in the Southwest: The Itinerary of Lieutenant A. W. Whipple during his Explorations for a Railway Route from Fort Smith to Los Angeles in the Years 1853 and 1854*. Norman: University of Oklahoma Press, 1941.

Frank, Ross. *From Settler to Citizen: New Mexican Economic Development and the Creation of Vecino Society, 1750–1820.* Berkeley: University of California Press, 2000.

Frazer, Robert W. *Forts and Supplies: The Role of the Army in the Economy of the Southwest, 1846–1861.* Albuquerque: University of New Mexico Press, 1983.

Frazier, Donald S. *Blood and Treasure: Confederate Empire in the Southwest.* College Station: Texas A&M University Press, 1995.

Ganaway, Loomis M. *New Mexico and the Sectional Controversy, 1846–1861.* Albuquerque: University of New Mexico Press, 1944.

Garber, Paul N. *The Gadsden Treaty.* Philadelphia: University of Pennsylvania Press, 1923.

Goetzmann, William H. *Exploration and Empire: The Explorer and the Scientist in the Winning of the American West.* New York: Alfred A. Knopf, 1966.

———. *Army Exploration in the American West, 1803–1863.* Lincoln: University of Nebraska Press, 1979.

Gómez, Laura E. *Manifest Destinies: The Making of the Mexican American Race.* New York: New York University Press, 2007.

González, Deena J. *Refusing the Favor: The Spanish-Mexican Women of Santa Fe, 1820–1880.* New York: Oxford University Press, 1999.

Gonzales, Manuel G. *The Hispanic Elite of the Southwest.* El Paso: Texas Western Press, 1989.

Greenberg, Amy S. *A Wicked War: Polk, Clay, Lincoln, and the 1846 U.S. Invasion of Mexico.* New York: Knopf, 2012.

Grenier, John. *The First Way of War: American War Making on the Frontier, 1607–1814.* Cambridge, MA: Cambridge University Press, 2005.

Griffen, William B. *Utmost Good Faith: Patterns of Apache-Mexican Hostilities in Northern Chihuahua Border Warfare, 1821–1848.* Albuquerque: University of New Mexico Press, 1988.

Gutiérrez, Ramón A. *When Jesus Came the Corn Mothers Went Away: Marriage, Sexuality, and Power in New Mexico, 1500–1846.* Stanford, CA: Stanford University Press, 1991.

Hall, Martin Hardwick. *The Confederate Army of New Mexico.* Austin, TX: Presidial Press, 1978.

———. *Sibley's New Mexico Campaign.* Austin: University of Texas Press, 1960.

Hall, Thomas D. *Social Change in the Southwest, 1350–1880.* Lawrence: University Press of Kansas, 1989.

Hämäläinen, Pekka. *The Comanche Empire.* New Haven, CT: Yale University Press, 2008.

Harris, Charles H., III. *A Mexican Family Empire: The Latifundio of the Sánchez Navarros, 1765–1867.* Austin: University of Texas Press, 1975.

Hietala, Thomas R. *Manifest Design: Anxious Aggrandizement in Late Jacksonian America.* Ithaca, NY: Cornell University Press, 1985.

Hine, Robert V. *Bartlett's West: Drawing the Mexican Boundary.* New Haven, CT: Yale University Press, 1968.

Hollon, W. Eugene. *The Lost Pathfinder: Zebulon Montgomery Pike.* Norman: University of Oklahoma Press, 1949.

Holt, Michael F. *The Political Crisis of the 1850s.* New York: Norton, 1978.

Horn, Calvin. *New Mexico's Troubled Years: The Story of the Early Territorial Governors.* Albuquerque, NM: Horn & Wallace, 1963.

Horsman, Reginald. *Race and Manifest Destiny: The Origins of American Racial Anglo-Saxonism.* Cambridge, MA: Harvard University Press, 1981.

Howe, Daniel Walker. *What Hath God Wrought: The Transformation of America, 1815–1848.* New York: Oxford University Press, 2007.

Hunt, Aurora. *Major General James Henry Carleton 1814–1873: Western Frontier Dragoon.* Glendale, CA: Arthur H. Clark, 1958.

———. *Kirby Benedict: Federal Frontier Judge.* Glendale, CA: Arthur H. Clark, 1961.

Hutton, Paul Andrew. *The Apache Wars: The Hunt for Geronimo, the Apache Kid, and the Captive Boy Who Started the Longest War in American History.* New York: Crown, 2016.

Hyde, Anne F. *Empires, Nations, and Families: A New History of the North American West, 1800–1860.* Lincoln: University of Nebraska Press, 2011.

Hyslop, Stephen G. *Bound for Santa Fe: The Road to New Mexico and the American Conquest, 1806–1848.* Norman: University of Oklahoma Press, 2002.

Iverson, Peter. *Diné: A History of the Navajos.* Albuquerque: University of New Mexico Press, 2002.

Johnson, Walter. *River of Dark Dreams: Slavery and Empire in the Cotton Kingdom.* Cambridge, MA: The Belknap Press of Harvard University Press, 2013.

Josephy, Alvin M., Jr. *The Civil War in the American West.* New York: Knopf, 1991.

Karp, Matthew. *This Vast Southern Empire: Slaveholders at the Helm of American Foreign Policy.* Cambridge, MA: Harvard University Press, 2016.

Keehn, David C. *Knights of the Golden Circle: Secret Empire, Southern Secession, Civil War.* Baton Rouge: Louisiana State University Press, 2013.

Keleher, William A. *Turmoil in New Mexico, 1846–1868.* Santa Fe: Rydal Press, 1952.

Kiser, William S. *Turmoil on the Rio Grande: The Territorial History of the Mesilla Valley, 1846–1865.* College Station: Texas A&M University Press, 2011.

———. *Dragoons in Apacheland: Conquest and Resistance in Southern New Mexico, 1846–1861.* Norman: University of Oklahoma Press, 2012.

———. *Borderlands of Slavery: The Struggle over Captivity and Peonage in the American Southwest.* Philadelphia: University of Pennsylvania Press, 2017.

Kluger, Richard. *Seizing Destiny: How America Grew from Sea to Shining Sea.* New York: Knopf, 2007.

Kvach, John F. *DeBow's Review: The Antebellum Vision of a New South.* Lexington: University Press of Kentucky, 2013.

Lamar, Howard R. *The Far Southwest, 1846–1912: A Territorial History.* Albuquerque: University of New Mexico Press, 2000.

Larson, Robert W. *New Mexico's Quest for Statehood, 1846–1912.* Albuquerque: University of New Mexico Press, 1968.

Lavender, David. *Bent's Fort: A Historical Account of the Adobe Empire That Shaped the Destiny of the American Southwest.* Garden City, NY: Doubleday, 1954.

Lecompte, Janet. *Rebellion in Rio Arriba, 1837.* Albuquerque: University of New Mexico Press, 1985.

LeFlouria, Talitha L. *Chained in Silence: Black Women and Convict Labor in the New South.* Chapel Hill: University of North Carolina Press, 2015.

Lichtenstein, Alex. *Twice the Work of Free Labor: The Political Economy of Convict Labor in the New South.* New York: Verso, 1996.

Loomis, Noel M. *The Texan–Santa Fe Pioneers.* Norman: University of Oklahoma Press, 1958.

Masich, Andrew E. *Civil War in the Southwest Borderlands, 1861–1867.* Norman: University of Oklahoma Press, 2017.

Matthews, George R. *Zebulon Pike: Thomas Jefferson's Agent for Empire.* Santa Barbara, CA: Praeger, 2016.

May, Robert E. *Manifest Destiny's Underworld: Filibustering in Antebellum America.* Chapel Hill: University of North Carolina Press, 2002.

McCaffrey, James M. *Army of Manifest Destiny: The American Soldier in the Mexican War, 1846–1848.* New York: New York University Press, 1992.

McNitt, Frank. *Navajo Wars: Military Campaigns, Slave Raids, and Reprisals.* Albuquerque: University of New Mexico Press, 1972.

Miller, Darlis. *The California Column in New Mexico.* Albuquerque: University of New Mexico Press, 1982.

Miner, H. Craig. *The St. Louis–San Francisco Transcontinental Railroad: The Thirty-Fifth Parallel Project, 1853–1890.* Lawrence: University Press of Kansas, 1972.

Montejano, David. *Anglos and Mexicans in the Making of Texas, 1836–1986.* Austin: University of Texas Press, 1987.

Montgomery, Charles. *The Spanish Redemption: Heritage, Power, and Loss on New Mexico's Upper Rio Grande.* Berkeley: University of California Press, 2002.

Moorhead, Max L. *New Mexico's Royal Road: Trade and Travel on the Chihuahua Trail.* Norman: University of Oklahoma Press, 1958.

Mora, Anthony. *Border Dilemmas: Racial and National Uncertainties in New Mexico, 1848–1912.* Durham, NC: Duke University Press, 2011.

Nieto-Phillips, John M. *The Language of Blood: The Making of Spanish-American Identity in New Mexico, 1880s–1930s.* Albuquerque: University of New Mexico Press, 2004.

Oakes, James. *Freedom National: The Destruction of Slavery in the United States, 1861–1865.* New York: Norton, 2012.

Oliva, Leo E. *Soldiers on the Santa Fe Trail.* Norman: University of Oklahoma Press, 1967.

Opler, Morris E. *An Apache Life-Way: The Economic, Social, and Religious Institutions of the Chiricahua Indians.* New York: Cooper Square Publishers, 1965.

Poldevaart, Arie W. *Black-Robed Justice: A History of the Administration of Justice in New Mexico from the American Occupation in 1846 until Statehood in 1912.* Holmes Beach, FL: Gaunt Publishing, 1999, reprint.

Potter, David M. *The Impending Crisis, 1848–1861.* New York: Harper & Row, 1973.

Prince, L. Bradford. *Historical Sketches of New Mexico from the Earliest Records to the American Occupation.* Kansas City, MO: Ramsey, Millett & Hudson, 1883.

Prucha, Francis Paul. *The Great Father: The United States Government and the American Indians.* 2 Vols. Lincoln: University of Nebraska Press, 1984.

———. *American Indian Treaties: The History of a Political Anomaly.* Berkeley: University of California Press, 1994.

Read, Benjamin M. *Illustrated History of New Mexico.* Santa Fe: New Mexican Printing Co., 1912.

Reid, John C. *Reid's Tramp, or a Journal of the Incidents of Ten Months Travel through Texas, New Mexico, Arizona, Sonora, and California.* Austin, TX: Steck, 1935.

Reséndez, Andrés. *Changing National Identities at the Frontier: Texas and New Mexico, 1800–1850.* New York: Cambridge University Press, 2005.

———. *The Other Slavery: The Uncovered Story of Indian Enslavement in America.* New York: Houghton Mifflin Harcourt, 2016.

Robbins, William G. *Colony and Empire: The Capitalist Transformation of the American West.* Lawrence: University Press of Kansas, 1994.

Ryan, John P. *Fort Stanton and Its Community, 1855–1896.* Las Cruces, NM: Yucca Tree Press, 1998.

Sánchez, George I. *Forgotten People: A Study of New Mexicans.* Albuquerque: University of New Mexico Press, 1940.

Sánchez, George J. *Becoming Mexican-American: Ethnicity, Culture, and Identity in Chicano Los Angeles, 1900–1945.* New York: Oxford University Press, 1993.

Schermerhorn, Calvin. *The Business of Slavery and the Rise of American Capitalism, 1815–1860.* New Haven, CT: Yale University Press, 2015.

Shalhope, Robert E. *Sterling Price: Portrait of a Southerner.* Columbia: University of Missouri Press, 1971.

Shinkle, James D. *Fort Sumner and the Bosque Redondo Indian Reservation.* Roswell, NM: Hall-Poorbaugh Press, 1965.

Simpson, Brooks D. *The Reconstruction Presidents.* Lawrence: University Press of Kansas, 1998.

Smith, Stacey L. *Freedom's Frontier: California and the Struggle over Unfree Labor, Emancipation, and Reconstruction.* Chapel Hill: University of North Carolina Press, 2013.

Sonnichsen, C. L. *The Mescalero Apaches.* Norman: University of Oklahoma Press, 1958.

Stegmaier, Mark J. *Texas, New Mexico, and the Compromise of 1850: Boundary Dispute and Sectional Crisis.* Kent, OH: Kent State University Press, 1996.

St. John, Rachel. *Line in the Sand: A History of the Western U.S.-Mexico Border.* Princeton, NJ: Princeton University Press, 2011.

Stover, John F. *History of the Baltimore and Ohio Railroad.* West Lafayette, IN: Purdue University Press, 1987.

Sunseri, Alvin R. *Seeds of Discord: New Mexico in the Aftermath of the American Conquest, 1846–1861.* Chicago: Nelson-Hall, 1979.

Swadesh, Frances Leon. *Los Primeros Pobladores: Hispanic Americans of the Ute Frontier.* Notre Dame, IN: University of Notre Dame Press, 1974.

Sweeney, Edwin R. *Cochise: Chiricahua Apache Chief.* Norman: University of Oklahoma Press, 1991.

———. *Mangas Coloradas: Chief of the Chiricahua Apaches.* Norman: University of Oklahoma Press, 1998.

Taylor, John. *Bloody Valverde: A Civil War Battle on the Rio Grande, February 21, 1862.* Albuquerque: University of New Mexico Press, 1995.

Thompson, Gerald. *The Army and the Navajo: The Bosque Redondo Reservation Experiment, 1863–1868.* Tucson: University of Arizona Press, 1976.

Thompson, Jerry D. *Colonel John Robert Baylor: Texas Indian Fighter and Confederate Soldier.* Hillsboro, TX: Hill Junior College Press, 1971.

———. *Henry Hopkins Sibley: Confederate General of the West.* Natchitoches, TX: Northwestern State University Press, 1987.

———. *A Civil War History of the New Mexico Volunteers and Militia.* Albuquerque: University of New Mexico Press, 2015.

Thrapp, Dan L. *Victorio and the Mimbres Apaches.* Norman: University of Oklahoma Press, 1974.

Torget, Andrew J. *Seeds of Empire: Cotton, Slavery, and the Transformation of the Texas Borderlands, 1800–1850.* Chapel Hill: University of North Carolina Press, 2015.

Trafzer, Clifford E. *The Kit Carson Campaign: The Last Great Navajo War.* Norman: University of Oklahoma Press, 1982.

Trennert, Robert A., Jr. *Alternative to Extinction: Federal Indian Policy and the Beginnings of the Reservation System, 1846–1851.* Philadelphia: Temple University Press, 1975.

Truett, Samuel. *Fugitive Landscapes: The Forgotten History of the U.S.-Mexico Borderlands.* New Haven, CT: Yale University Press, 2006.

Tsesis, Alexander. *The Thirteenth Amendment and American Freedom: A Legal History.* New York: New York University Press, 2004.

Twitchell, Ralph Emerson. *The History of the Military Occupation of the Territory of New Mexico from 1846 to 1851 by the Government of the United States.* 1909; reprint, Chicago: Rio Grande, 1963.

———. *Leading Facts of New Mexican History.* 5 vols. Cedar Rapids, IA: Torch Press, 1912.

Underhill, Ruth M. *The Navajos.* Norman: University of Oklahoma Press, 1956.

Usner, Daniel H., Jr. *Indians, Settlers, and Slaves in a Frontier Exchange Economy: The Lower Mississippi Valley Before 1783.* Chapel Hill: University of North Carolina Press, 1992.

Utley, Robert M. *Frontiersmen in Blue: The United States Army and the Indian, 1848–1865.* New York: MacMillan, 1967.

———. *Fort Union and the Santa Fe Trail.* El Paso: Texas Western Press, 1989.

Vorenberg, Michael. *Final Freedom: The Civil War, the Abolition of Slavery, and the Thirteenth Amendment.* Cambridge, UK: Cambridge University Press, 2001.

Wadsworth, Richard. *Incident at San Augustine Springs: A Hearing for Major Isaac Lynde.* Las Cruces, NM: Yucca Tree Press, 2002.

Walker, Henry Pickering. *The Wagonmasters: High Plains Freighting from the Earliest Days of the Santa Fe Trail to 1880.* Norman: University of Oklahoma Press, 1966.

Wallace, Edward S. *The Great Reconnaissance: Soldiers, Artists, and Scientists on the Frontier, 1848–1861.* Boston: Little, Brown & Co., 1955.

Weber, David J. *The Taos Trappers: The Fur Trade in the Far Southwest, 1540–1846.* Norman: University of Oklahoma Press, 1971.

————. *The Mexican Frontier, 1821–1846: The American Southwest under Mexico.* Albuquerque: University of New Mexico Press, 1982.

————. *Richard H. Kern: Expeditionary Artist in the Far Southwest, 1848–1853.* Albuquerque: University of New Mexico Press, 1985.

————. *Bárbaros: Spaniards and Their Savages in the Age of Enlightenment.* New Haven, CT: Yale University Press, 2005.

Weinberg, Albert K. *Manifest Destiny: A Study of Nationalist Expansionism in American History.* Baltimore: Johns Hopkins University Press, 1935.

Werne, Joseph Richard. *The Imaginary Line: A History of the United States and Mexican Boundary Survey, 1848–1857.* Fort Worth: Texas Christian University Press, 2007.

White, Richard. *Railroaded: The Transcontinentals and the Making of Modern America.* New York: Norton, 2011.

Wooster, Robert. *The American Military Frontiers: The United States Army in the West, 1783–1900.* Albuquerque: University of New Mexico Press, 2009.

Articles and Book Chapters

Abel, Annie H., ed. "The Journal of John Greiner." *Old Santa Fe* 3 (July 1916): 189–243.

Ayers, John. "A Soldier's Experience in New Mexico." *New Mexico Historical Review* 24 (Oct. 1949): 259–66.

Barbour, Barton H. "Kit Carson and the 'Americanization' of New Mexico." In *New Mexican Lives: Profiles and Historical Stories,* edited by Richard W. Etulain, 163–92. Albuquerque: University of New Mexico Press, 2002.

Bieber, Ralph P., ed. "Letters of William Carr Lane, 1852–1854." *New Mexico Historical Review* 3 (April 1928): 179–203.

Bloom, Lansing B. "New Mexico under Mexican Administration: Part 3—New Mexico as a Department, 1837–1846." *Old Santa Fe* 2 (April 1915): 351–80.

Burton, E. Bennett. "The Taos Rebellion." *Old Santa Fe* 1 (Oct. 1913): 176–209.

Carson, William G. B., ed. "William Carr Lane Diary." *New Mexico Historical Review* 39 (Oct. 1964): 274–332.

Faragher, John Mack. "North, South, and West: Sectional Controversies and the U.S.-Mexico Boundary Survey." In *Drawing the Borderline: Artist-Explorers of the U.S.-Mexico Boundary Survey,* edited by Dawn Hall, 1–11. Albuquerque, NM: Albuquerque Museum, 1996.

Gómez, Laura E. "Off-White in an Age of White Supremacy: Mexican Elites and the Rights of Indians and Blacks in Nineteenth-Century New Mexico." In *Colored Men and Hombres Aqui: Hernandez v. Texas and the Emergence of Mexican-American Lawyering,* edited by Michael A. Olivas, 1–40. Houston: Arte Público Press, 2006.

González, Deena J. "La Tules of Image and Reality: Euro-American Attitudes and Legend Formation on a Spanish-Mexican Frontier." In *Building with Our Hands: New Directions in Chicana Studies,* edited by Adela de la Torre and Beatríz M. Pesquera, 75–90. Berkeley: University of California Press, 1993.

Goodrich, James W. "Revolt at Mora, 1847." *New Mexico Historical Review* 47 (Jan. 1972): 49–60.

Gorenfeld, Will, and David M. Johnson. "The Battle of Cieneguilla." In *Battles and Massacres on the Southwestern Frontier: Historical and Archaeological Perspectives,* edited by Ronald K. Wetherington and Frances Levine, 9–76. Norman: University of Oklahoma Press, 2014.

Hahn, Steven. "The Widest Implications of Disorienting the Civil War Era." In *Civil War Wests,* edited by Adam Arenson and Andrew R. Graybill, 265–274.

Hall, Martin Hardwick. "Colonel James Reily's Diplomatic Missions to Chihuahua and Sonora." *New Mexico Historical Review* 31 (July 1956): 232–45.

Jett, Stephen C., ed. "The Destruction of Navajo Orchards in 1864: Captain John Thompson's Report." *Arizona and the West* 16 (Winter 1974): 365–78.

Jordan, Weymouth T., Jr., John D. Chapla, and Shan C. Sutton. "'Notorious as the Noonday Sun': Capt. Alexander Welch Reynolds and the New Mexico Territory, 1849–1859." *New Mexico Historical Review* 75 (Oct. 2000): 457–508.

Kellogg, Deren Earl. "Lincoln's New Mexico Patronage: Saving the Far Southwest for the Union." *New Mexico Historical Review* 75 (Oct. 2000): 511–33.

Kessell, John L. "General Sherman and the Navajo Treaty of 1868: A Basic and Expedient Misunderstanding." *Western Historical Quarterly* 12 (July 1981): 251–72.

Kiser, William S. "'A charming name for a species of slavery': Political Debate over Debt Peonage in the Southwest, 1840s–1860s." *Western Historical Quarterly* 45, no. 2 (Summer 2014): 169–89.

———. "Louis Geck." In *Soldiers in the Southwest Borderlands, 1848–1886,* edited by Janne Lahti, 35–56. Norman: University of Oklahoma Press, 2017.

Kraemer, Paul. "Sickliest Post in the Territory of New Mexico: Fort Thorn and Malaria, 1853–1860." *New Mexico Historical Review* 71 (July 1996): 221–35.

Lecompte, Janet. "The Independent Women of Hispanic New Mexico, 1821–1846." *Western Historical Quarterly* 12 (Jan. 1981): 17–35.

Martinez, Oscar J. "Surveying and Marking the U.S.-Mexico Boundary: The Mexican Perspective." In *Drawing the Borderline: Artist-Explorers of the U.S.-Mexico Boundary Survey,* edited by Dawn Hall, 13–22. Albuquerque, NM: Albuquerque Museum, 1996.

Meyer, Roy W. "New Light on Lewis Garrard." *Western Historical Quarterly* 6 (July 1975): 261–78.

Moorhead, Max L., ed. "Notes and Documents." *New Mexico Historical Review* 26 (Jan. 1951): 68–82.

Murphy, Lawrence R. "Reconstruction in New Mexico." *New Mexico Historical Review* 43 (April 1968): 99–115.

———. "The United States Army in Taos, 1847–1852." *New Mexico Historical Review* 47 (Jan. 1972): 33–48.

Nelson, Megan Kate. "Death in the Distance: Confederate Manifest Destiny and the Campaign for New Mexico, 1861–1862." In *Civil War Wests,* edited by Adam Arenson and Andrew R. Graybill, 33–52.

Osburn, Katherine M. B. "The Navajo at the Bosque Redondo: Cooperation, Resistance, and Initiative, 1864–1868." *New Mexico Historical Review* 60 (Oct. 1985): 399–413.

"The Pacific Railroad." *North American Review* 82 (Jan. 1856): 211–36.

Paredes, Raymund A. "The Mexican Image in American Travel Literature, 1831–1869." *New Mexico Historical Review* 52 (Jan. 1977): 5–29.

Reeve, Frank D., ed. "Puritan and Apache." *New Mexico Historical Review* 24 (Jan. 1949): 12–53.

Reséndez, Andrés. "National Identity on a Shifting Border: Texas and New Mexico in the Age of Transition, 1821–1848." *Journal of American History* 86 (Sept. 1999): 668–88.

Simmons, Marc. "The Chacón Economic Report of 1803." *New Mexico Historical Review* 60 (Jan. 1985): 81–88.

Stegmaier, Mark. "'An Imaginary Negro in an Impossible Place?': The Issue of New Mexico Statehood in the Secession Crisis, 1860–1861." *New Mexico Historical Review* 84 (Spring 2009): 263–90.

———. "New Mexico's Delegate in the Secession Winter Congress, Part 1: Two Newspaper Accounts of Miguel Otero in 1861." *New Mexico Historical Review* 86 (Summer 2011): 385–92.

———. "New Mexico's Delegate in the Secession Winter Congress, Part 2: Miguel A. Otero Responds to Horace Greeley, and Greeley takes Revenge." *New Mexico Historical Review* 86 (Fall 2011): 513–23.

———. "A Law that Would Make Caligula Blush? New Mexico Territory's Unique Slave Code, 1859–1861." *New Mexico Historical Review* 87 (Spring 2012): 209–42.

Teel, T. T. "Sibley's New Mexican Campaign—Its Objects and the Causes of its Failure." In *Battles and Leaders of the Civil War.* Edited by Robert Underwood Johnson and Clarence Clough Buel. 4 vols. New York: Century Co., 1887.

Thompson, Jerry, ed. "'Is This to Be the Glory of Our Brave Men?': The New Mexico Civil War Journal and Letters of Dr. Henry Jacob 'Hal' Hunter." *New Mexico Historical Review* 75 (Oct. 2000): 535–603.

Tyler, Daniel. "Gringo Views of Governor Manuel Armijo." *New Mexico Historical Review* 45 (Jan. 1970): 23–46.

———. "Governor Armijo's Moment of Truth." *Journal of the West* 11 (April 1972): 307–16.

Wadsworth, Richard. "The Battle of Mesilla: A Rebel View." *Southern New Mexico Historical Review* (Jan. 2005): 8–9.

Weber, David J. "'Scarce more than apes': Historical Roots of Anglo-American Stereotypes of Mexicans." In *New Spain's Far Northern Frontier: Essays on Spain in the American West, 1540–1821,* edited by David J. Weber, 293–307. Albuquerque: University of New Mexico Press, 1979.

———. "Señor Escudero Goes to Washington: Diplomacy, Indians, and the Santa Fe Trade." *Western Historical Quarterly* 43 (Winter 2012): 417–35.

Wilson, John P. "Retreat to the Rio Grande: The Report of Captain Isaiah N. Moore." *Rio Grande History* 2 (1975): 4–8.

———. "Whiskey at Fort Fillmore: A Story of the Civil War." *New Mexico Historical Review* 68 (April 1993): 109–32.

INDEX

Wilson, Henry, 123
Wislizenus, Adolph, 4–5, 8, 45, 53, 91
women, 22, 40, 46, 56, 59, 65, 83, 94–95,
    112, 154, 155, 173, 174; as peons, 114–15,
    124
Wool, John, 43, 53
Wootton, Uncle Dick, 63

Yerger, George S., 146
Ylarregui, José Salazar, 141
Young, Brigham, 10
Young, Richard M., 228n64

Zarcillos Largos (Navajo), 89–90, 97, 98
Zuñi Pueblo, N.Mex., 137